THREEEEEE!

KOYOHARU GOTOUGE

Hi, I'm Gotouge. Volume 3 is finally out! And it's thanks to me relying on a lot of people, getting help and receiving encouragement. Thank you. Even I'm shocked. I'm the type who jumps to the conclusion that things are sure to fail, but if I offer my cowardly self tasty bananas and other treats, and tell myself that maybe there's still hope, I'll keep doing my very best.

DEMON SLAYER: KIMETSU NO YAIBA VOLUME 3

Shonen Jump Edition

Story and Art by
KOYOHARU GOTOUGE

KIMETSU NO YAIBA
© 2016 by Koyoharu Gotouge
All rights reserved. First published in Japan
in 2016 by SHUEISHA Inc., Tokyo. English
translation rights arranged by SHUEISHA Inc.

TRANSLATION John Werry
ENGLISH ADAPTATION Stan!
TOUCH-UP ART & LETTERING John Hunt
DESIGN Adam Grano
EDITOR Mike Montesa

Printed in Canada

Published by VIZ Media, LLC
P.O. Box 77010
San Francisco, CA 94107

10 9 8 7 6
First printing, November 2018
Sixth printing, December 2020

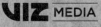

viz.com

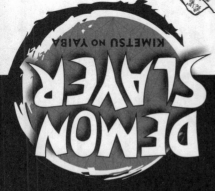

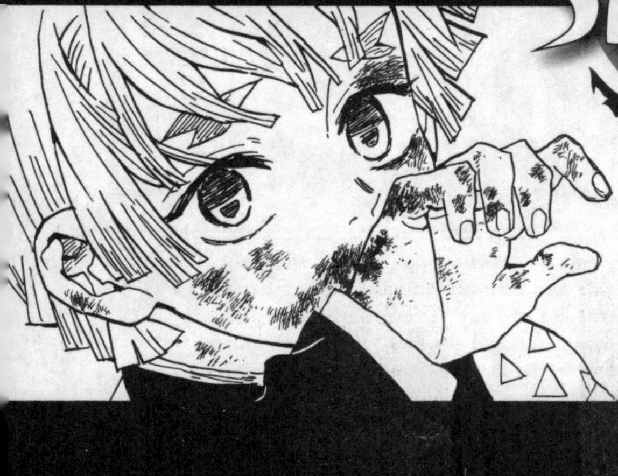

3 BELIEVE IN YOURSELF

DEMON SLAYER

KIMETSU NO YAIBA

KOYOHARU GOTOUGE

CHARACTERS

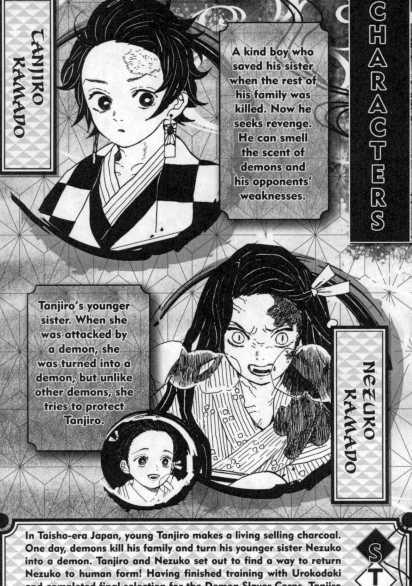

TANJIRO KAMADO

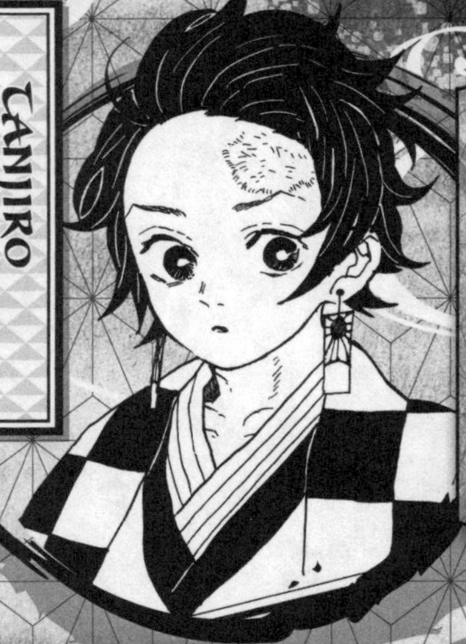

A kind boy who saved his sister when the rest of his family was killed. Now he seeks revenge. He can smell the scent of demons and his opponents' weaknesses.

NEZUKO KAMADO

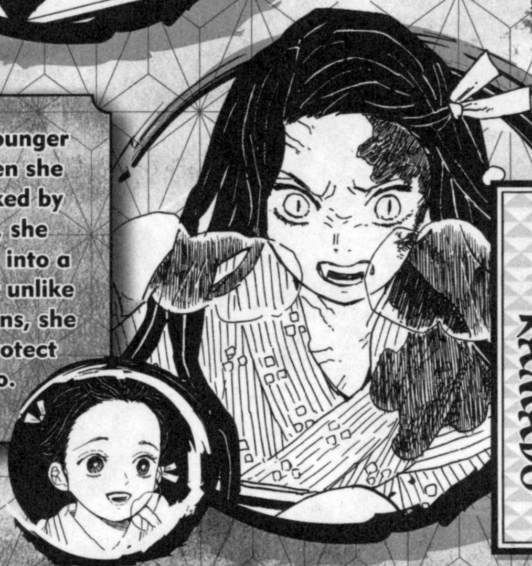

Tanjiro's younger sister. When she was attacked by a demon, she was turned into a demon, but unlike other demons, she tries to protect Tanjiro.

STORY

In Taisho-era Japan, young Tanjiro makes a living selling charcoal. One day, demons kill his family and turn his younger sister Nezuko into a demon. Tanjiro and Nezuko set out to find a way to return Nezuko to human form! Having finished training with Urokodaki and completed final selection for the Demon Slayer Corps, Tanjiro accepts a mission and brings Nezuko with him. During the mission, Tanjiro encounters his most hated enemy, Kibutsuji, but the demon escapes. Then Tanjiro meets Tamayo and Yushiro, who are demons but also want to kill Kibutsuji. They provide Tanjiro with a clue as to how Nezuko may return to being human. Before he can do anything with this information, Tanjiro is suddenly attacked by members of the Twelve Kizuki, who directly serve Kibutsuji!

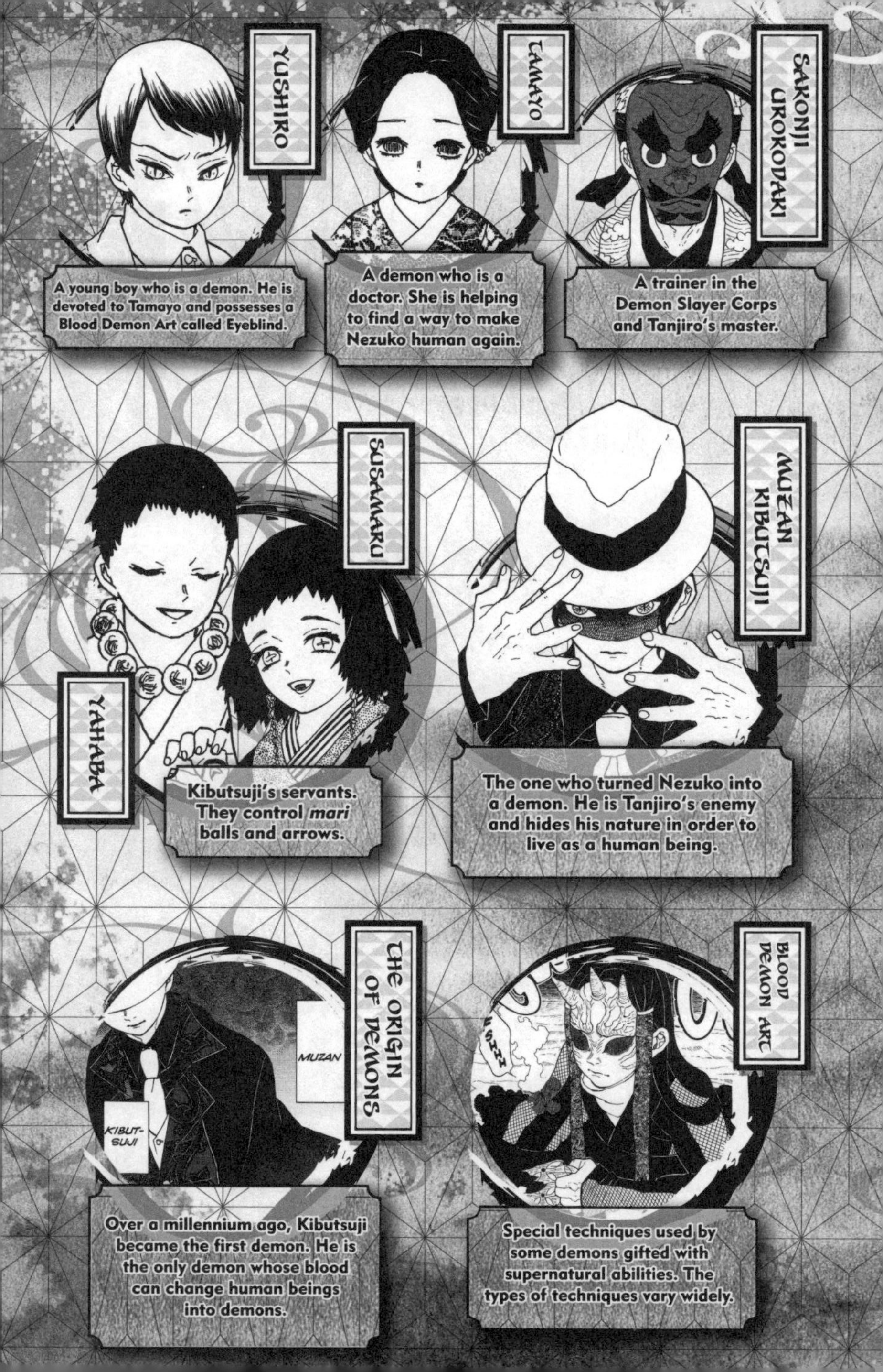
SAKONJI UROKODAKI
A trainer in the Demon Slayer Corps and Tanjiro's master.
TAMAYO
A demon who is a doctor. She is helping to find a way to make Nezuko human again.
YUSHIRO
A young boy who is a demon. He is devoted to Tamayo and possesses a Blood Demon Art called Eyeblind.
MUZAN KIBUTSUJI
The one who turned Nezuko into a demon. He is Tanjiro's enemy and hides his nature in order to live as a human being.
SUSAMARU
YAHABA
Kibutsuji's servants. They control *mari* balls and arrows.
BLOOD DEMON ART
Special techniques used by some demons gifted with supernatural abilities. The types of techniques vary widely.
THE ORIGIN OF DEMONS
MUZAN
KIBUT-SUJI
Over a millennium ago, Kibutsuji became the first demon. He is the only demon whose blood can change human beings into demons.

CONTENTS

DEMON SLAYER
KIMETSU NO YAIBA

3

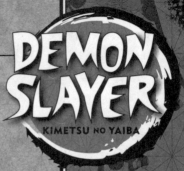

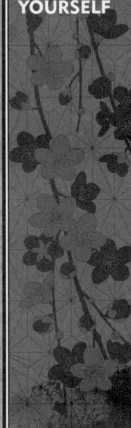

BELIEVE IN YOURSELF

CHAPTER 17: ARROW DEMON

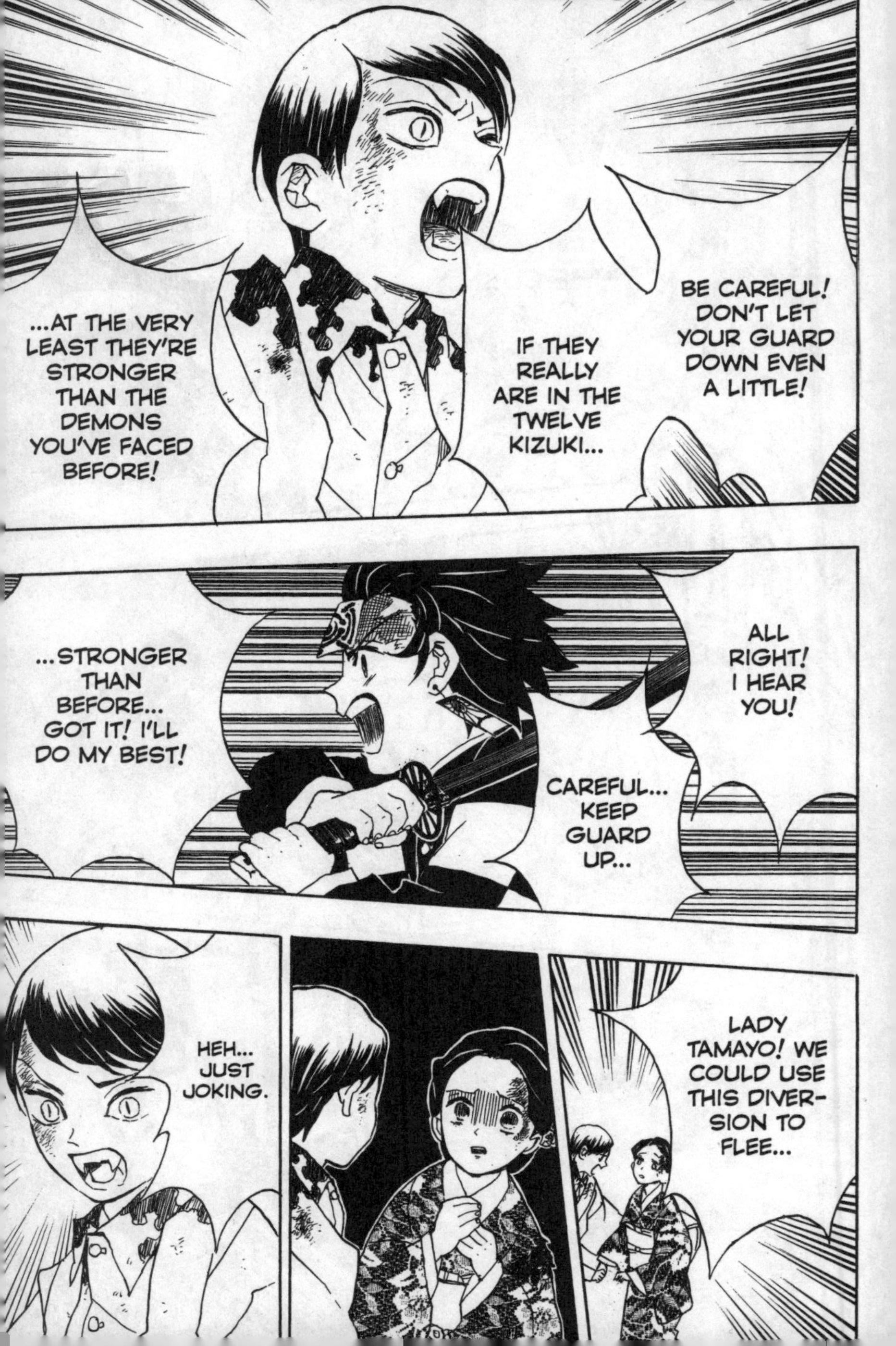
BE CAREFUL! DON'T LET YOUR GUARD DOWN EVEN A LITTLE!
IF THEY REALLY ARE IN THE TWELVE KIZUKI...
...AT THE VERY LEAST THEY'RE STRONGER THAN THE DEMONS YOU'VE FACED BEFORE!
ALL RIGHT! I HEAR YOU!
CAREFUL... KEEP GUARD UP...
...STRONGER THAN BEFORE... GOT IT! I'LL DO MY BEST!
LADY TAMAYO! WE COULD USE THIS DIVER-SION TO FLEE...
HEH... JUST JOKING.

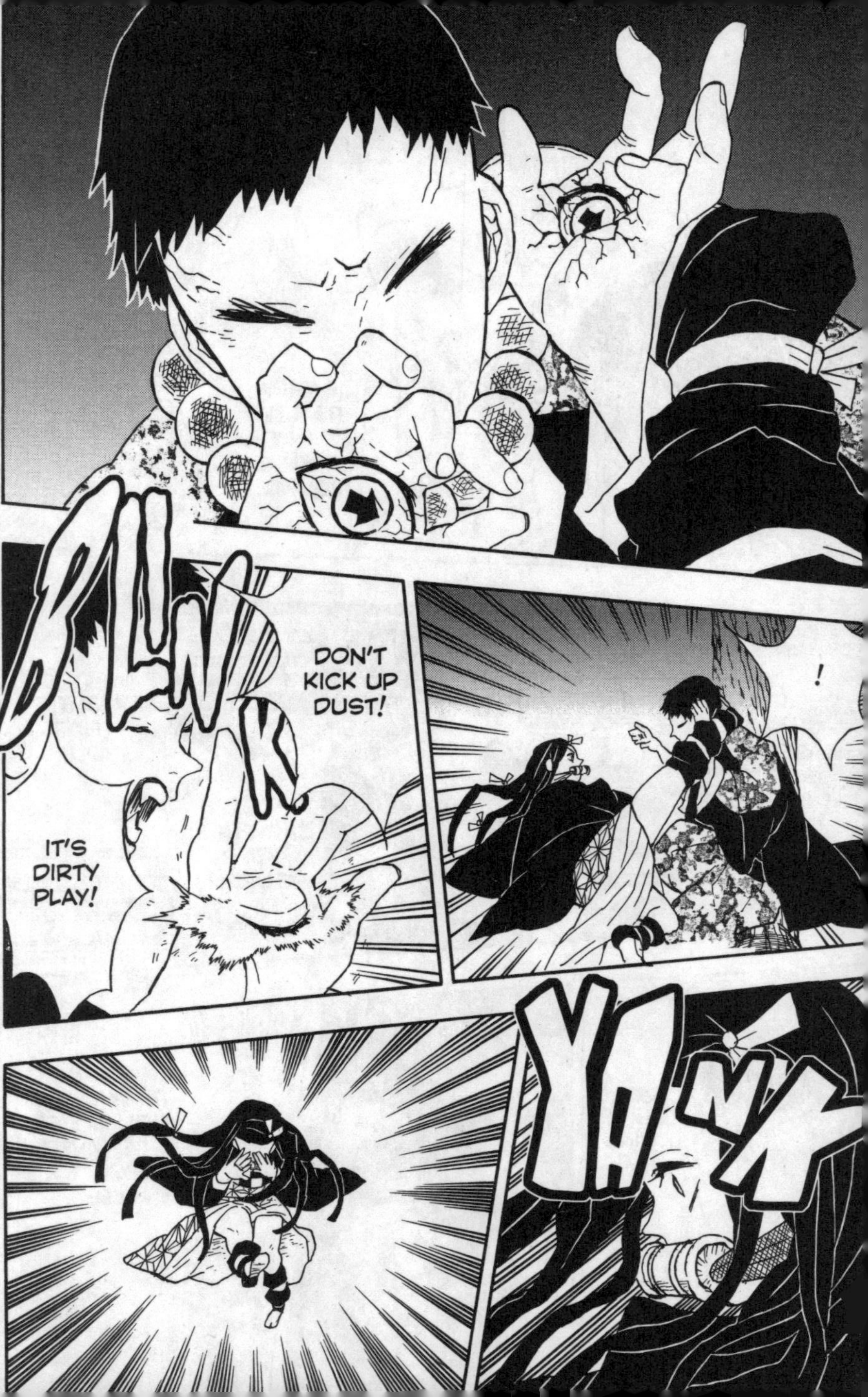
!
BLINK
DON'T KICK UP DUST!
IT'S DIRTY PLAY!
YANK

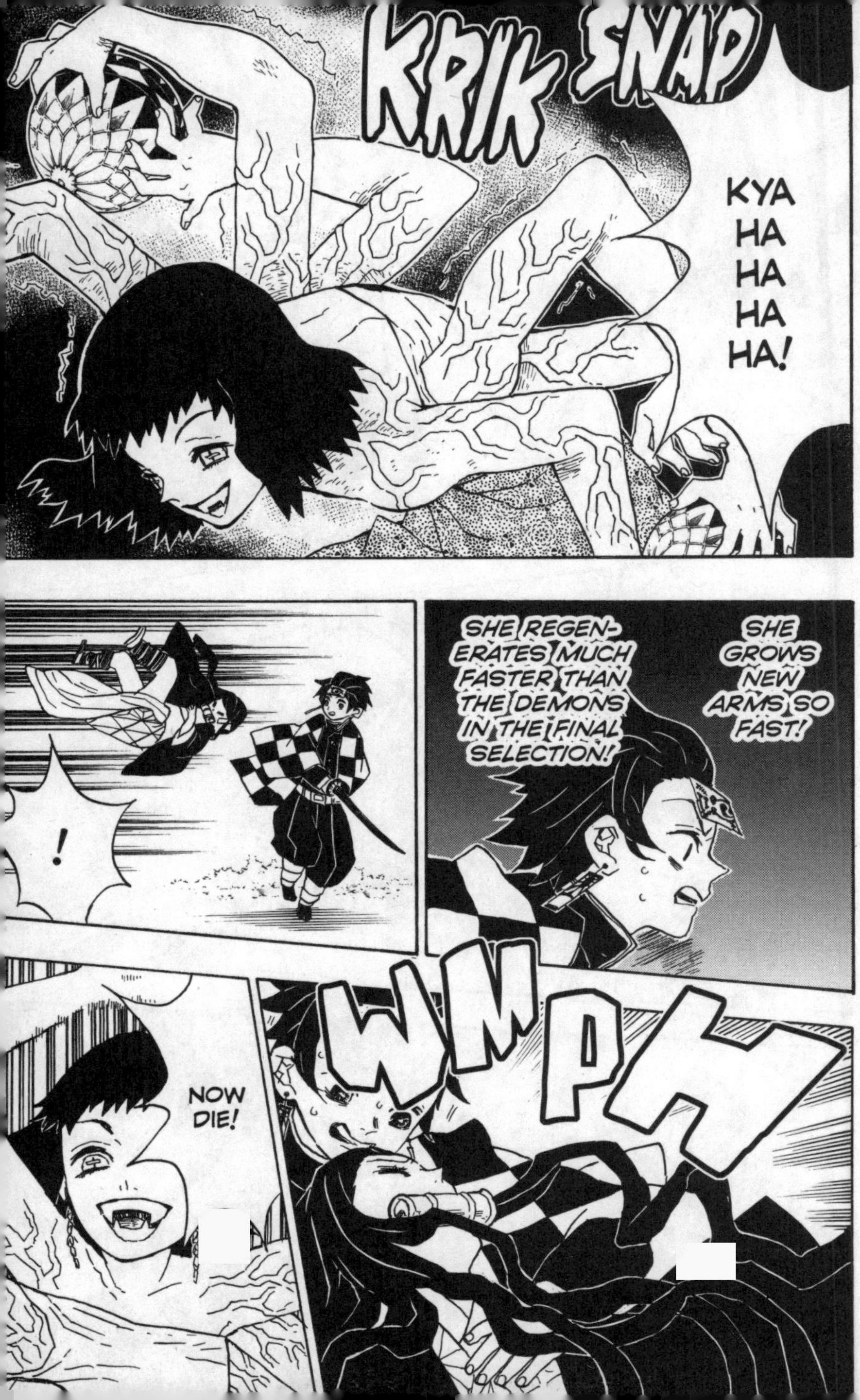
KRIK SNAP
KYA HA HA HA HA!
SHE GROWS NEW ARMS SO FAST!
SHE REGEN-ERATES MUCH FASTER THAN THE DEMONS IN THE FINAL SELECTION!
!
WMPH
NOW DIE!

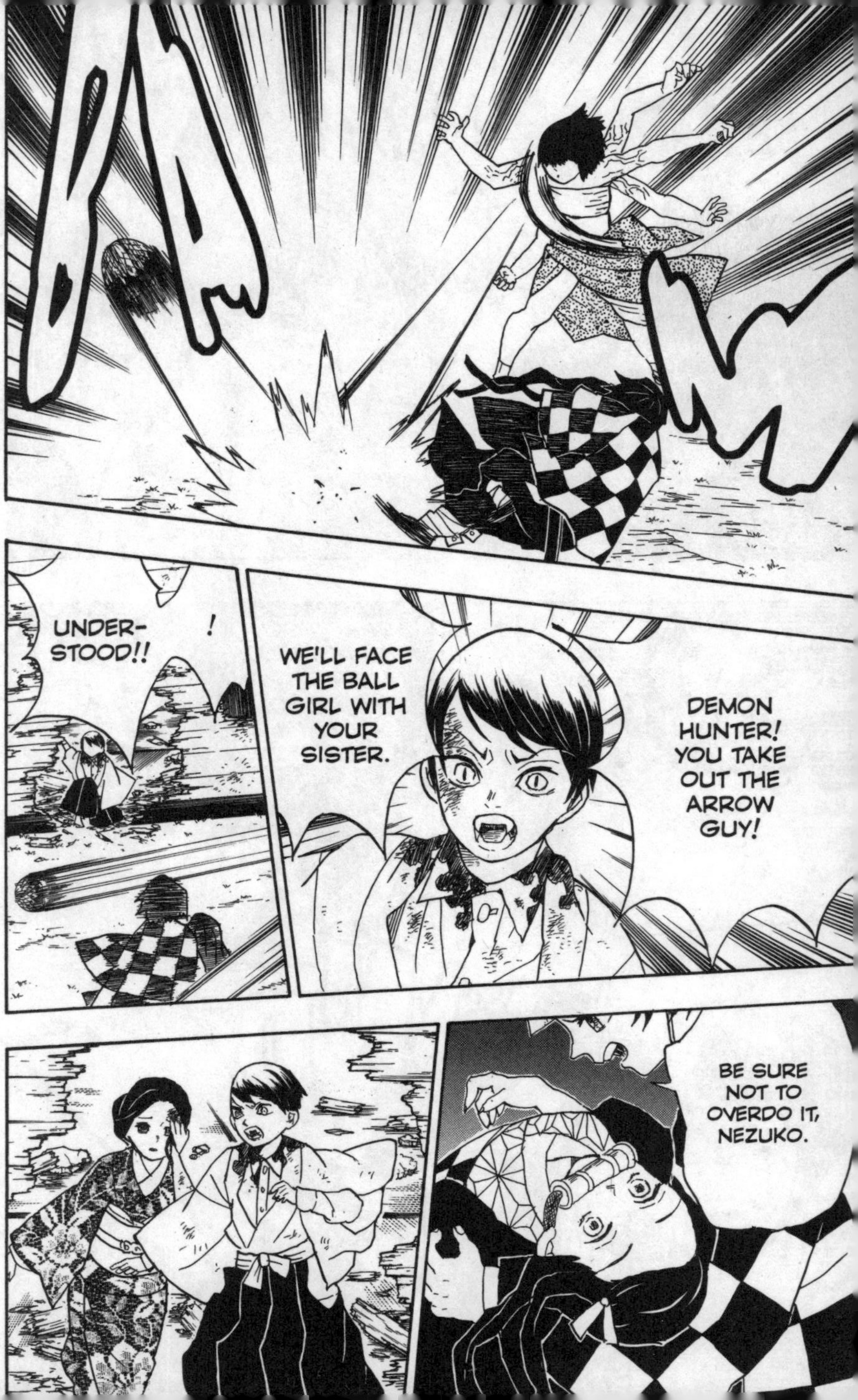
DEMON HUNTER! YOU TAKE OUT THE ARROW GUY!
WE'LL FACE THE BALL GIRL WITH YOUR SISTER.
!
UNDER-STOOD!!
BE SURE NOT TO OVERDO IT, NEZUKO.

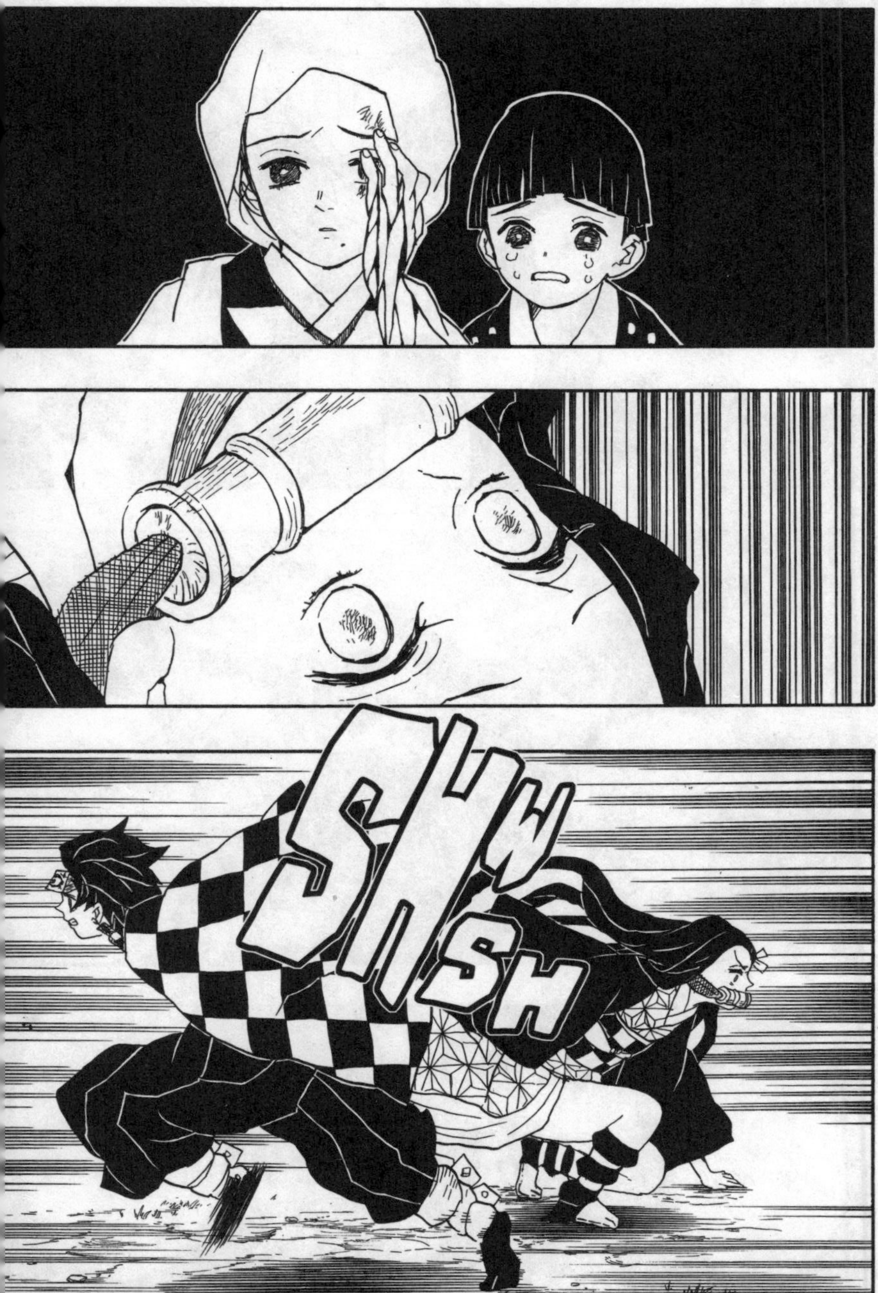
SWISH

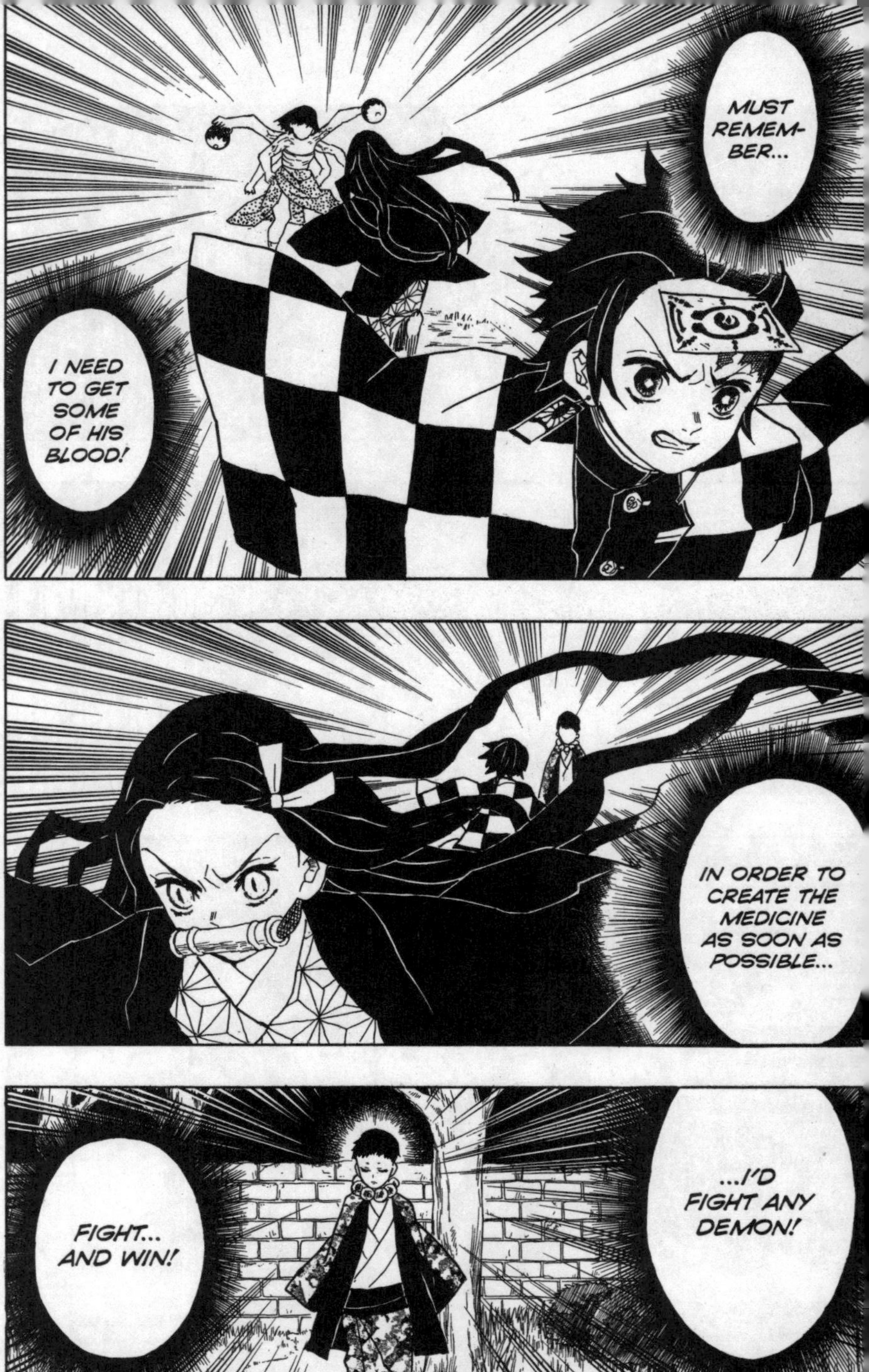
MUST REMEMBER-BER...
I NEED TO GET SOME OF HIS BLOOD!
IN ORDER TO CREATE THE MEDICINE AS SOON AS POSSIBLE...
...I'D FIGHT ANY DEMON!
FIGHT... AND WIN!

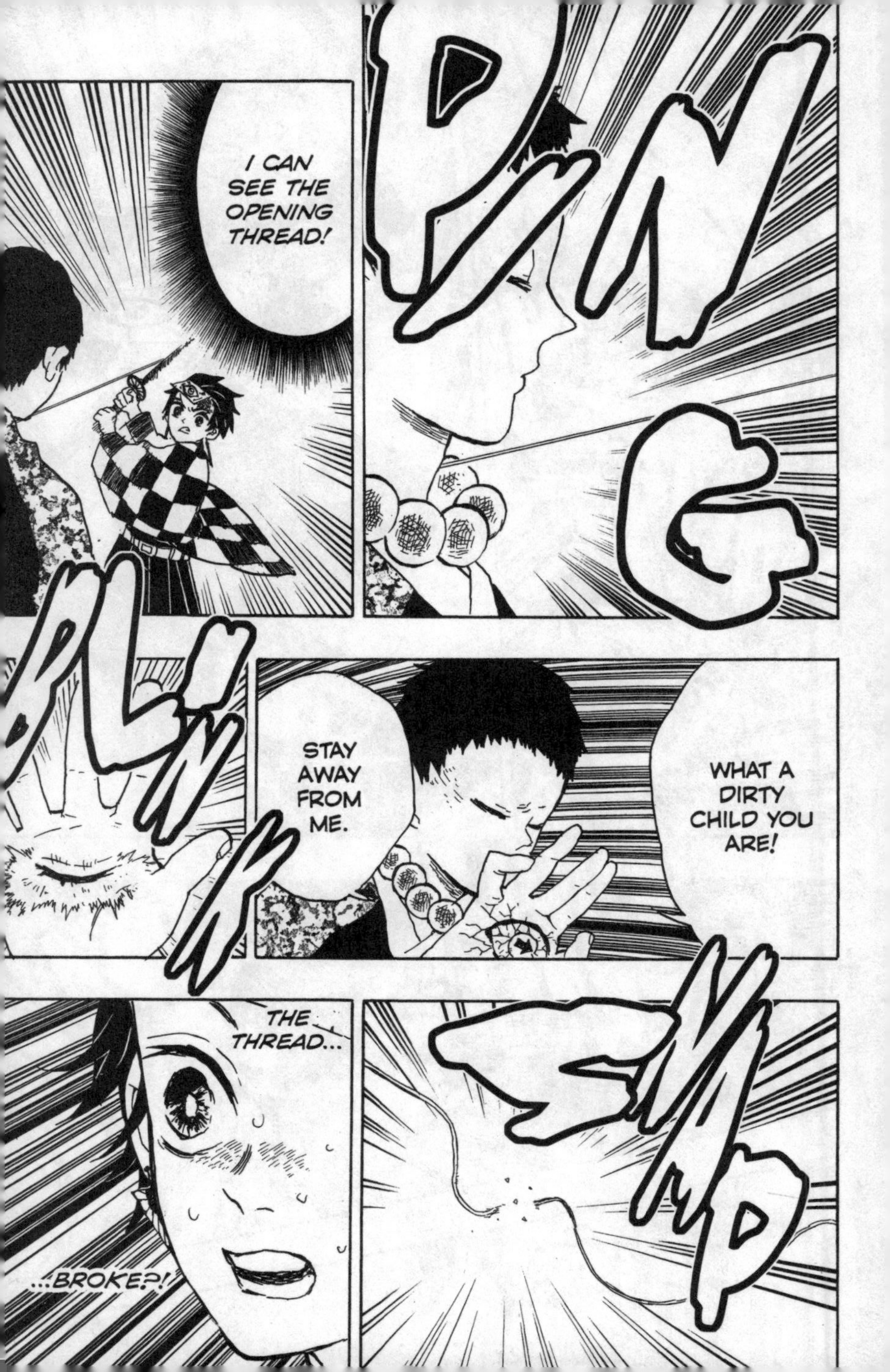
I CAN SEE THE OPENING THREAD!
WHAT A DIRTY CHILD YOU ARE!
STAY AWAY FROM ME.
THE THREAD...
...BROKE?!

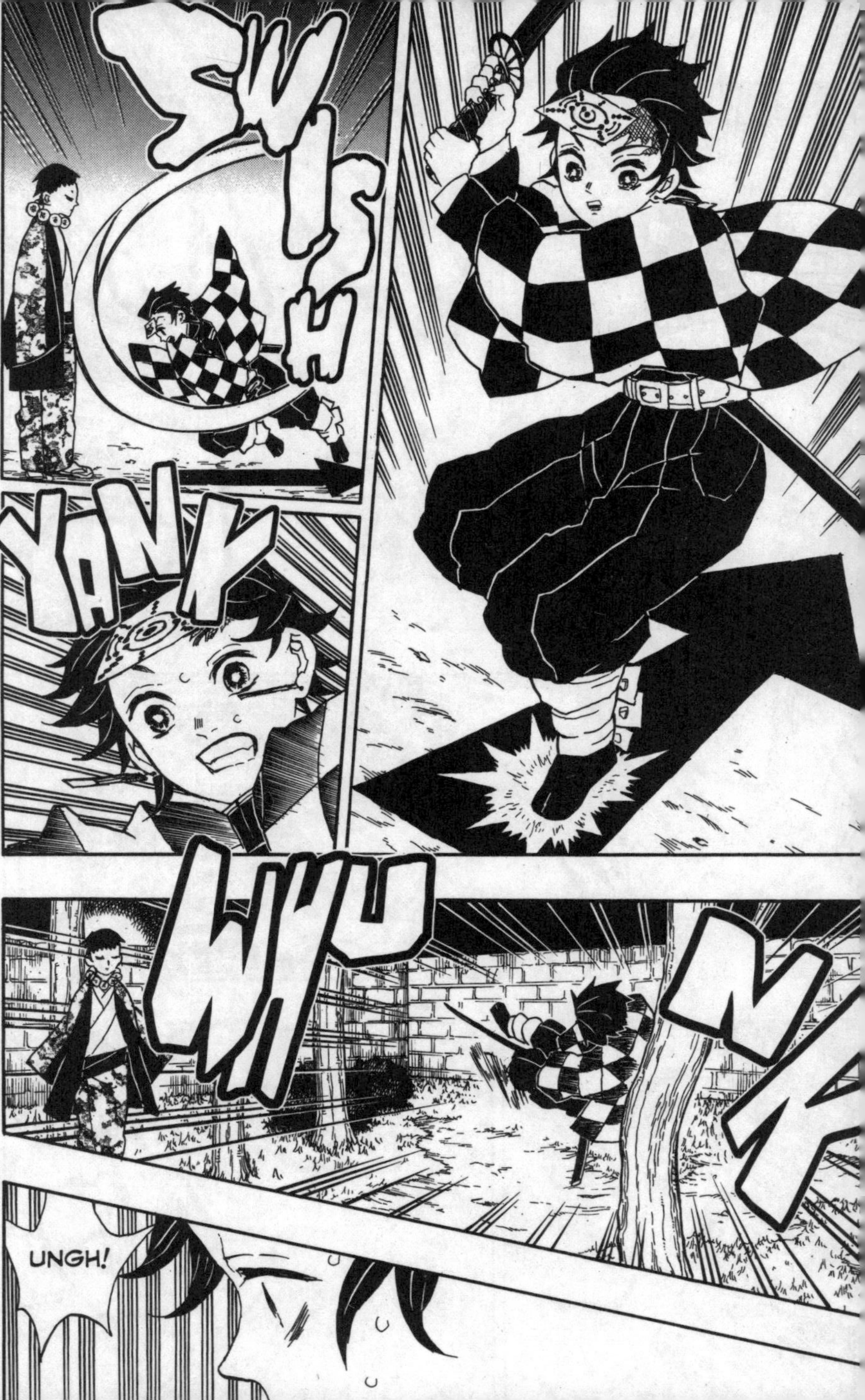
SWISH
YANK
WHUNK
UNGH!

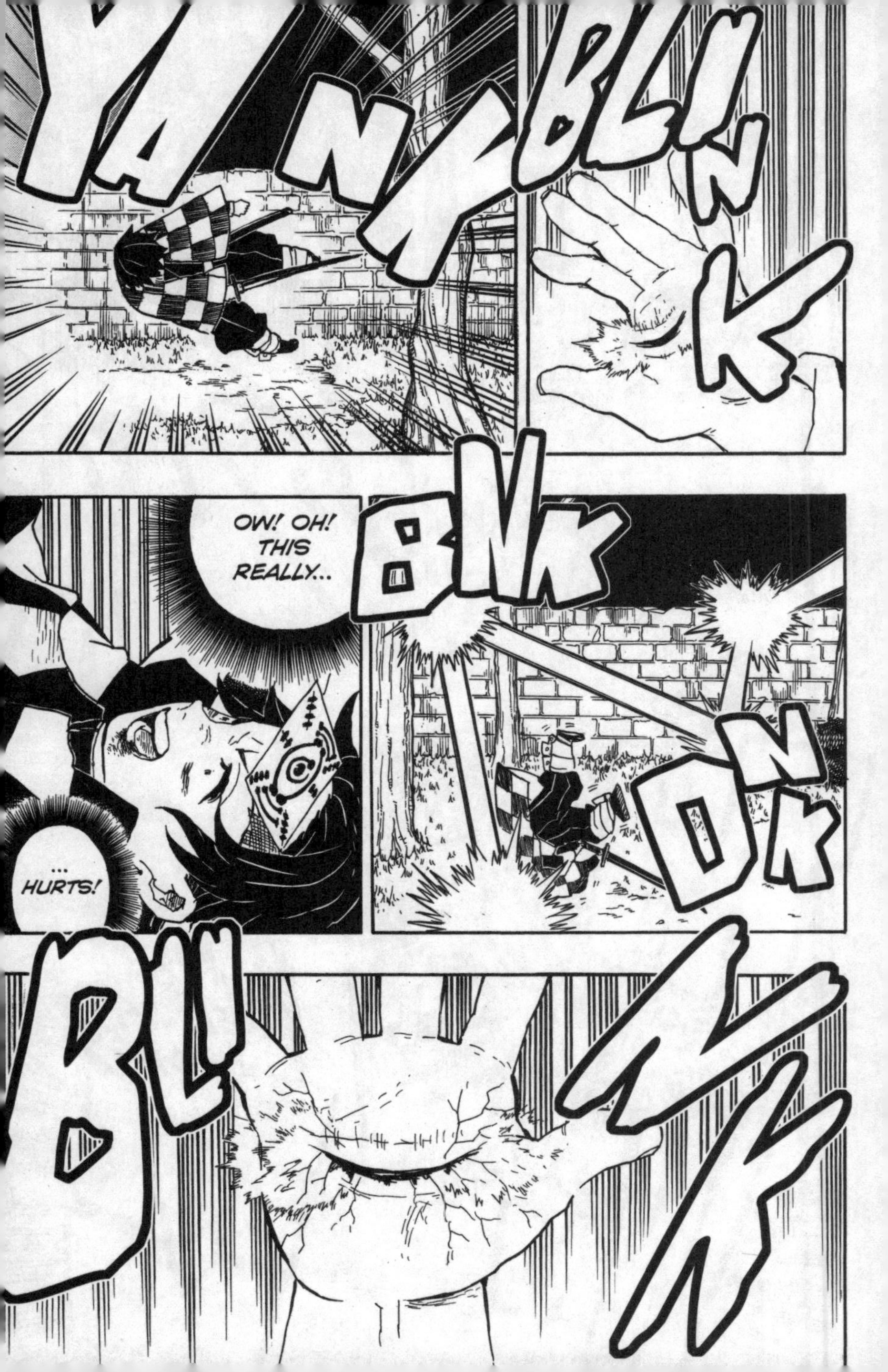
BLINK
YANK
DONK
BNK
OW! OH! THIS REALLY...
...HURTS!
BLINK

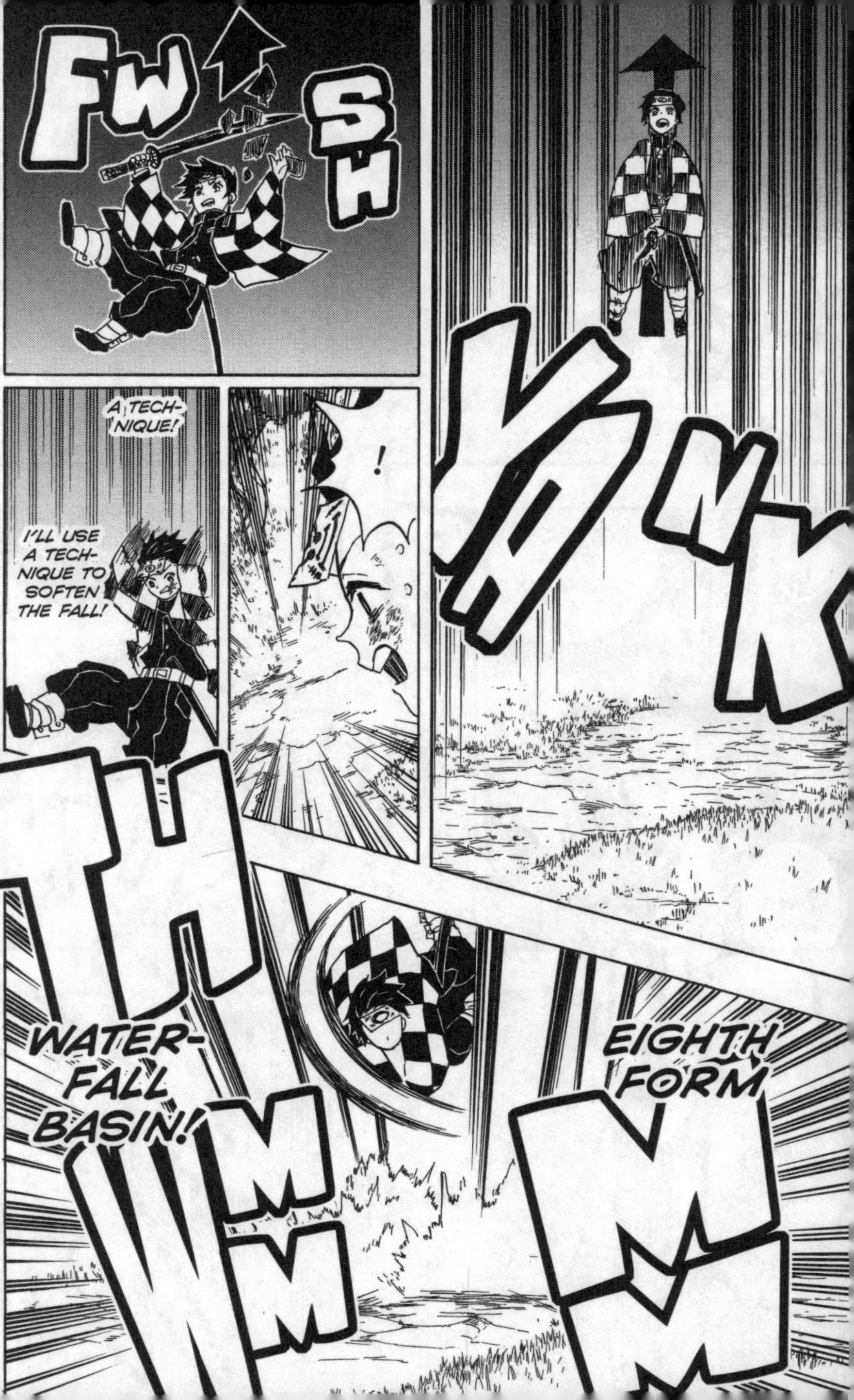
KNK
FWSH
!
A TECHNIQUE!
I'LL USE A TECHNIQUE TO SOFTEN THE FALL!
EIGHTH FORM
WATERFALL BASIN!

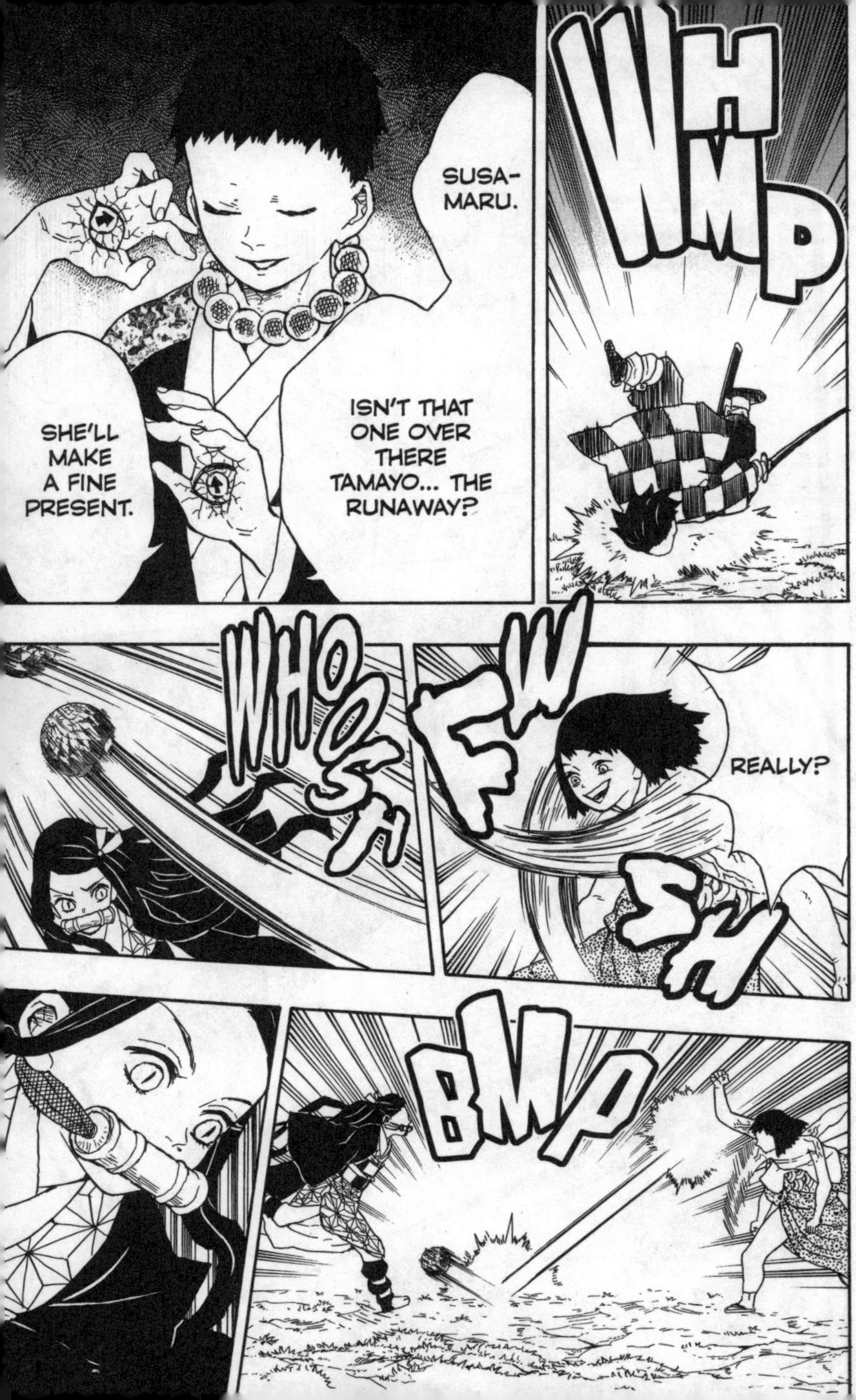
WHMP
SUSA-MARU.
ISN'T THAT ONE OVER THERE TAMAYO... THE RUNAWAY?
SHE'LL MAKE A FINE PRESENT.
REALLY?
FW
SH
WHOOSH
BMP

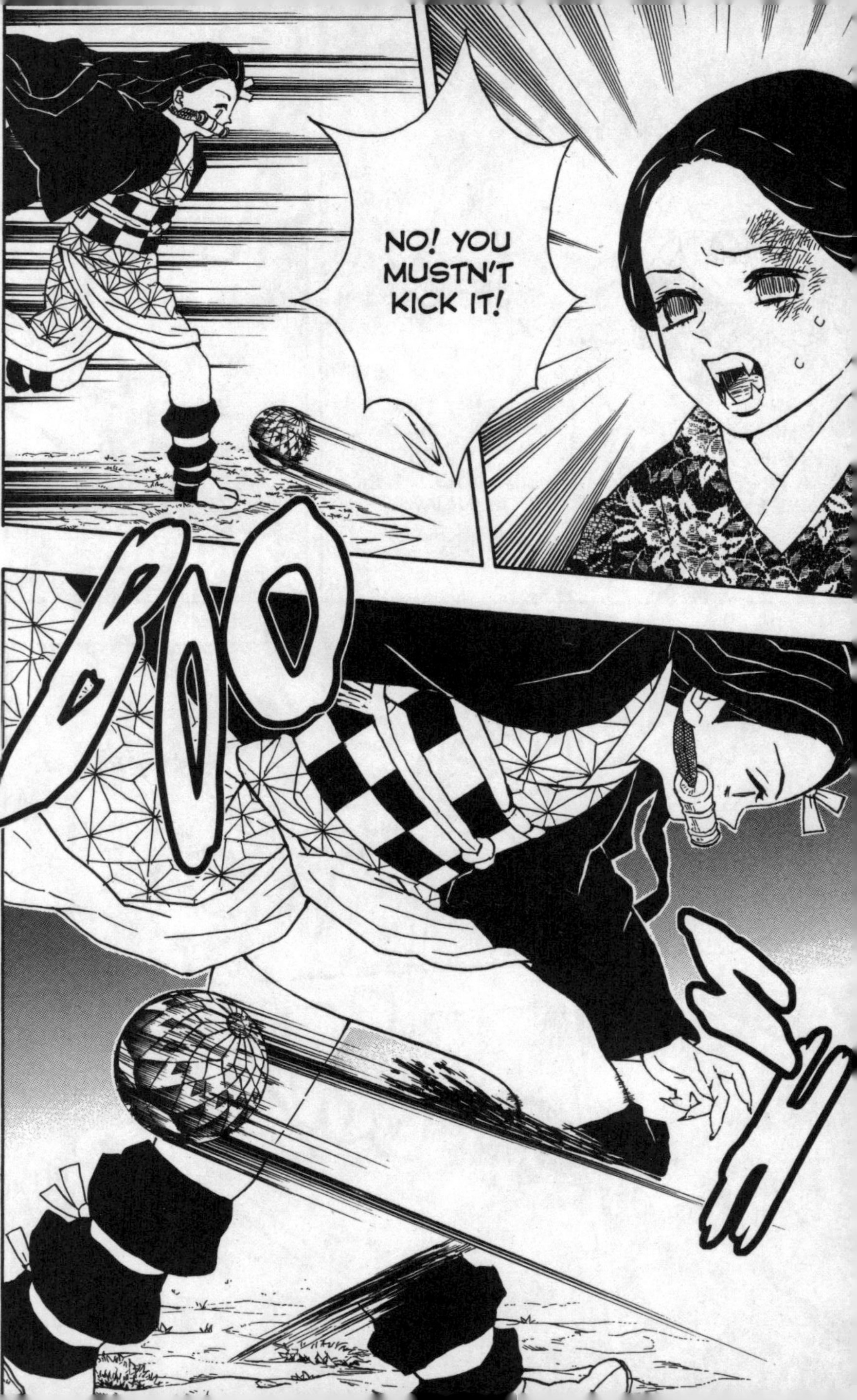
NO! YOU MUSTN'T KICK IT!
BOOM

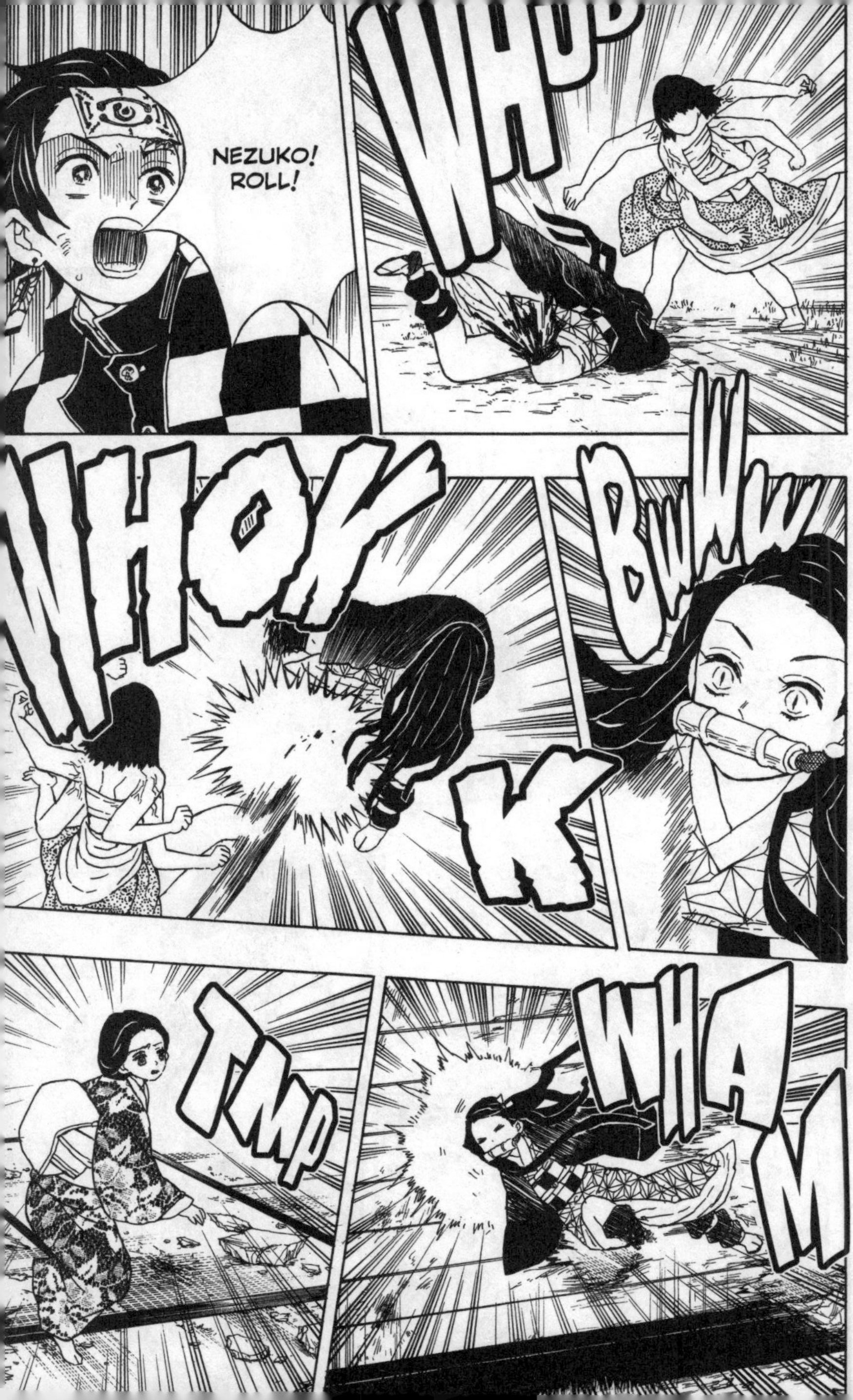
WHUD
NEZUKO! ROLL!
BWUW
WHOK
K
WHAM
TMP

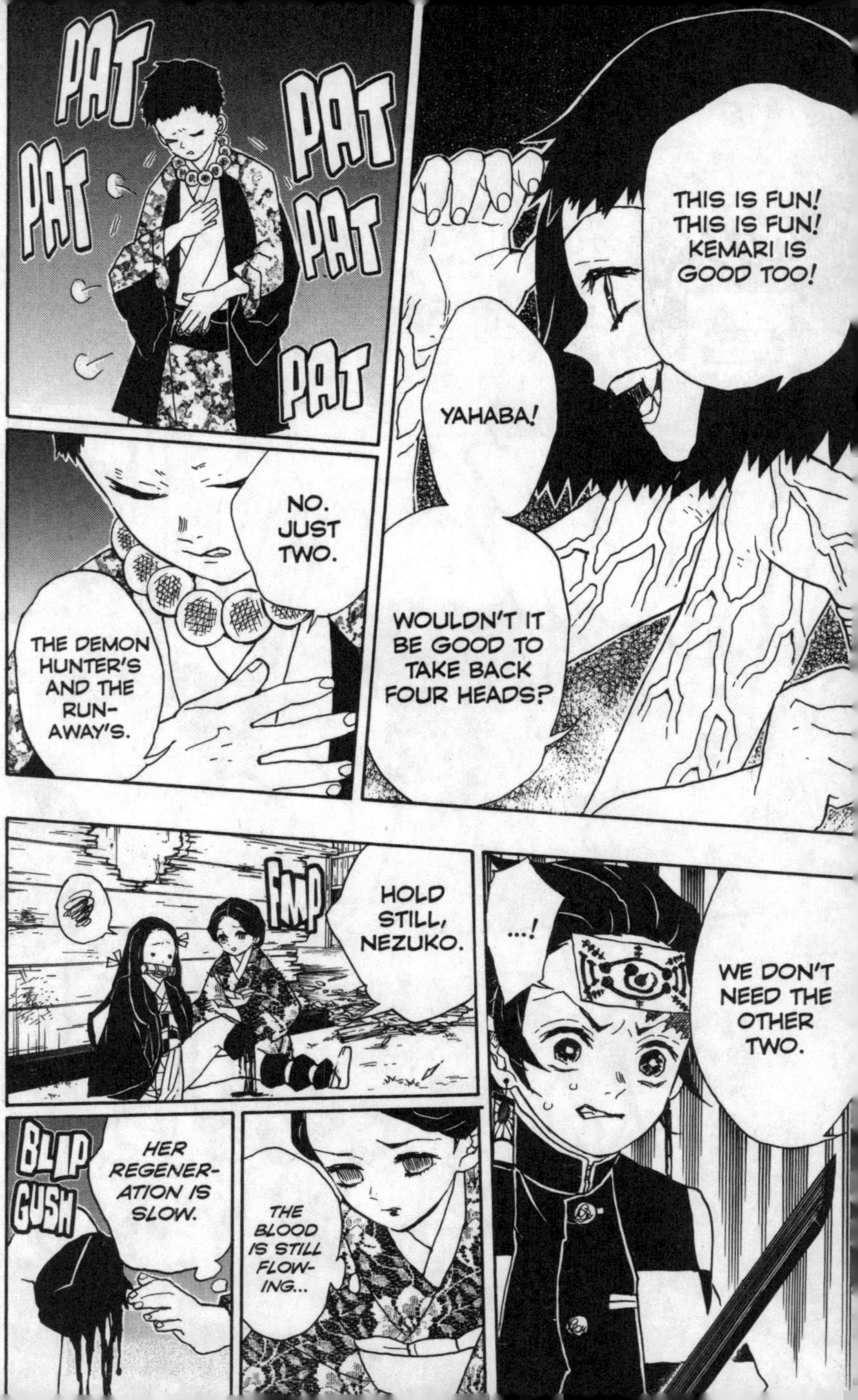
THIS IS FUN! THIS IS FUN! KEMARI IS GOOD TOO!
YAHABA!
WOULDN'T IT BE GOOD TO TAKE BACK FOUR HEADS?
PAT PAT PAT PAT PAT
NO. JUST TWO.
THE DEMON HUNTER'S AND THE RUN-AWAY'S.
...!
WE DON'T NEED THE OTHER TWO.
FMP
HOLD STILL, NEZUKO.
THE BLOOD IS STILL FLOWING...
HER REGENER-ATION IS SLOW.
BLIP
GUSH

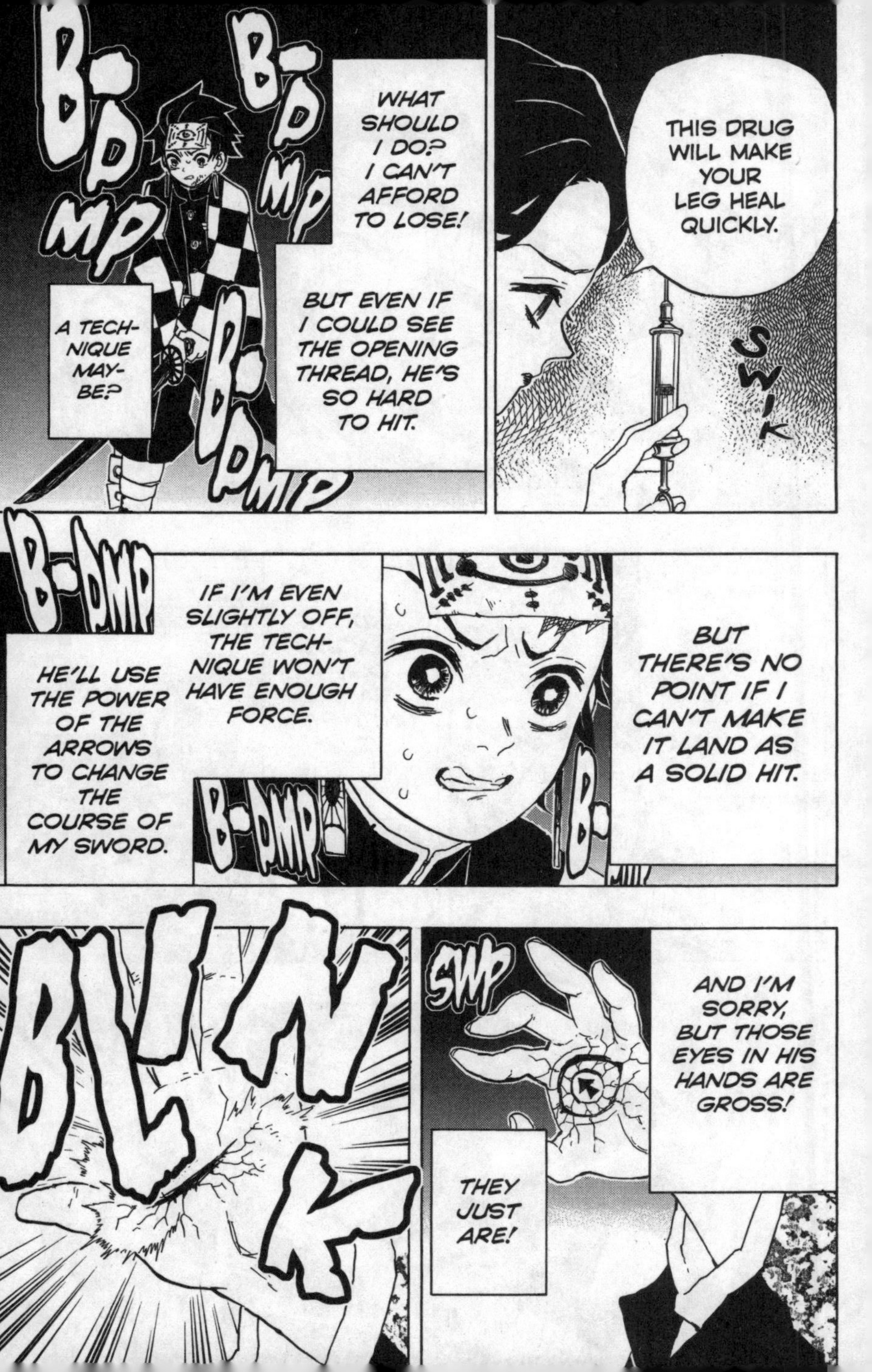
THIS DRUG WILL MAKE YOUR LEG HEAL QUICKLY.
SWIK
WHAT SHOULD I DO? I CAN'T AFFORD TO LOSE!
BUT EVEN IF I COULD SEE THE OPENING THREAD, HE'S SO HARD TO HIT.
A TECH-NIQUE MAY-BE?
B-B-MP
B-D-MP
B-DMP
B-DMP
BUT THERE'S NO POINT IF I CAN'T MAKE IT LAND AS A SOLID HIT.
IF I'M EVEN SLIGHTLY OFF, THE TECH-NIQUE WON'T HAVE ENOUGH FORCE.
HE'LL USE THE POWER OF THE ARROWS TO CHANGE THE COURSE OF MY SWORD.
B-DMP
AND I'M SORRY, BUT THOSE EYES IN HIS HANDS ARE GROSS!
SWP
THEY JUST ARE!
BLINK

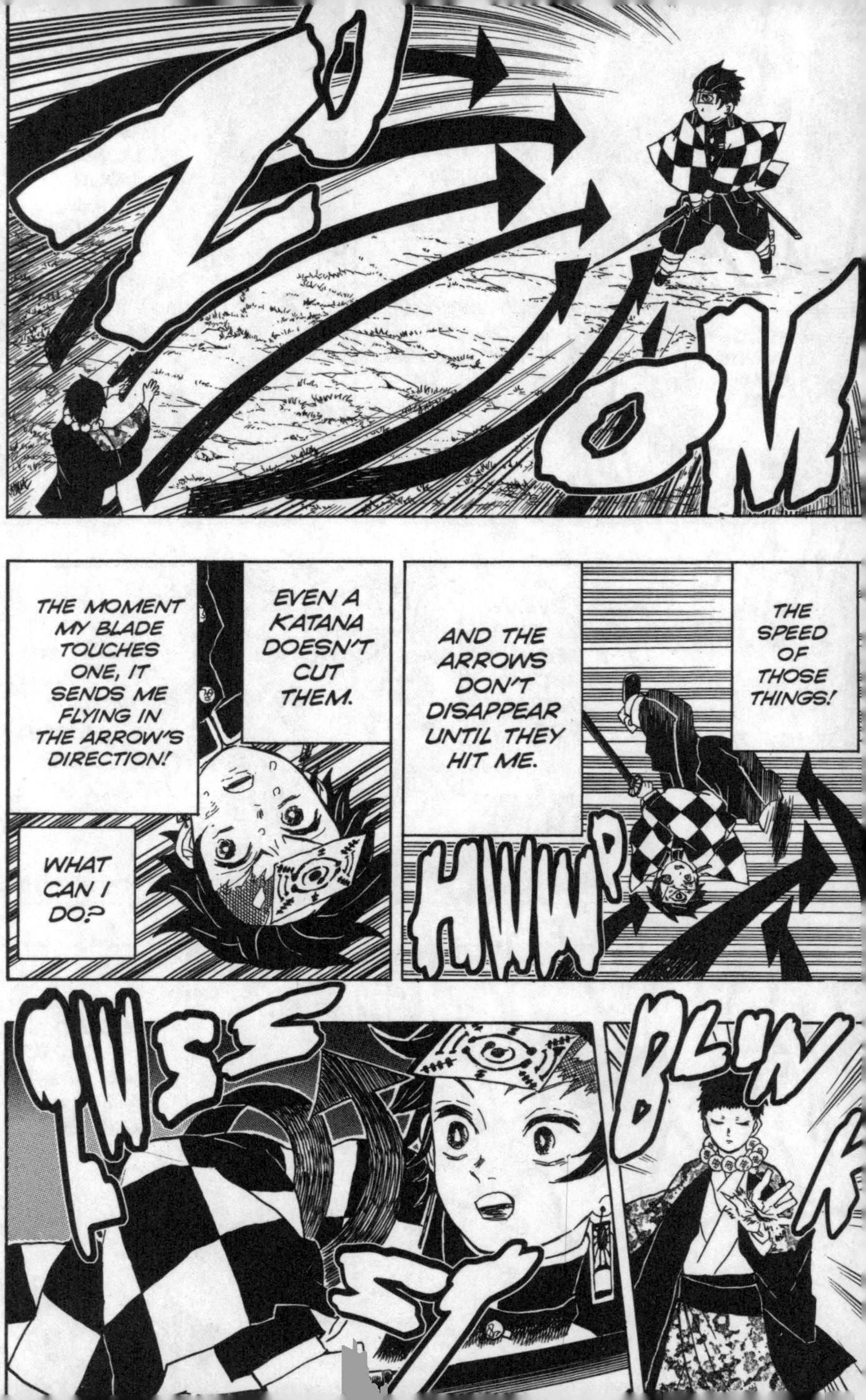
THE SPEED OF THOSE THINGS!
AND THE ARROWS DON'T DISAPPEAR UNTIL THEY HIT ME.
HWWP
EVEN A KATANA DOESN'T CUT THEM.
THE MOMENT MY BLADE TOUCHES ONE, IT SENDS ME FLYING IN THE ARROW'S DIRECTION!
WHAT CAN I DO?
BLINK

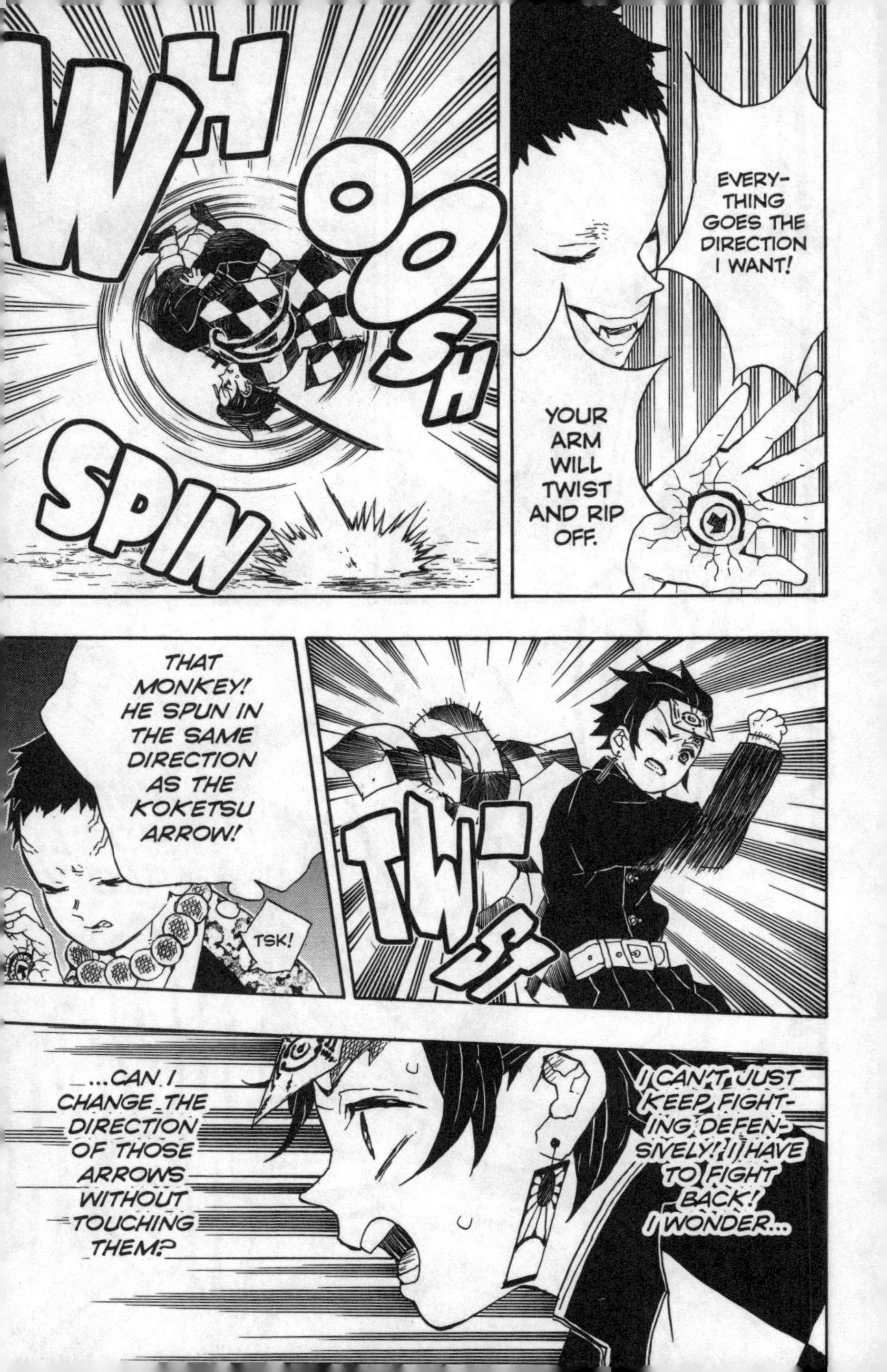
EVERYTHING GOES THE DIRECTION I WANT!
YOUR ARM WILL TWIST AND RIP OFF.
WHOOSH
SPIN
TWIST
THAT MONKEY! HE SPUN IN THE SAME DIRECTION AS THE KOKETSU ARROW!
TSK!
I CAN'T JUST KEEP FIGHTING DEFENSIVELY! I HAVE TO FIGHT BACK! I WONDER...
...CAN I CHANGE THE DIRECTION OF THOSE ARROWS WITHOUT TOUCHING THEM?

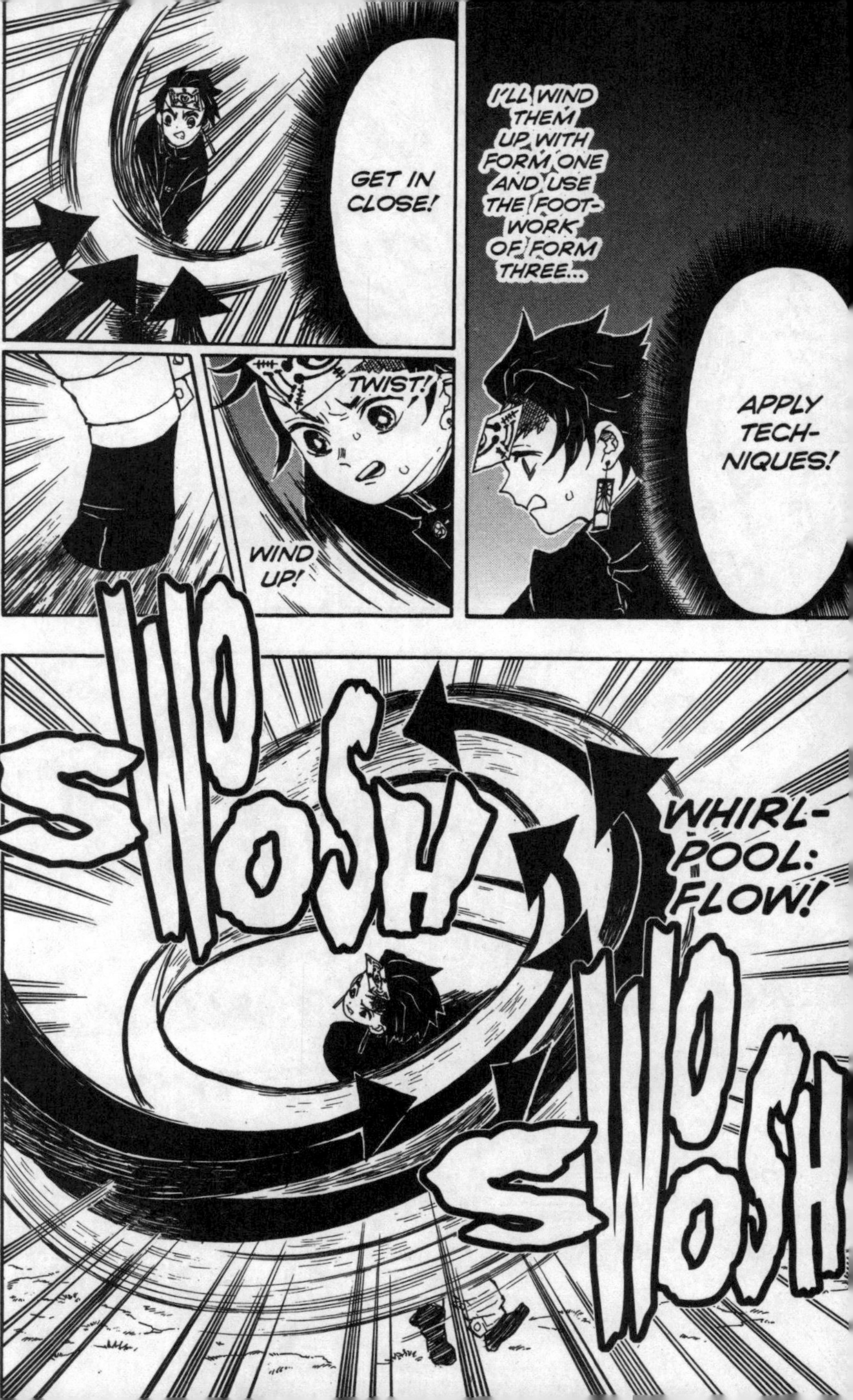
I'LL WIND THEM UP WITH FORM ONE AND USE THE FOOT-WORK OF FORM THREE...
APPLY TECH-NIQUES!
GET IN CLOSE!
TWIST!
WIND UP!
SWOOSH
WHIRL-POOL: FLOW!
SWOOSH

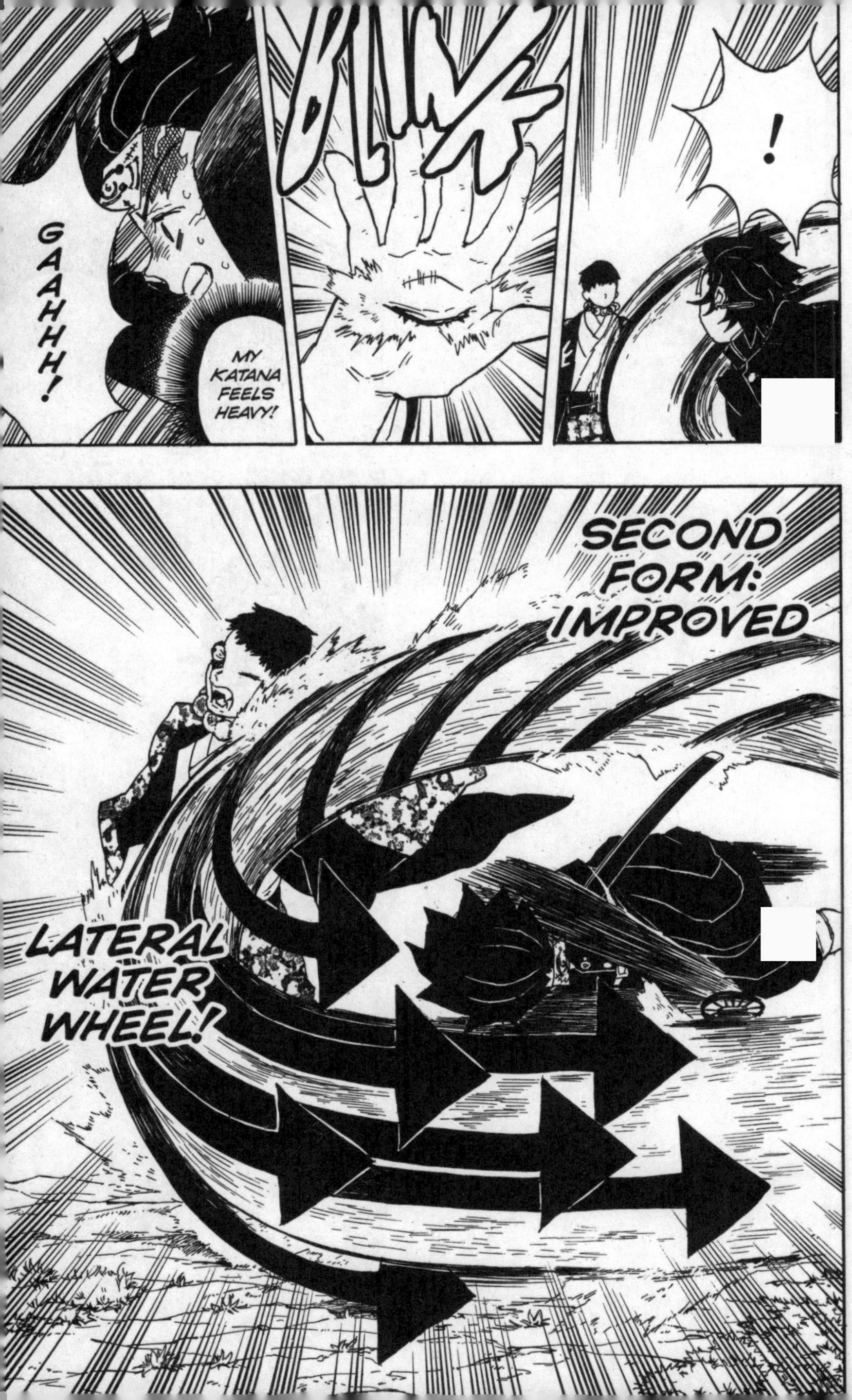
!
MY KATANA FEELS HEAVY!
GAAHHH!
SECOND FORM: IMPROVED
LATERAL WATER WHEEL!

2016
Combined cover, issue 36/37

CHAPTER 18: THE CURSE

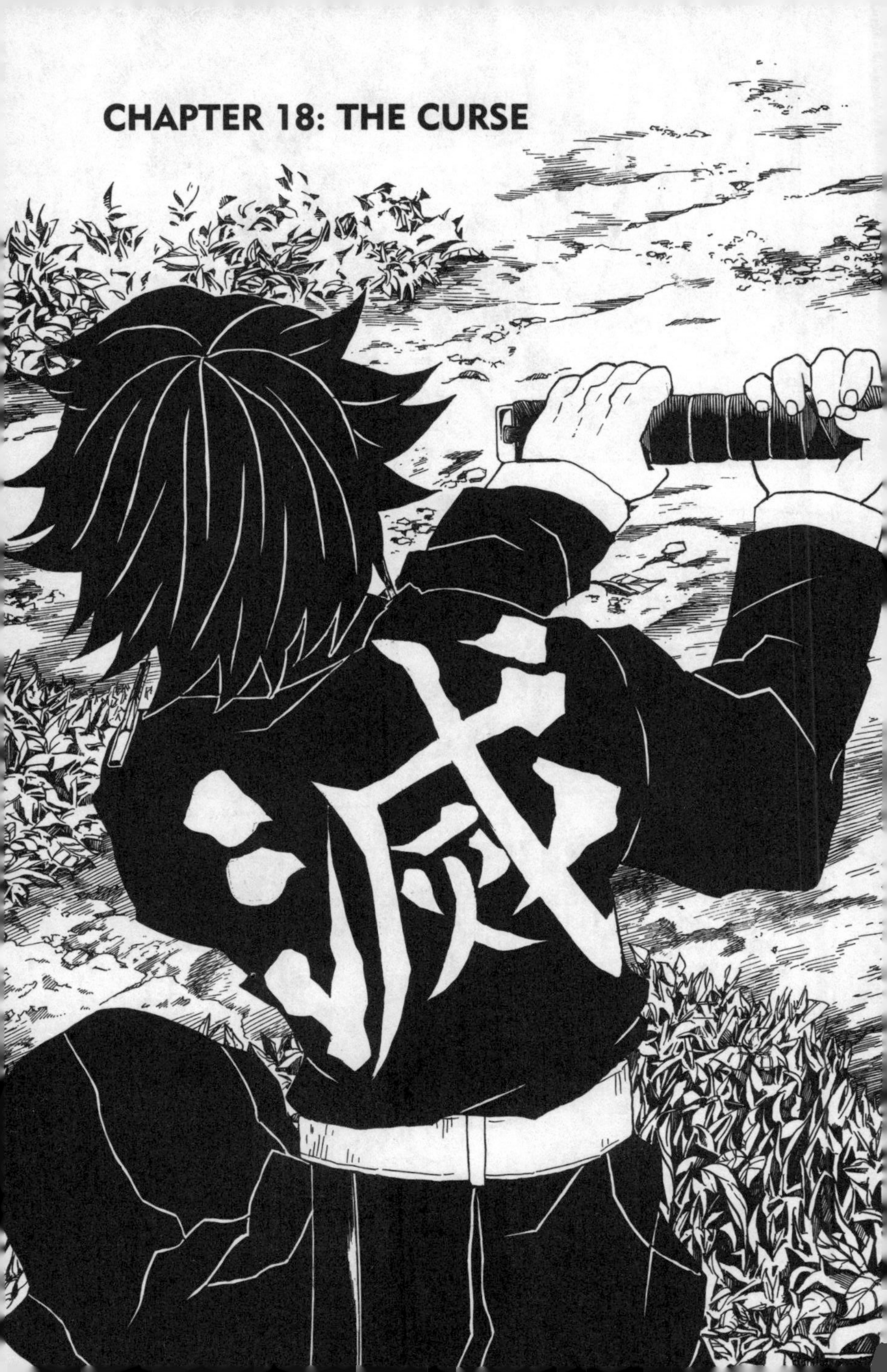
滅

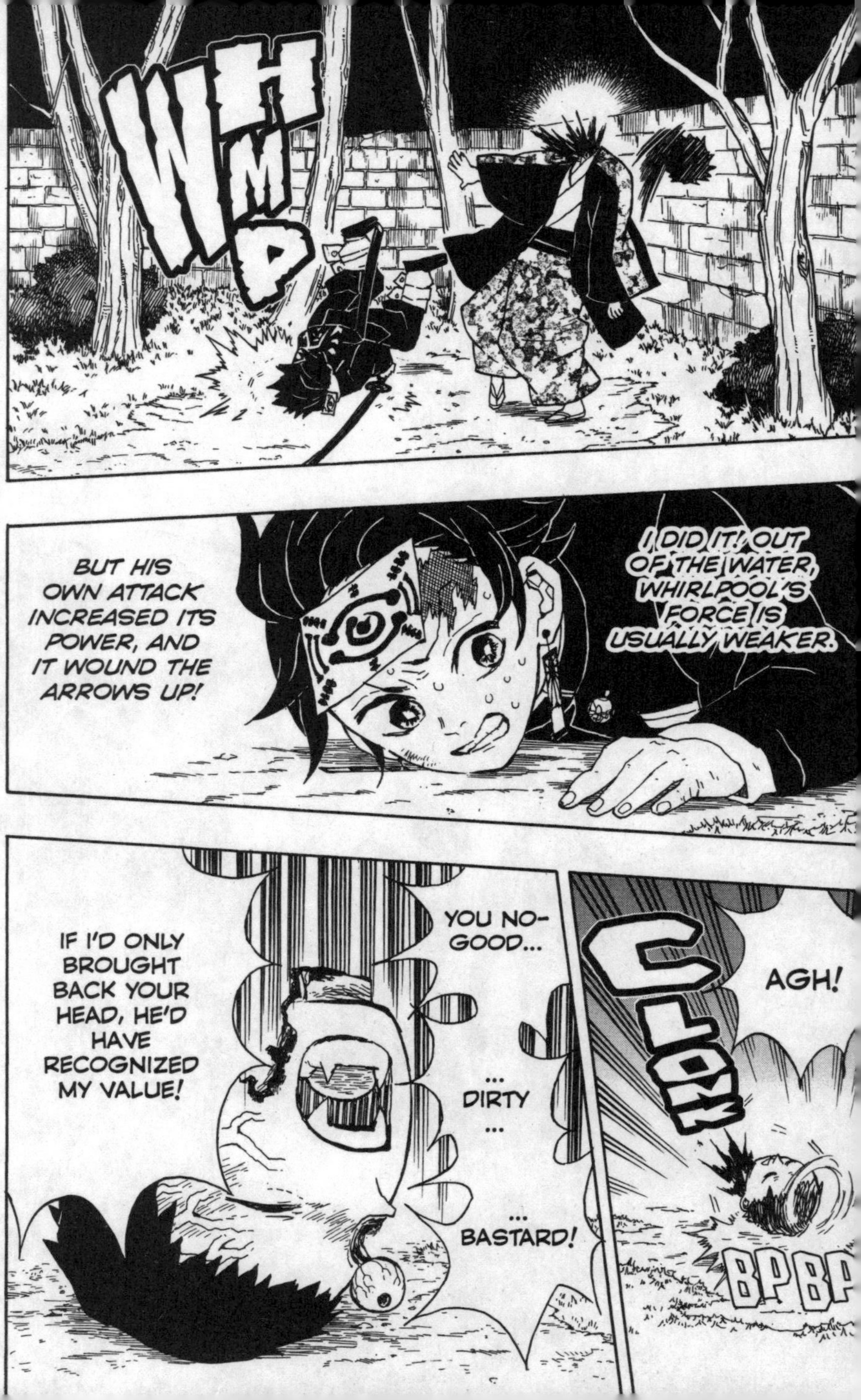
WHMP
I DID IT! OUT OF THE WATER, WHIRLPOOL'S FORCE IS USUALLY WEAKER.
BUT HIS OWN ATTACK INCREASED ITS POWER, AND IT WOUND THE ARROWS UP!
AGH!
CLOM
BPBP
YOU NO-GOOD...
... DIRTY ...
... BASTARD!
IF I'D ONLY BROUGHT BACK YOUR HEAD, HE'D HAVE RECOGNIZED MY VALUE!

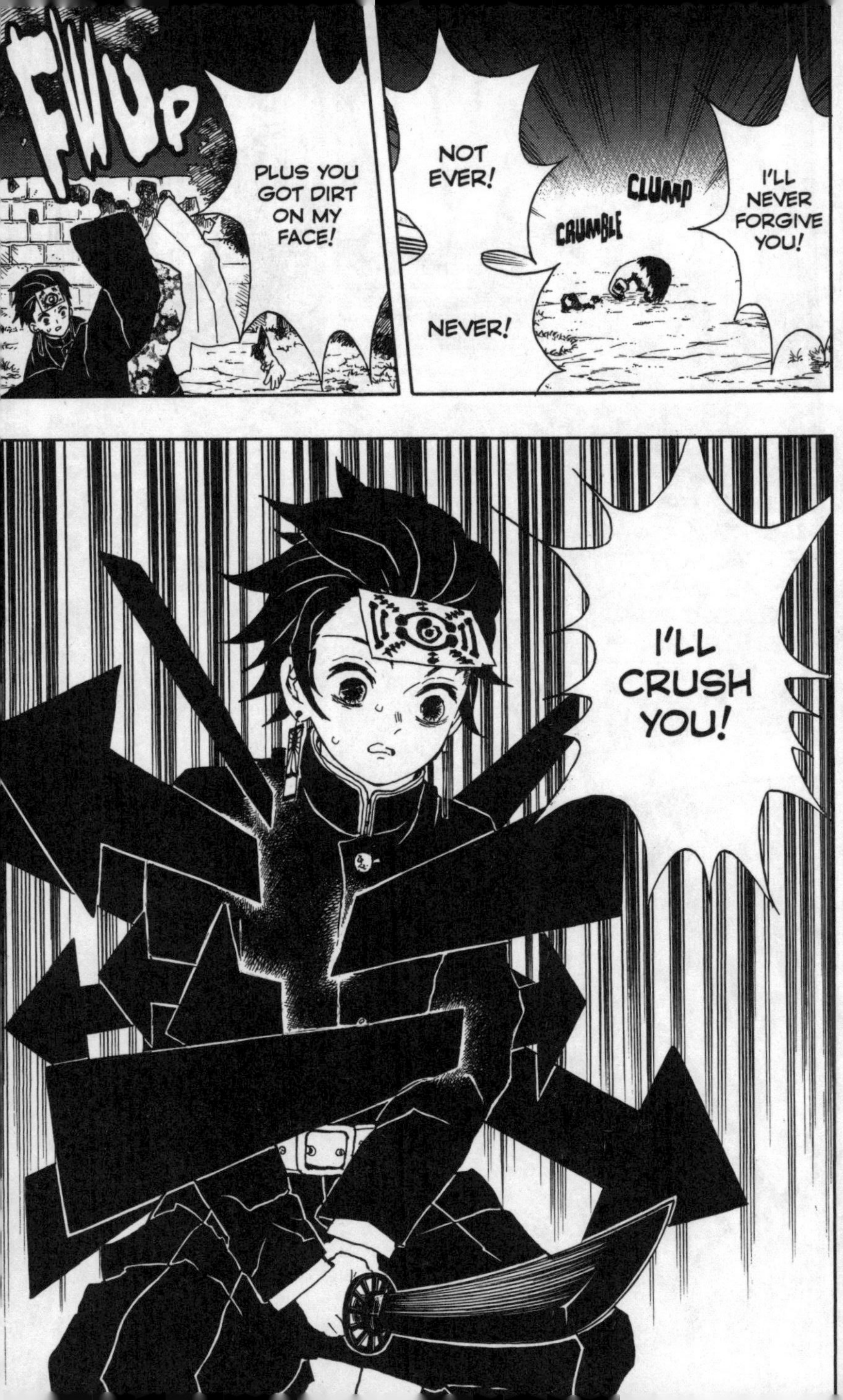
I'LL NEVER FORGIVE YOU!
CLUMP
CRUMBLE
NOT EVER!
NEVER!
PLUS YOU GOT DIRT ON MY FACE!
FWUP
I'LL CRUSH YOU!

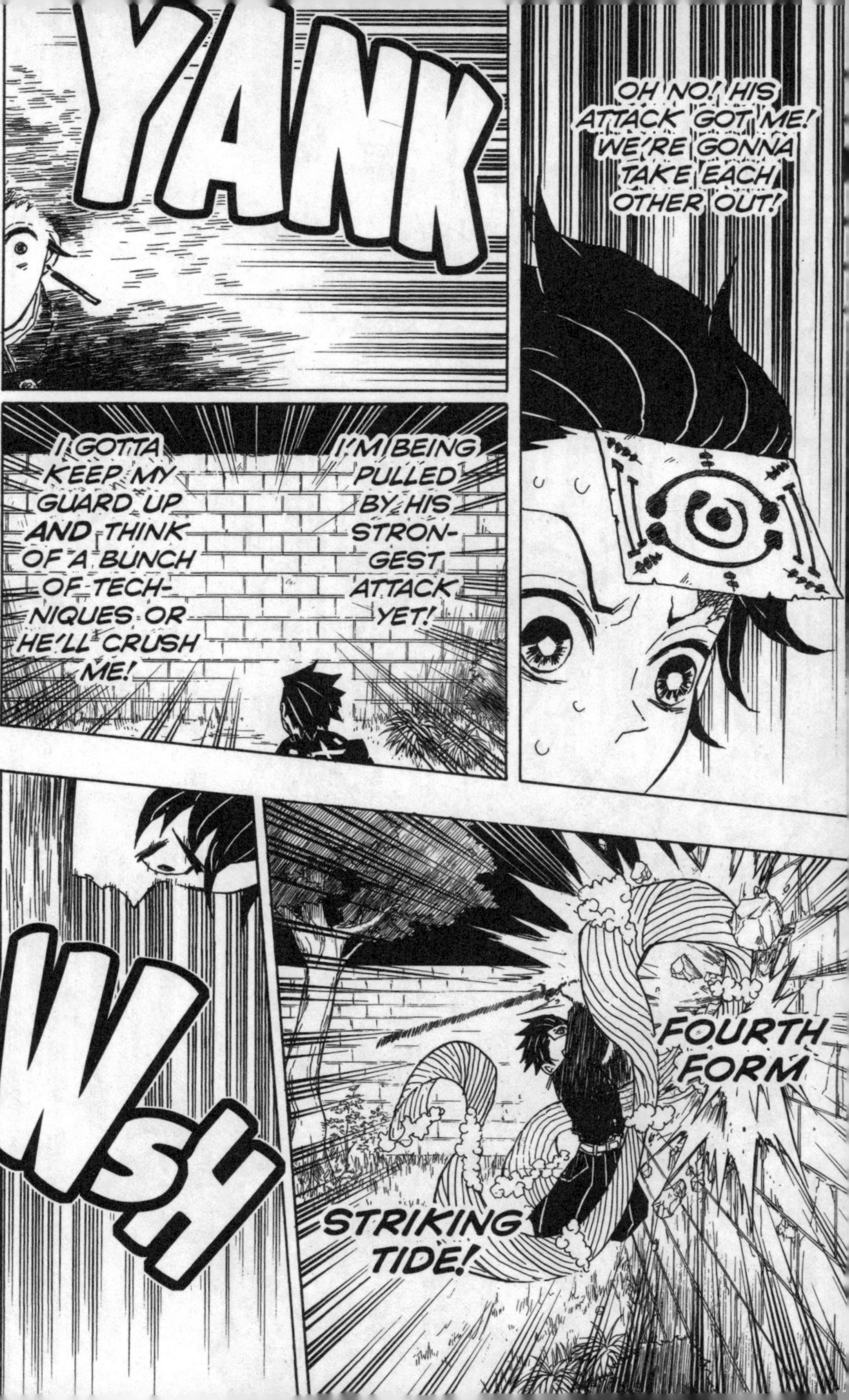
OH NO! HIS ATTACK GOT ME! WE'RE GONNA TAKE EACH OTHER OUT!
YANK
I'M BEING PULLED BY HIS STRONGEST ATTACK YET!
I GOTTA KEEP MY GUARD UP AND THINK OF A BUNCH OF TECHNIQUES OR HE'LL CRUSH ME!
FOURTH FORM
STRIKING TIDE!
WSH

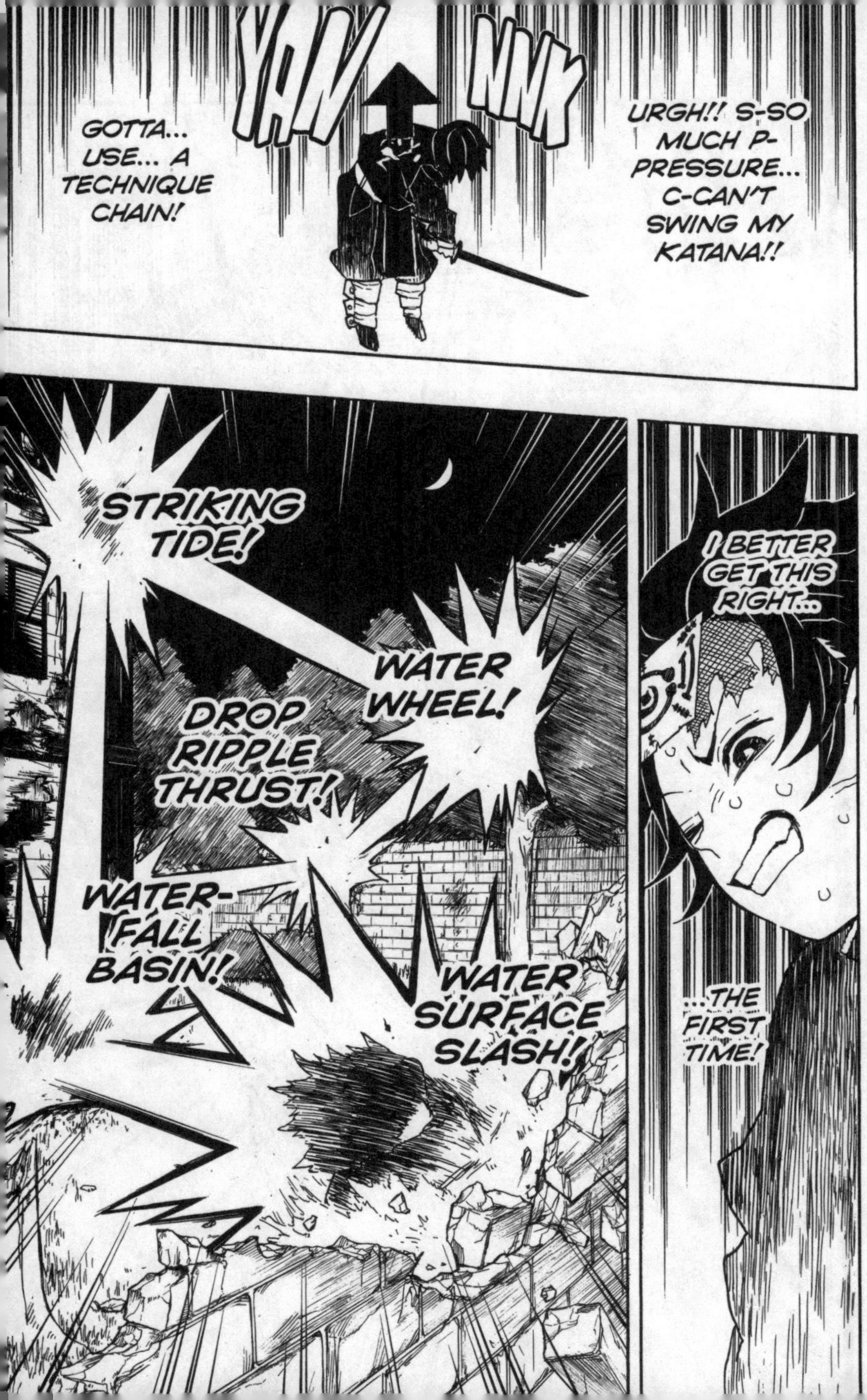
URGH!! S-SO MUCH P-PRESSURE... C-CAN'T SWING MY KATANA!!
YAN NNK
GOTTA... USE... A TECHNIQUE CHAIN!
I BETTER GET THIS RIGHT...
...THE FIRST TIME!
STRIKING TIDE!
WATER WHEEL!
DROP RIPPLE THRUST!
WATER-FALL BASIN!
WATER SURFACE SLASH!

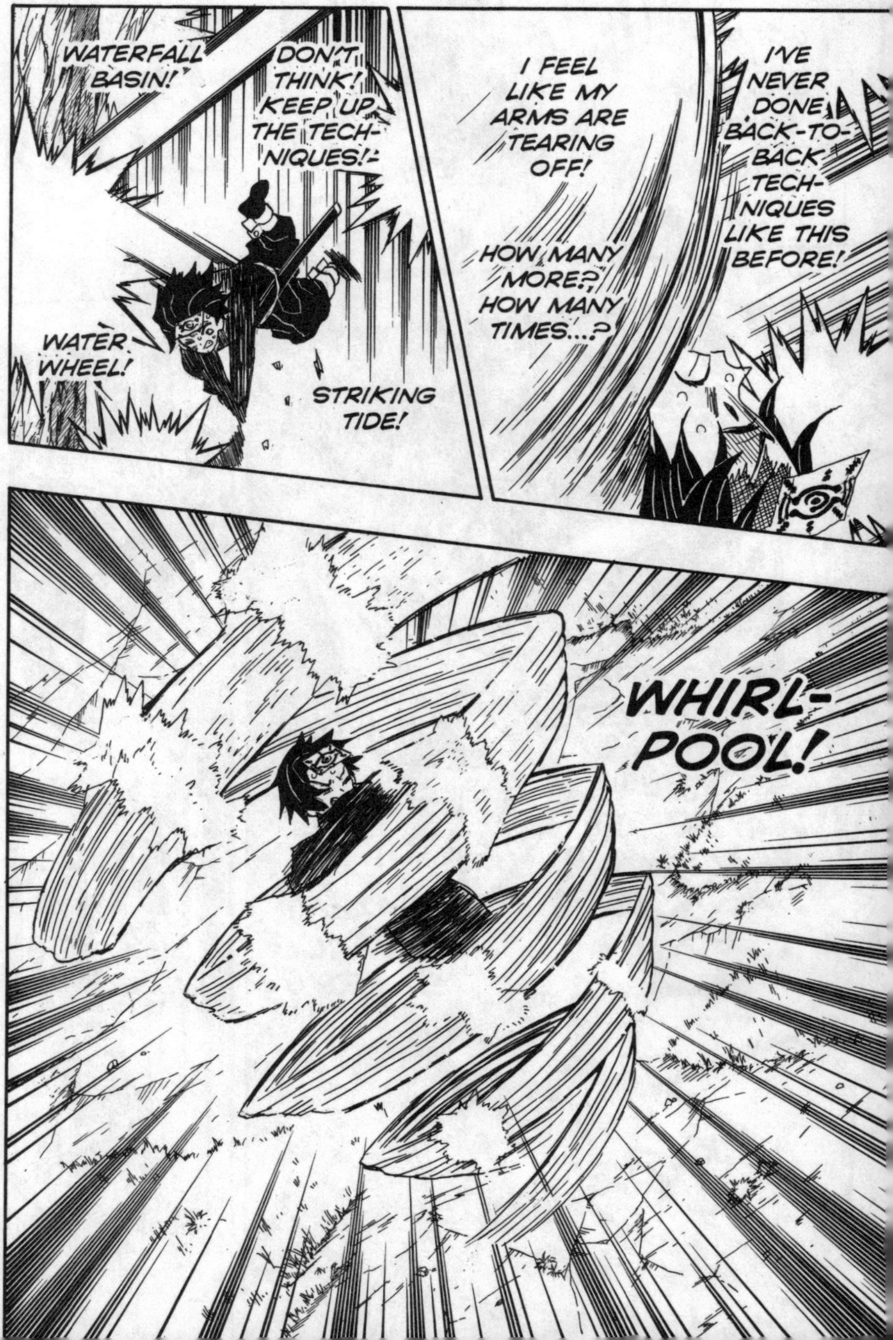
I'VE NEVER DONE BACK-TO-BACK TECHNIQUES LIKE THIS BEFORE!
I FEEL LIKE MY ARMS ARE TEARING OFF!
HOW MANY MORE? HOW MANY TIMES...?
DON'T THINK! KEEP UP THE TECHNIQUES!
WATERFALL BASIN!
STRIKING TIDE!
WATER WHEEL!
WHIRLPOOL!

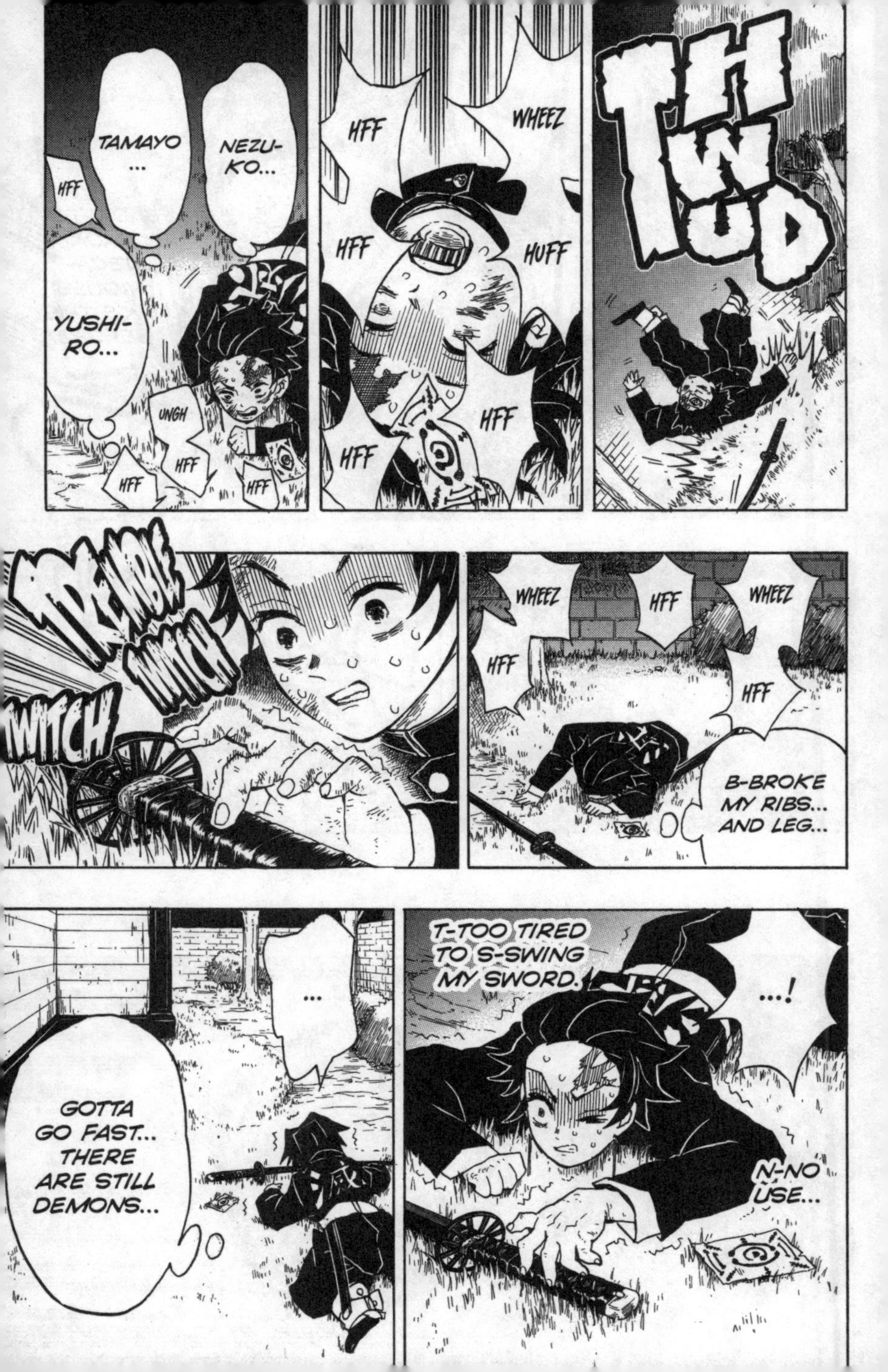
THUD
WHEEZ
HFF
HUFF
HFF
HFF
HFF
HFF
NEZU-KO...
TAMAYO...
YUSHI-RO...
UNGH
HFF
HFF
HFF
WHEEZ
HFF
WHEEZ
HFF
HFF
B-BROKE MY RIBS... AND LEG...
TWITCH
T-TOO TIRED TO S-SWING MY SWORD.
...!
N-NO USE...
...
GOTTA GO FAST... THERE ARE STILL DEMONS...

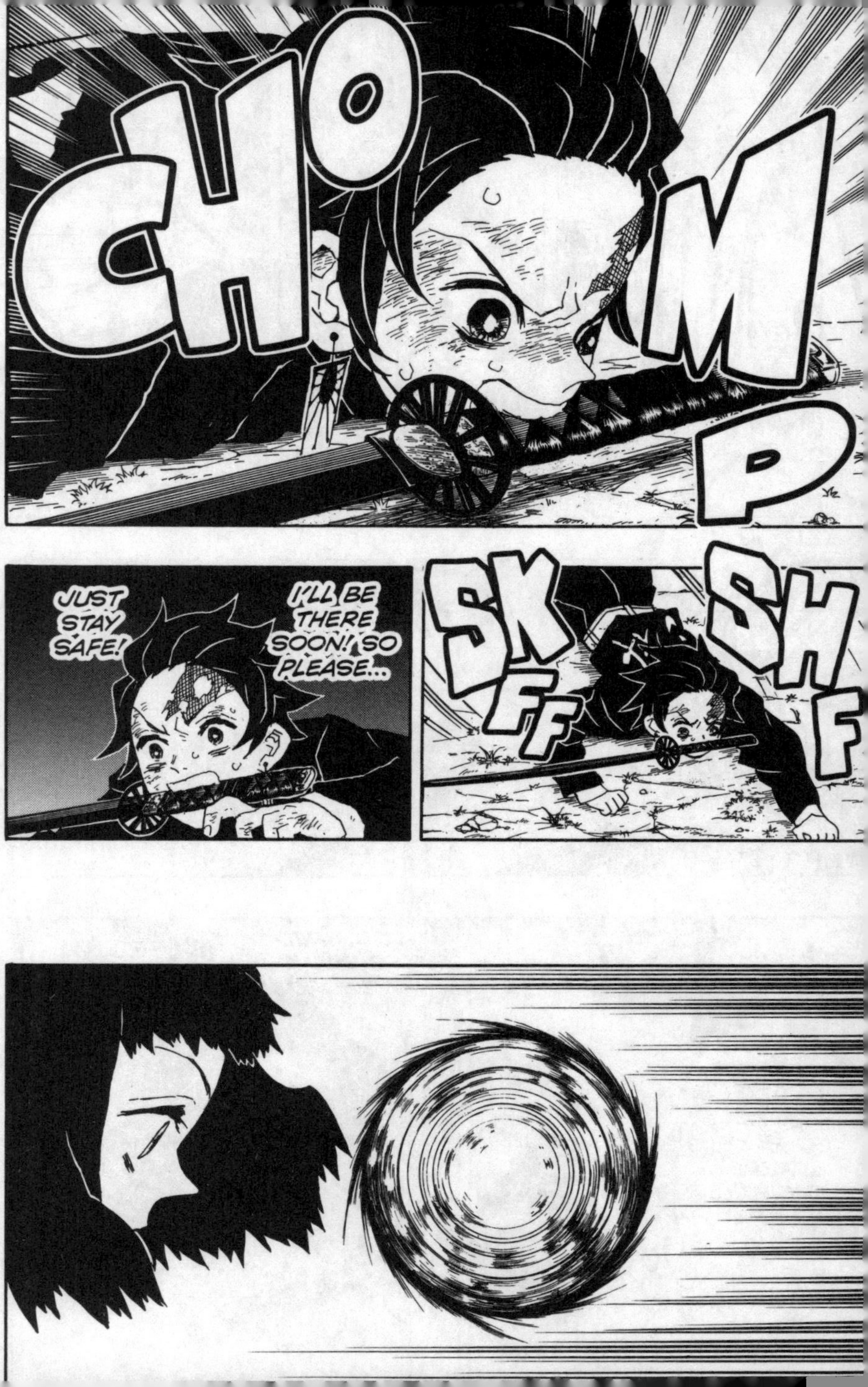
CHOMP
SHF
SKFF
I'LL BE THERE SOON! SO PLEASE...
JUST STAY SAFE!

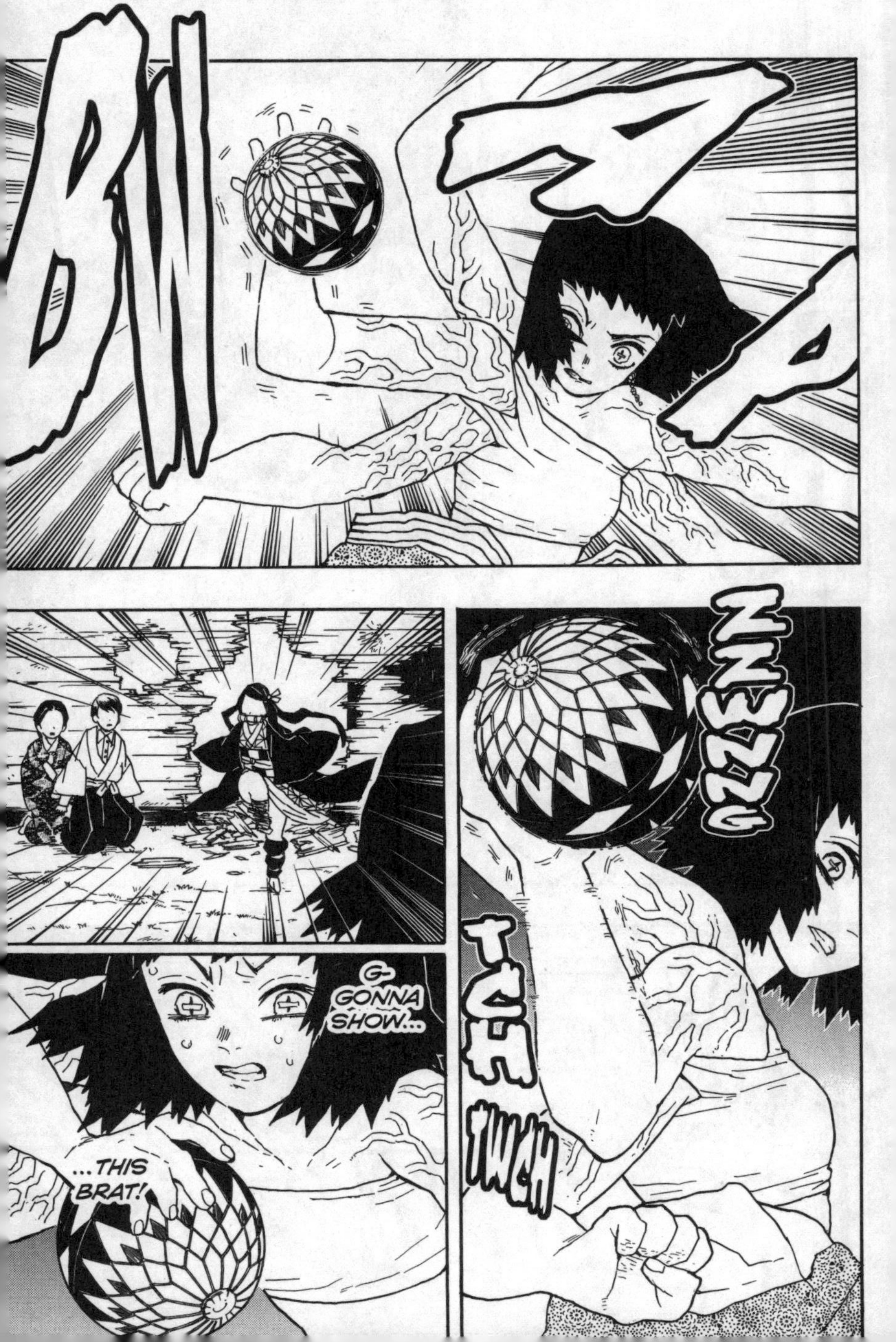
BAM
NNNNG
TCH
TWCH
G-GONNA SHOW...
...THIS BRAT!

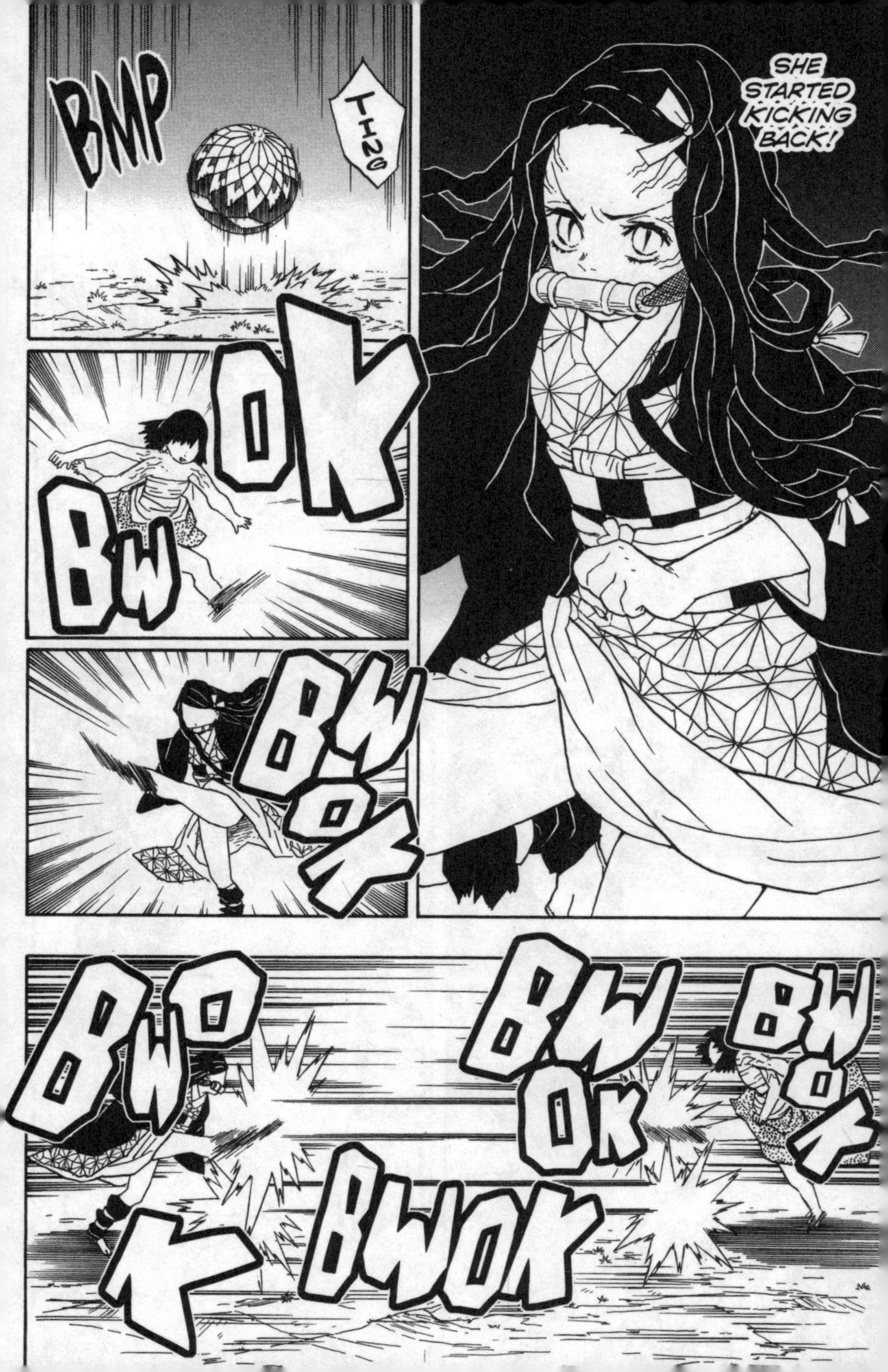
SHE STARTED KICKING BACK!
TING
BMP
BWOK
BWOK
BWOK
BWOK
BWOK
BWOK

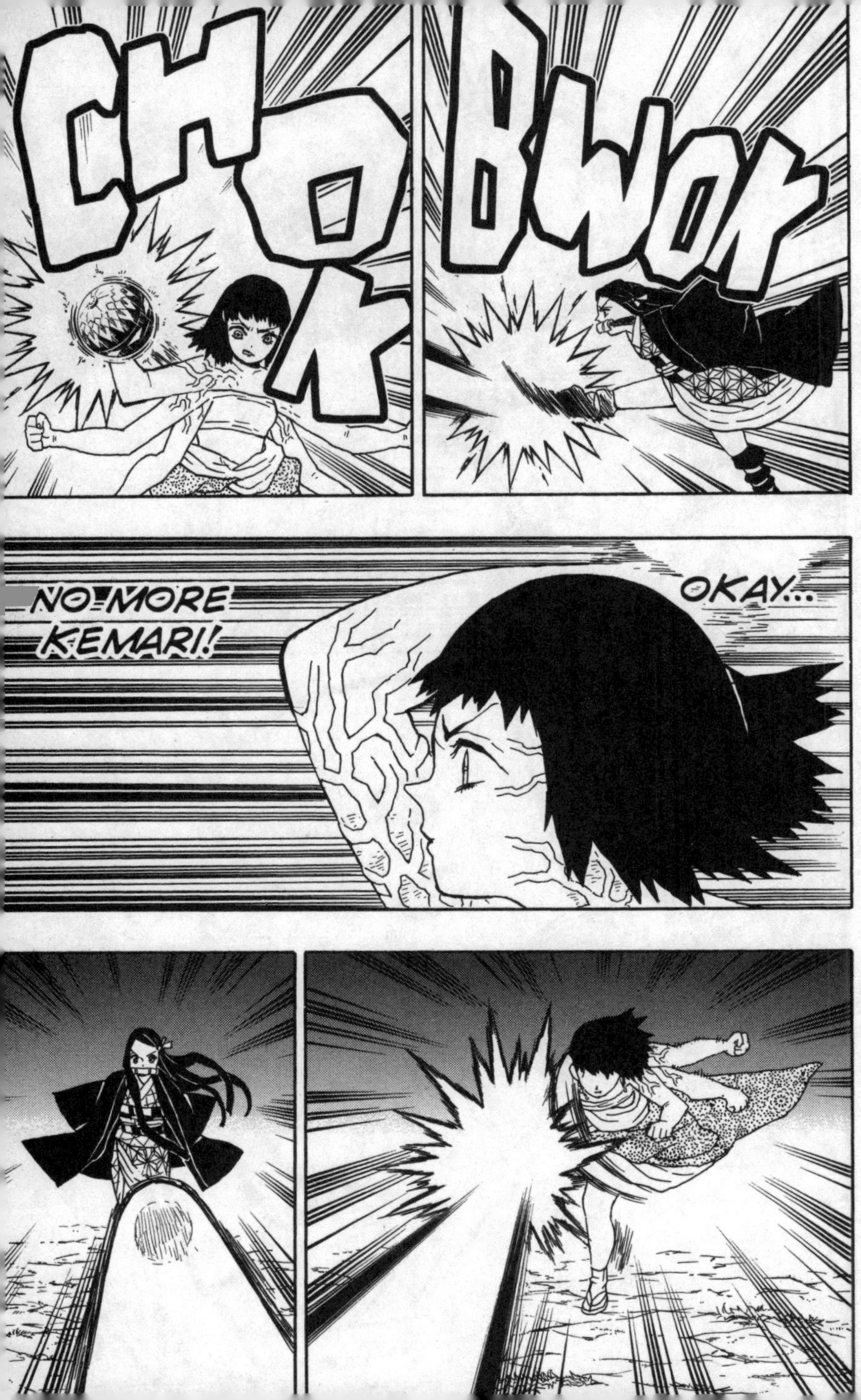
BWOK
CHOK
OKAY...
NO MORE KEMARI!

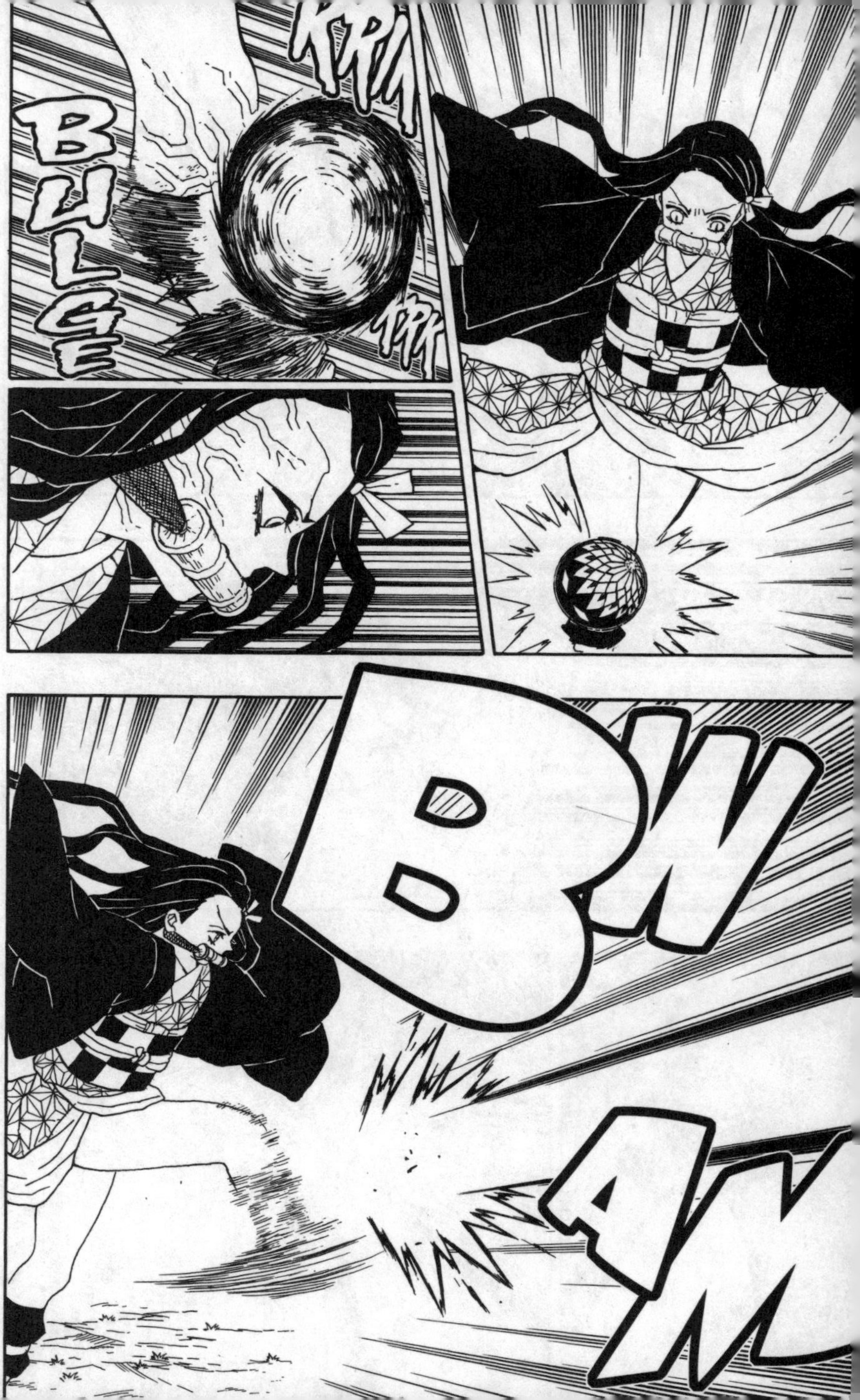
KRRK
BULGE
KRRK
BWAM

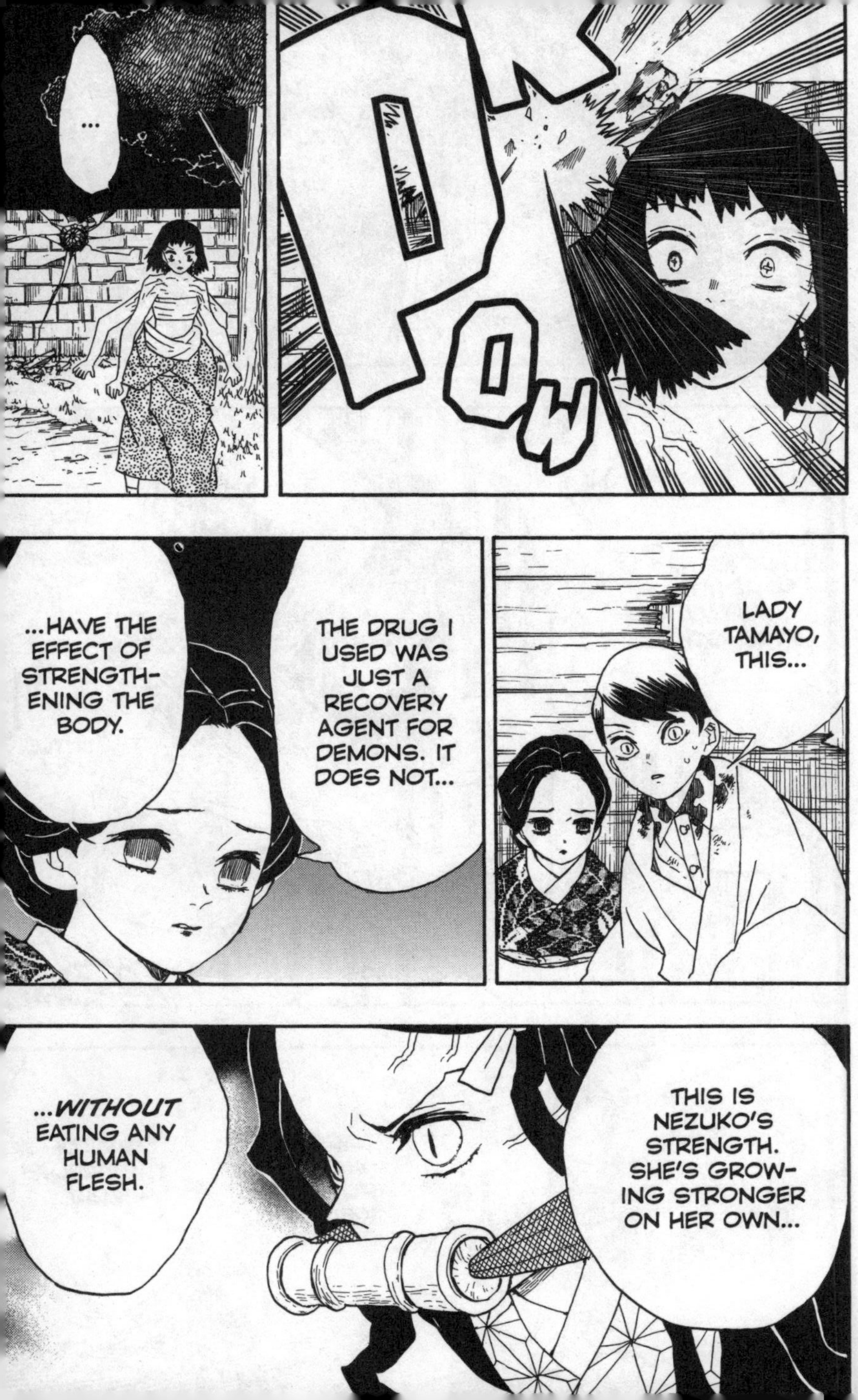
POW
...
LADY TAMAYO, THIS...
THE DRUG I USED WAS JUST A RECOVERY AGENT FOR DEMONS. IT DOES NOT...
...HAVE THE EFFECT OF STRENGTH-ENING THE BODY.
THIS IS NEZUKO'S STRENGTH. SHE'S GROW-ING STRONGER ON HER OWN...
...*WITHOUT* EATING ANY HUMAN FLESH.

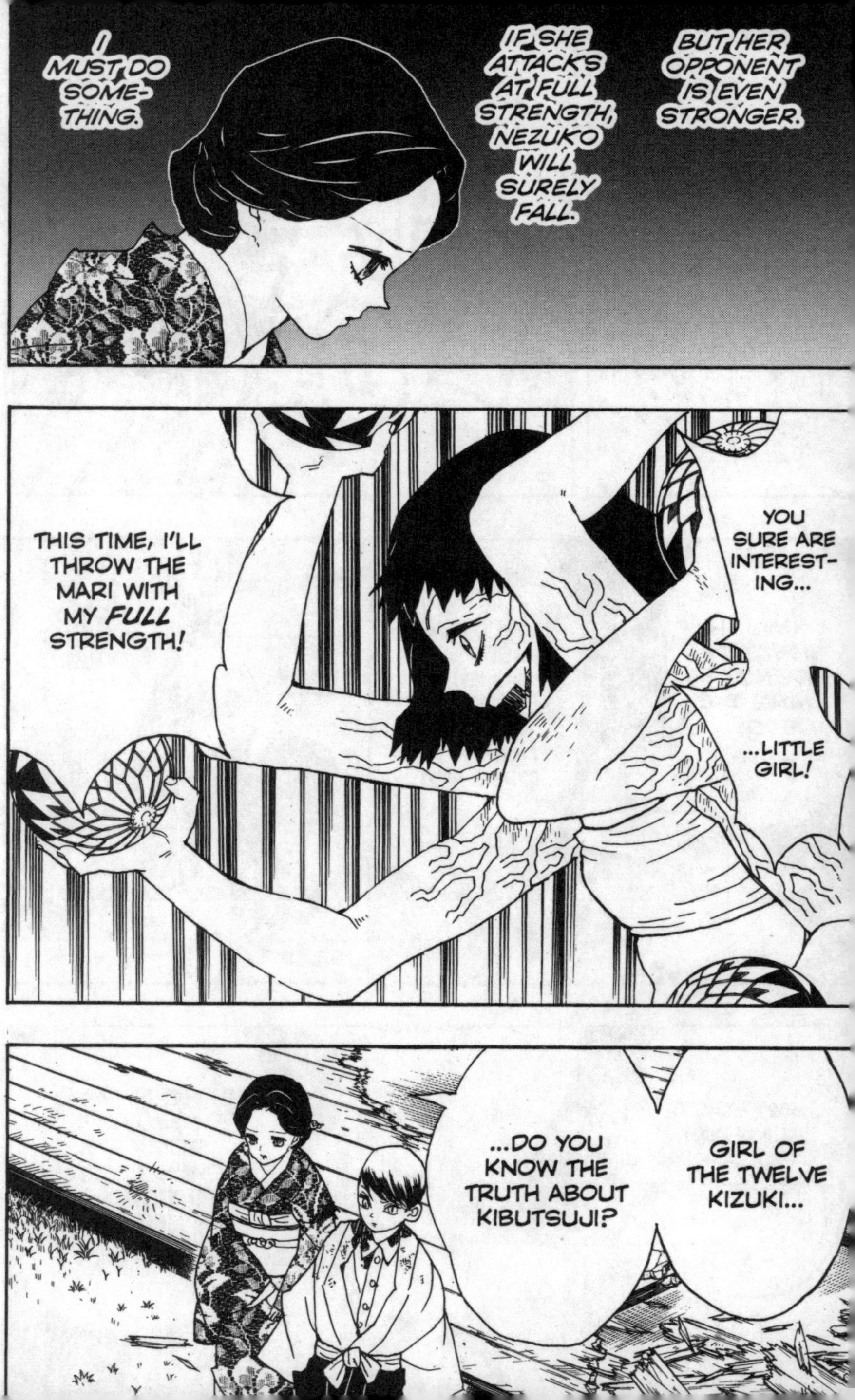
BUT HER OPPONENT IS EVEN STRONGER.
IF SHE ATTACKS AT FULL STRENGTH, NEZUKO WILL SURELY FALL.
I MUST DO SOME-THING.
YOU SURE ARE INTEREST-ING...
...LITTLE GIRL!
THIS TIME, I'LL THROW THE MARI WITH MY *FULL* STRENGTH!
GIRL OF THE TWELVE KIZUKI...
...DO YOU KNOW THE TRUTH ABOUT KIBUTSUJI?

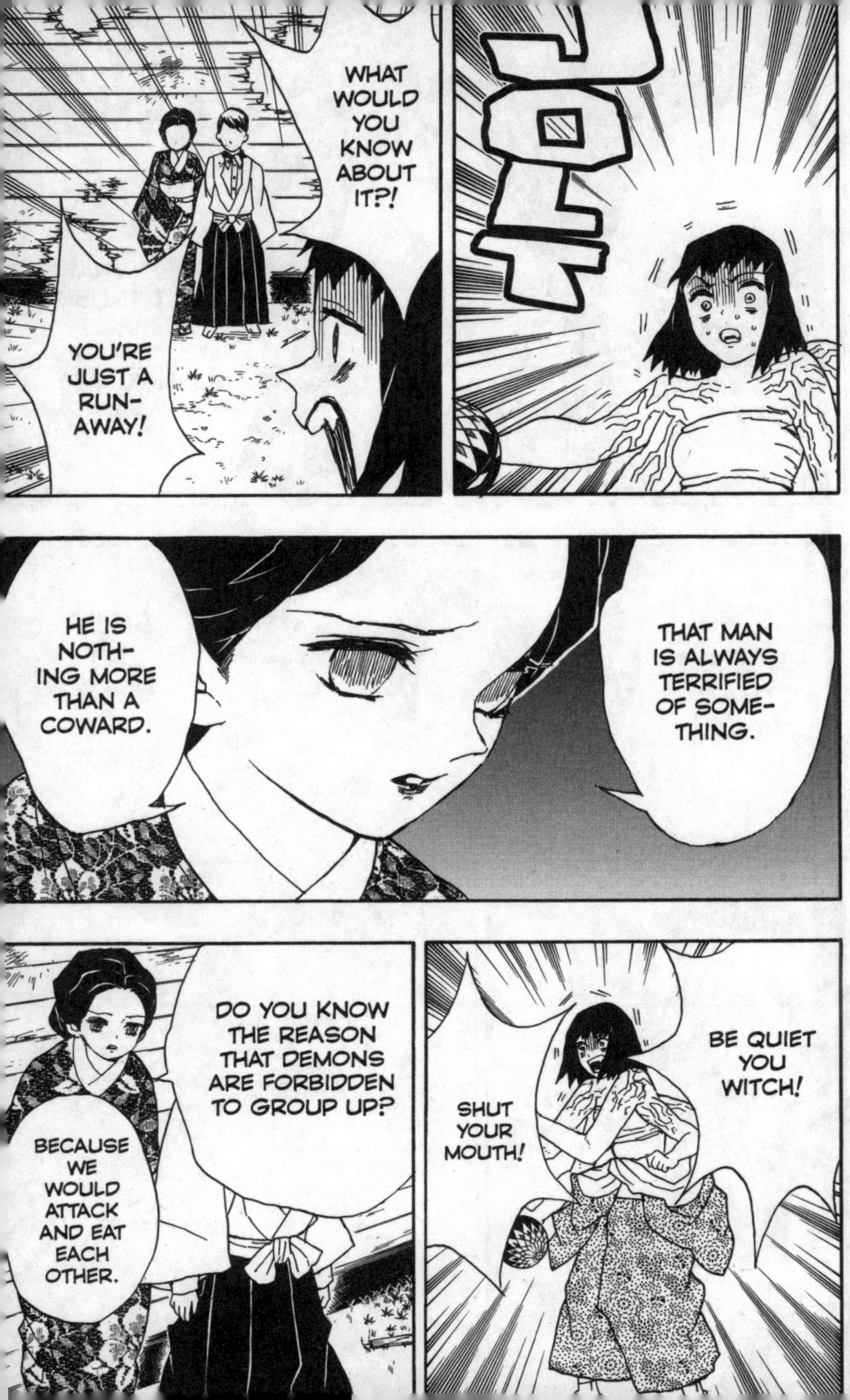
WHAT WOULD YOU KNOW ABOUT IT?!
YOU'RE JUST A RUN-AWAY!
THAT MAN IS ALWAYS TERRIFIED OF SOME-THING.
HE IS NOTH-ING MORE THAN A COWARD.
BE QUIET YOU WITCH!
SHUT YOUR MOUTH!
DO YOU KNOW THE REASON THAT DEMONS ARE FORBIDDEN TO GROUP UP?
BECAUSE WE WOULD ATTACK AND EAT EACH OTHER.

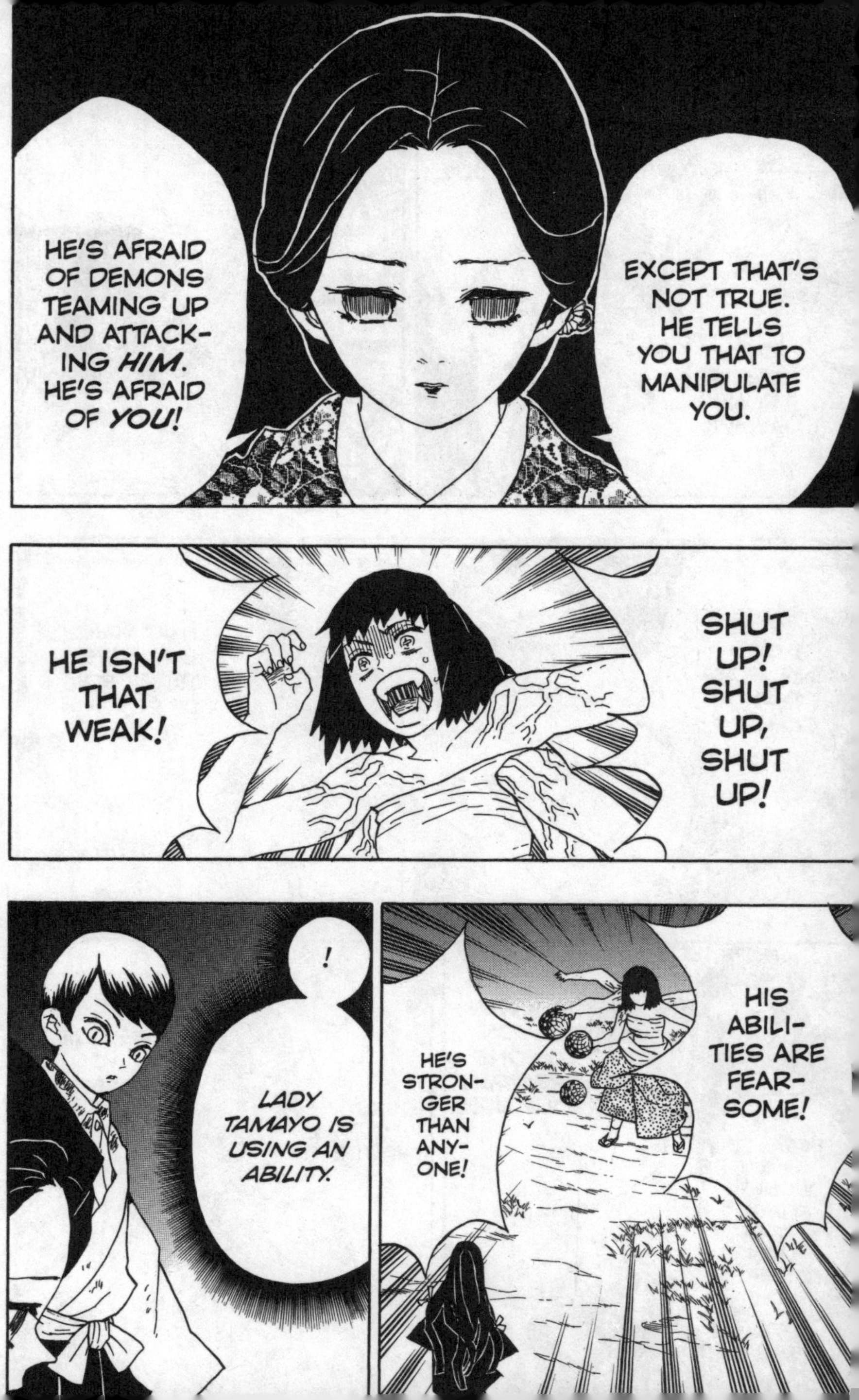
EXCEPT THAT'S NOT TRUE. HE TELLS YOU THAT TO MANIPULATE YOU.
HE'S AFRAID OF DEMONS TEAMING UP AND ATTACKING *HIM*. HE'S AFRAID OF *YOU*!
SHUT UP! SHUT UP, SHUT UP!
HE ISN'T THAT WEAK!
HIS ABILITIES ARE FEARSOME!
HE'S STRONGER THAN ANYONE!
!
LADY TAMAYO IS USING AN ABILITY.

MAGICAL AROMA OF DAYLIGHT...

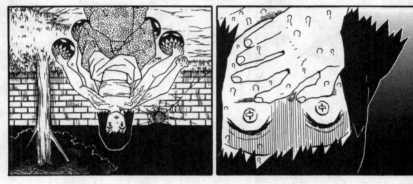

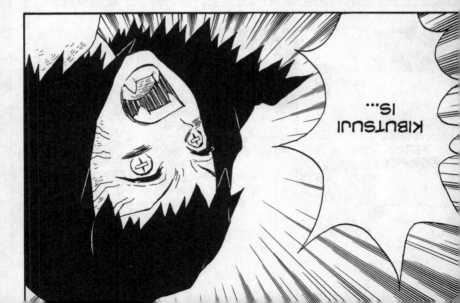

KIBUTSUJI IS...

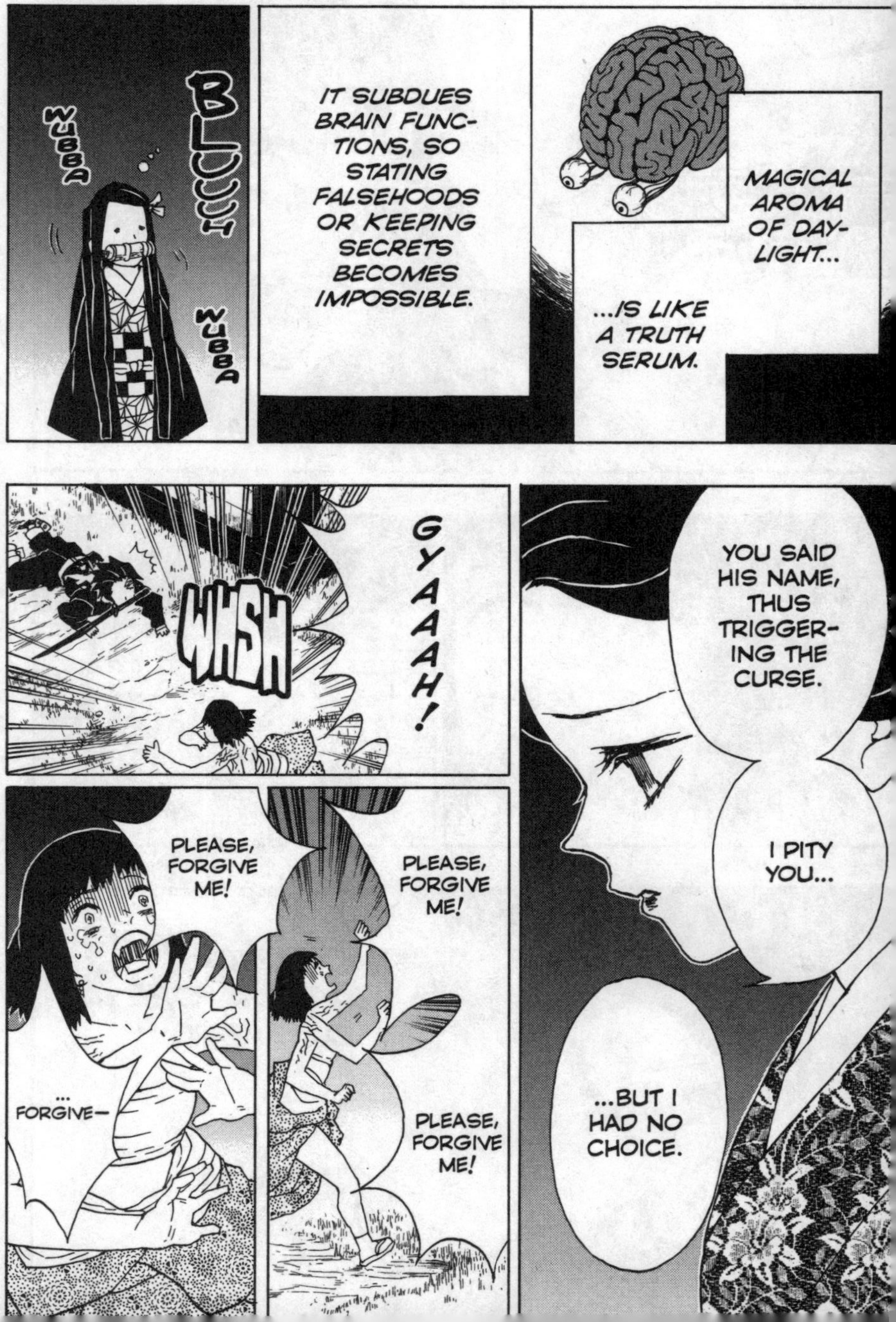
MAGICAL AROMA OF DAYLIGHT...
...IS LIKE A TRUTH SERUM.
IT SUBDUES BRAIN FUNCTIONS, SO STATING FALSEHOODS OR KEEPING SECRETS BECOMES IMPOSSIBLE.
BLUUUH
WUBBA
WUBBA
YOU SAID HIS NAME, THUS TRIGGERING THE CURSE.
I PITY YOU...
...BUT I HAD NO CHOICE.
GYAAAAH!
WHSH
PLEASE, FORGIVE ME!
PLEASE, FORGIVE ME!
PLEASE, FORGIVE ME!
... FORGIVE—

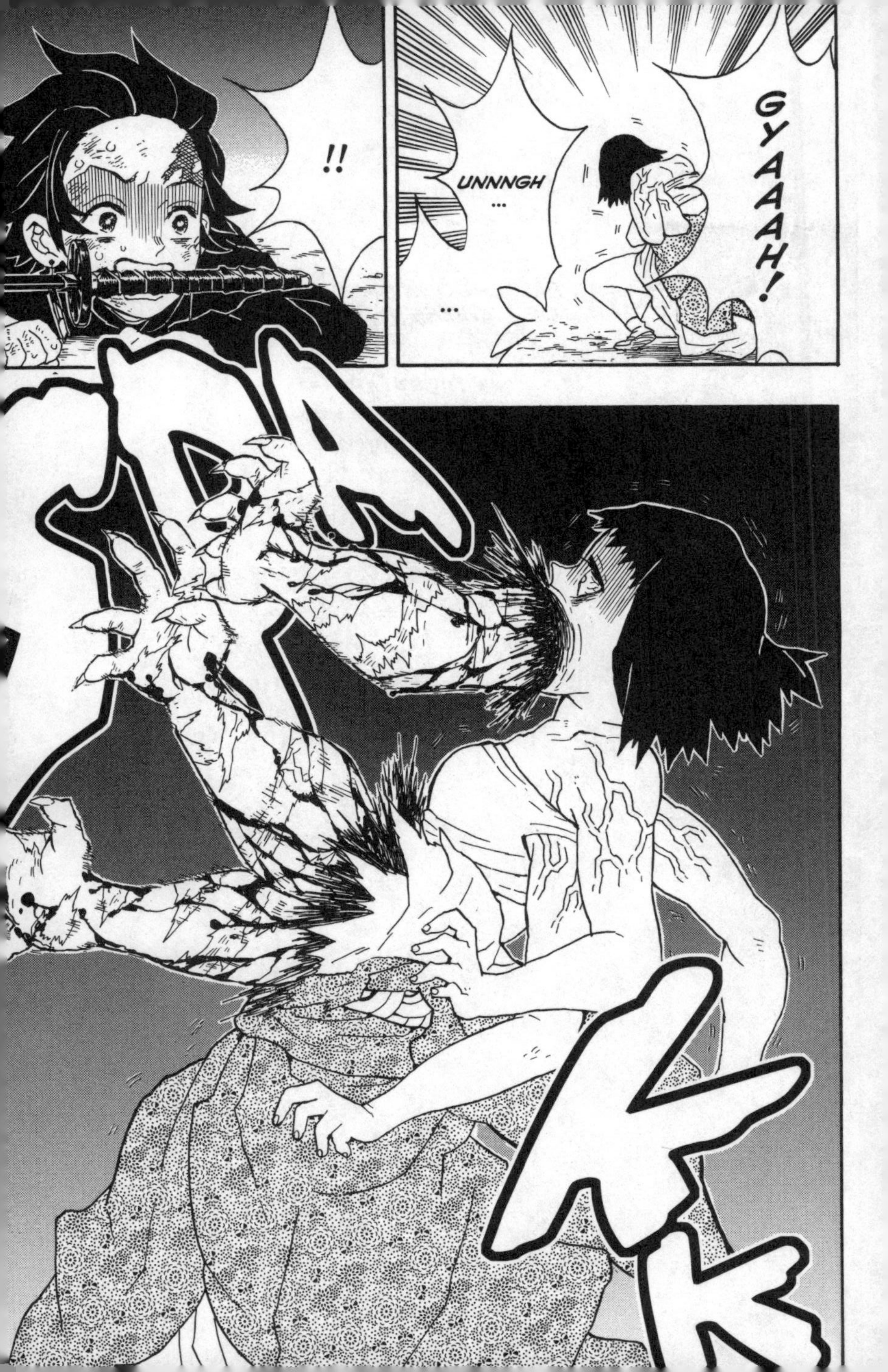
GYAAAH!
UNNNGH
...
...
!!

DRESS NEZUKO

The request for the combined issue was just for Tanjiro, but I drew Nezuko too.

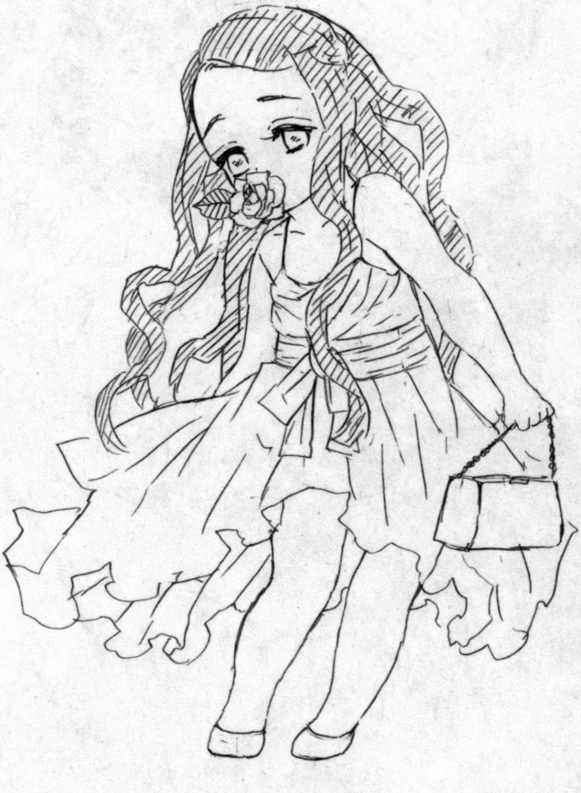

CHAPTER 19: TOGETHER FOREVER

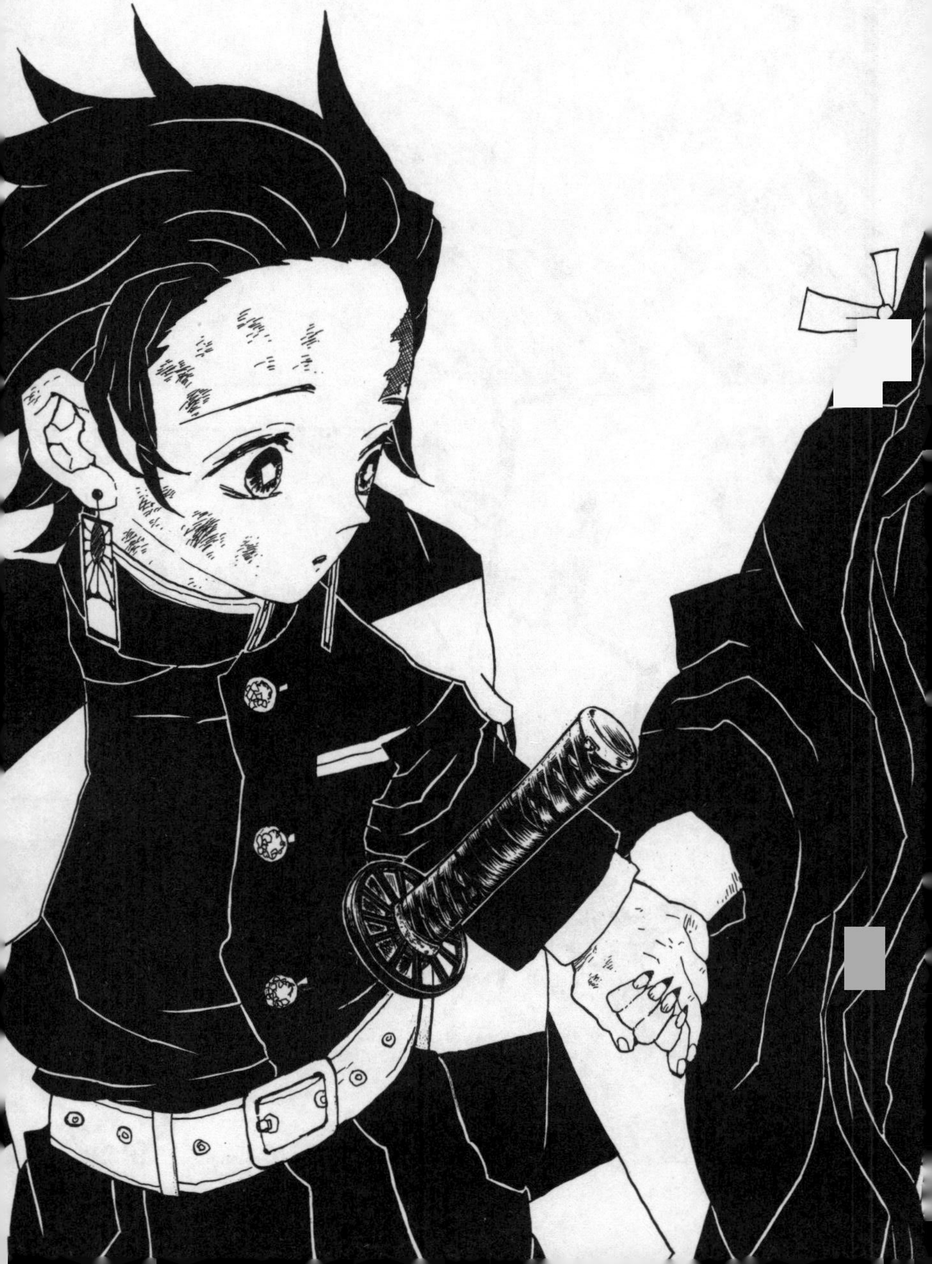

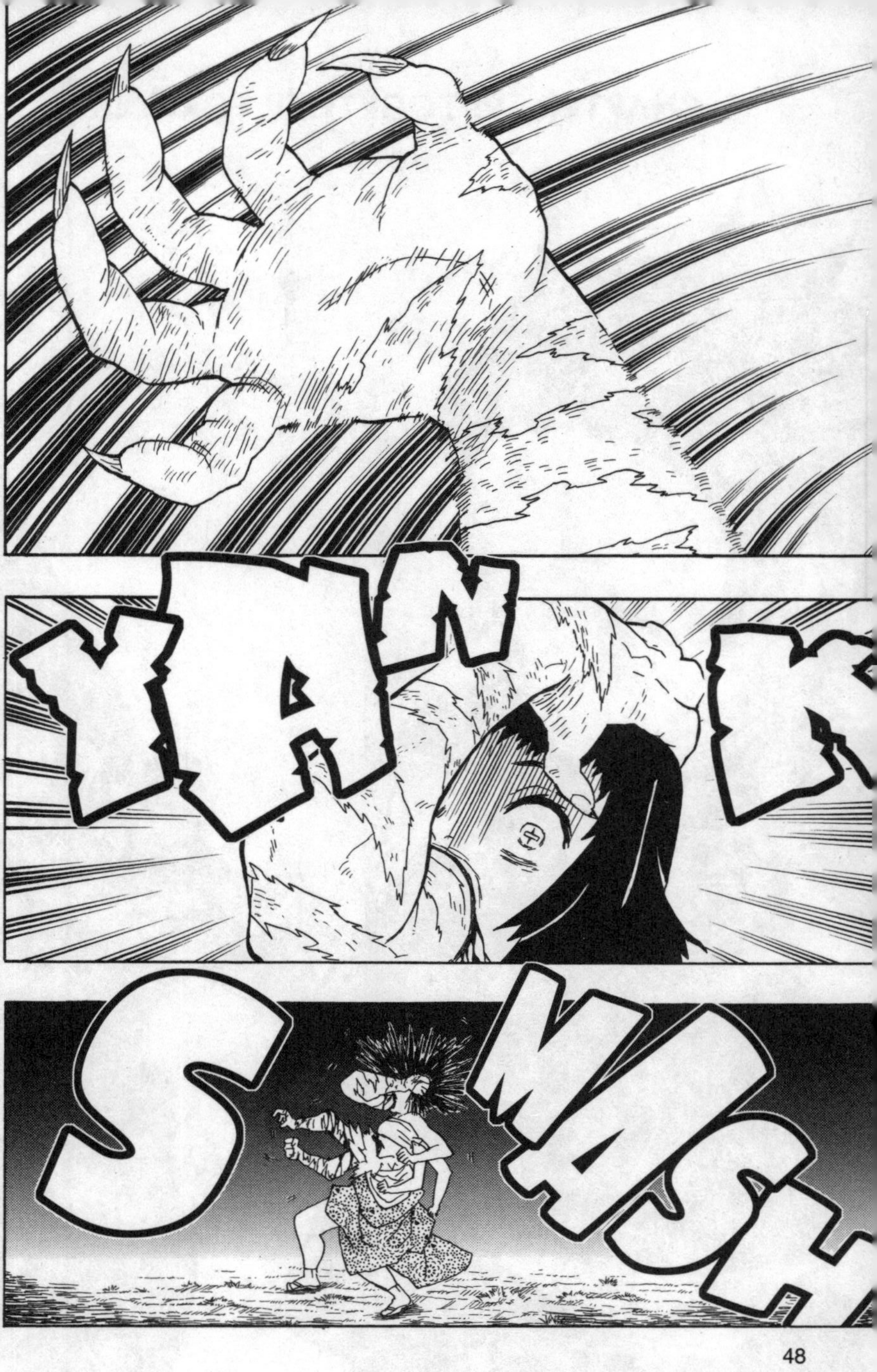
YANK
SMASH

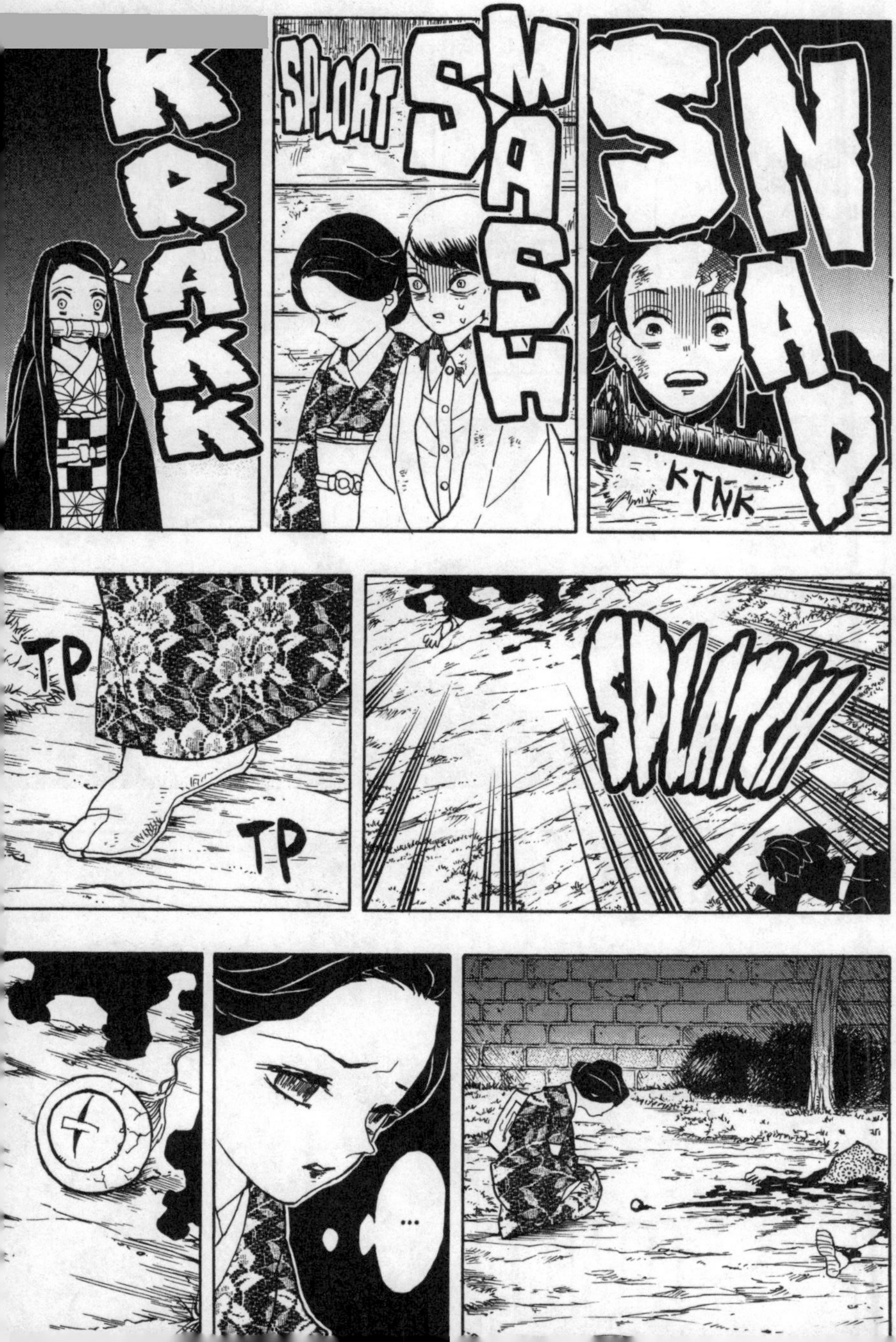
SNAP
KTNK
SMASH
SPLORT
KRAKK
SPLATCH
TP
TP
...

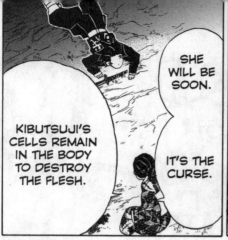

IS SHE DEAD?
SHE WILL BE SOON.
IT'S THE CURSE.
KIBUTSUJI'S CELLS REMAIN IN THE BODY TO DESTROY THE FLESH.
BASI-CALLY...
...FIGHTING BETWEEN DEMONS IS MEANING-LESS.
IT IS IMPOSSIBLE TO STRIKE A FATAL BLOW...
...UNLESS IT'S DONE BY SUN-LIGHT OR THE KATANA OF A DEMON SLAYER.
HOWEVER, KIBUTSUJI CAN DESTROY A DEMON'S CELLS.
KLOMP
WAH!
MMPH

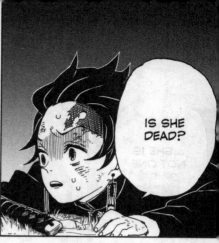

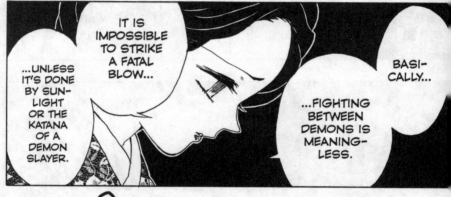

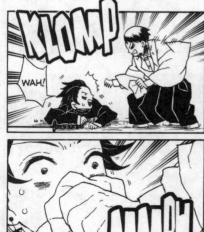

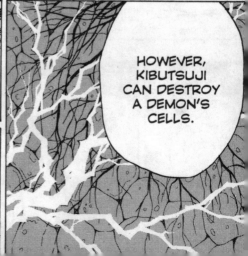

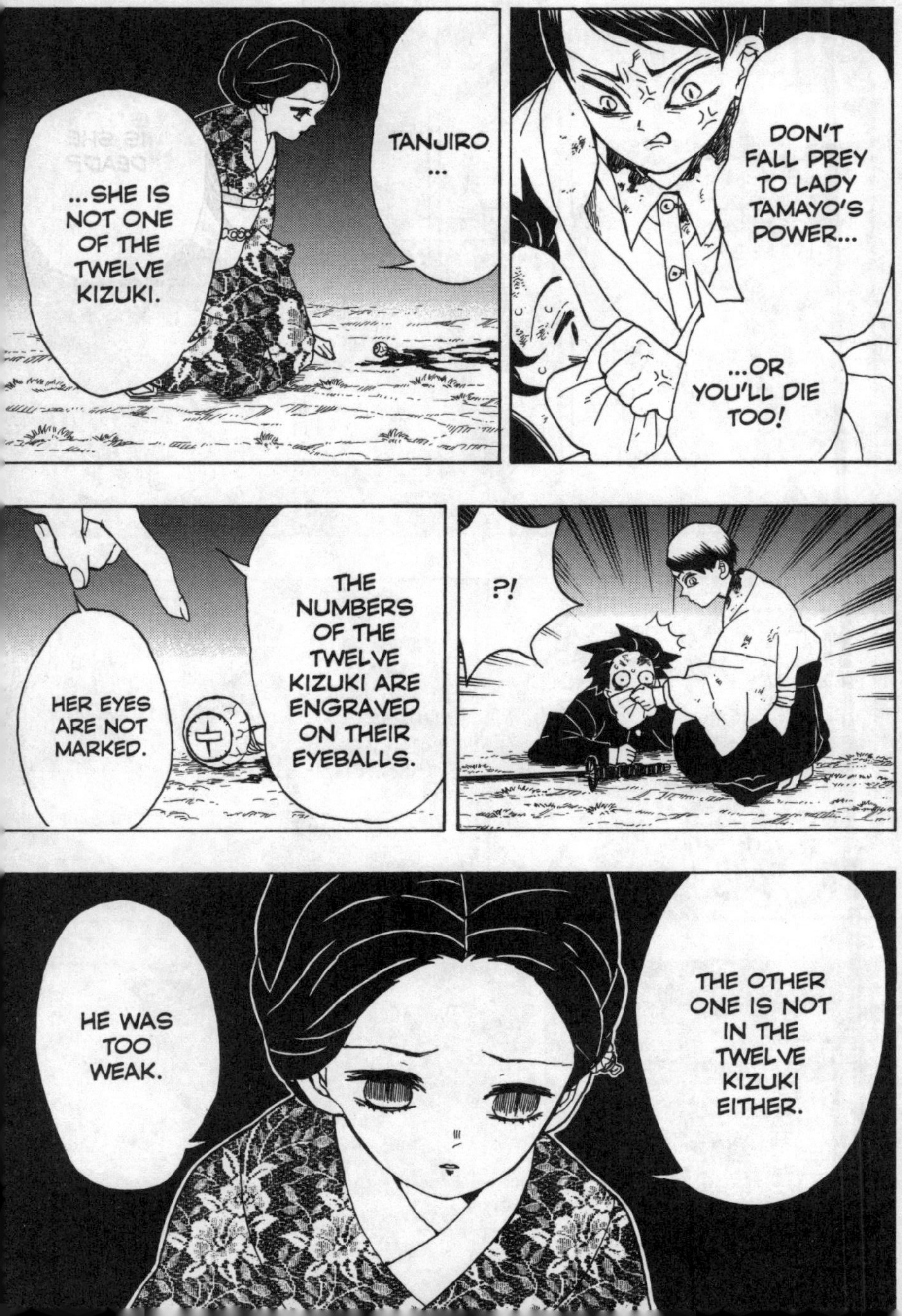
DON'T FALL PREY TO LADY TAMAYO'S POWER...
...OR YOU'LL DIE TOO!
TANJIRO ...
...SHE IS NOT ONE OF THE TWELVE KIZUKI.
?!
THE NUMBERS OF THE TWELVE KIZUKI ARE ENGRAVED ON THEIR EYEBALLS.
HER EYES ARE NOT MARKED.
THE OTHER ONE IS NOT IN THE TWELVE KIZUKI EITHER.
HE WAS TOO WEAK.

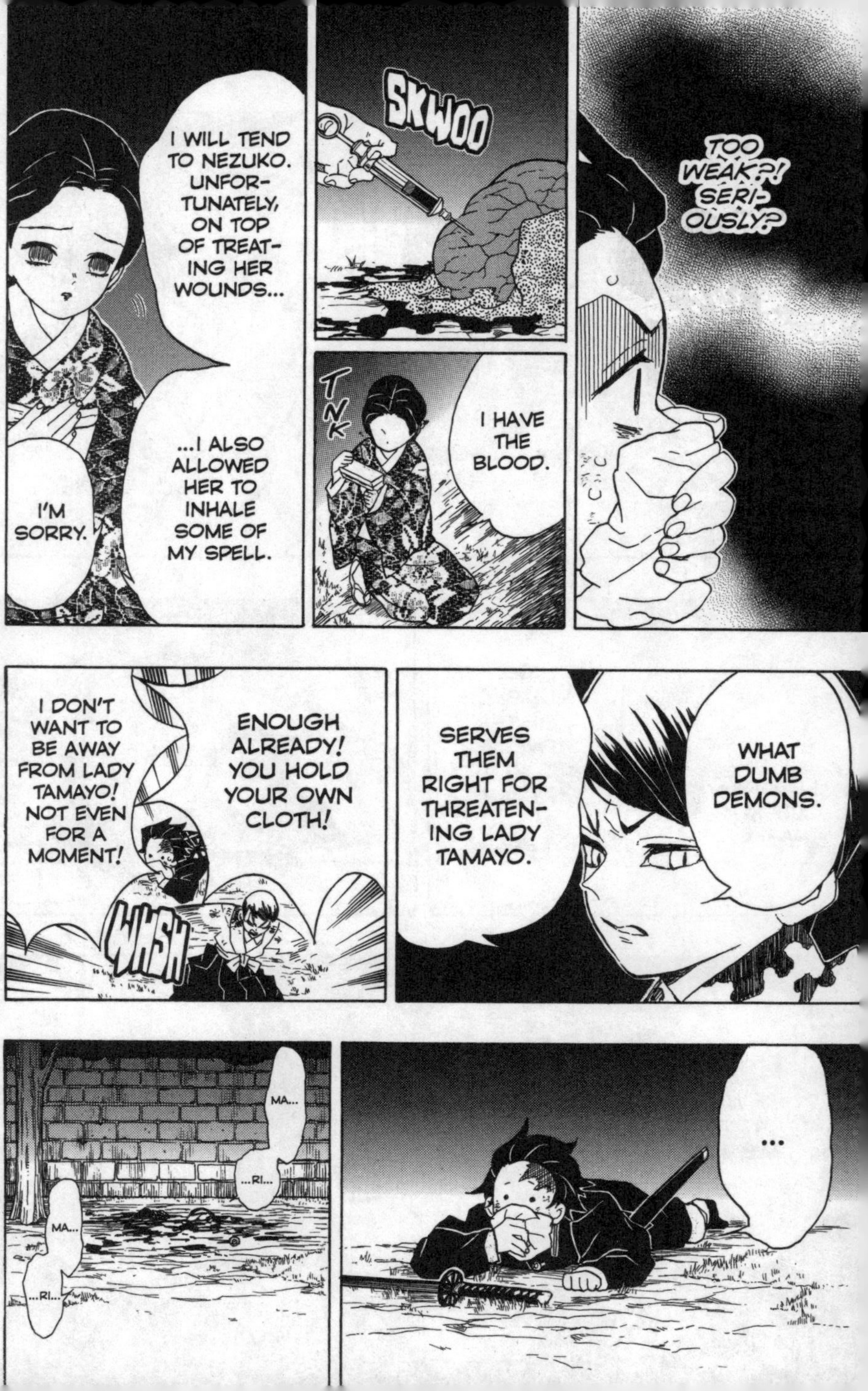
TOO WEAK?! SERI-OUSLY?
SKWOO
TNK
I HAVE THE BLOOD.
I WILL TEND TO NEZUKO. UNFOR-TUNATELY, ON TOP OF TREAT-ING HER WOUNDS...
...I ALSO ALLOWED HER TO INHALE SOME OF MY SPELL.
I'M SORRY.
WHAT DUMB DEMONS.
SERVES THEM RIGHT FOR THREATEN-ING LADY TAMAYO.
ENOUGH ALREADY! YOU HOLD YOUR OWN CLOTH!
I DON'T WANT TO BE AWAY FROM LADY TAMAYO! NOT EVEN FOR A MOMENT!
WHSH
...
MA...
...RI...
MA...
...RI...

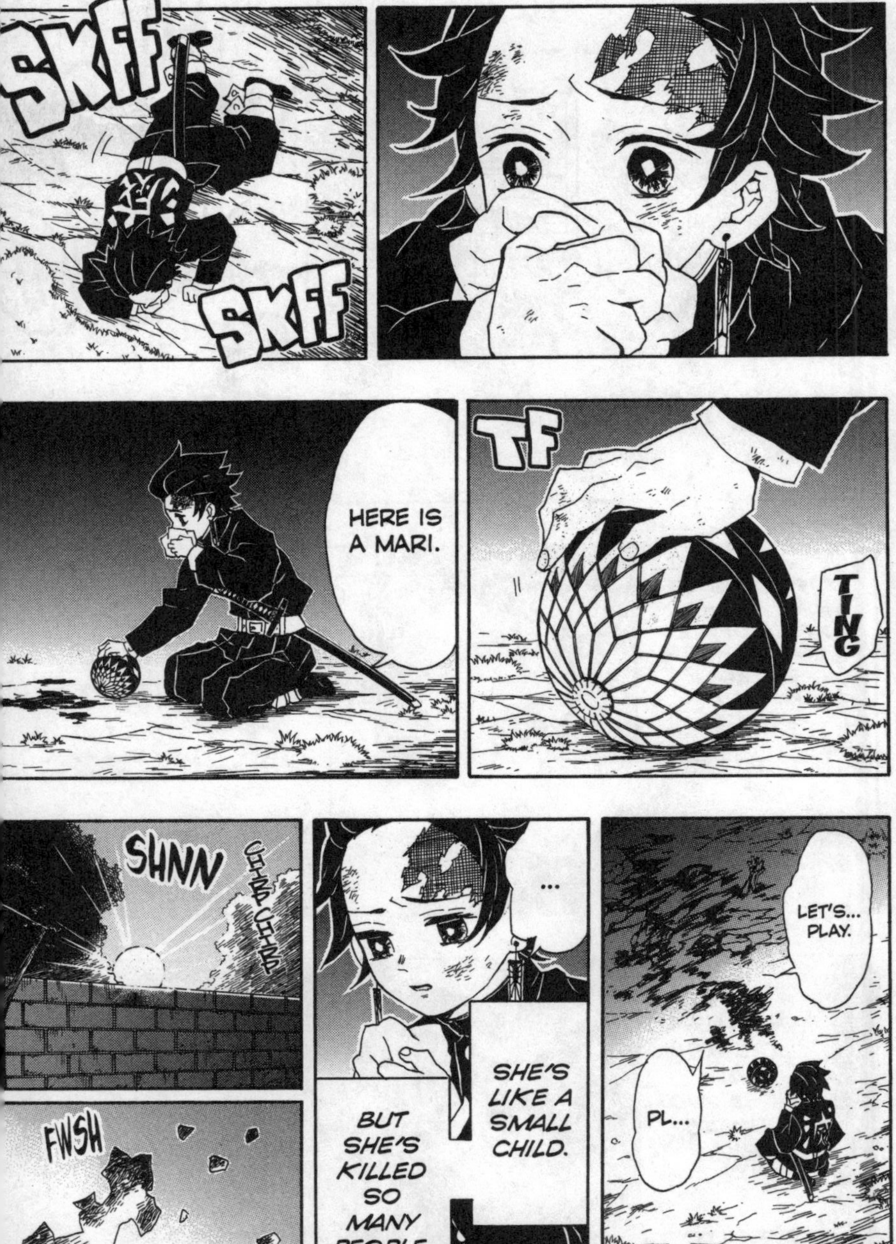
SKFF
SKFF
TF
TING
HERE IS A MARI.
LET'S... PLAY.
PL...
...
SHE'S LIKE A SMALL CHILD.
BUT SHE'S KILLED SO MANY PEOPLE.
SHUNN
CHIRP CHIRP
FWSH

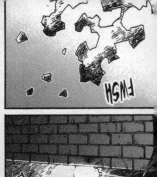

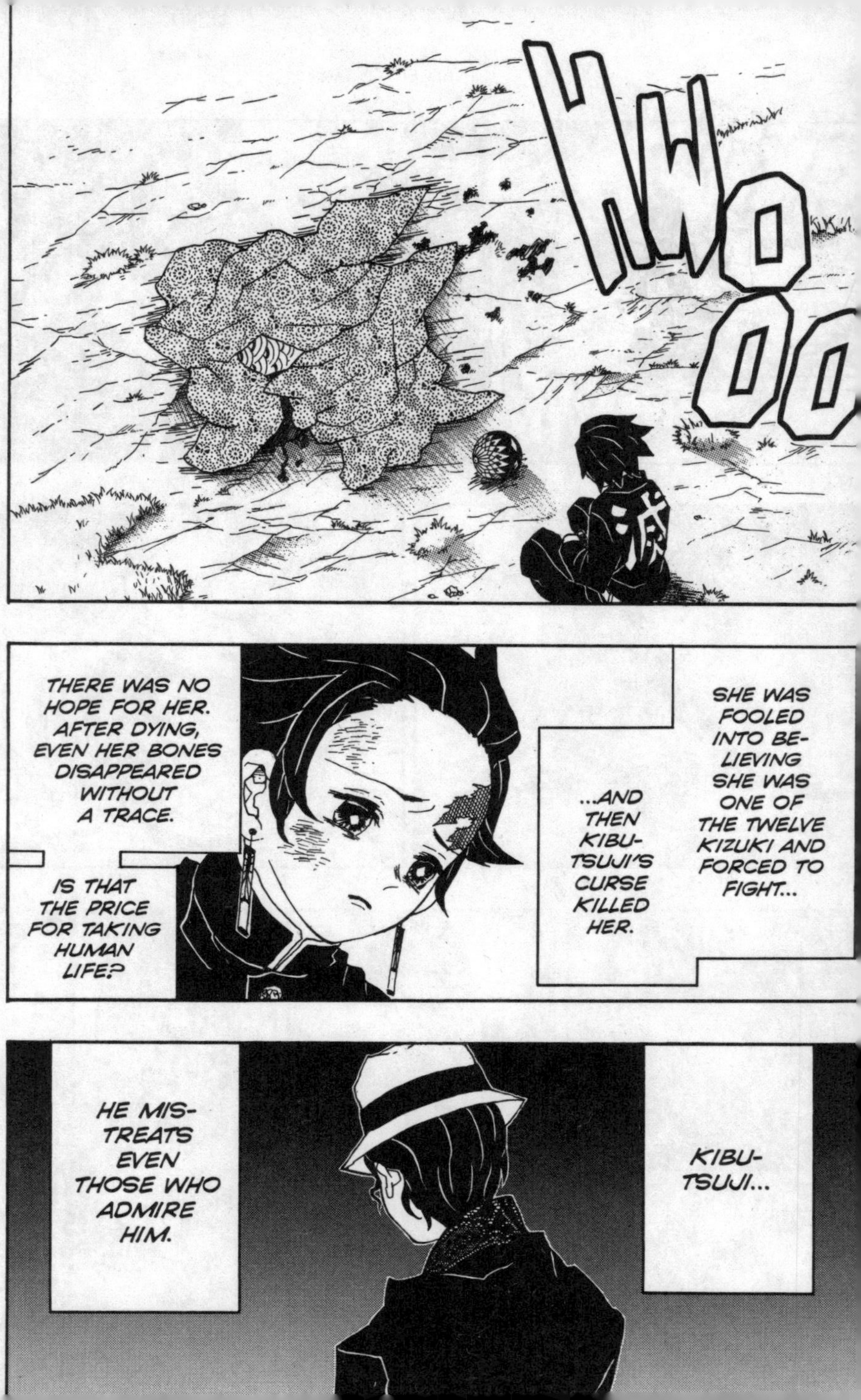
HWOOO
SHE WAS FOOLED INTO BELIEVING SHE WAS ONE OF THE TWELVE KIZUKI AND FORCED TO FIGHT...
...AND THEN KIBUTSUJI'S CURSE KILLED HER.
THERE WAS NO HOPE FOR HER. AFTER DYING, EVEN HER BONES DISAPPEARED WITHOUT A TRACE.
IS THAT THE PRICE FOR TAKING HUMAN LIFE?
KIBUTSUJI...
HE MISTREATS EVEN THOSE WHO ADMIRE HIM.

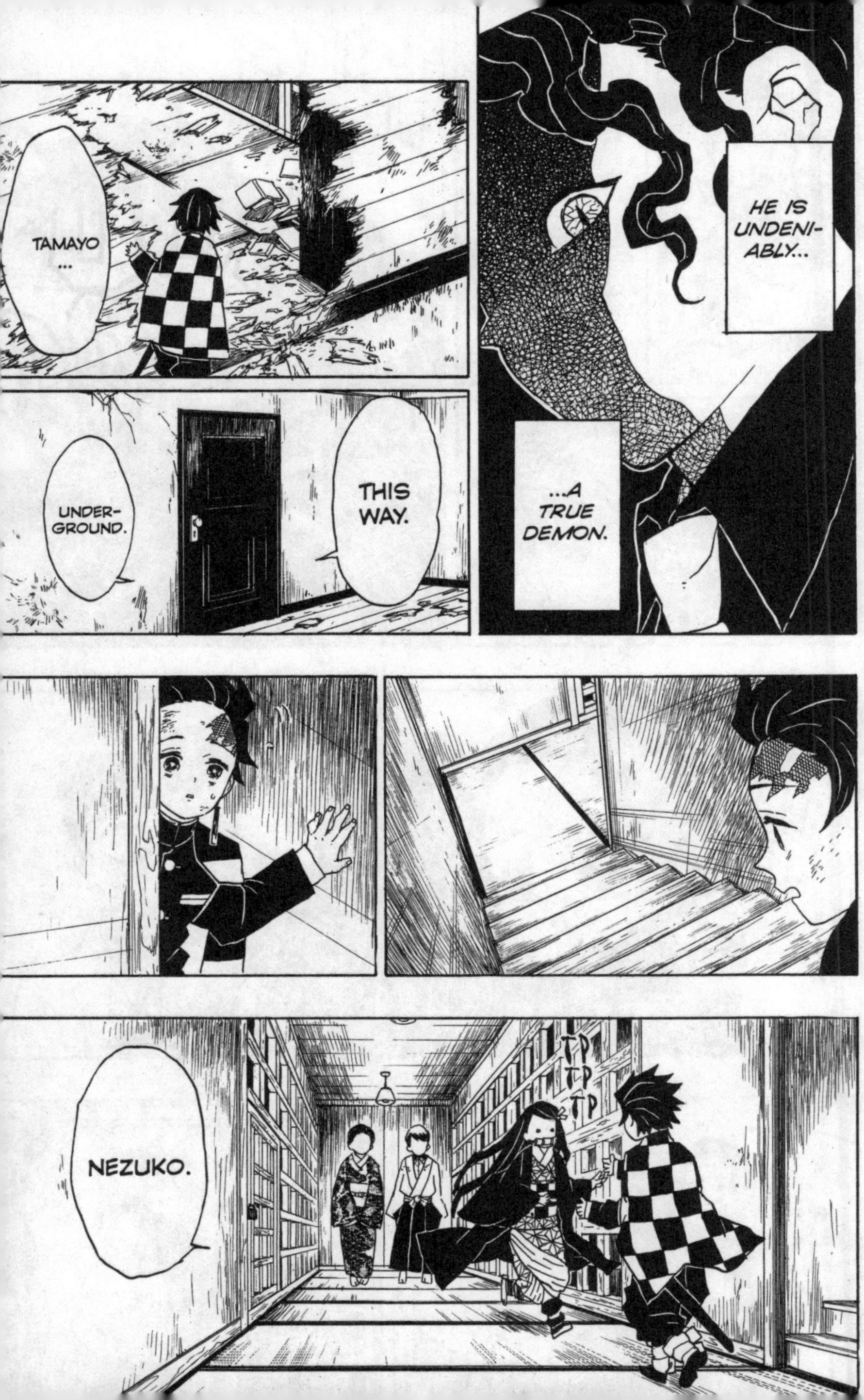
HE IS UNDENI-ABLY...
...A TRUE DEMON.
TAMAYO ...
THIS WAY.
UNDER-GROUND.
TP TP TP
NEZUKO.

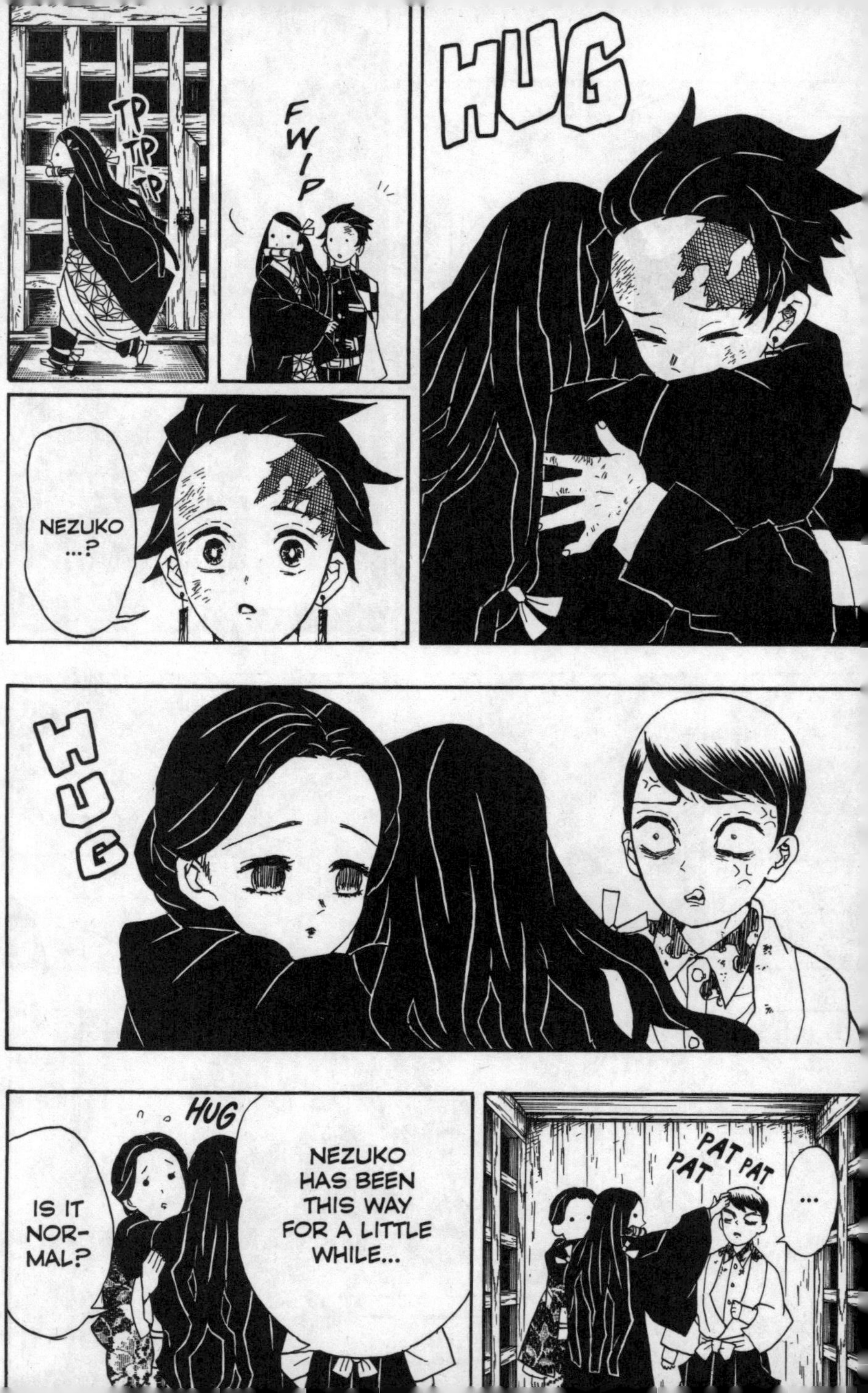
HUG
FWIP
TP TP TP
NEZUKO ...?
HUG
PAT PAT PAT
...
HUG
NEZUKO HAS BEEN THIS WAY FOR A LITTLE WHILE...
IS IT NOR-MAL?

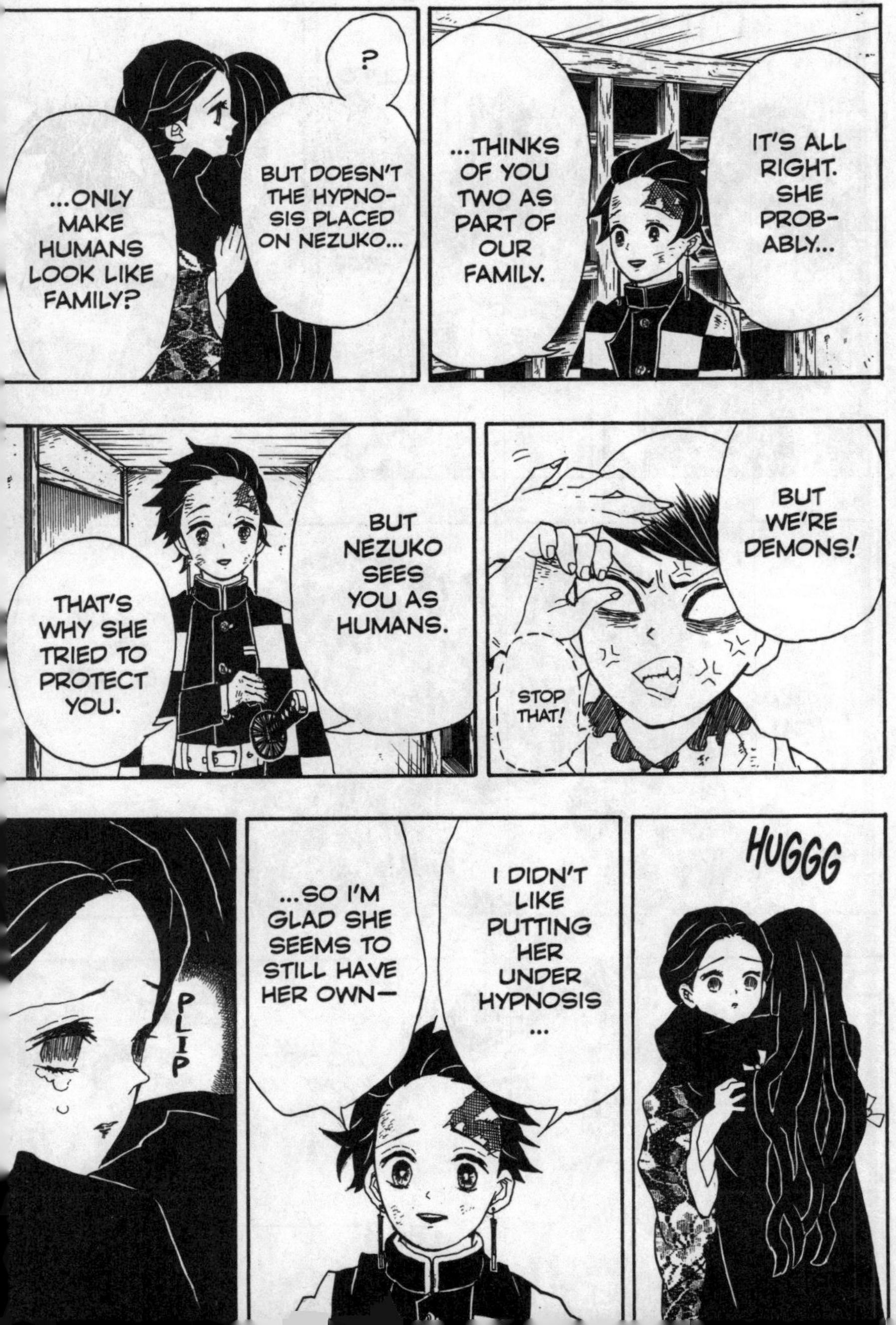
IT'S ALL RIGHT. SHE PROB-ABLY...
...THINKS OF YOU TWO AS PART OF OUR FAMILY.
?
BUT DOESN'T THE HYPNO-SIS PLACED ON NEZUKO...
...ONLY MAKE HUMANS LOOK LIKE FAMILY?
BUT WE'RE DEMONS!
STOP THAT!
BUT NEZUKO SEES YOU AS HUMANS.
THAT'S WHY SHE TRIED TO PROTECT YOU.
HUGGG
I DIDN'T LIKE PUTTING HER UNDER HYPNOSIS ...
...SO I'M GLAD SHE SEEMS TO STILL HAVE HER OWN—
PLIP

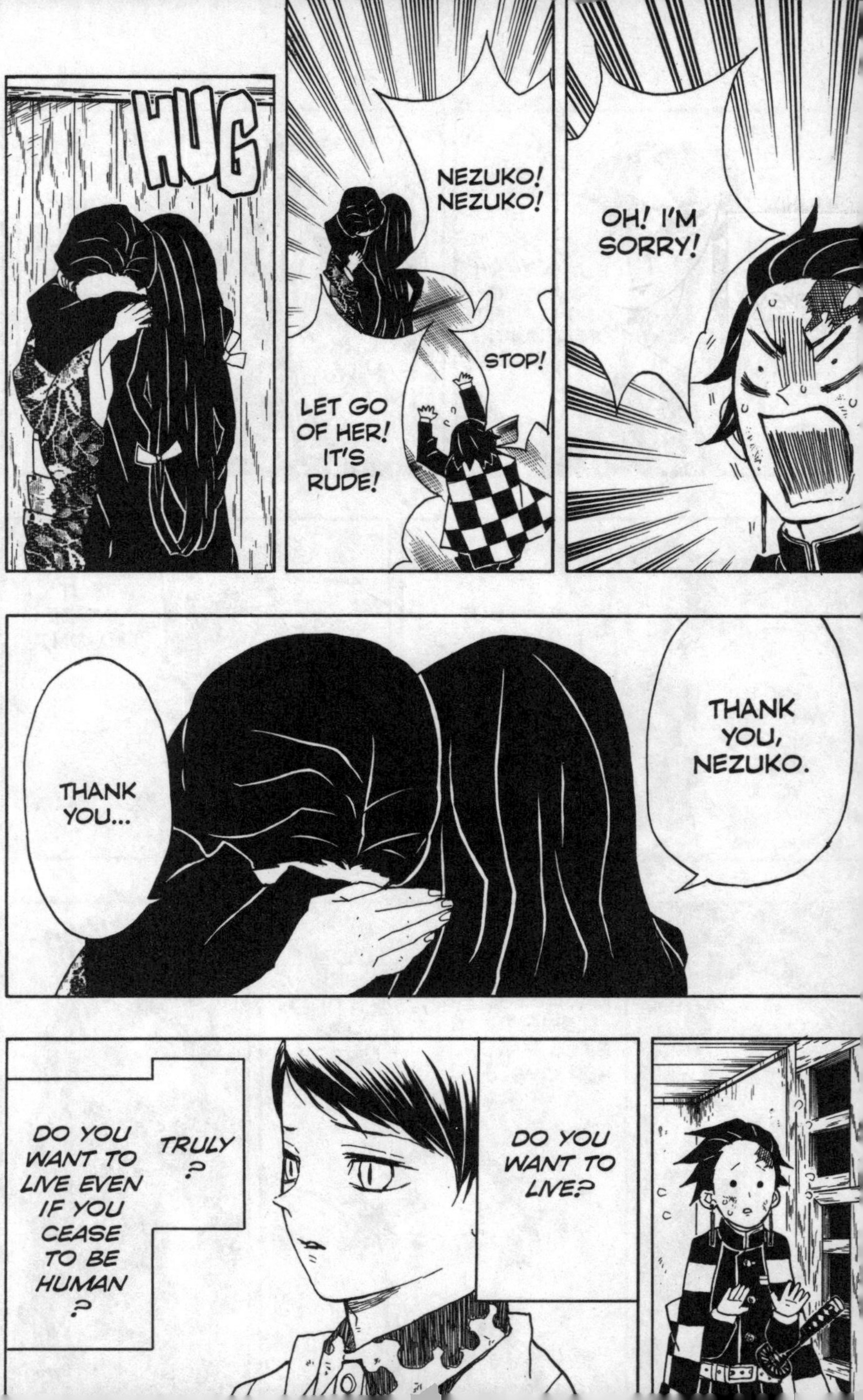
OH! I'M SORRY!
NEZUKO! NEZUKO!
STOP!
LET GO OF HER! IT'S RUDE!
HUG
THANK YOU, NEZUKO.
THANK YOU...
DO YOU WANT TO LIVE?
TRULY?
DO YOU WANT TO LIVE EVEN IF YOU CEASE TO BE HUMAN?

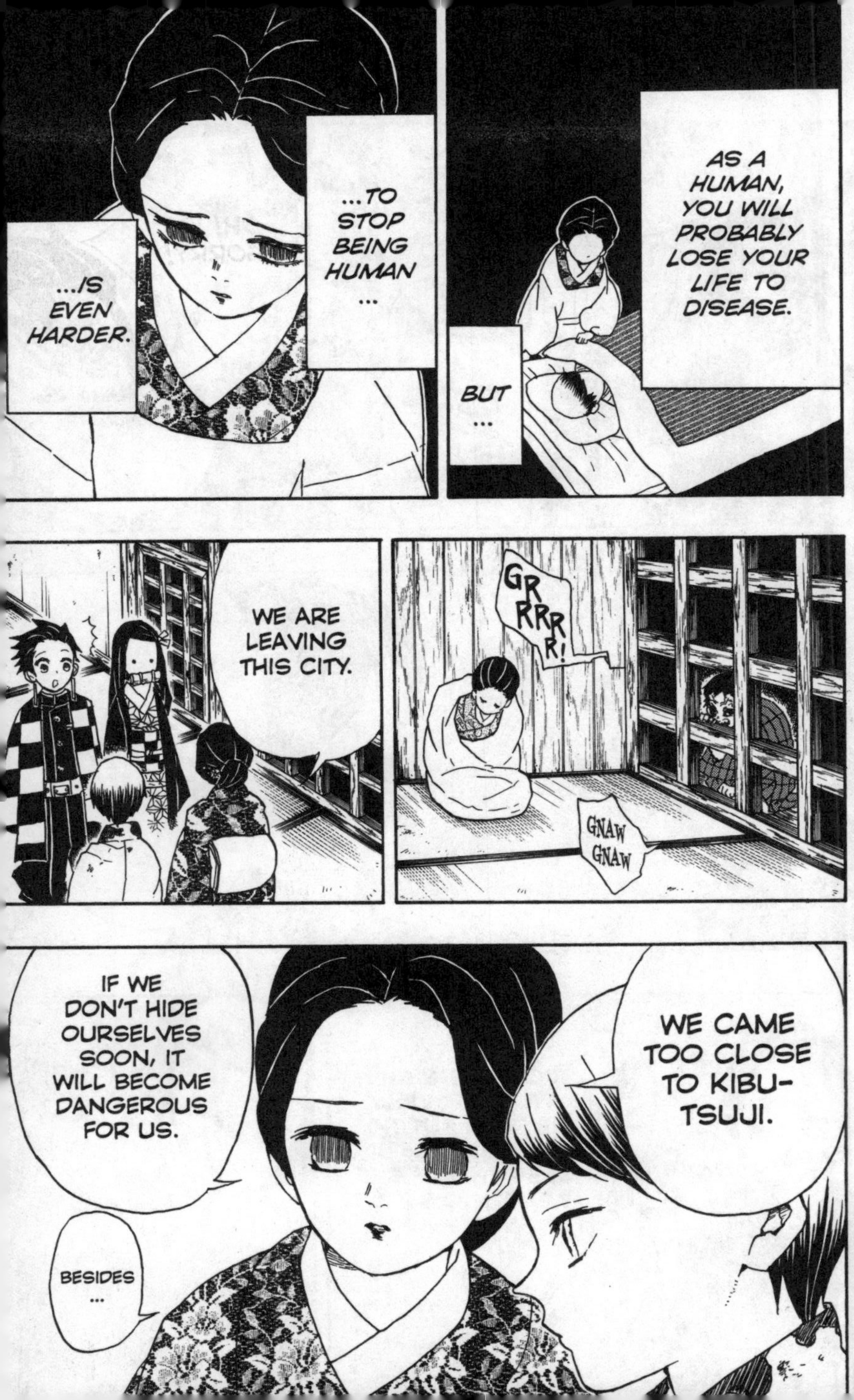
AS A HUMAN, YOU WILL PROBABLY LOSE YOUR LIFE TO DISEASE.
BUT ...
...TO STOP BEING HUMAN ...
...IS EVEN HARDER.
GRRRR!
GNAW GNAW
WE ARE LEAVING THIS CITY.
WE CAME TOO CLOSE TO KIBU-TSUJI.
IF WE DON'T HIDE OURSELVES SOON, IT WILL BECOME DANGEROUS FOR US.
BESIDES ...

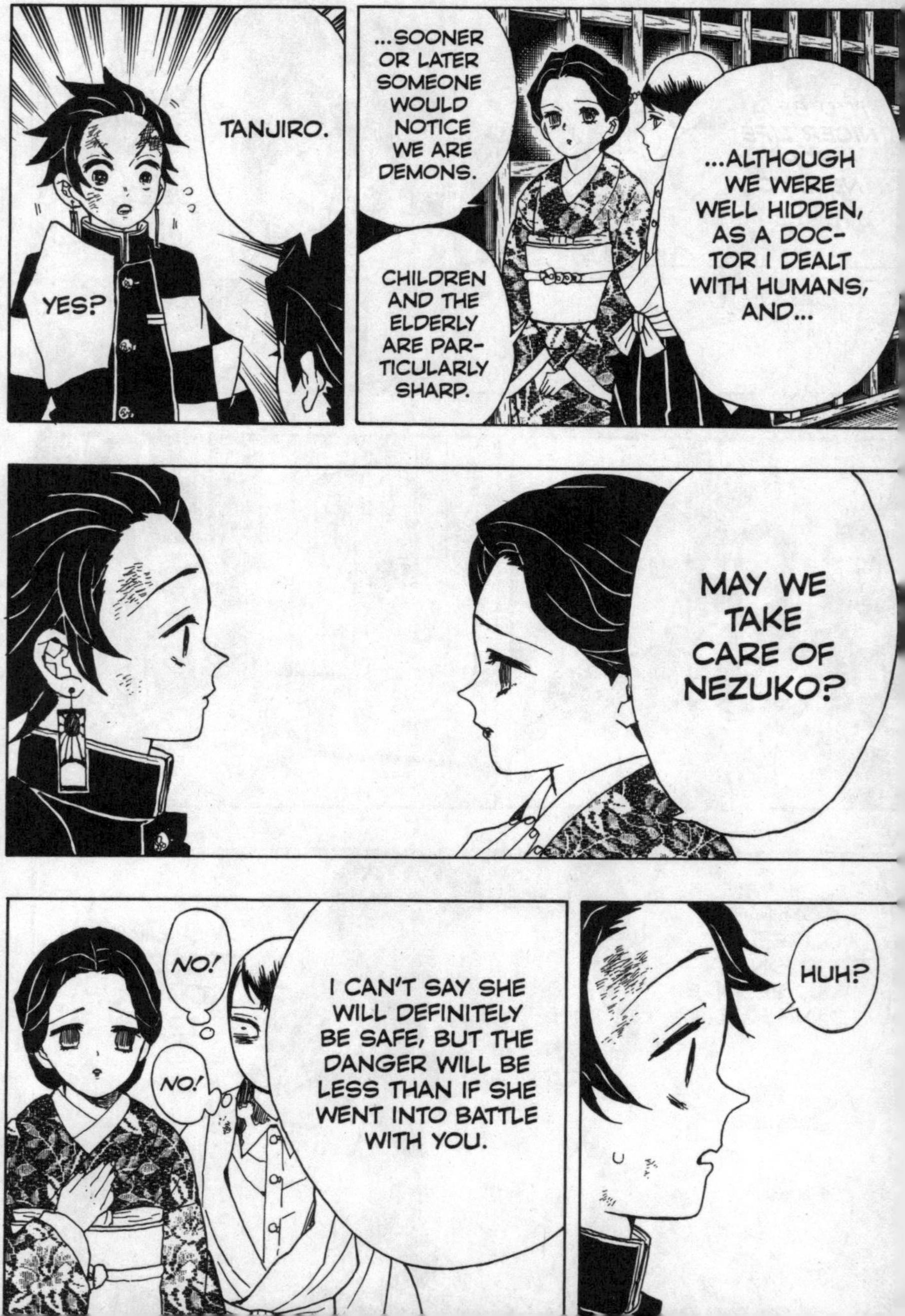
...ALTHOUGH WE WERE WELL HIDDEN, AS A DOCTOR I DEALT WITH HUMANS, AND...
...SOONER OR LATER SOMEONE WOULD NOTICE WE ARE DEMONS.
CHILDREN AND THE ELDERLY ARE PARTICULARLY SHARP.
TANJIRO.
YES?
MAY WE TAKE CARE OF NEZUKO?
HUH?
I CAN'T SAY SHE WILL DEFINITELY BE SAFE, BUT THE DANGER WILL BE LESS THAN IF SHE WENT INTO BATTLE WITH YOU.
NO!
NO!

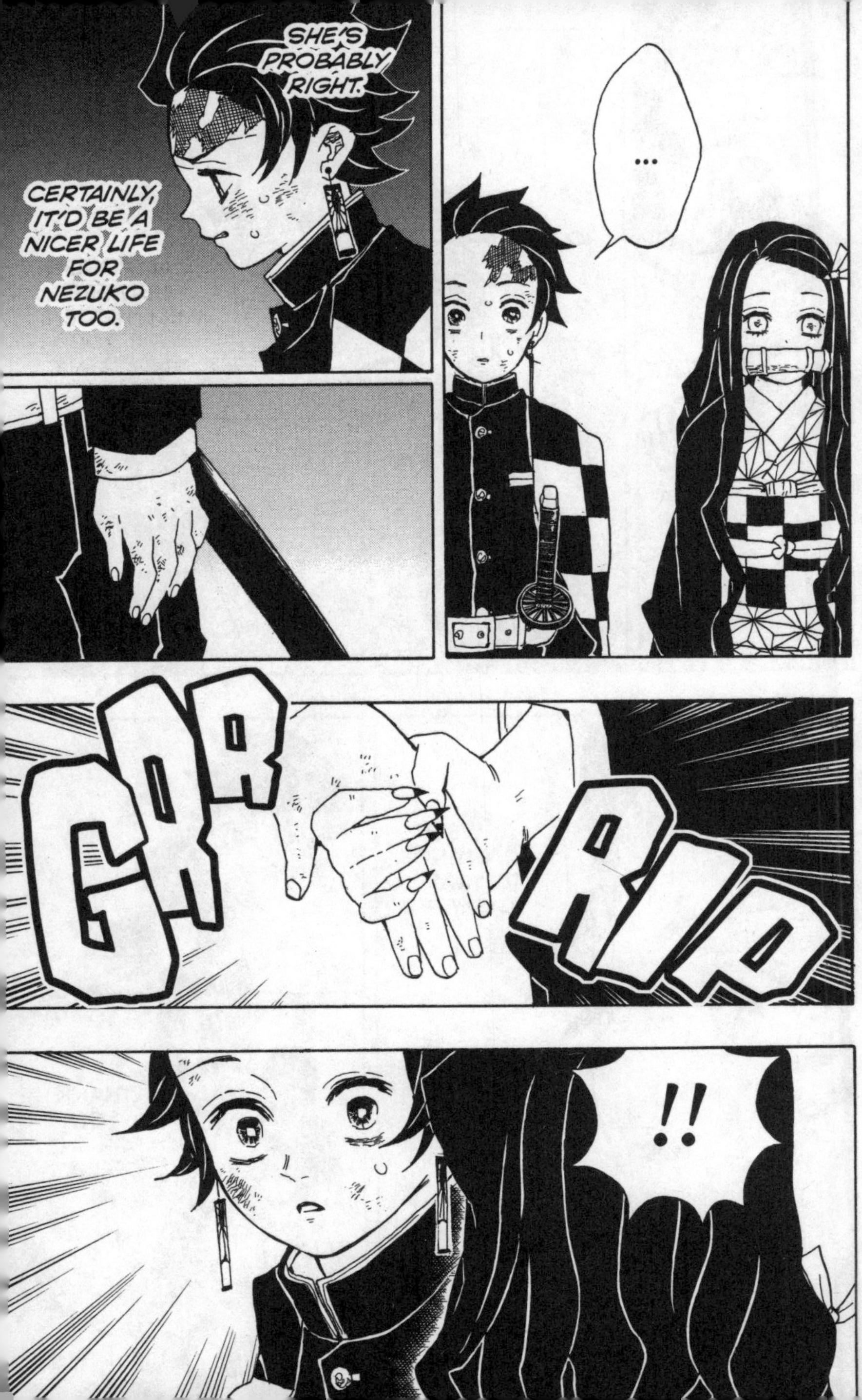
...
SHE'S PROBABLY RIGHT.
CERTAINLY, IT'D BE A NICER LIFE FOR NEZUKO TOO.
GRR RIP
!!

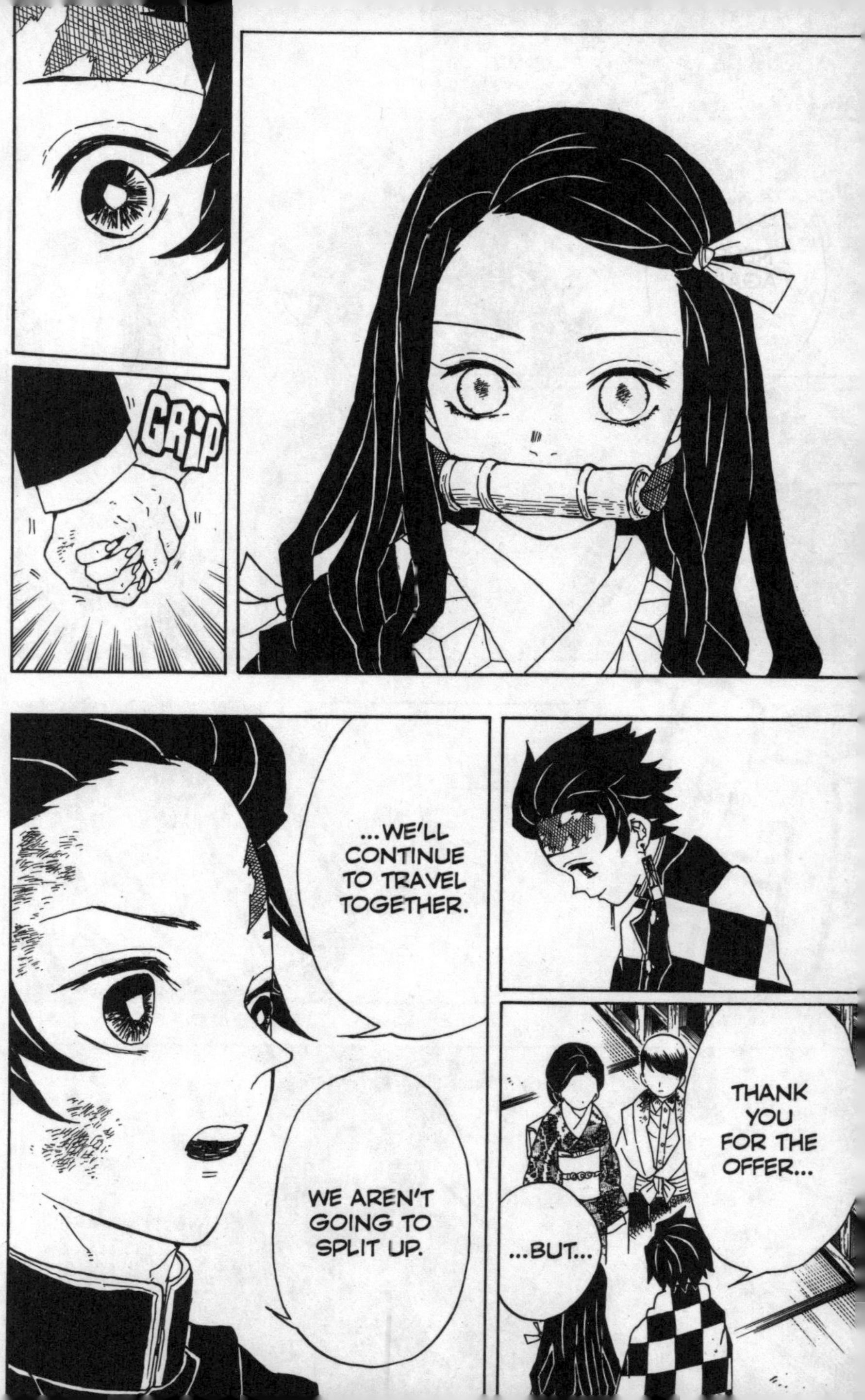
GRIP
THANK YOU FOR THE OFFER...
...BUT...
...WE'LL CONTINUE TO TRAVEL TOGETHER.
WE AREN'T GOING TO SPLIT UP.

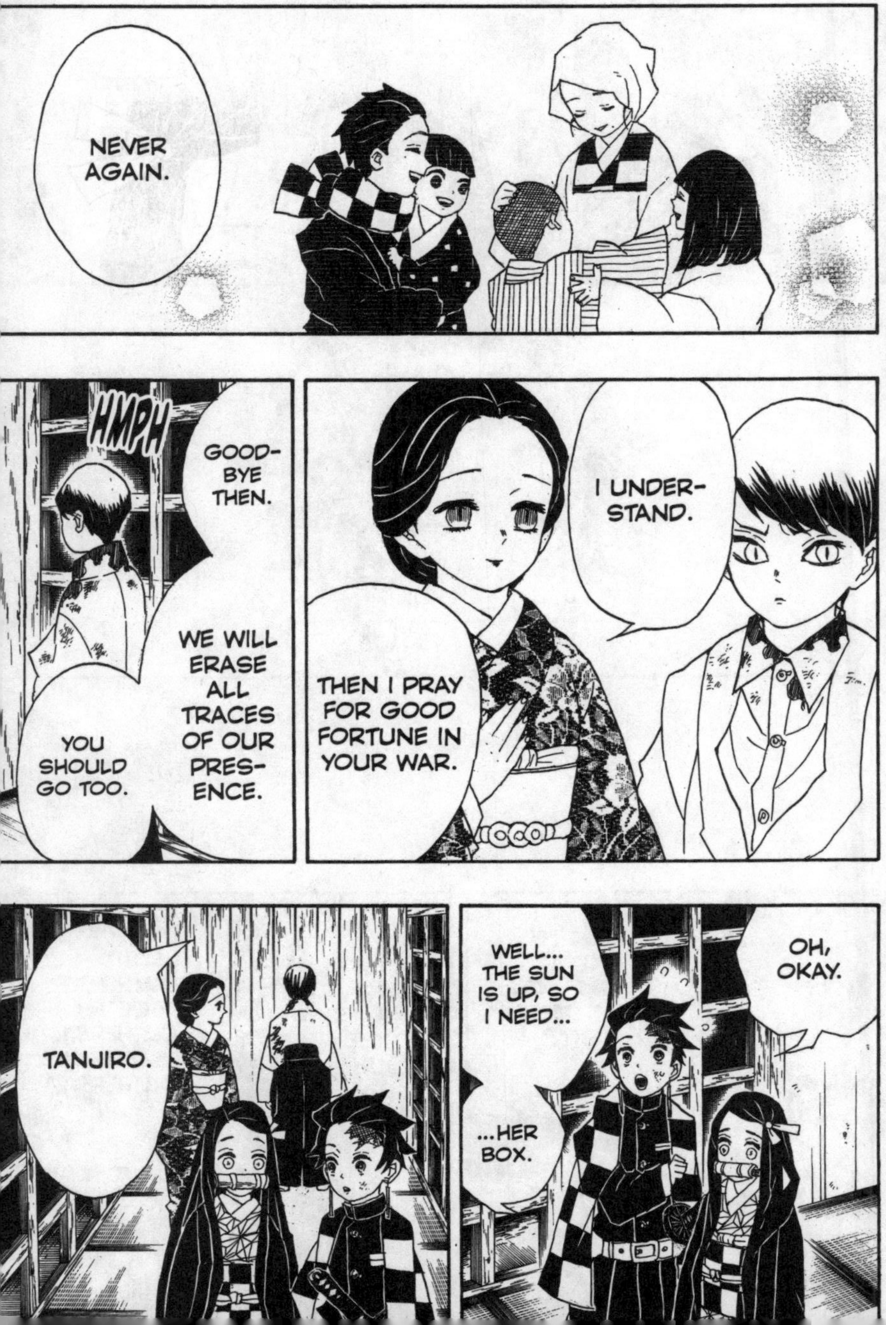
NEVER AGAIN.
I UNDER-STAND.
THEN I PRAY FOR GOOD FORTUNE IN YOUR WAR.
GOOD-BYE THEN.
HMPH
WE WILL ERASE ALL TRACES OF OUR PRES-ENCE.
YOU SHOULD GO TOO.
OH, OKAY.
WELL... THE SUN IS UP, SO I NEED...
...HER BOX.
TANJIRO.

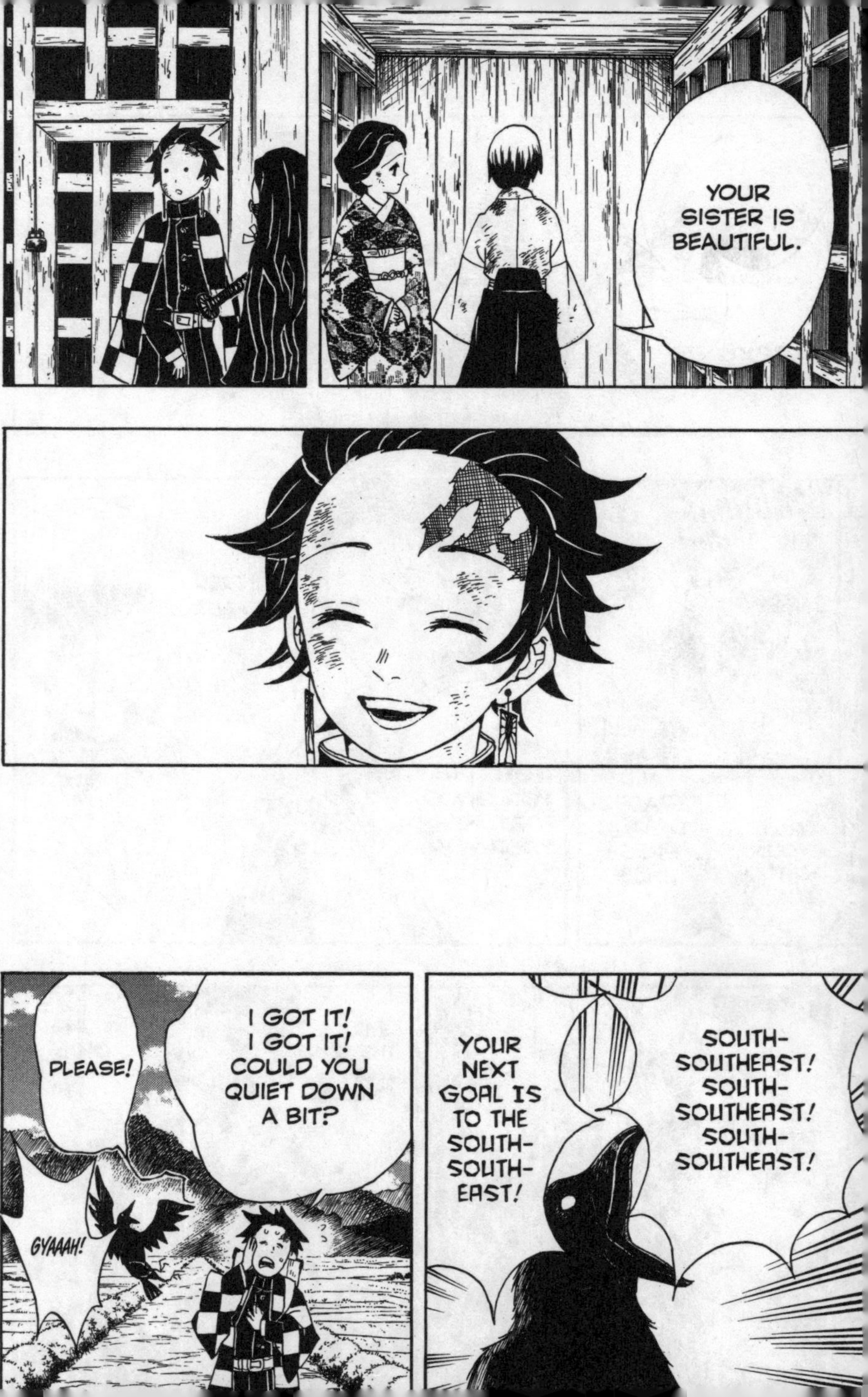
YOUR SISTER IS BEAUTIFUL.
SOUTH-SOUTHEAST! SOUTH-SOUTHEAST! SOUTH-SOUTHEAST!
YOUR NEXT GOAL IS TO THE SOUTH-SOUTH-EAST!
I GOT IT! I GOT IT! COULD YOU QUIET DOWN A BIT?
PLEASE!
GYAAAH!

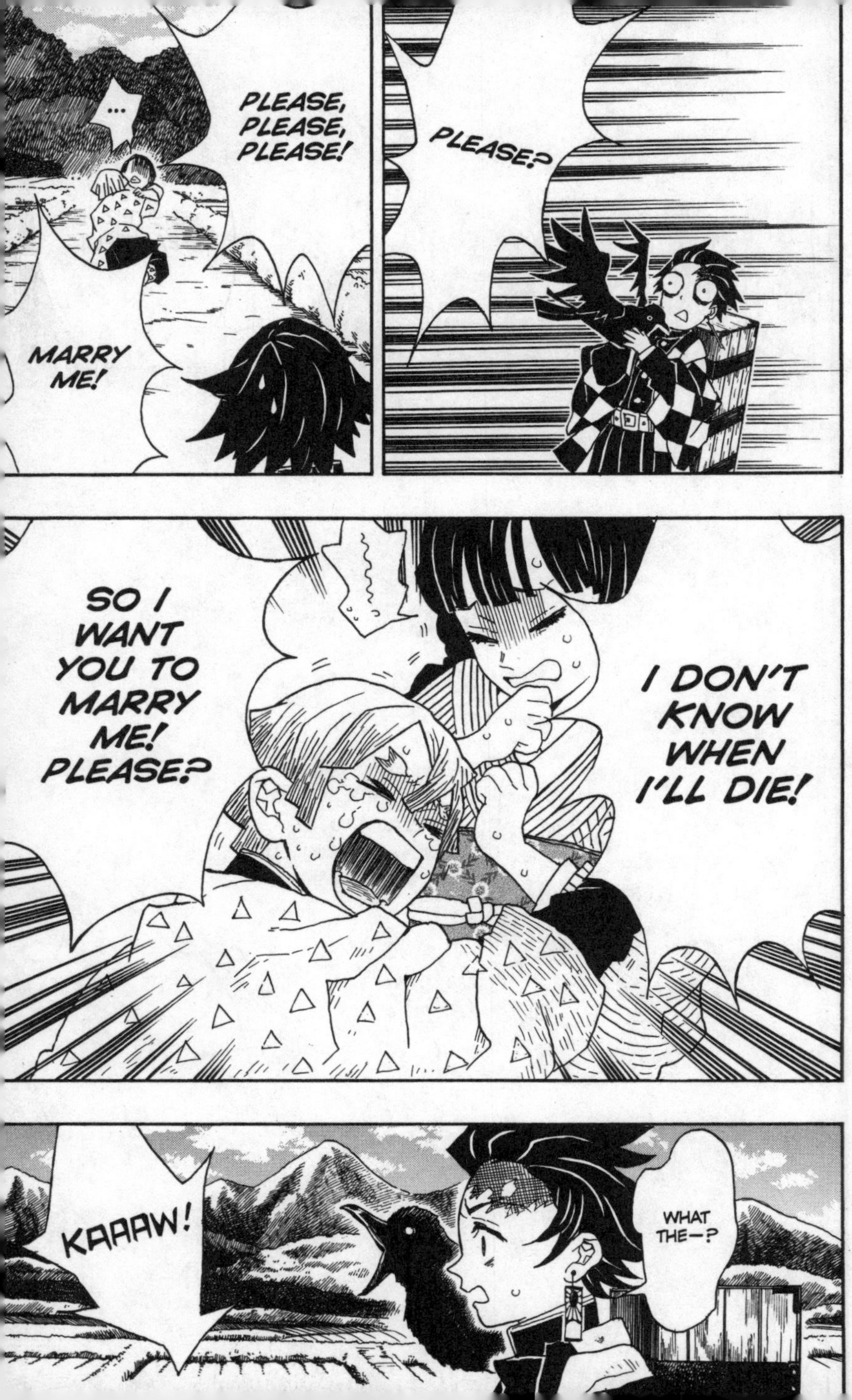
PLEASE?
PLEASE, PLEASE, PLEASE!
...
MARRY ME!
I DON'T KNOW WHEN I'LL DIE!
SO I WANT YOU TO MARRY ME! PLEASE?
WHAT THE—?
KAAAW!

THE CROW IN...

~THE HEART'S VOICE~

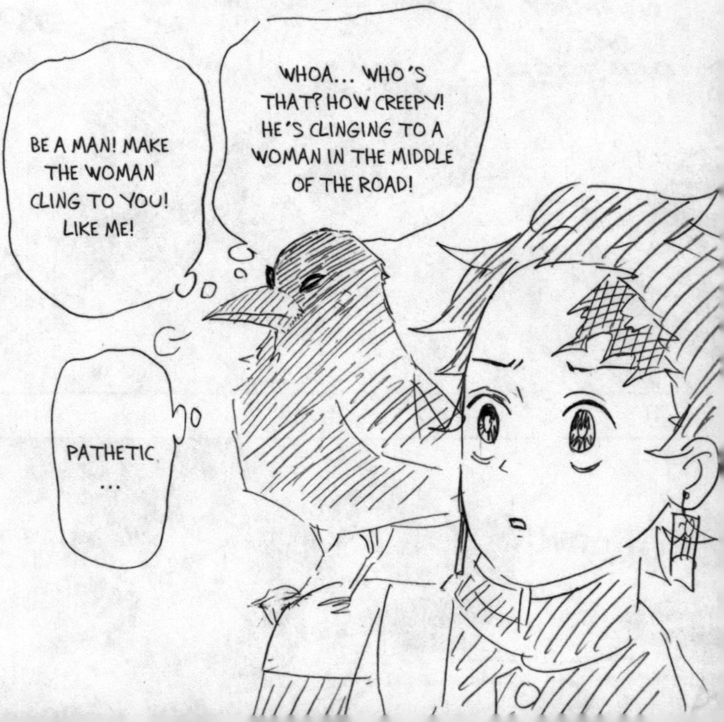
WHOA... WHO'S THAT? HOW CREEPY! HE'S CLINGING TO A WOMAN IN THE MIDDLE OF THE ROAD!
BE A MAN! MAKE THE WOMAN CLING TO YOU! LIKE ME!
PATHETIC...

CHAPTER 20: ZENITSU AGATSUMA

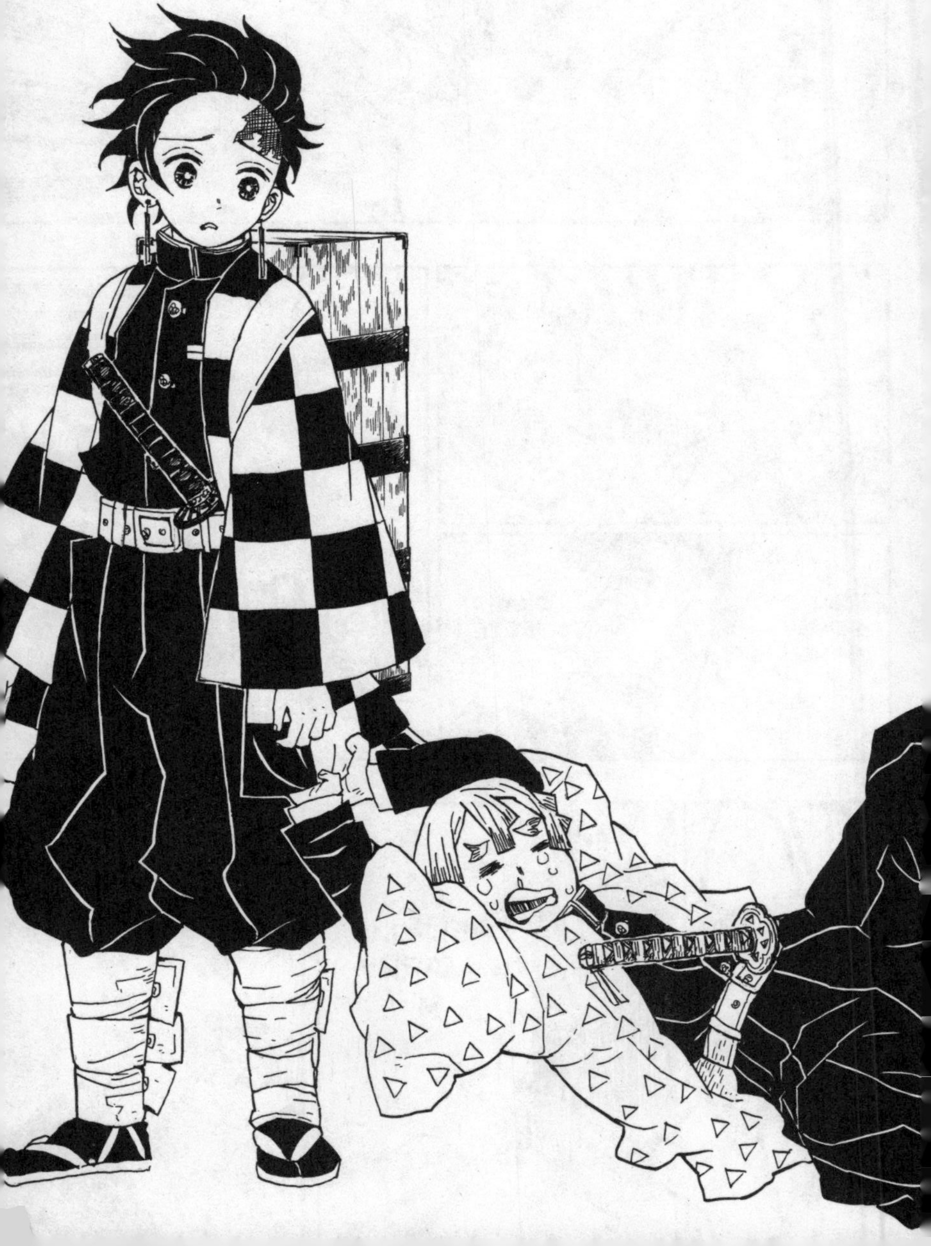

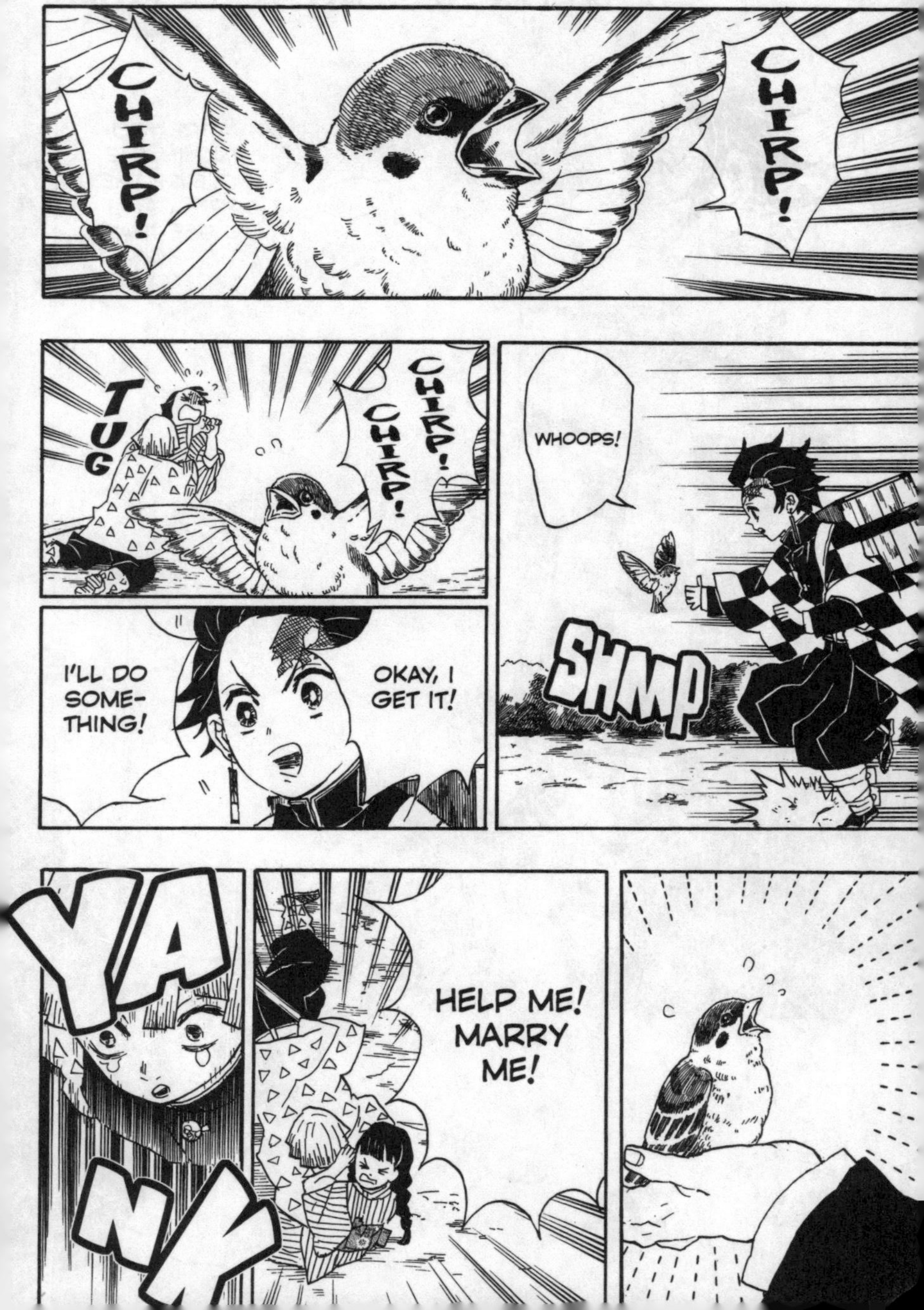
CHIRP!
CHIRP!
WHOOPS!
SHMP
CHIRP! CHIRP!
TUG
OKAY, I GET IT!
I'LL DO SOMETHING!
HELP ME! MARRY ME!
YANK

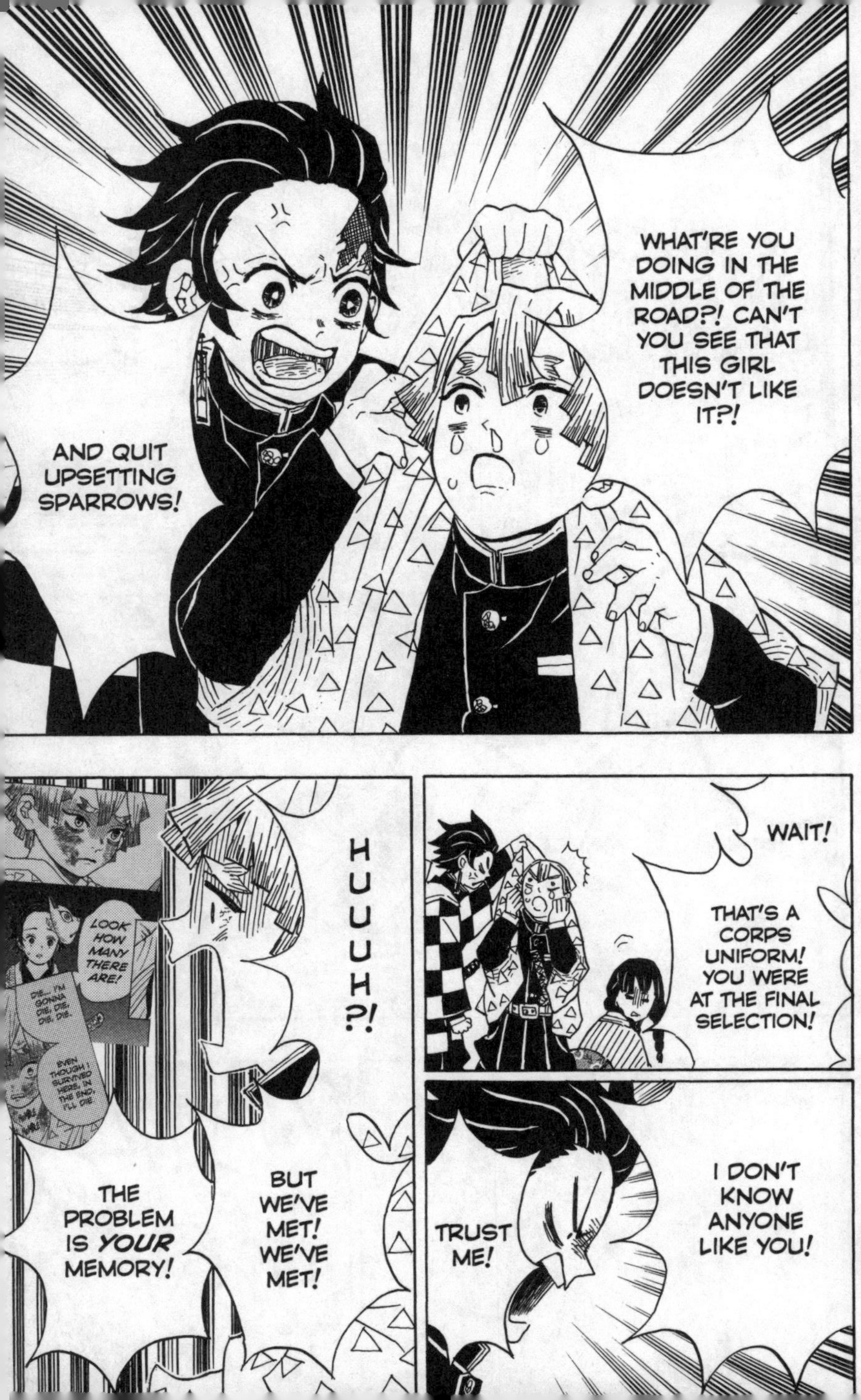
WHAT'RE YOU DOING IN THE MIDDLE OF THE ROAD?! CAN'T YOU SEE THAT THIS GIRL DOESN'T LIKE IT?!
AND QUIT UPSETTING SPARROWS!
WAIT!
THAT'S A CORPS UNIFORM! YOU WERE AT THE FINAL SELECTION!
I DON'T KNOW ANYONE LIKE YOU!
TRUST ME!
BUT WE'VE MET! WE'VE MET!
THE PROBLEM IS *YOUR* MEMORY!
HUUUUH?!
LOOK HOW MANY THERE ARE!
DIE... I'M GONNA DIE. DIE. DIE.
EVEN THOUGH I SURVIVED HERE, IN THE END, I'LL DIE

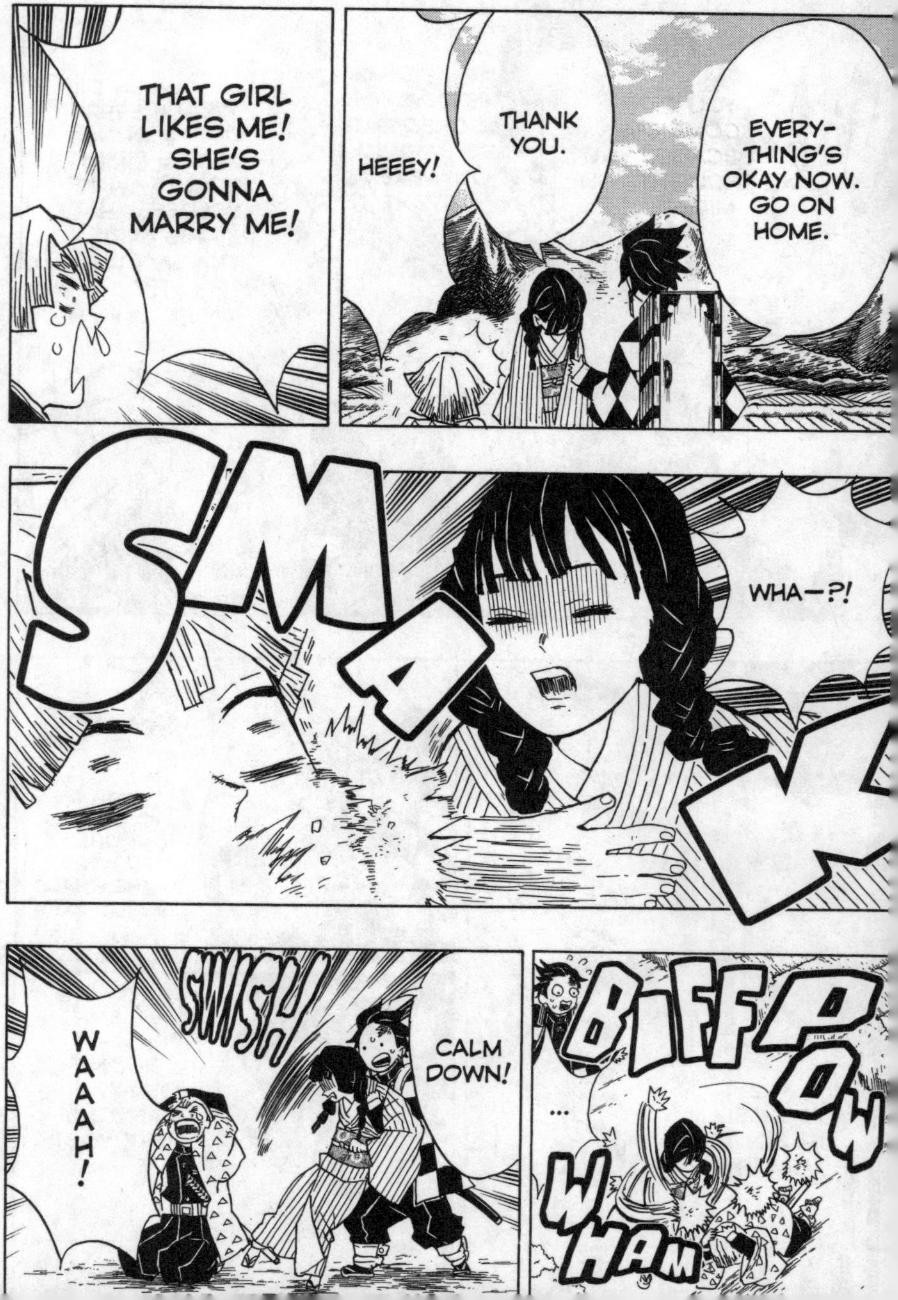
EVERY-THING'S OKAY NOW. GO ON HOME.
THANK YOU.
HEEEY!
THAT GIRL LIKES ME! SHE'S GONNA MARRY ME!
WHA—?!
SMA
K
BIFF
POW
...
WHAM
CALM DOWN!
SWISH
WAAAH!

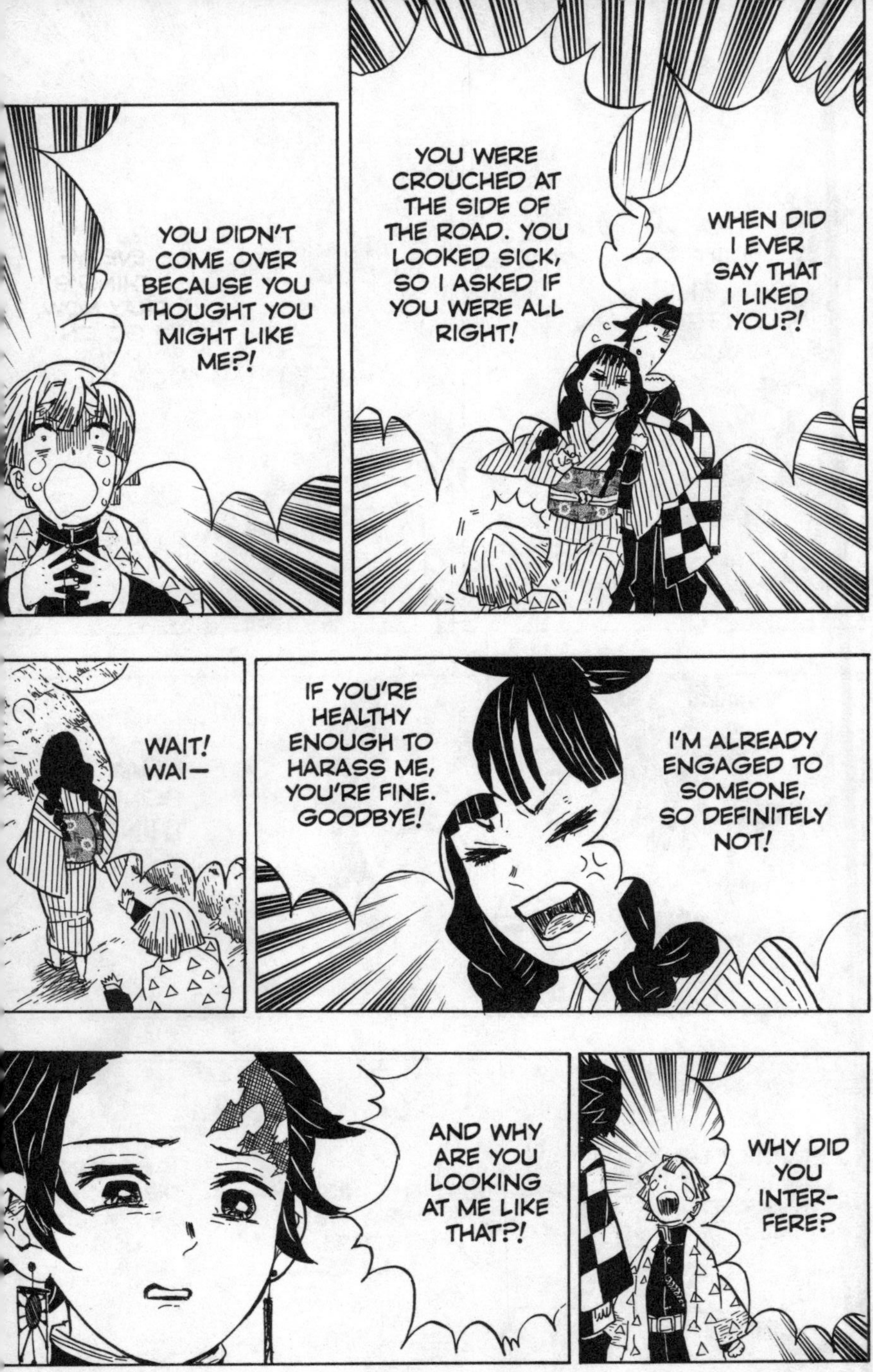
WHEN DID I EVER SAY THAT I LIKED YOU?!
YOU WERE CROUCHED AT THE SIDE OF THE ROAD. YOU LOOKED SICK, SO I ASKED IF YOU WERE ALL RIGHT!
YOU DIDN'T COME OVER BECAUSE YOU THOUGHT YOU MIGHT LIKE ME?!
I'M ALREADY ENGAGED TO SOMEONE, SO DEFINITELY NOT!
IF YOU'RE HEALTHY ENOUGH TO HARASS ME, YOU'RE FINE. GOODBYE!
WAIT! WAI—
WHY DID YOU INTER-FERE?
AND WHY ARE YOU LOOKING AT ME LIKE THAT?!

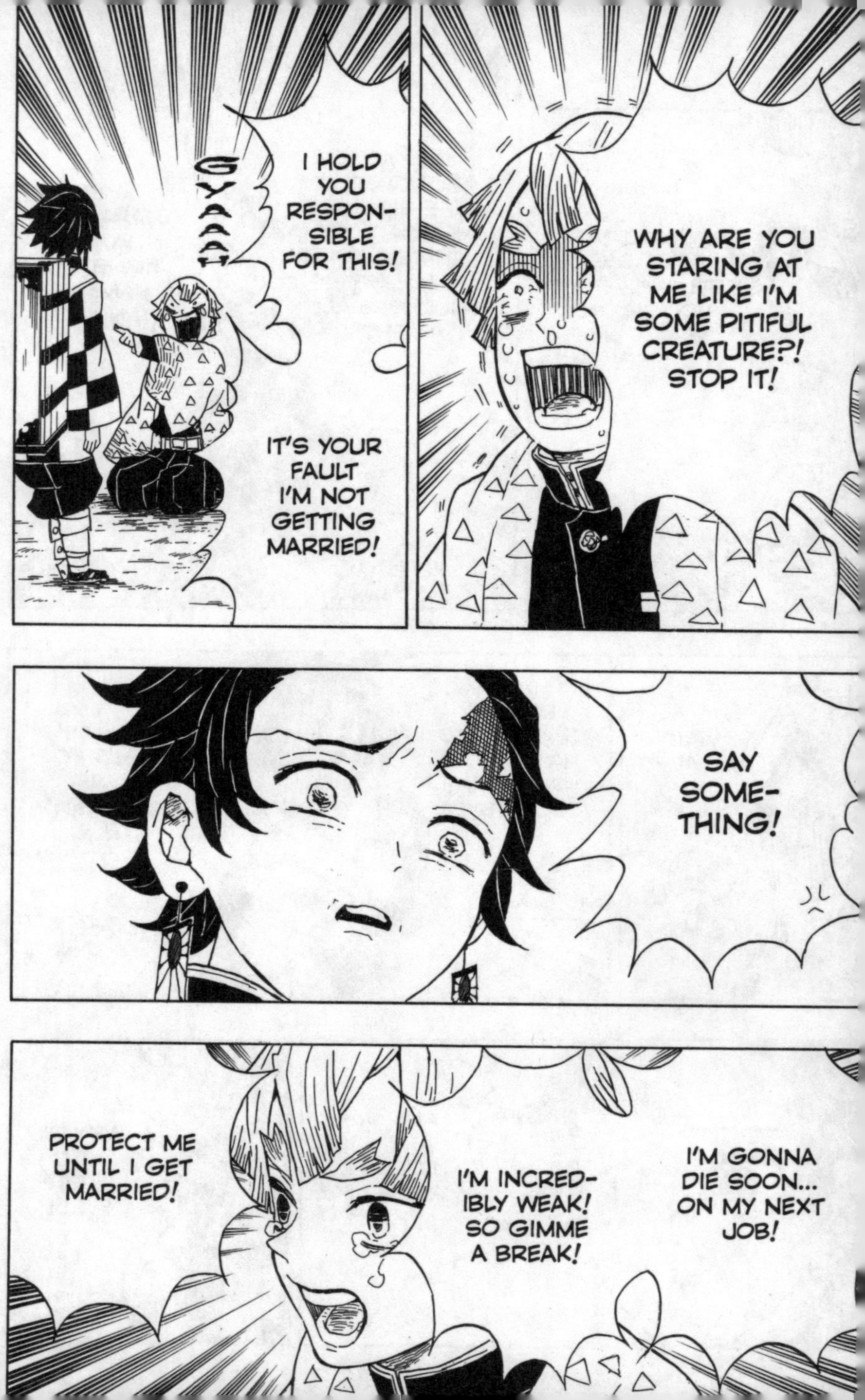
WHY ARE YOU STARING AT ME LIKE I'M SOME PITIFUL CREATURE?! STOP IT!
GYAAAH
I HOLD YOU RESPONSIBLE FOR THIS!
IT'S YOUR FAULT I'M NOT GETTING MARRIED!
SAY SOMETHING!
I'M GONNA DIE SOON... ON MY NEXT JOB!
I'M INCREDIBLY WEAK! SO GIMME A BREAK!
PROTECT ME UNTIL I GET MARRIED!

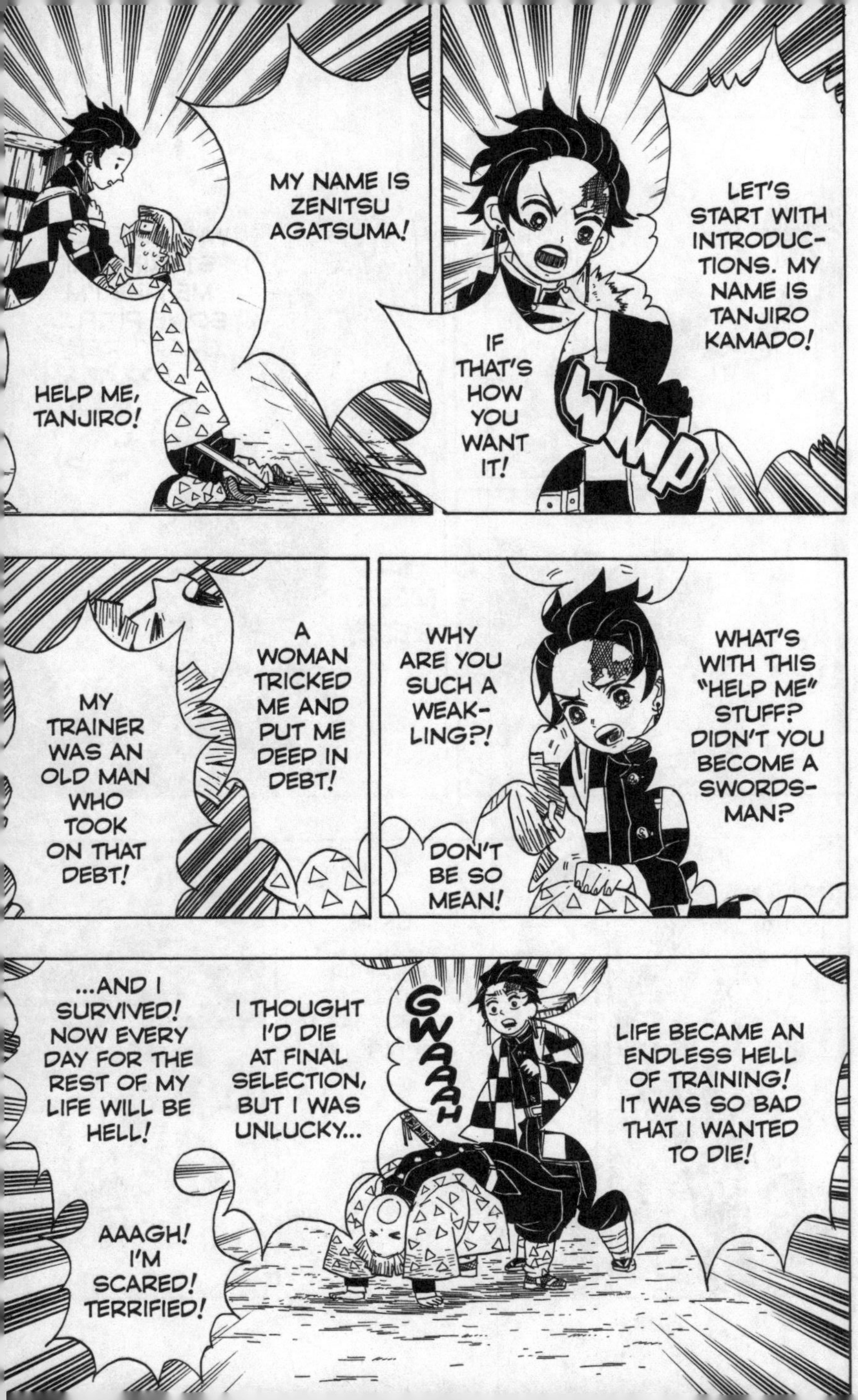
LET'S START WITH INTRODUCTIONS. MY NAME IS TANJIRO KAMADO!
WMP
IF THAT'S HOW YOU WANT IT!
MY NAME IS ZENITSU AGATSUMA!
HELP ME, TANJIRO!
WHAT'S WITH THIS "HELP ME" STUFF? DIDN'T YOU BECOME A SWORDSMAN?
WHY ARE YOU SUCH A WEAKLING?!
DON'T BE SO MEAN!
A WOMAN TRICKED ME AND PUT ME DEEP IN DEBT!
MY TRAINER WAS AN OLD MAN WHO TOOK ON THAT DEBT!
LIFE BECAME AN ENDLESS HELL OF TRAINING! IT WAS SO BAD THAT I WANTED TO DIE!
GWAAAH
I THOUGHT I'D DIE AT FINAL SELECTION, BUT I WAS UNLUCKY...
...AND I SURVIVED! NOW EVERY DAY FOR THE REST OF MY LIFE WILL BE HELL!
AAAGH! I'M SCARED! TERRIFIED!

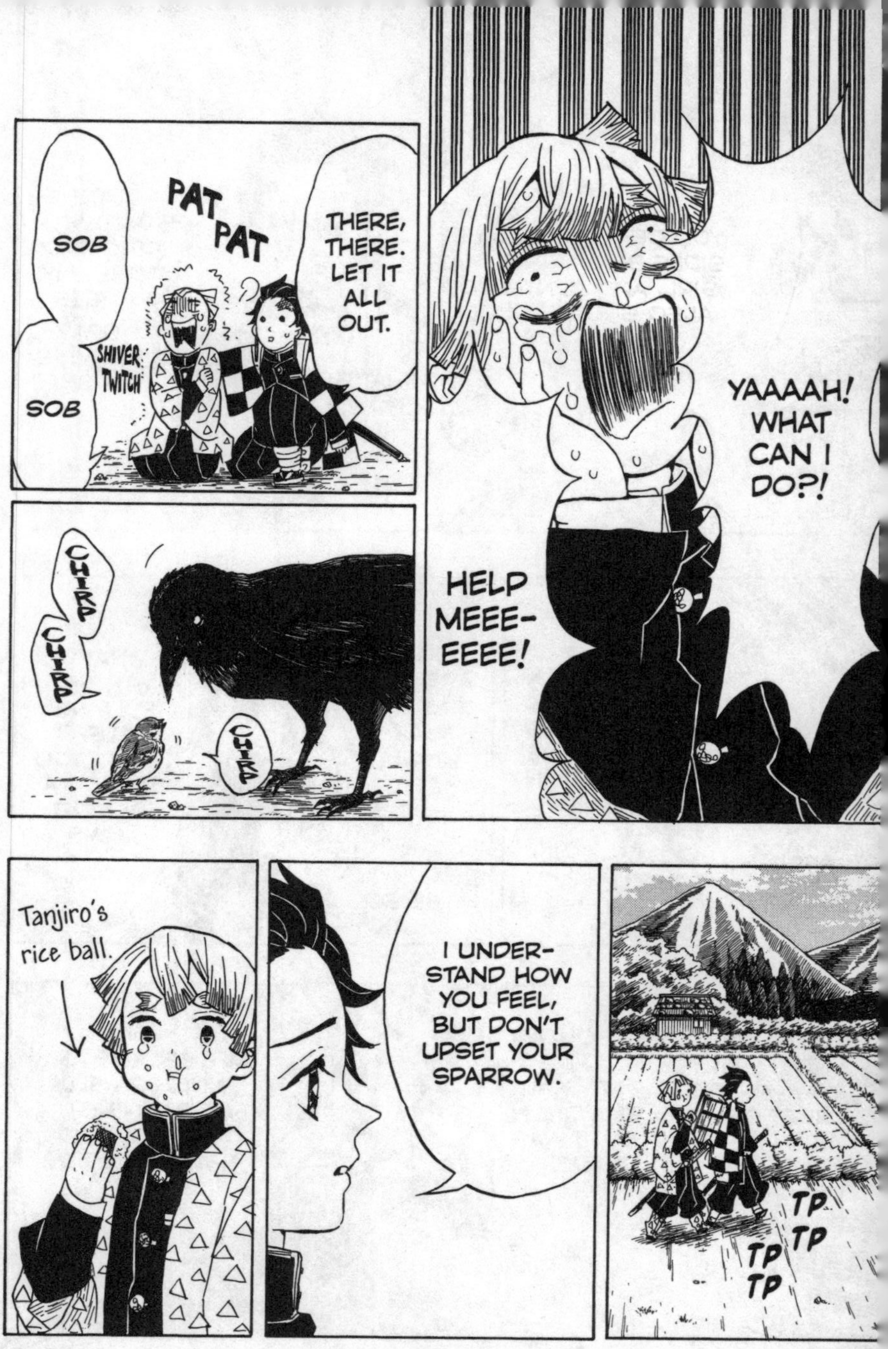

YAAAAH! WHAT CAN I DO?!
HELP MEEE-EEEE!
THERE, THERE. LET IT ALL OUT.
PAT PAT
SOB
SHIVER TWITCH
SOB
CHIRP
CHIRP
CHIRP
CHIRP
TP TP TP TP
I UNDER-STAND HOW YOU FEEL, BUT DON'T UPSET YOUR SPARROW.
Tanjiro's rice ball.

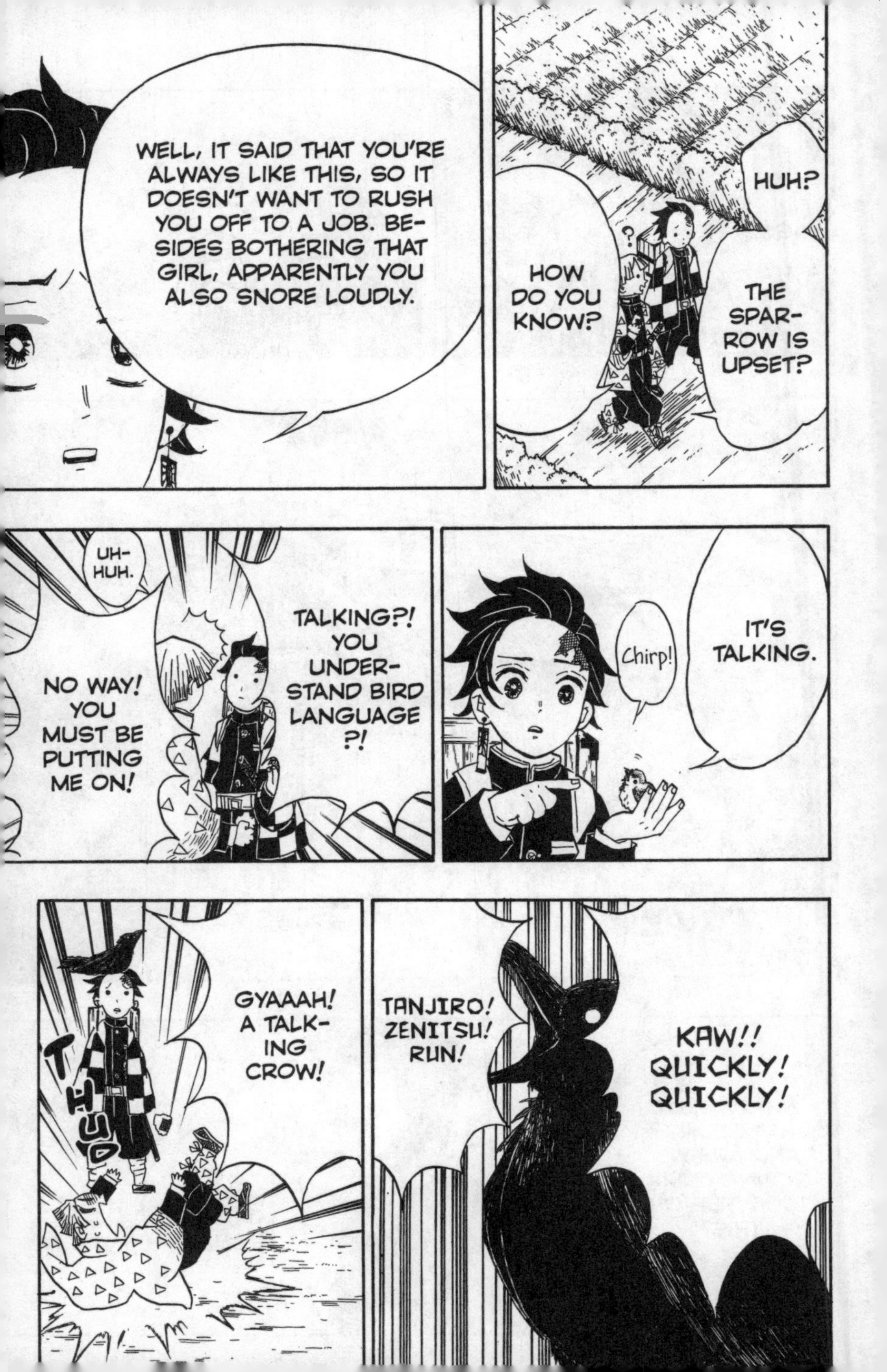
HUH?
THE SPARROW IS UPSET?
HOW DO YOU KNOW?
WELL, IT SAID THAT YOU'RE ALWAYS LIKE THIS, SO IT DOESN'T WANT TO RUSH YOU OFF TO A JOB. BESIDES BOTHERING THAT GIRL, APPARENTLY YOU ALSO SNORE LOUDLY.
IT'S TALKING.
Chirp!
UH-HUH.
TALKING?! YOU UNDERSTAND BIRD LANGUAGE?!
NO WAY! YOU MUST BE PUTTING ME ON!
KAW!! QUICKLY! QUICKLY!
TANJIRO! ZENITSU! RUN!
GYAAAH! A TALKING CROW!
THUD

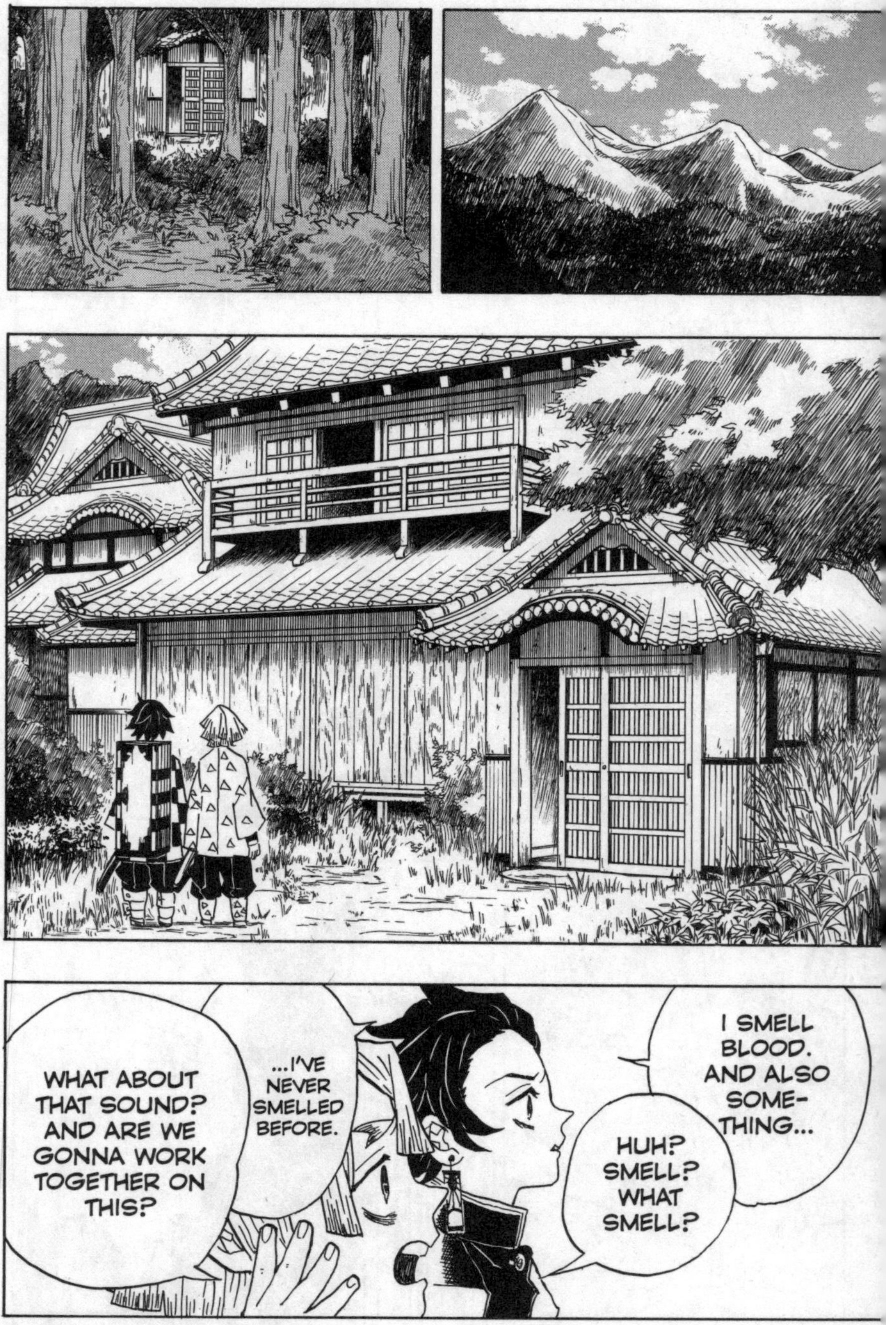
I SMELL BLOOD. AND ALSO SOME-THING...
...I'VE NEVER SMELLED BEFORE.
HUH? SMELL? WHAT SMELL?
WHAT ABOUT THAT SOUND? AND ARE WE GONNA WORK TOGETHER ON THIS?

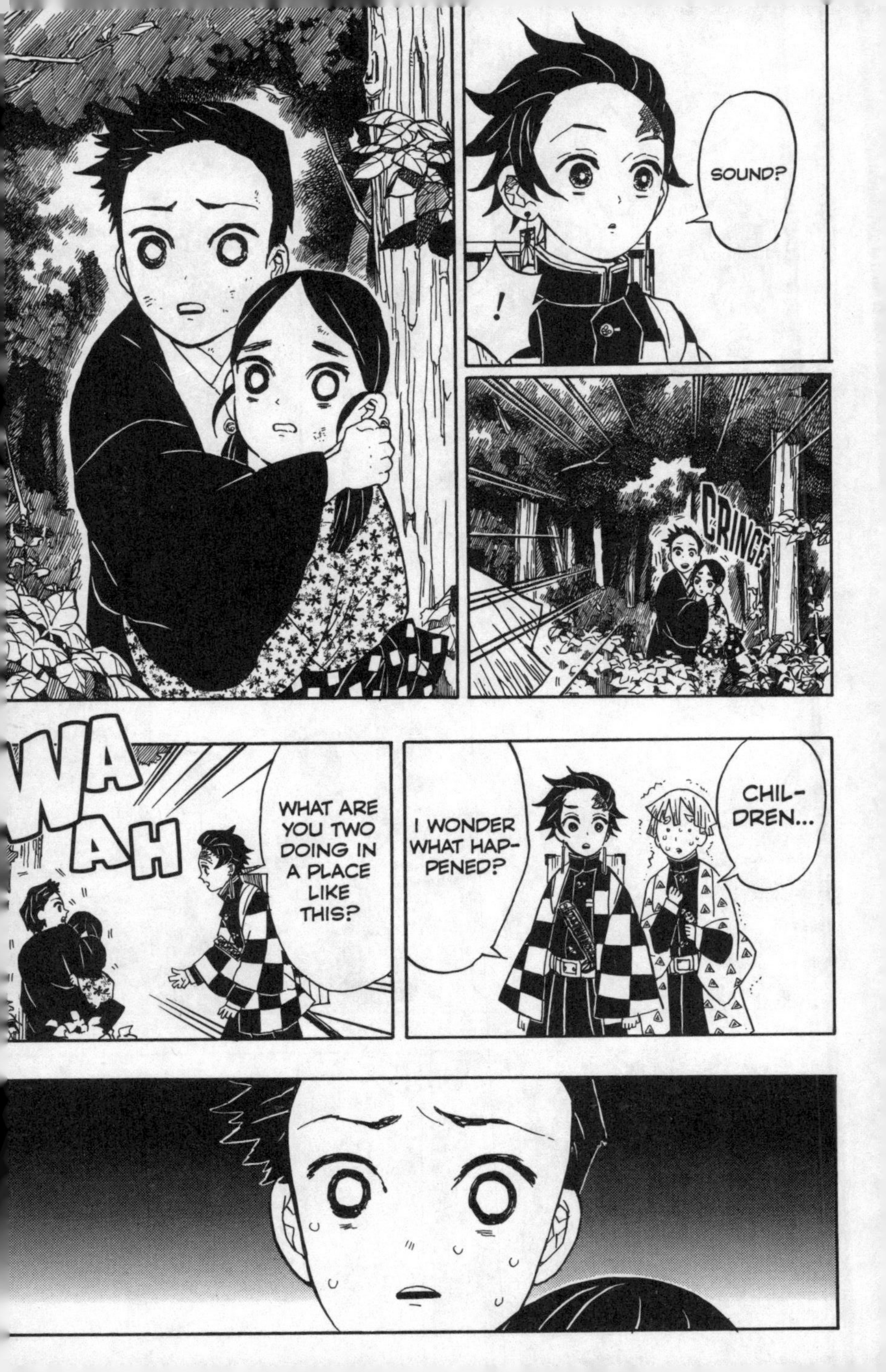
SOUND?
!
CRINGE
CHIL-
DREN...
I WONDER
WHAT HAP-
PENED?
WHAT ARE
YOU TWO
DOING IN
A PLACE
LIKE
THIS?
WA
AH

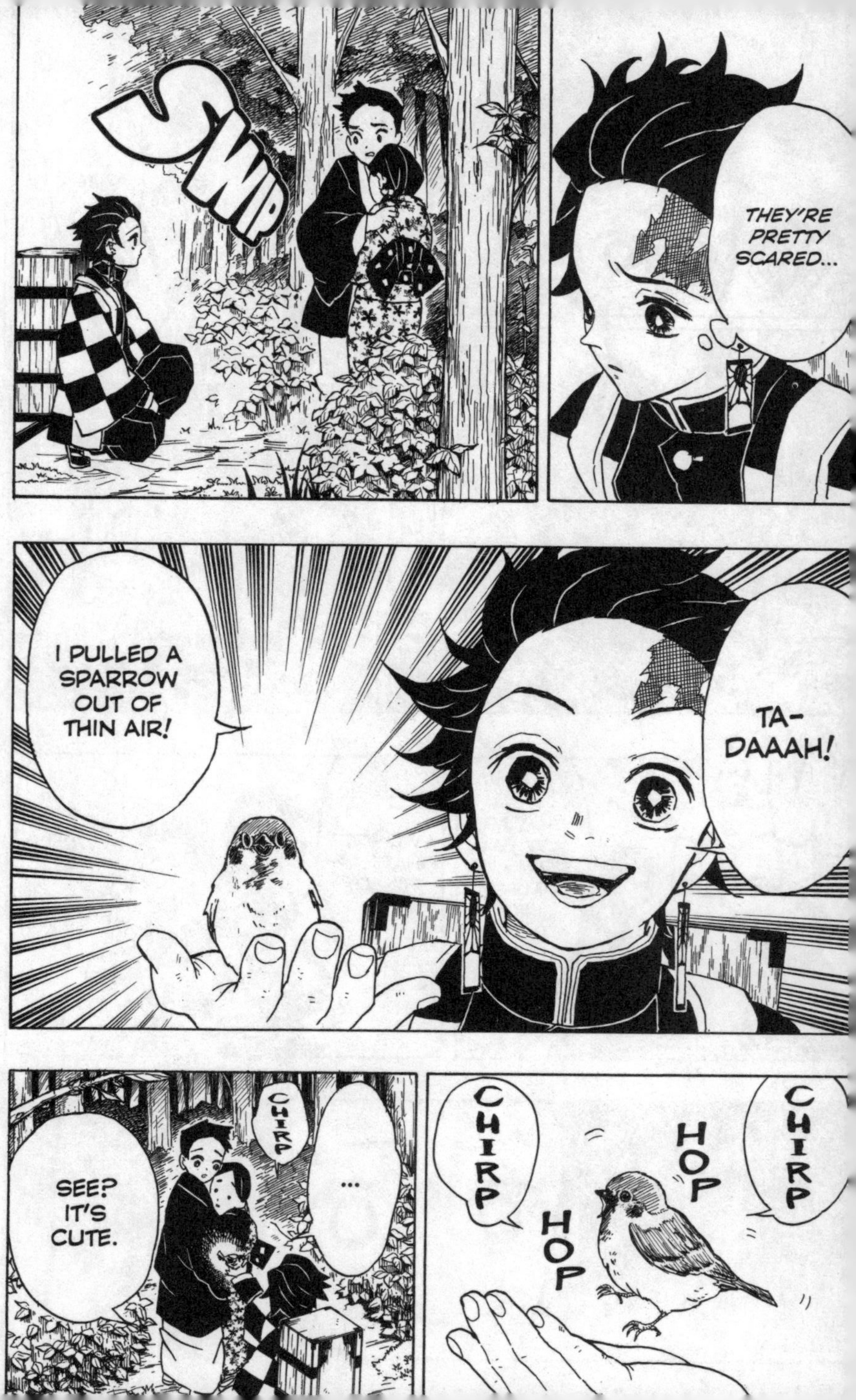
THEY'RE PRETTY SCARED...
SWIP
TA-DAAAH!
I PULLED A SPARROW OUT OF THIN AIR!
CHIRP
HOP
HOP
CHIRP
...
CHIRP
SEE? IT'S CUTE.

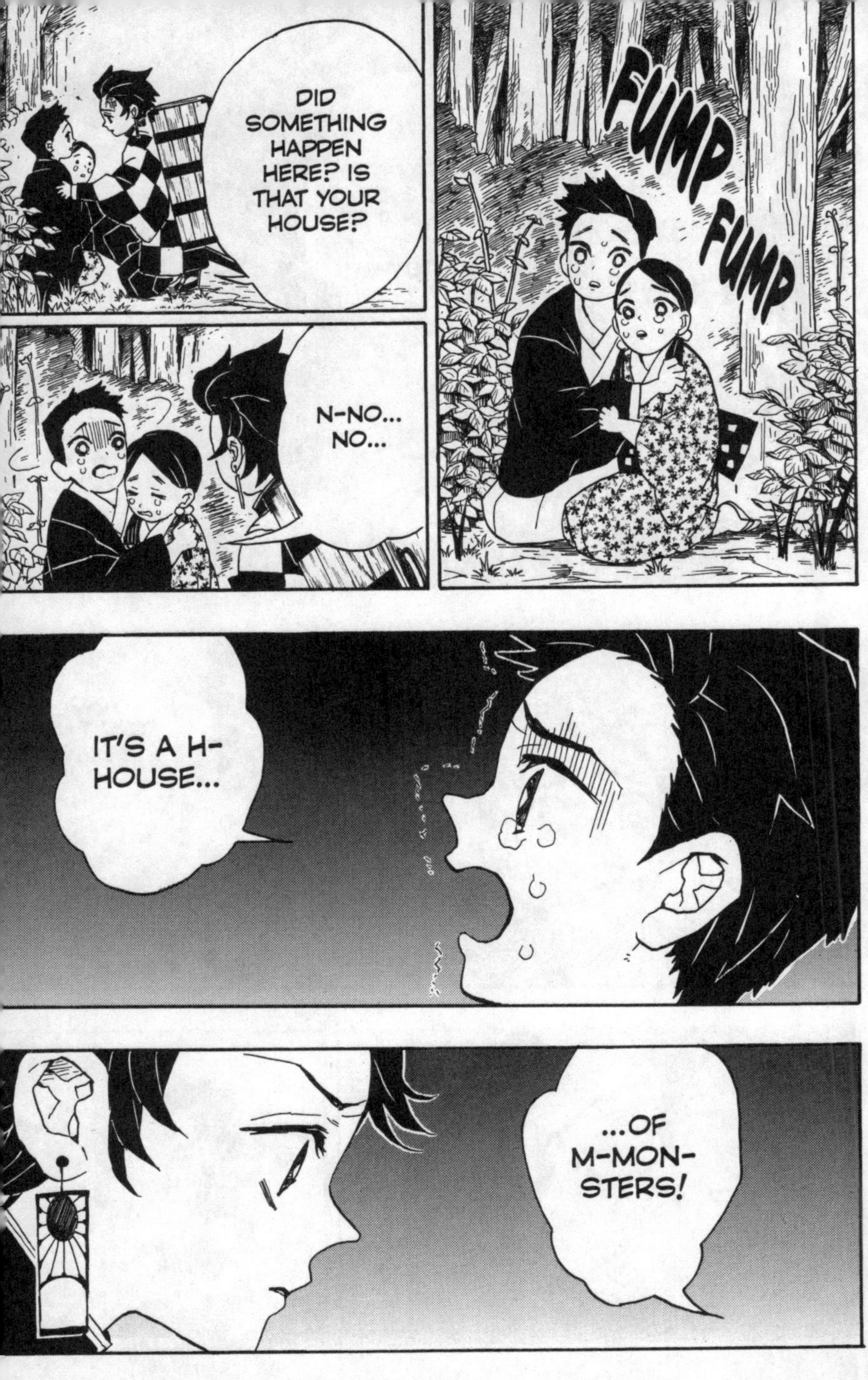
FUMP FUMP
DID SOMETHING HAPPEN HERE? IS THAT YOUR HOUSE?
N-NO... NO...
IT'S A H-HOUSE...
...OF M-MON-STERS!

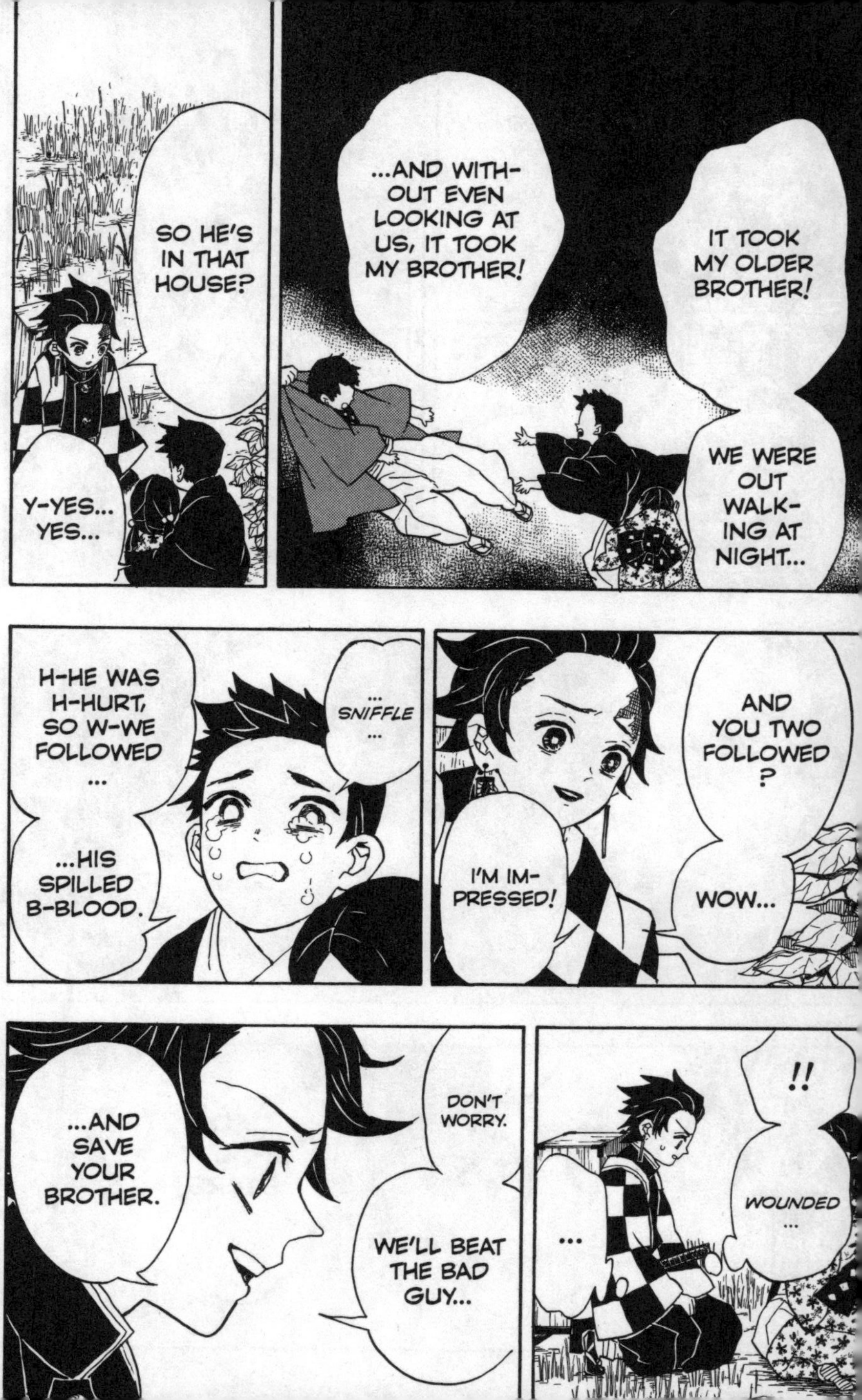
IT TOOK MY OLDER BROTHER!
WE WERE OUT WALKING AT NIGHT...
...AND WITHOUT EVEN LOOKING AT US, IT TOOK MY BROTHER!
SO HE'S IN THAT HOUSE?
Y-YES... YES...
AND YOU TWO FOLLOWED?
WOW...
I'M IMPRESSED!
...SNIFFLE...
H-HE WAS H-HURT, SO W-WE FOLLOWED...
...HIS SPILLED B-BLOOD.
!!
WOUNDED...
...
DON'T WORRY.
WE'LL BEAT THE BAD GUY...
...AND SAVE YOUR BROTHER.

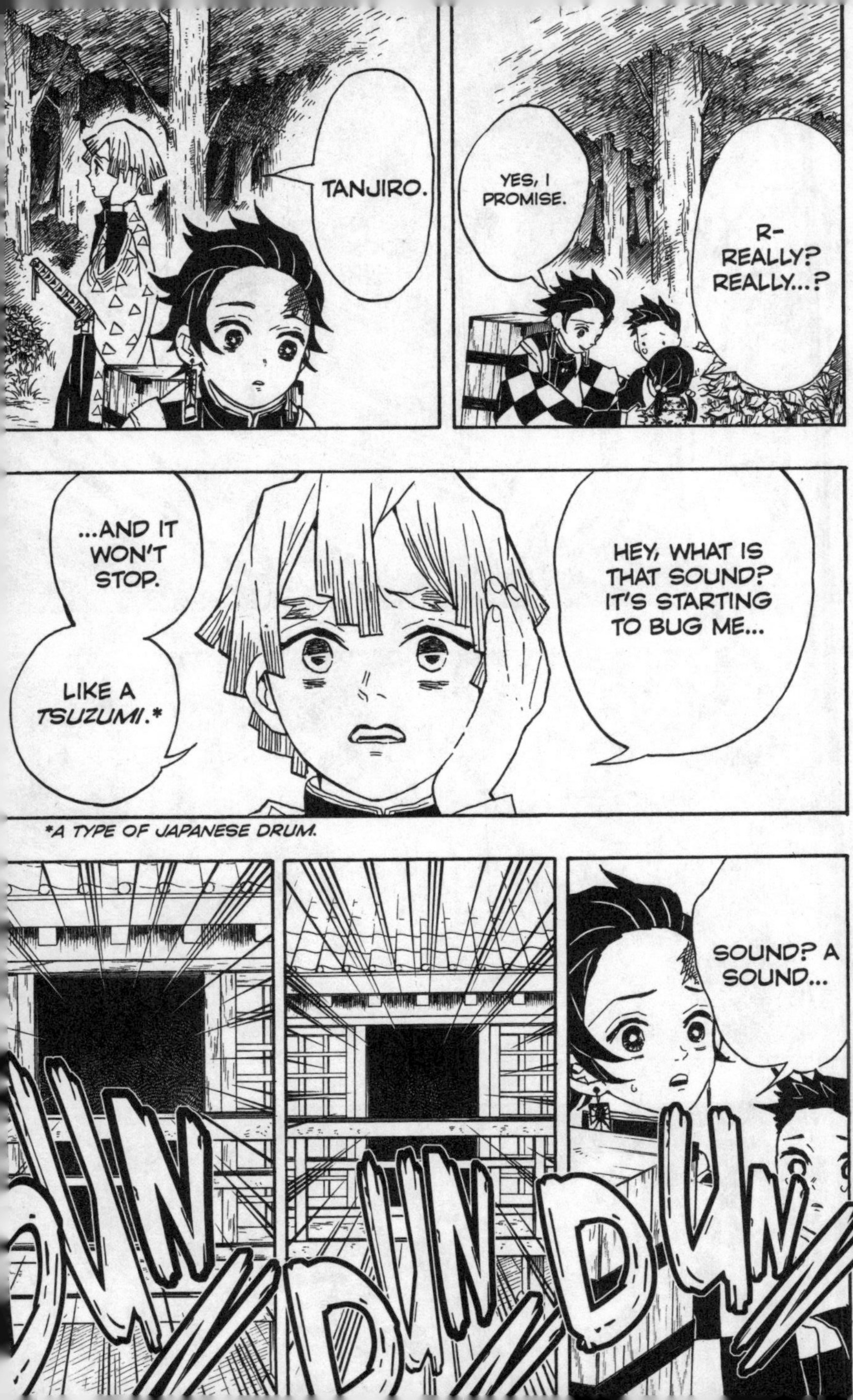
R- REALLY? REALLY...?
YES, I PROMISE.
TANJIRO.
HEY, WHAT IS THAT SOUND? IT'S STARTING TO BUG ME...
...AND IT WON'T STOP.
LIKE A *TSUZUMI*.*
SOUND? A SOUND...
DUN DUN DUN DUN

**A TYPE OF JAPANESE DRUM.*

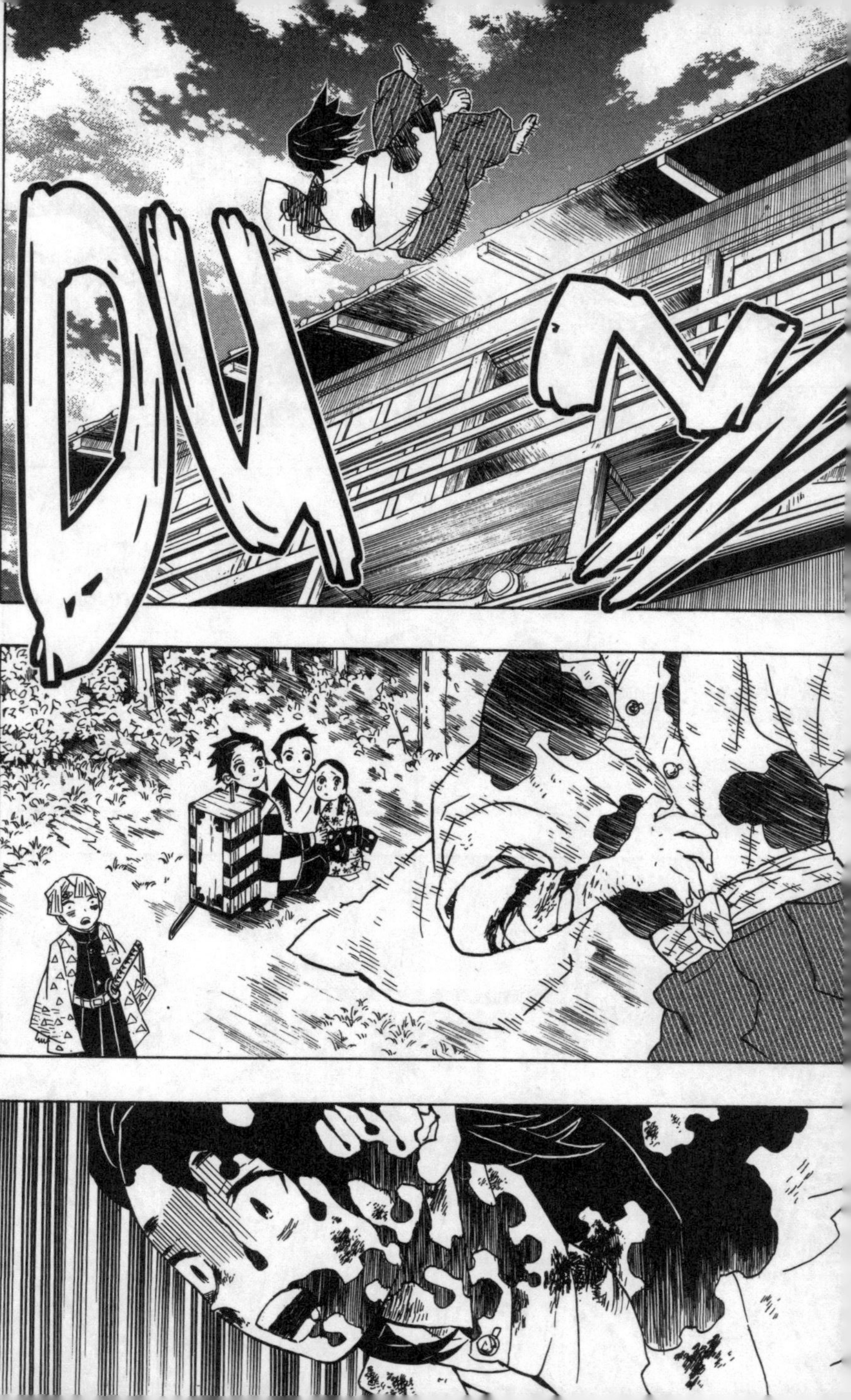
DUN

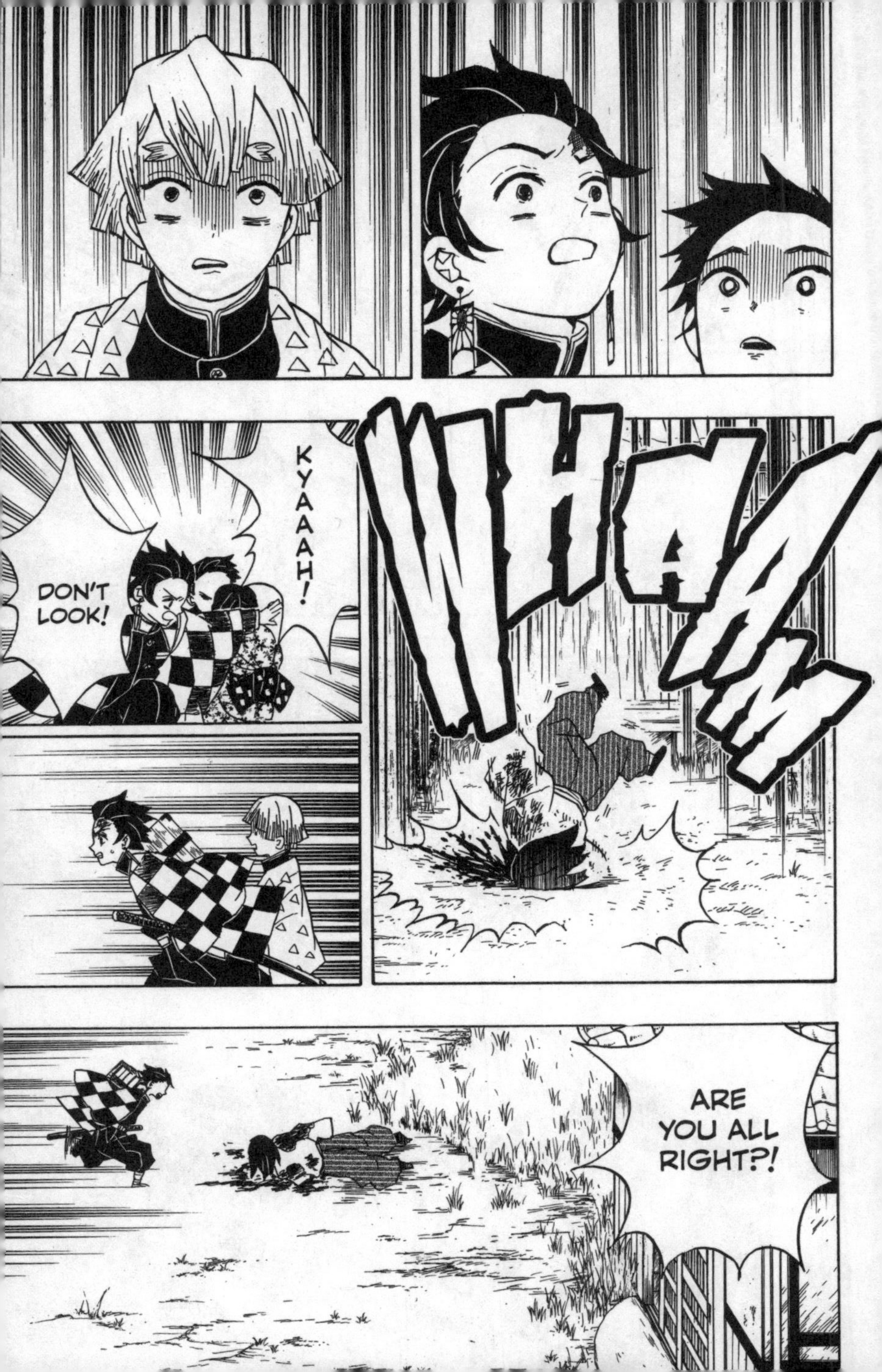
WHAM
KYAAAH!
DON'T LOOK!
ARE YOU ALL RIGHT?!

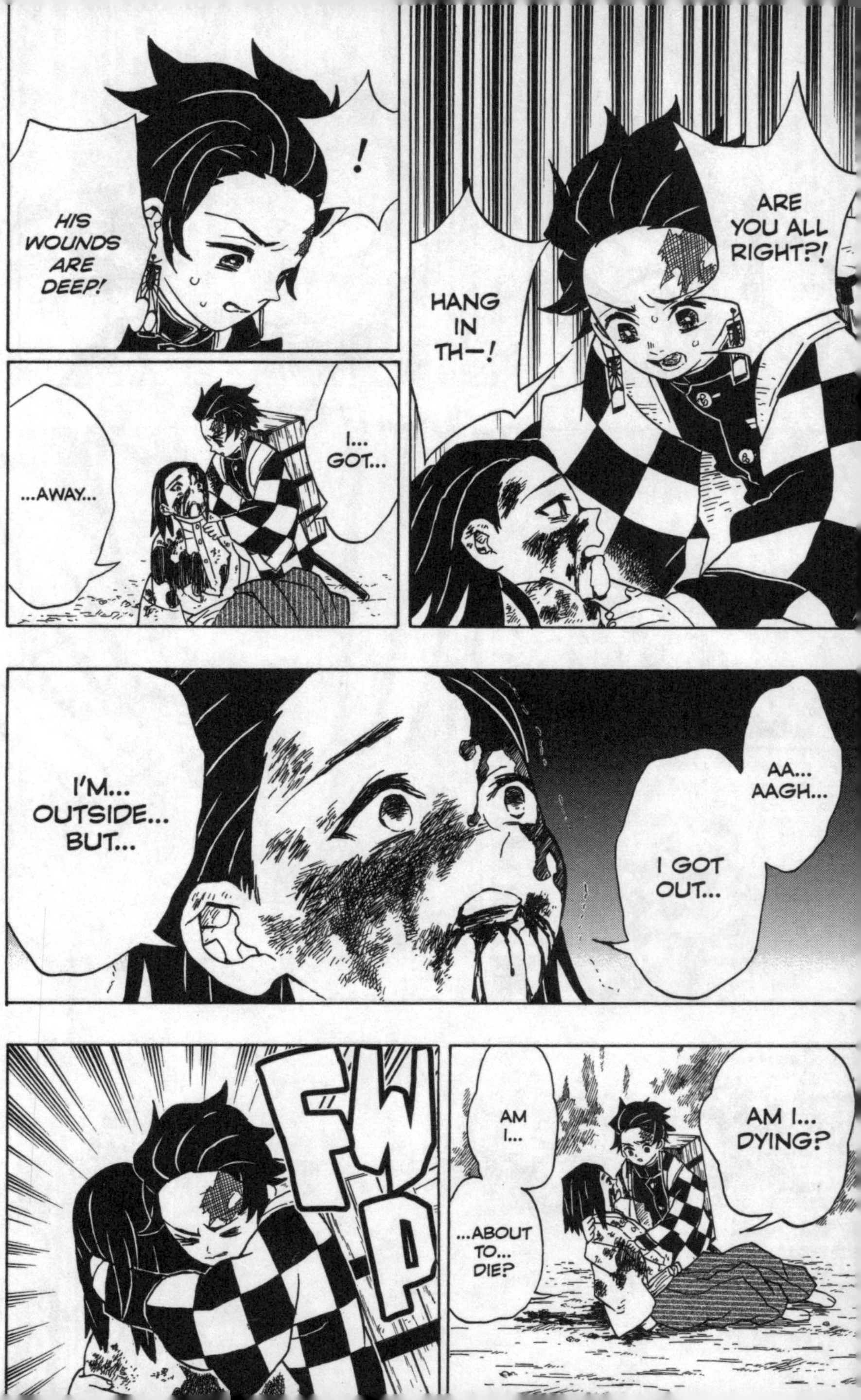
ARE YOU ALL RIGHT?!
HANG IN TH—!
!
HIS WOUNDS ARE DEEP!
I... GOT...
...AWAY...
AA... AAGH...
I GOT OUT...
I'M... OUTSIDE... BUT...
AM I... DYING?
AM I...
...ABOUT TO... DIE?
FWP

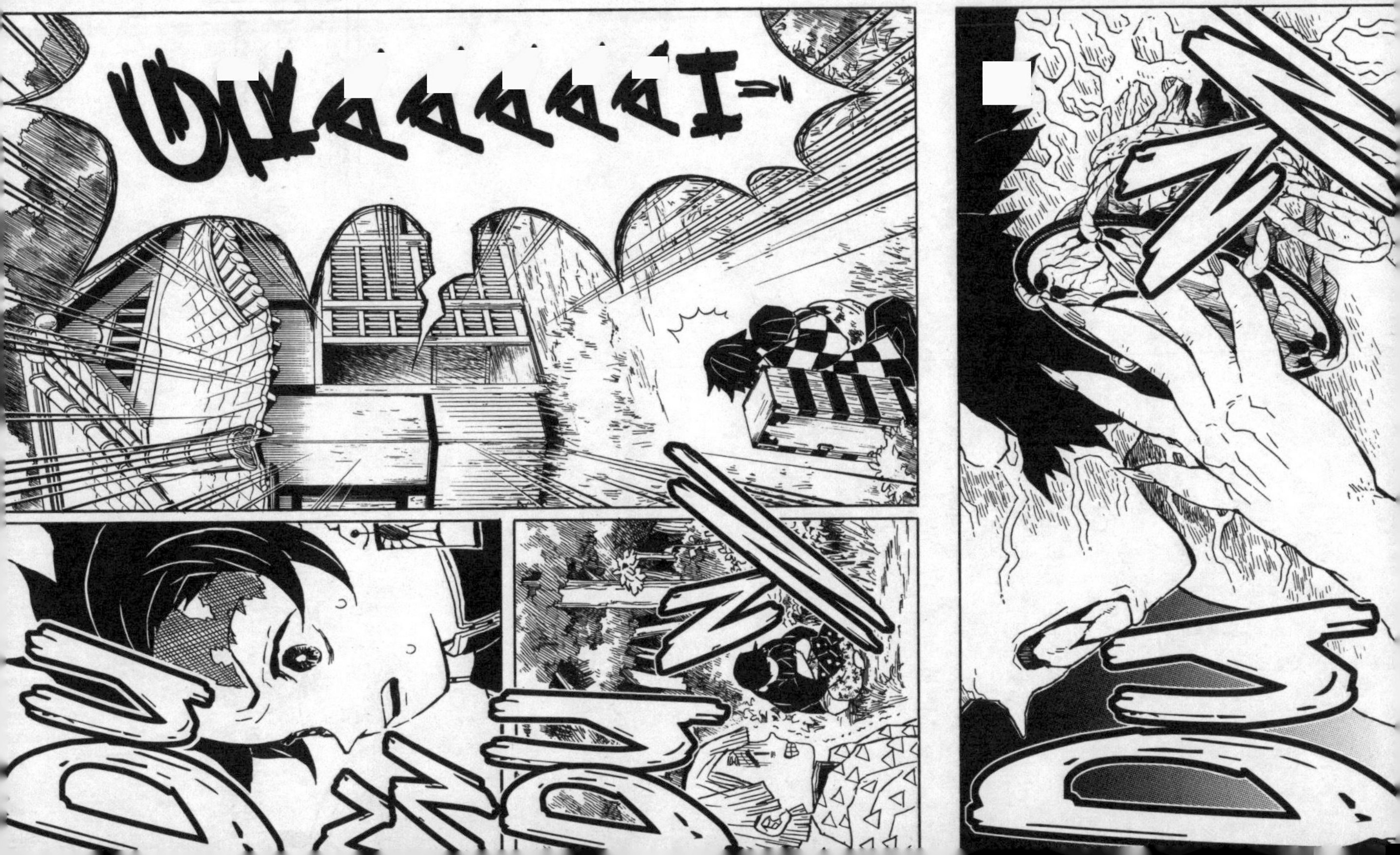
WAAAAAH!!

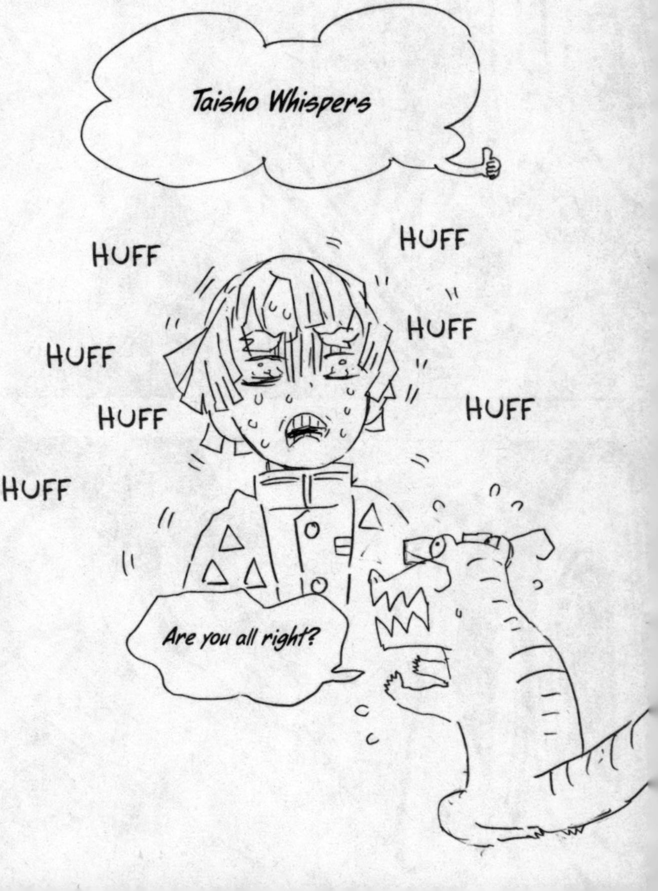
Taisho Whispers
HUFF
HUFF
HUFF
HUFF
HUFF
HUFF
HUFF
Are you all right?

CHAPTER 21: TSUZUMI MANSION

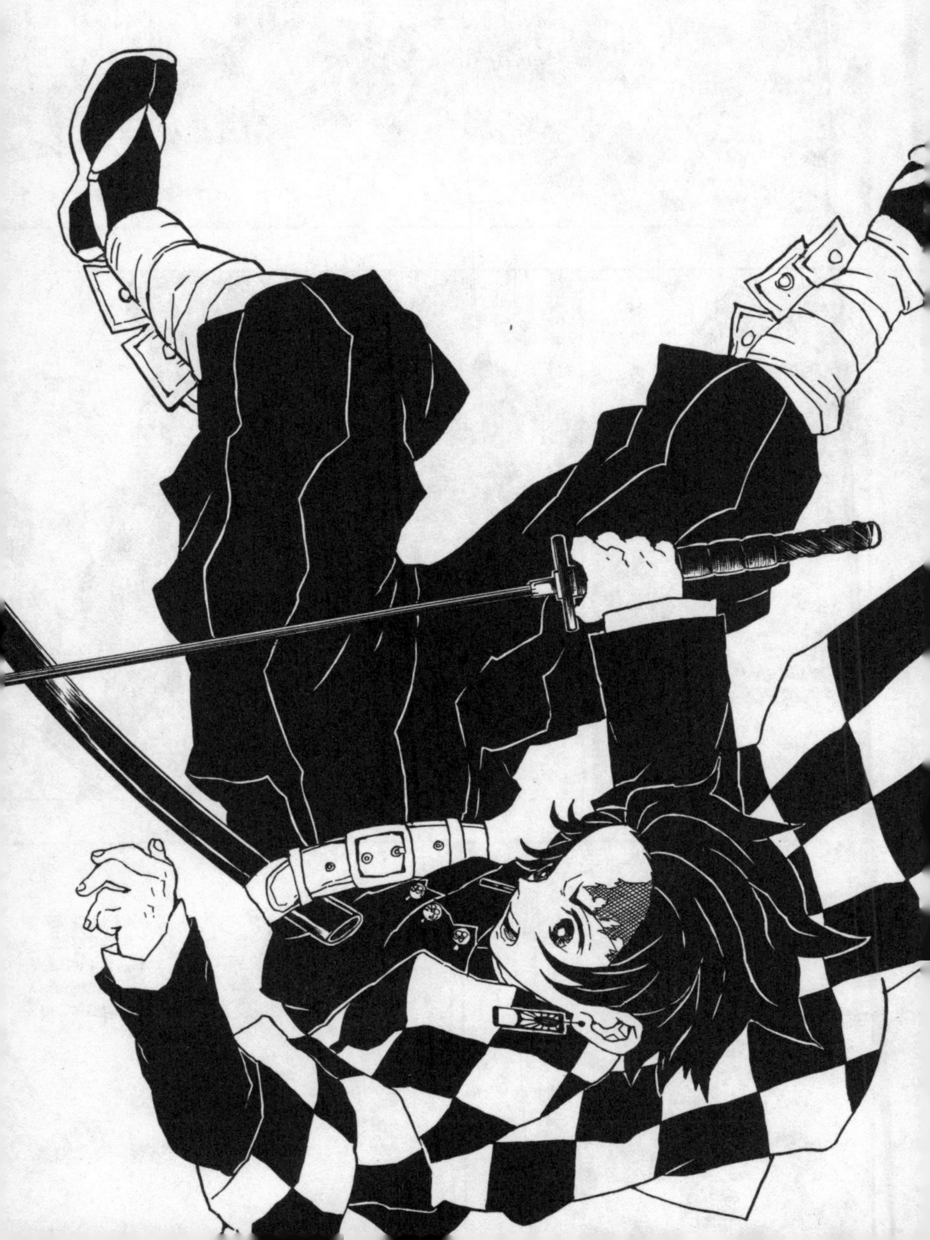

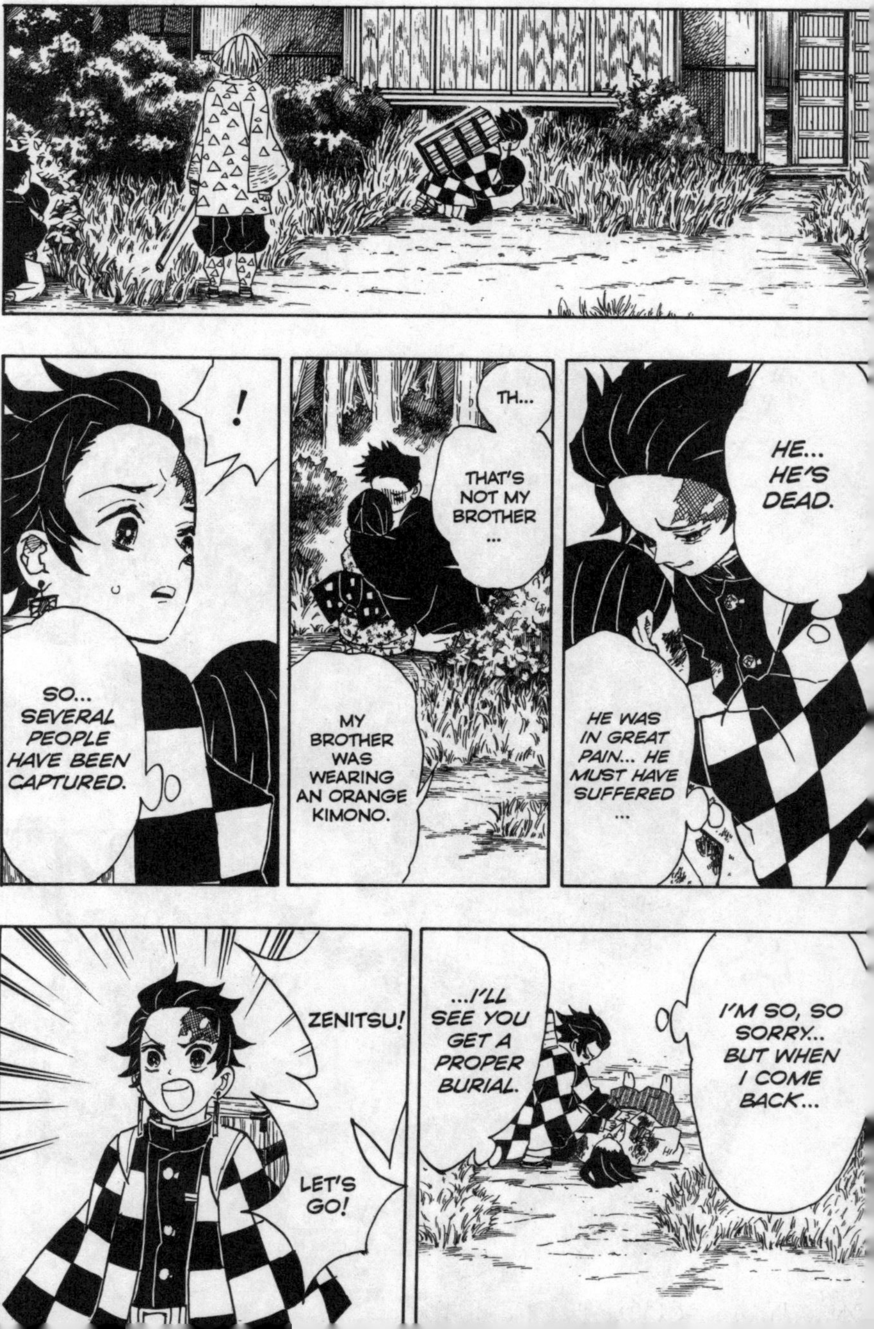
HE... HE'S DEAD.
HE WAS IN GREAT PAIN... HE MUST HAVE SUFFERED ...
TH...
THAT'S NOT MY BROTHER ...
MY BROTHER WAS WEARING AN ORANGE KIMONO.
!
SO... SEVERAL PEOPLE HAVE BEEN CAPTURED.
I'M SO, SO SORRY... BUT WHEN I COME BACK...
...I'LL SEE YOU GET A PROPER BURIAL.
ZENITSU!
LET'S GO!

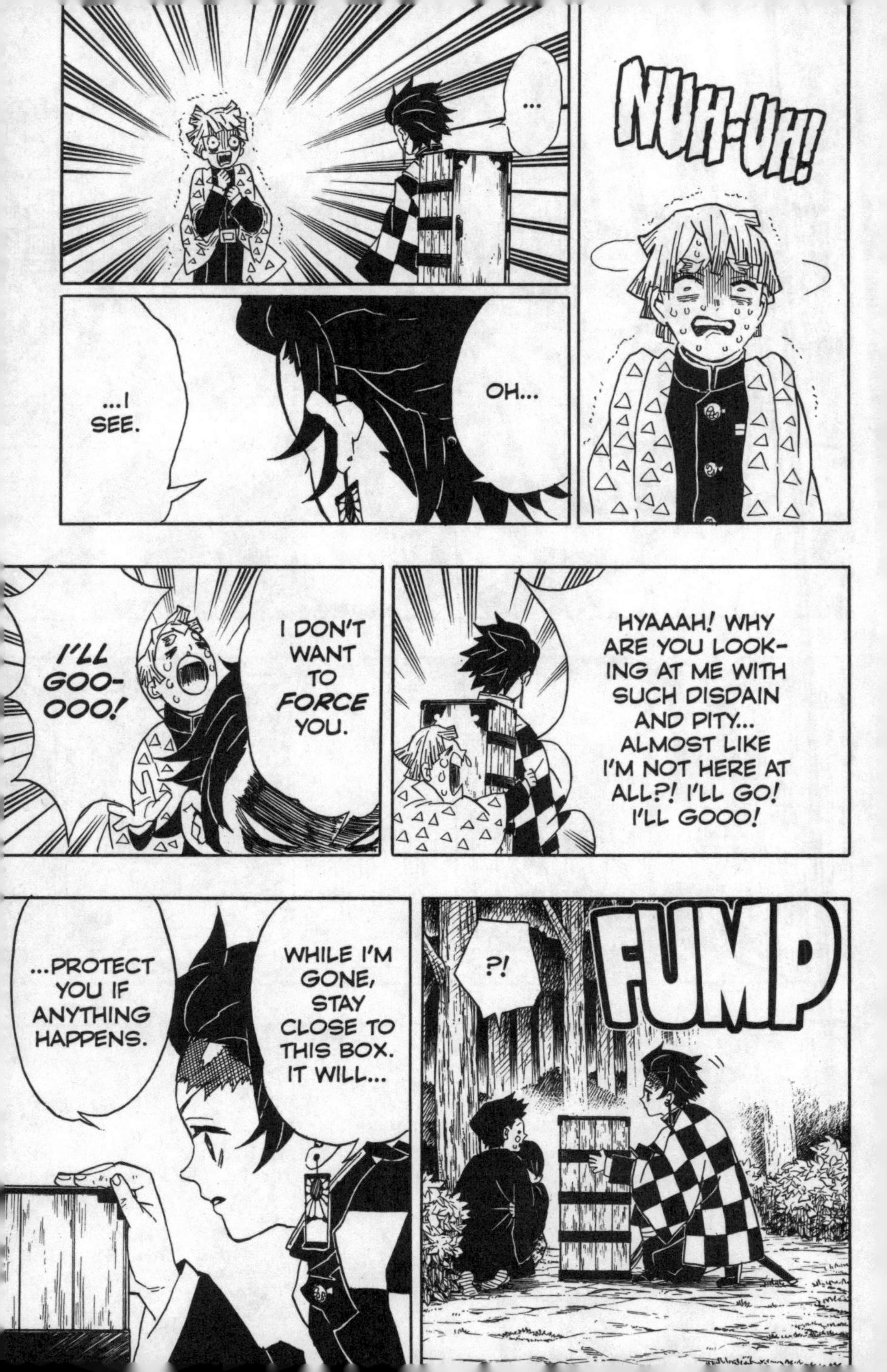
NUH-UH!
...
OH...
...I SEE.
HYAAAH! WHY ARE YOU LOOK-ING AT ME WITH SUCH DISDAIN AND PITY... ALMOST LIKE I'M NOT HERE AT ALL?! I'LL GO! I'LL GOOO!
I DON'T WANT TO FORCE YOU.
I'LL GOO-OOO!
FUMP
?!
WHILE I'M GONE, STAY CLOSE TO THIS BOX. IT WILL...
...PROTECT YOU IF ANYTHING HAPPENS.

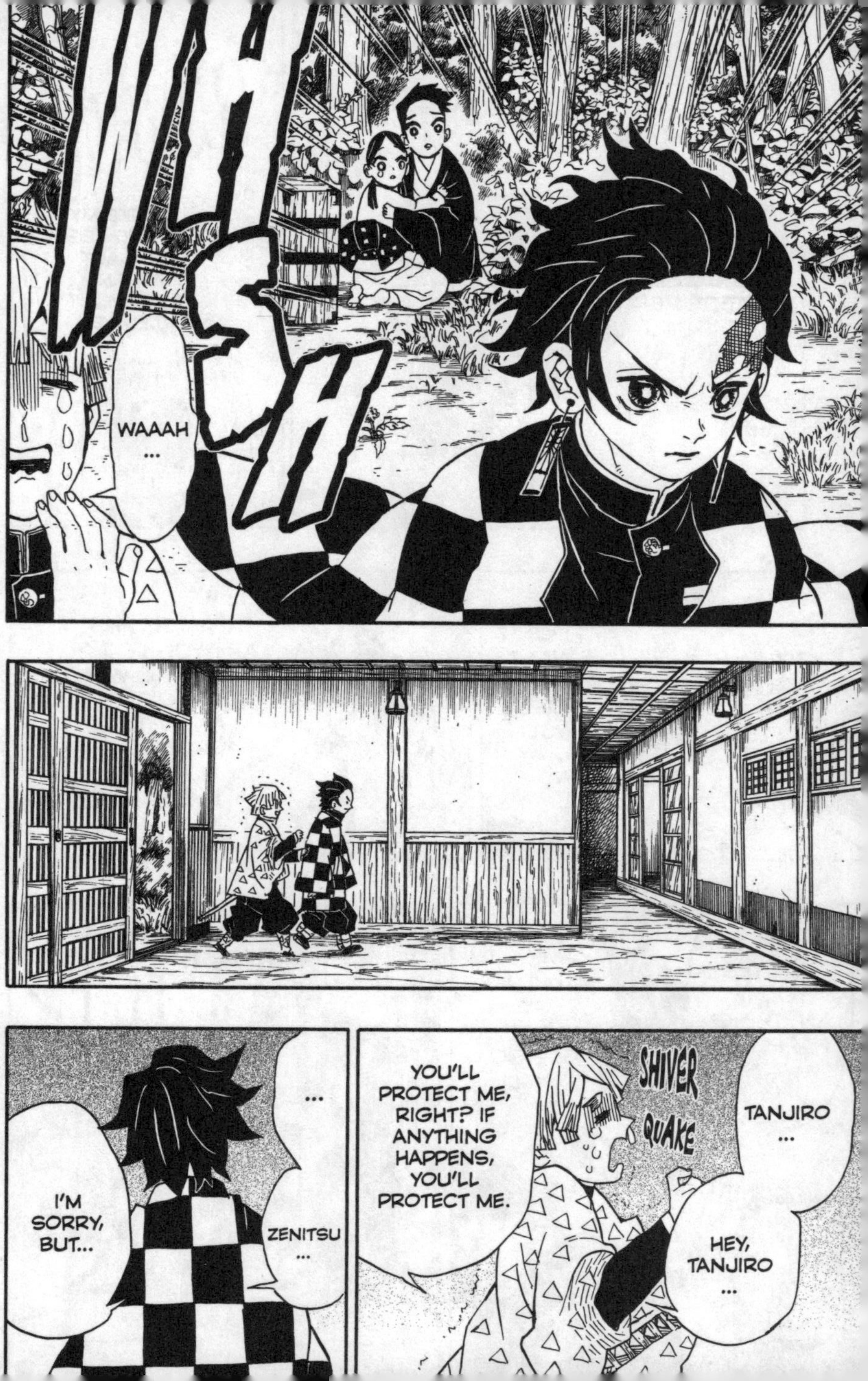
WAAAH ...
TANJIRO ...
SHIVER
QUAKE
HEY, TANJIRO ...
YOU'LL PROTECT ME, RIGHT? IF ANYTHING HAPPENS, YOU'LL PROTECT ME.
...
ZENITSU ...
I'M SORRY, BUT...

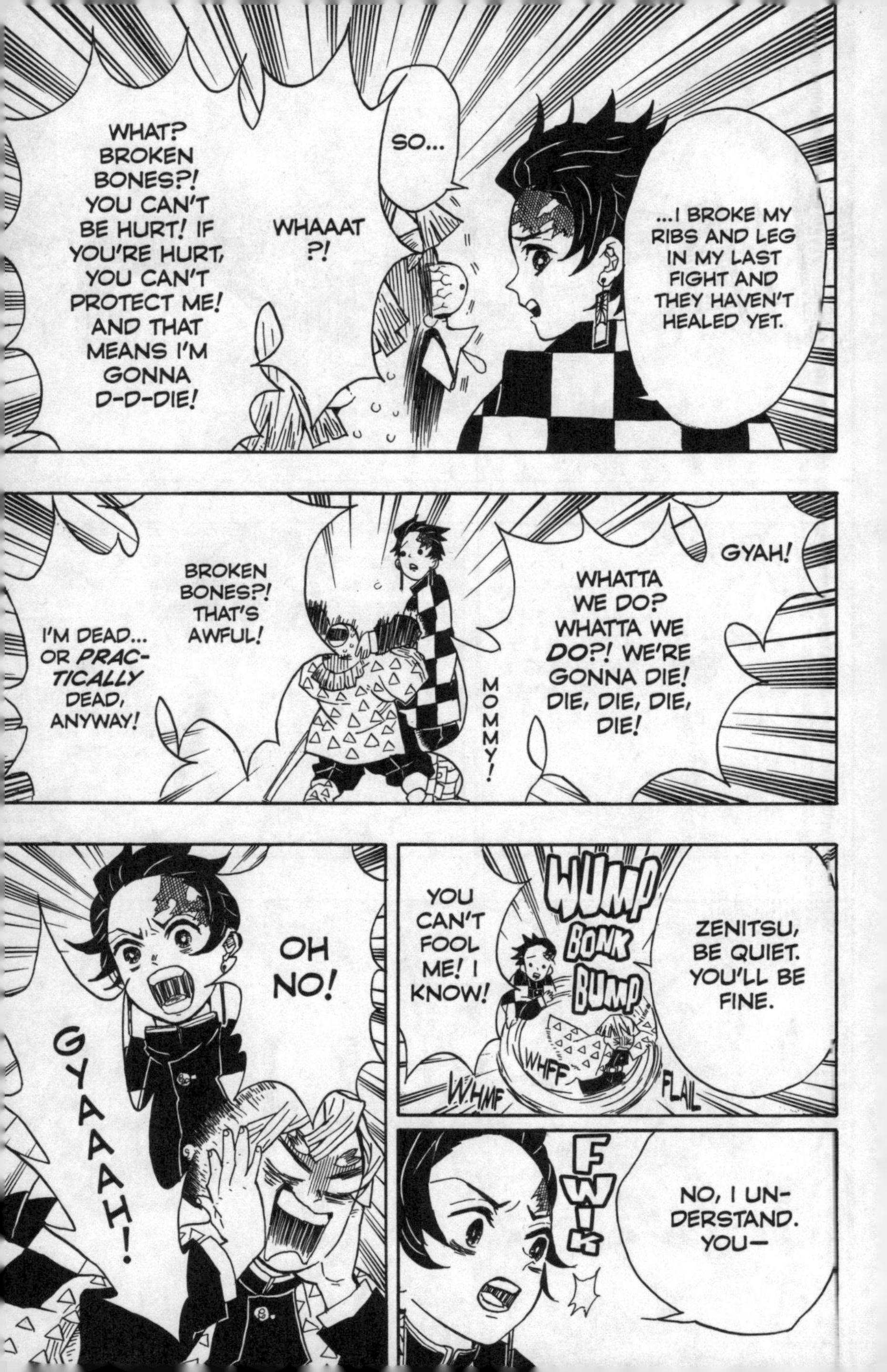
...I BROKE MY RIBS AND LEG IN MY LAST FIGHT AND THEY HAVEN'T HEALED YET.
SO...
WHAAAT ?!
WHAT? BROKEN BONES?! YOU CAN'T BE HURT! IF YOU'RE HURT, YOU CAN'T PROTECT ME! AND THAT MEANS I'M GONNA D-D-DIE!
GYAH!
WHATTA WE DO? WHATTA WE DO?! WE'RE GONNA DIE! DIE, DIE, DIE, DIE!
MOMMY!
BROKEN BONES?! THAT'S AWFUL!
I'M DEAD... OR PRACTICALLY DEAD, ANYWAY!
ZENITSU, BE QUIET. YOU'LL BE FINE.
WUMP
BONK
BUMP
YOU CAN'T FOOL ME! I KNOW!
WHFF
WHMF
FLAIL
NO, I UNDERSTAND. YOU—
FWIK
OH NO!
GYAAAH!

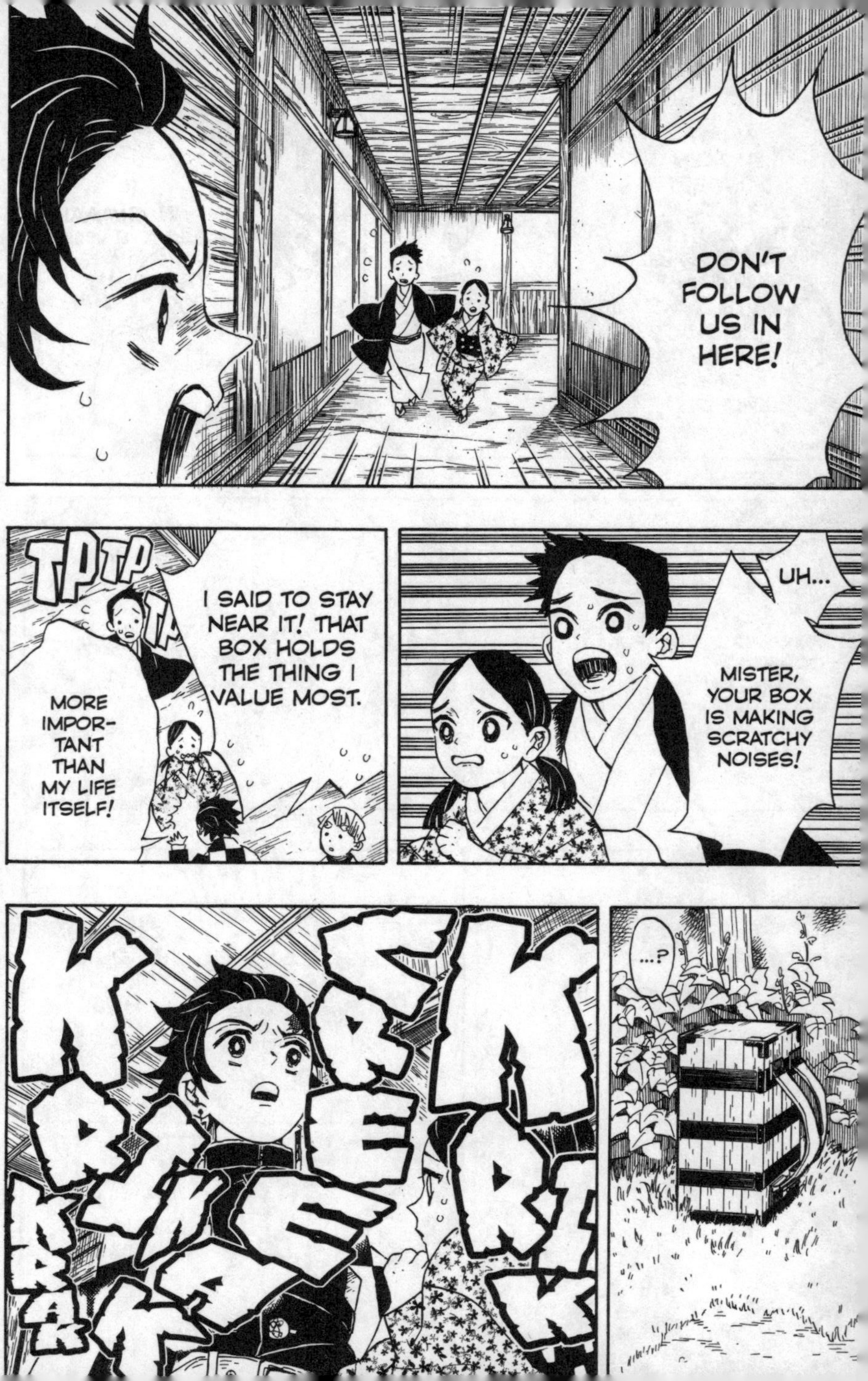
DON'T FOLLOW US IN HERE!
UH...
MISTER, YOUR BOX IS MAKING SCRATCHY NOISES!
TP TP TP
I SAID TO STAY NEAR IT! THAT BOX HOLDS THE THING I VALUE MOST.
MORE IMPORTANT THAN MY LIFE ITSELF!
...?

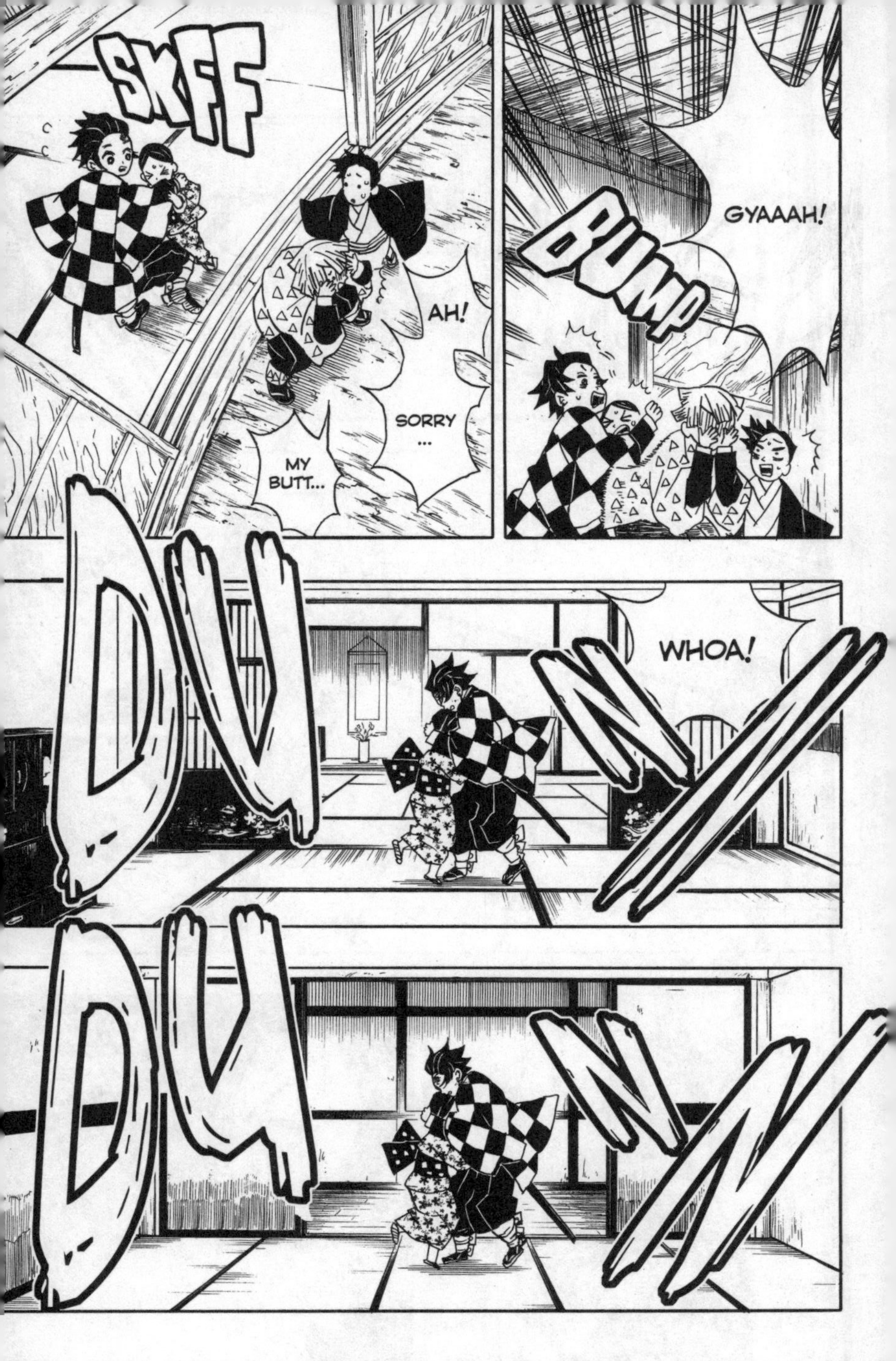
GYAAAH!
BUMP
SKFF
AH!
SORRY ...
MY BUTT...
WHOA!
DUNN
DUNN

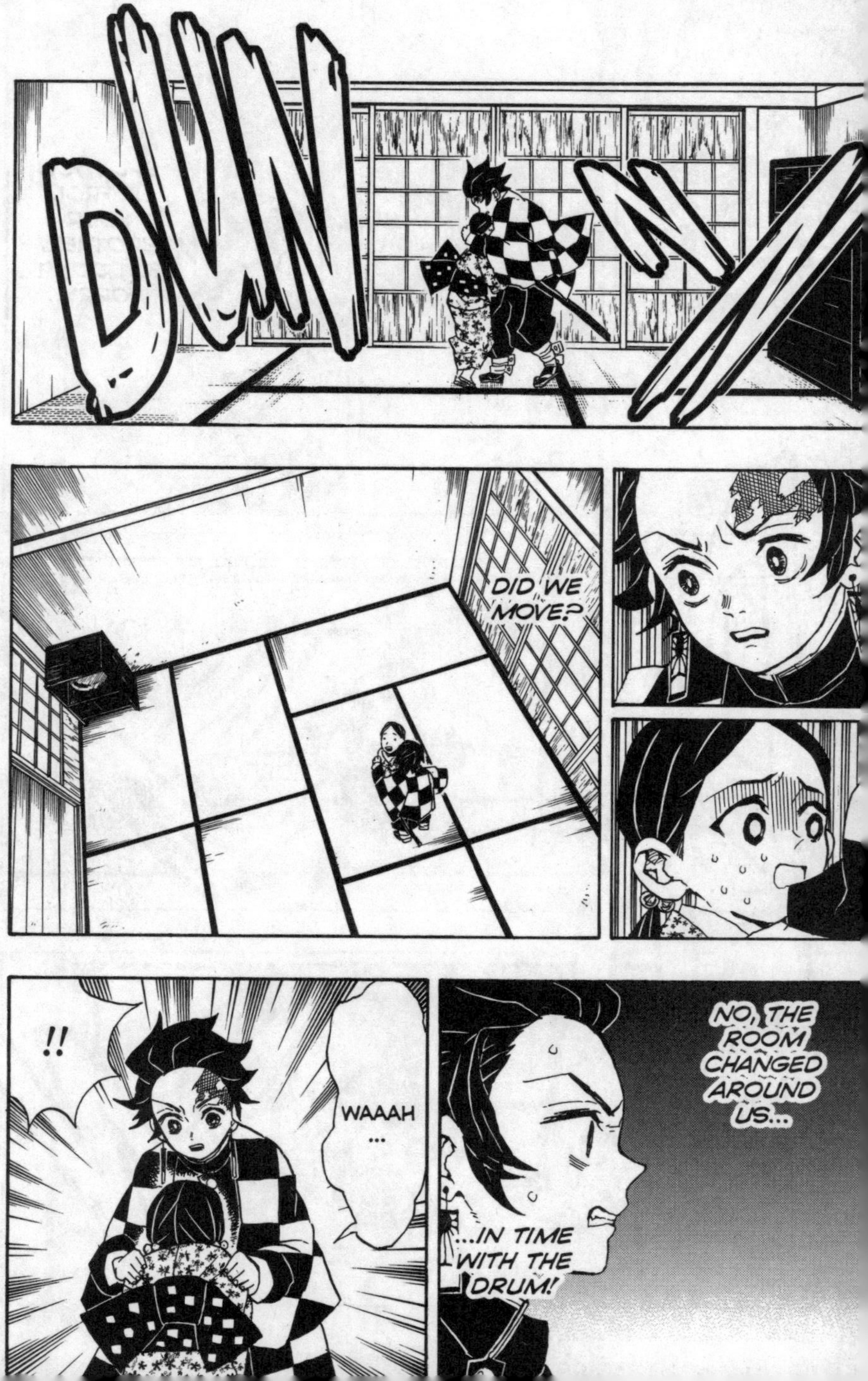

DUN
N
DID WE MOVE?
NO, THE ROOM CHANGED AROUND US...
...IN TIME WITH THE DRUM!
WAAAH ...
!!

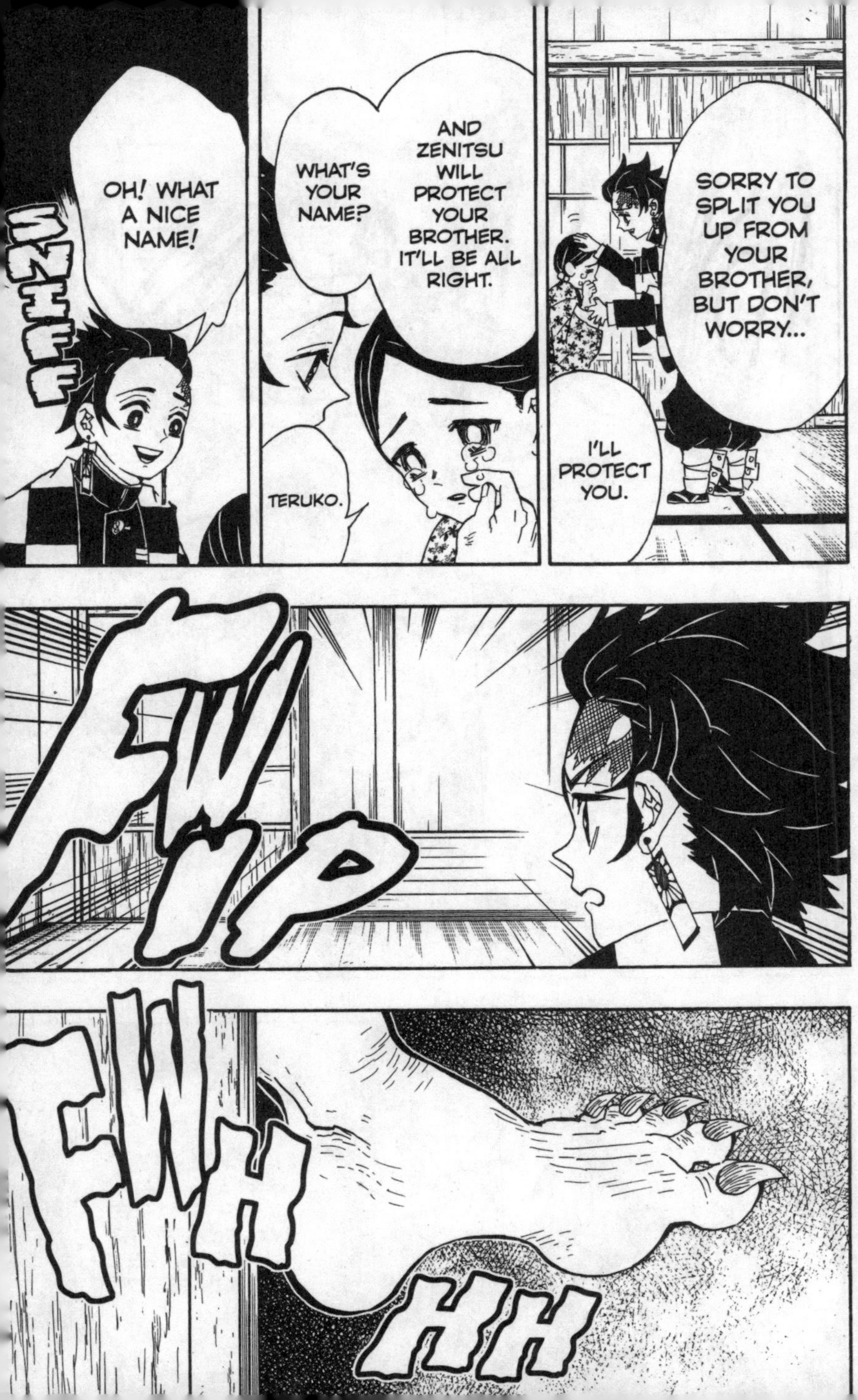
SORRY TO SPLIT YOU UP FROM YOUR BROTHER, BUT DON'T WORRY...
I'LL PROTECT YOU.
AND ZENITSU WILL PROTECT YOUR BROTHER. IT'LL BE ALL RIGHT.
WHAT'S YOUR NAME?
TERUKO.
OH! WHAT A NICE NAME!
SNIFF
FWIP
FWHHH

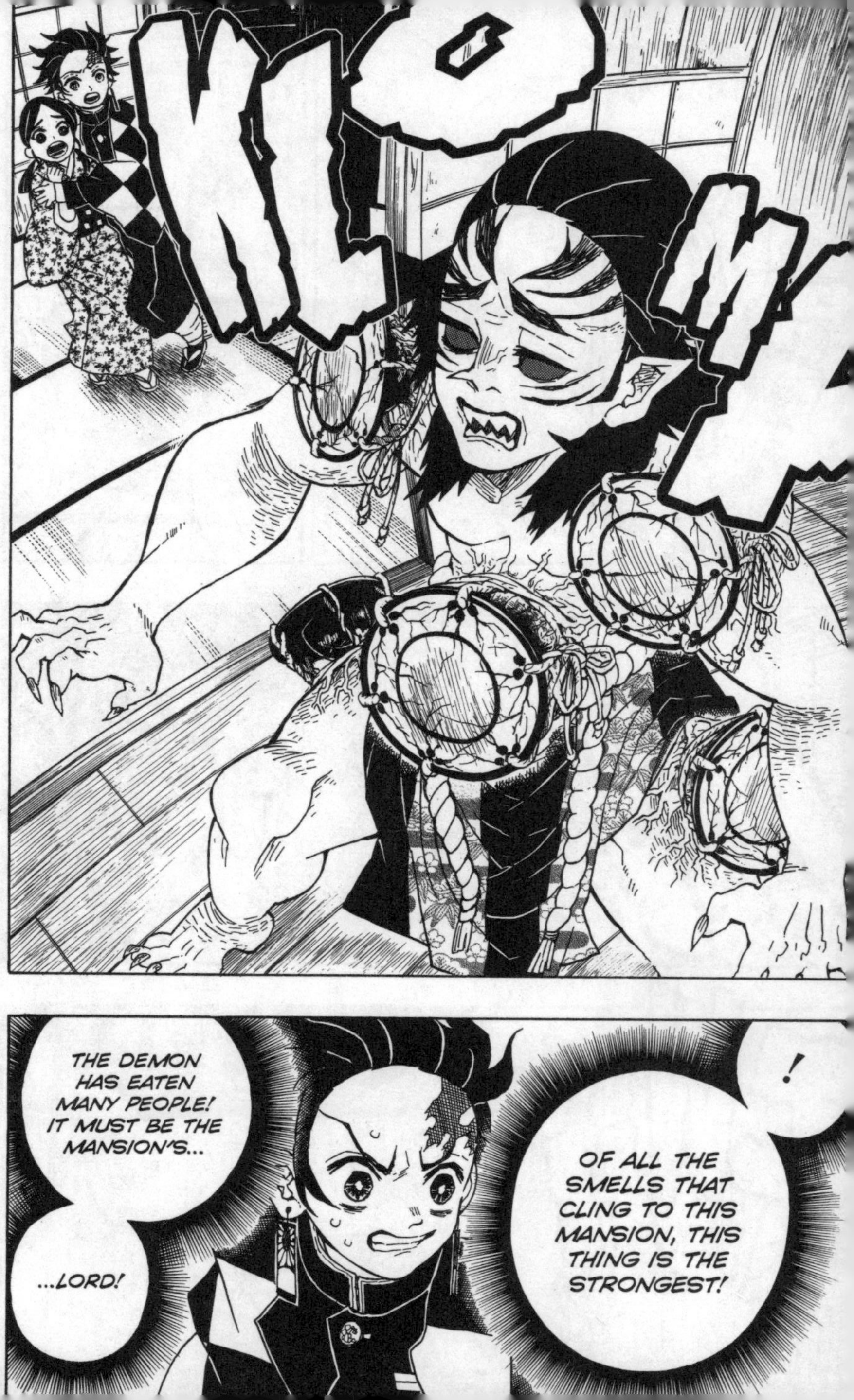
!
OF ALL THE SMELLS THAT CLING TO THIS MANSION, THIS THING IS THE STRONGEST!
THE DEMON HAS EATEN MANY PEOPLE! IT MUST BE THE MANSION'S...
...LORD!

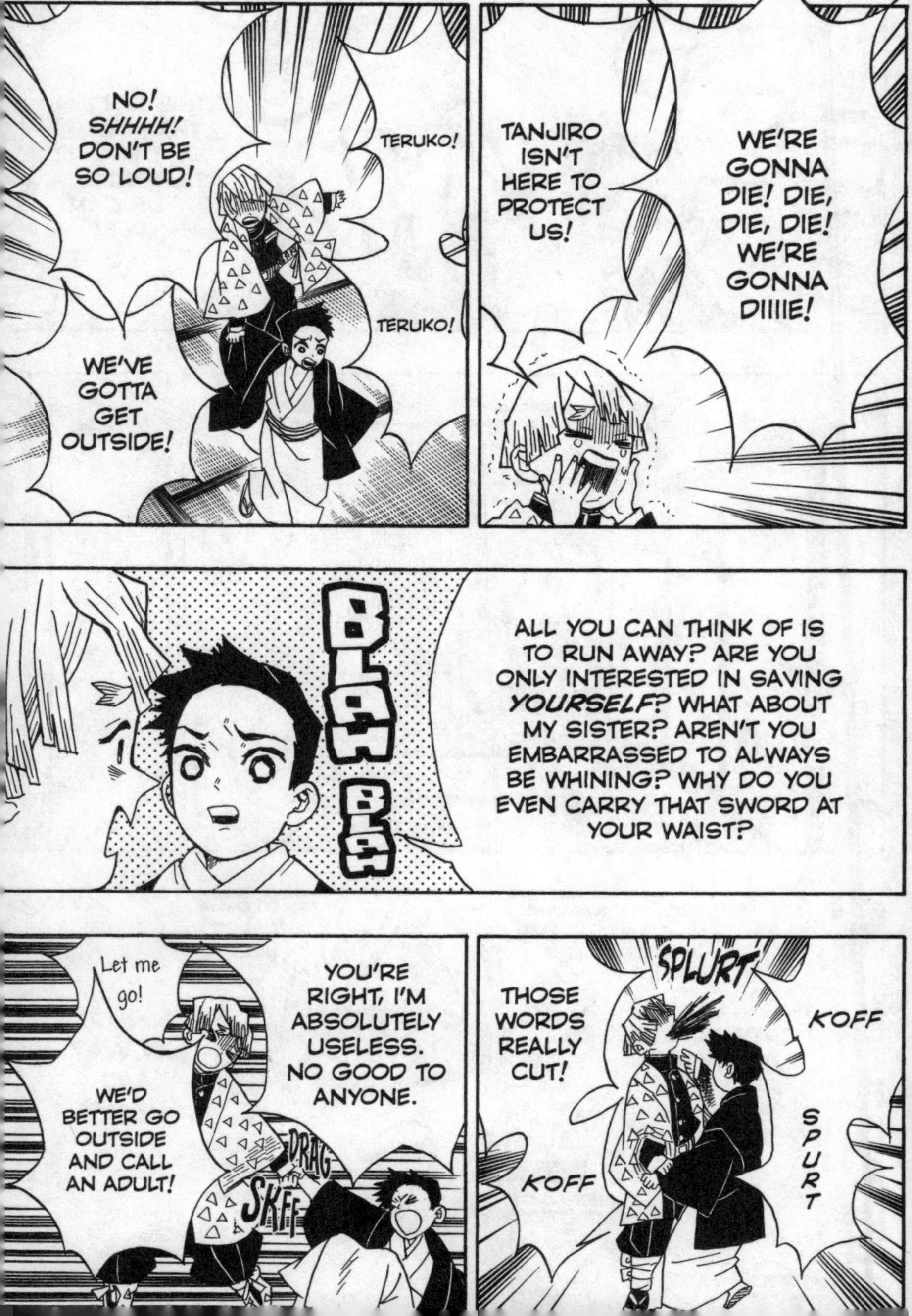
WE'RE GONNA DIE! DIE, DIE, DIE! WE'RE GONNA DIIIIE!
TANJIRO ISN'T HERE TO PROTECT US!
NO! SHHHH! DON'T BE SO LOUD!
TERUKO!
TERUKO!
WE'VE GOTTA GET OUTSIDE!
ALL YOU CAN THINK OF IS TO RUN AWAY? ARE YOU ONLY INTERESTED IN SAVING YOURSELF? WHAT ABOUT MY SISTER? AREN'T YOU EMBARRASSED TO ALWAYS BE WHINING? WHY DO YOU EVEN CARRY THAT SWORD AT YOUR WAIST?
BLAH BLAH
SPLURT
KOFF
THOSE WORDS REALLY CUT!
SPURT
KOFF
YOU'RE RIGHT, I'M ABSOLUTELY USELESS. NO GOOD TO ANYONE.
Let me go!
WE'D BETTER GO OUTSIDE AND CALL AN ADULT!
DRAG
SKFF

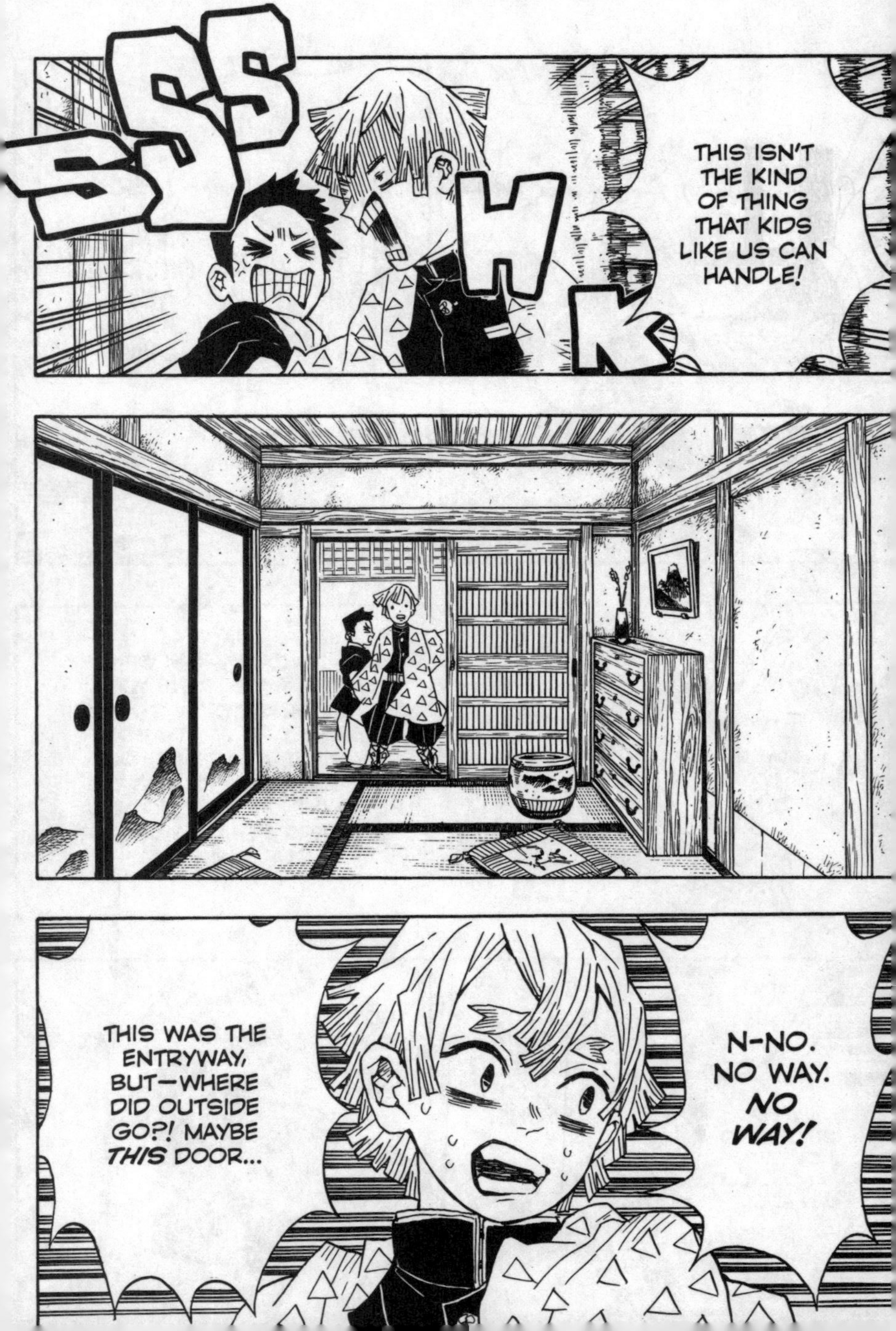
SSSHK
THIS ISN'T THE KIND OF THING THAT KIDS LIKE US CAN HANDLE!
N-NO. NO WAY. *NO WAY!*
THIS WAS THE ENTRYWAY, BUT—WHERE DID OUTSIDE GO?! MAYBE *THIS* DOOR...

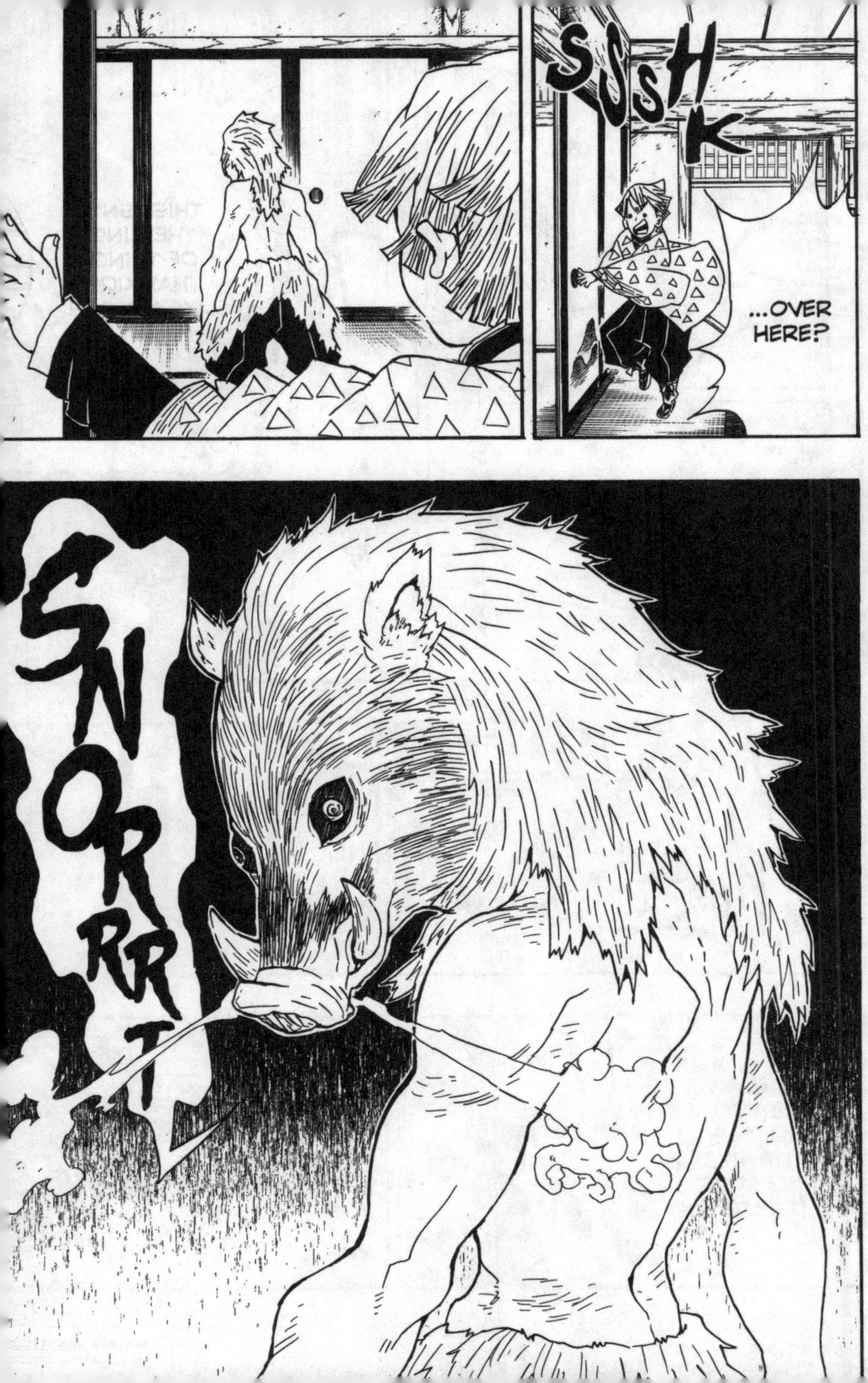
SSSH
K
...OVER HERE?
SNORRRT

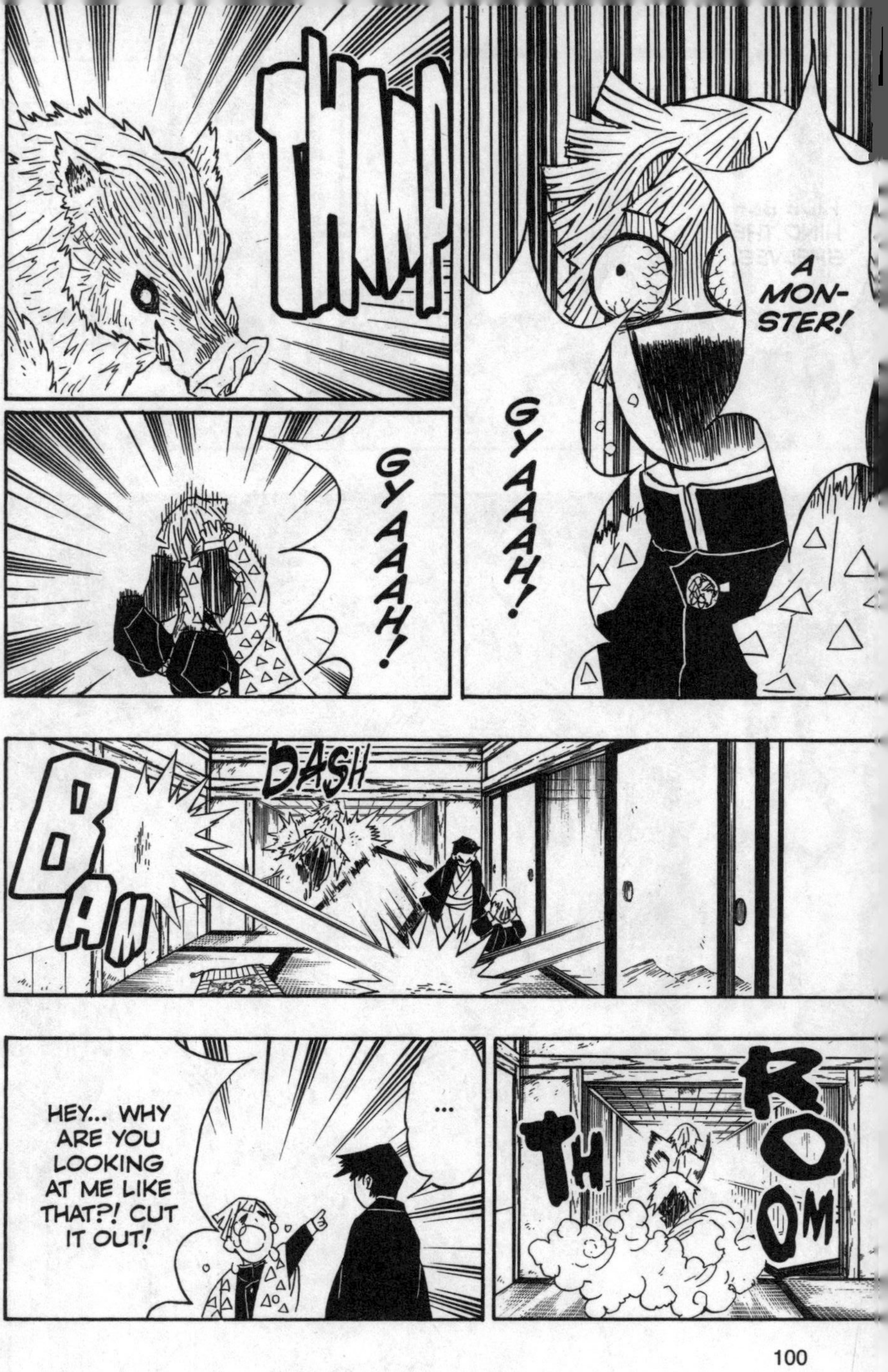
A MONSTER!
GYAAAAH!
THMP
GYAAAAH!
BASH
BAM
THROOM
...
HEY... WHY ARE YOU LOOKING AT ME LIKE THAT?! CUT IT OUT!

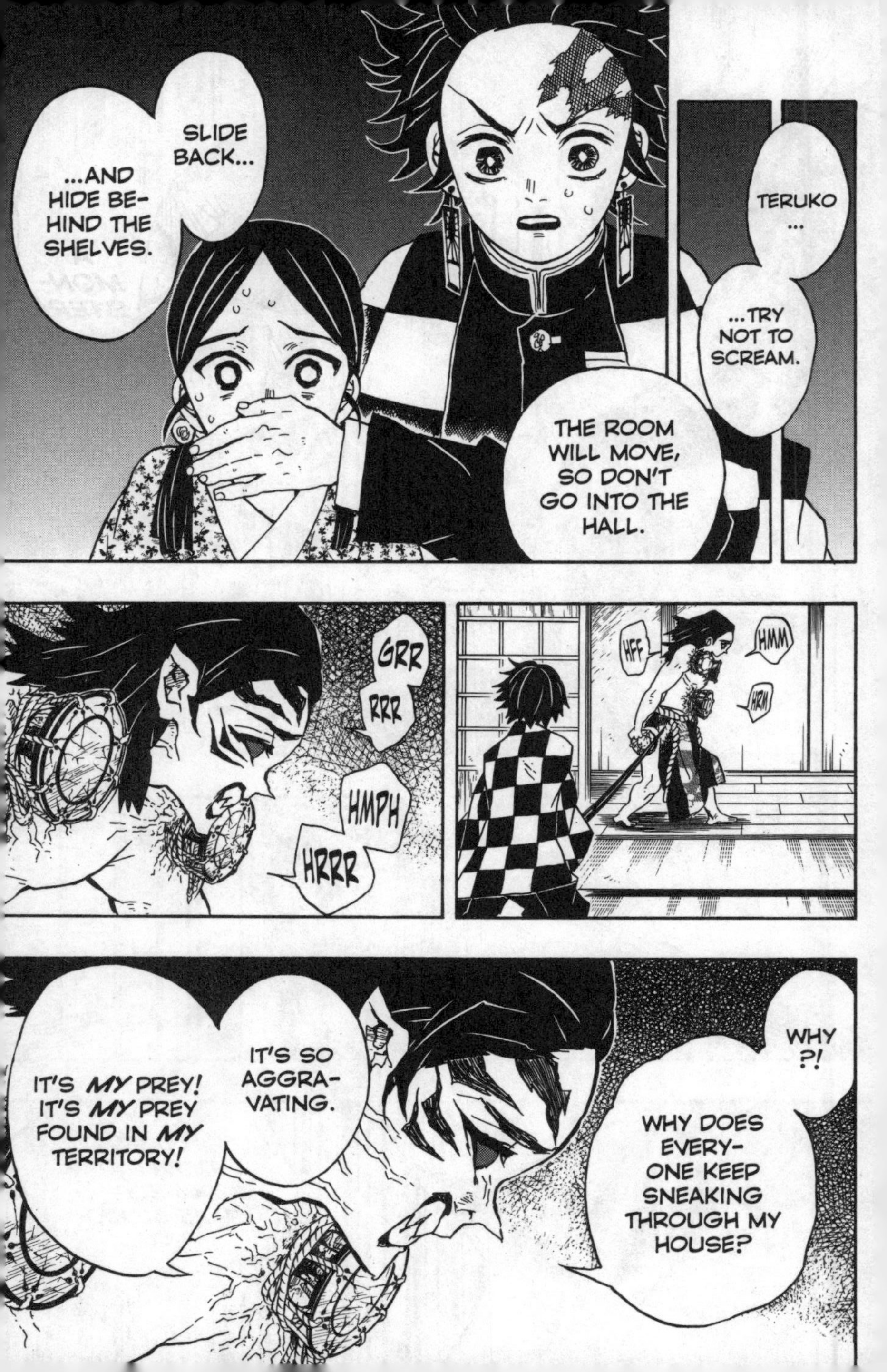
TERUKO ...
...TRY NOT TO SCREAM.
THE ROOM WILL MOVE, SO DON'T GO INTO THE HALL.
SLIDE BACK...
...AND HIDE BE-HIND THE SHELVES.
HMM
HFF
HRM
GRR RRR
HMPH
HRRR
WHY ?!
WHY DOES EVERY-ONE KEEP SNEAKING THROUGH MY HOUSE?
IT'S SO AGGRA-VATING.
IT'S MY PREY! IT'S MY PREY FOUND IN MY TERRITORY!

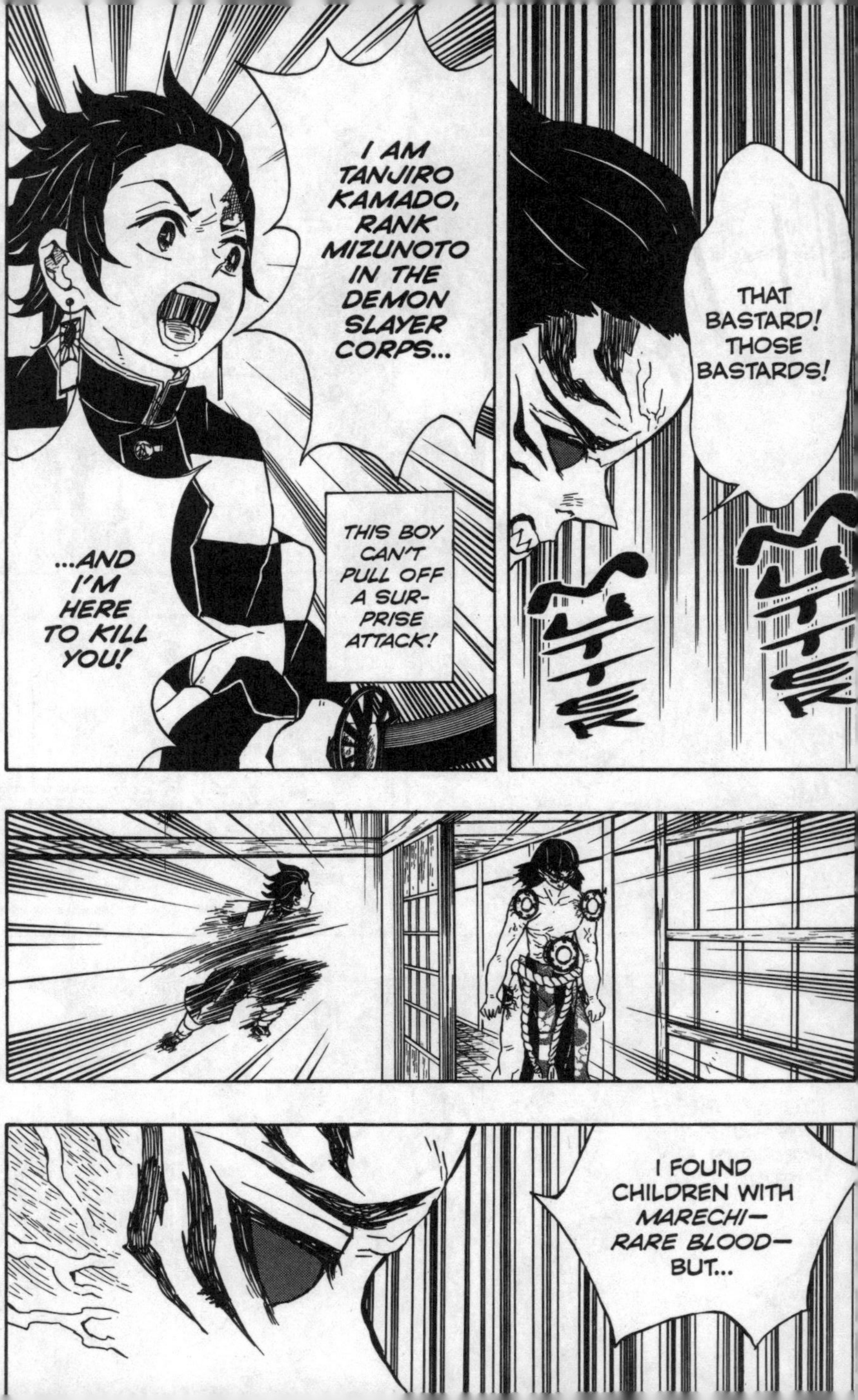
THAT BASTARD! THOSE BASTARDS!
I AM TANJIRO KAMADO, RANK MIZUNOTO IN THE DEMON SLAYER CORPS...
THIS BOY CAN'T PULL OFF A SUR-PRISE ATTACK!
...AND I'M HERE TO KILL YOU!
I FOUND CHILDREN WITH *MARECHI*—RARE BLOOD—BUT...

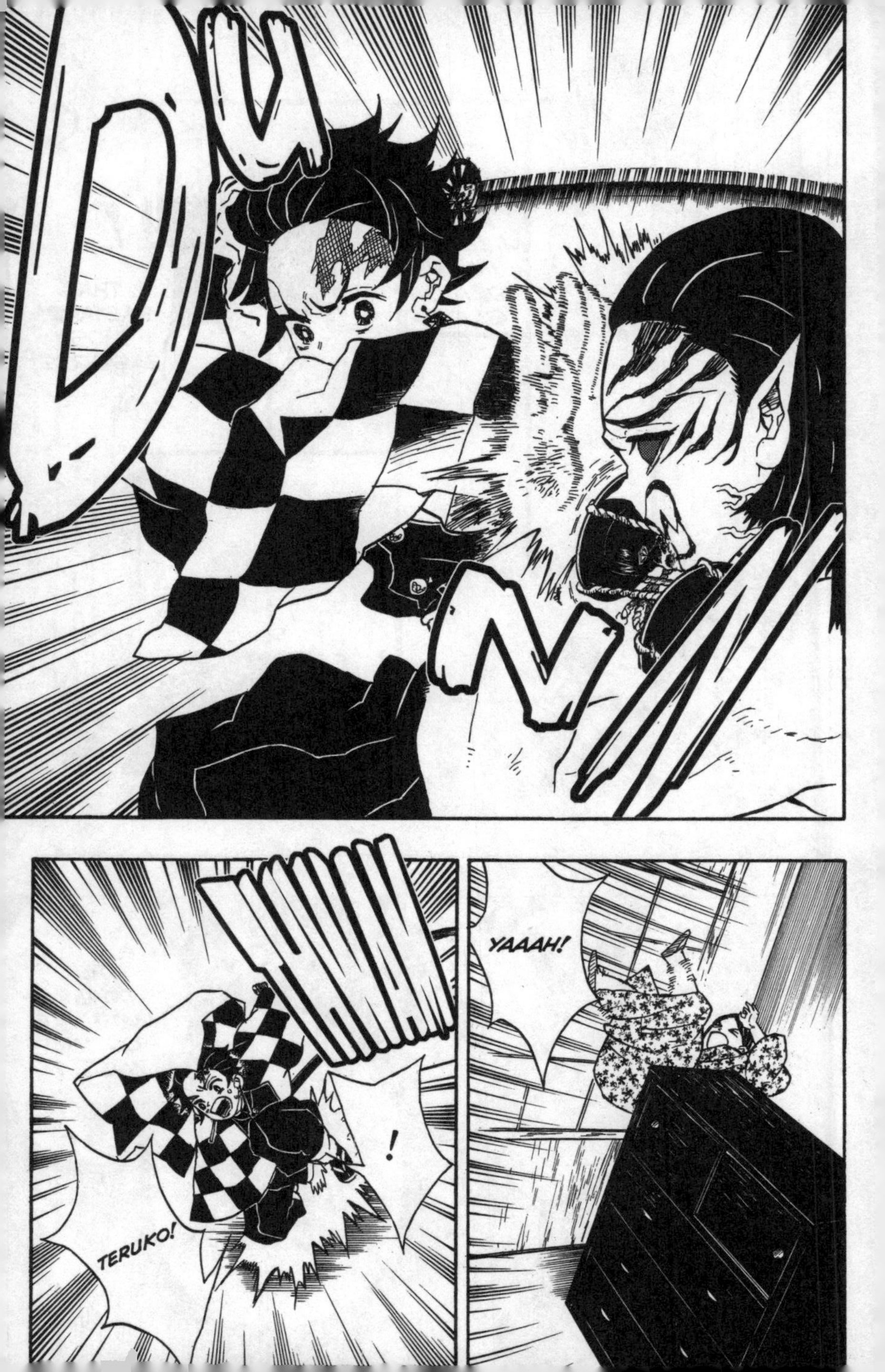
YAAAH!
!
TERUKO!

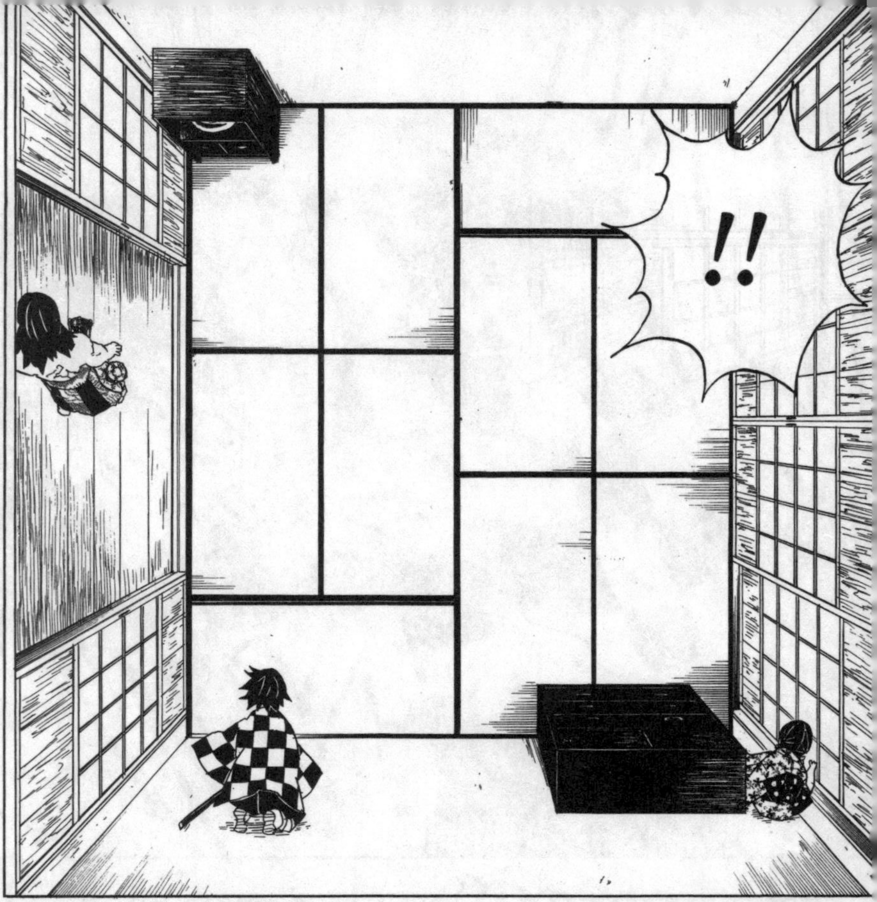
!!
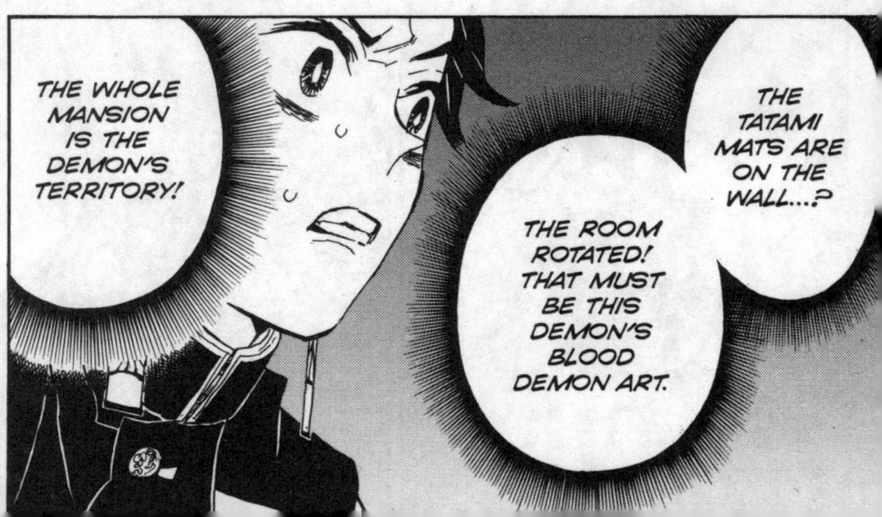
THE TATAMI MATS ARE ON THE WALL...?
THE ROOM ROTATED! THAT MUST BE THIS DEMON'S BLOOD DEMON ART.
THE WHOLE MANSION IS THE DEMON'S TERRITORY!

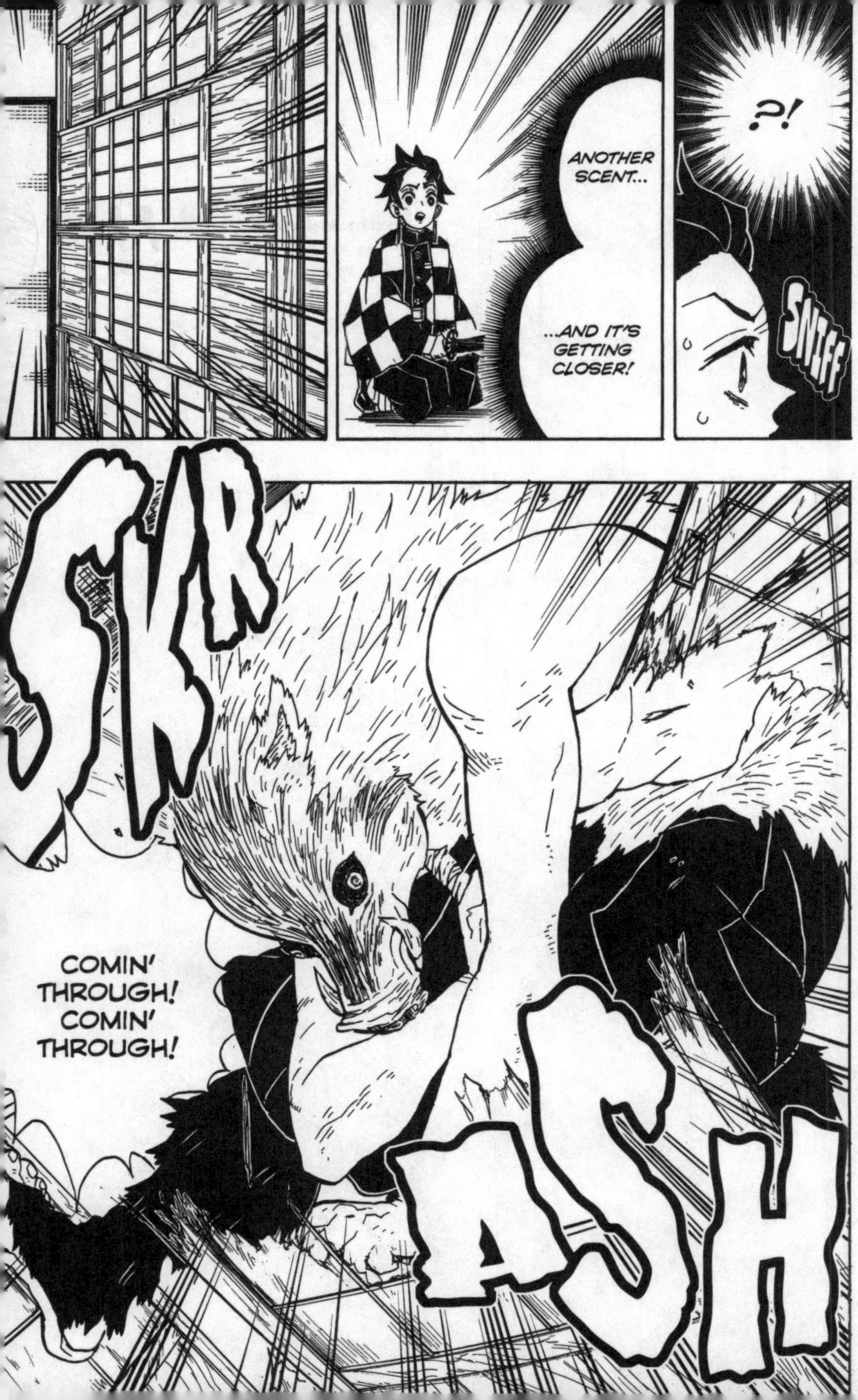
?!
SNIFF
ANOTHER SCENT...
...AND IT'S GETTING CLOSER!
SKR
ASH
COMIN' THROUGH! COMIN' THROUGH!

Boar hair

Deer hair

Bear hair

CHAPTER 22: RUSHING BOAR

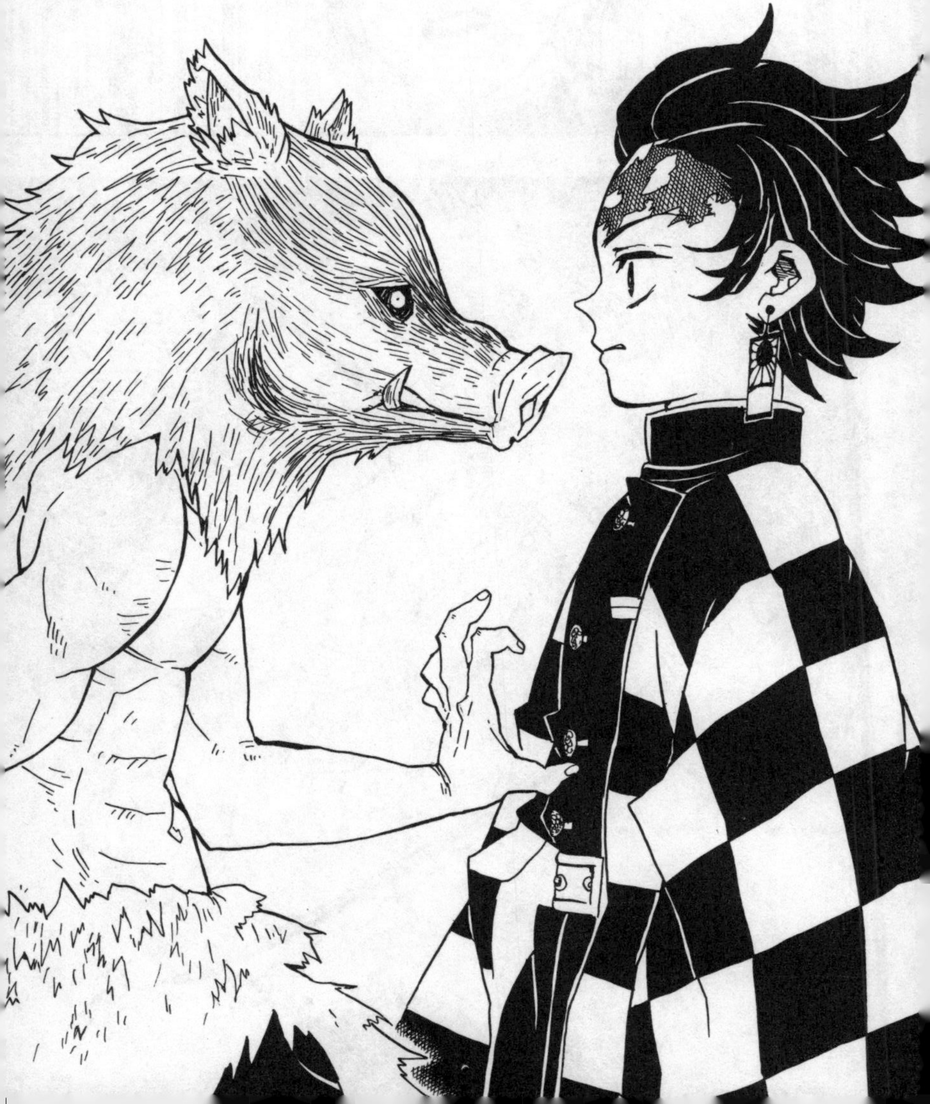

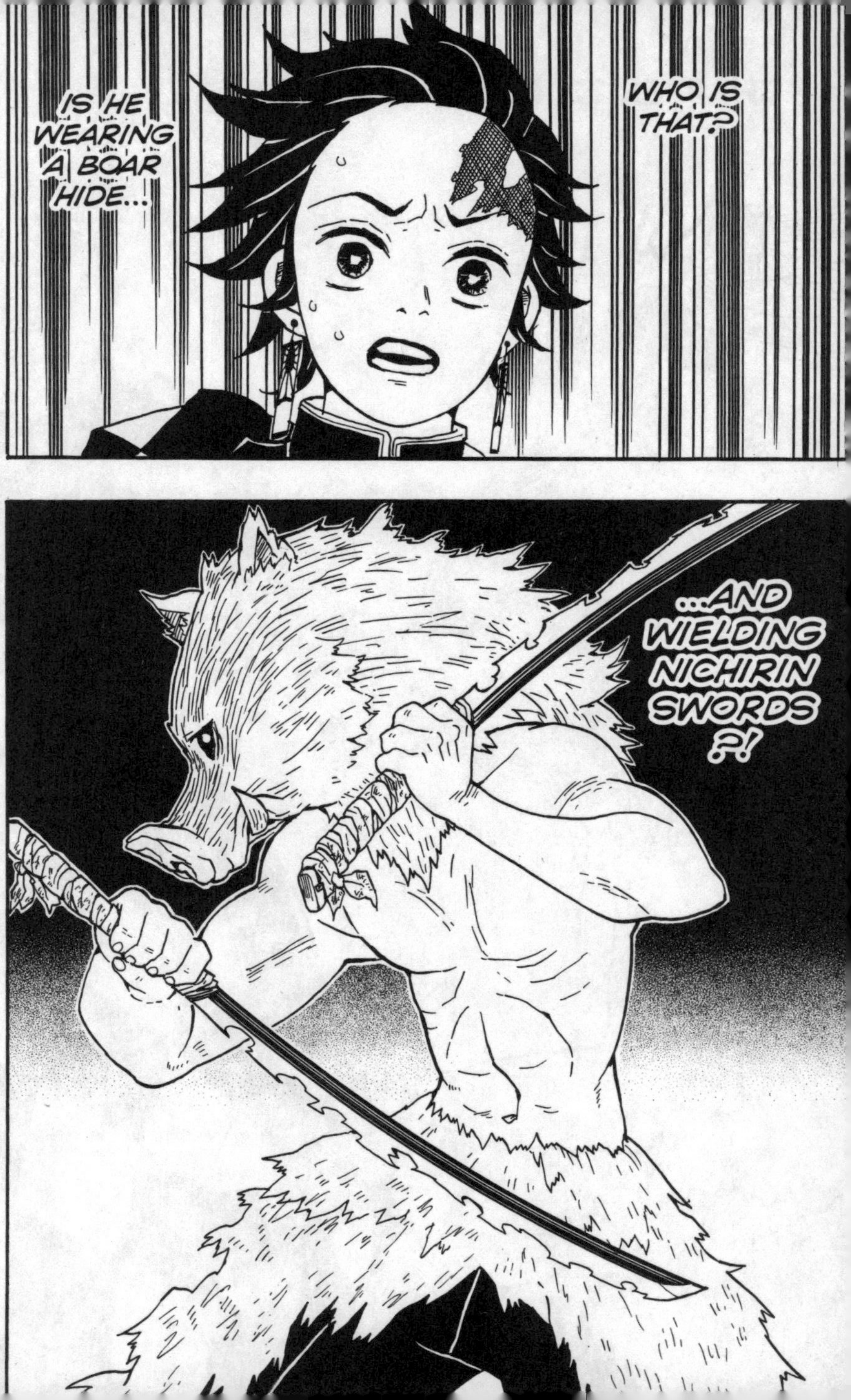
WHO IS THAT?
IS HE WEARING A BOAR HIDE...
...AND WIELDING NICHIRIN SWORDS ?!

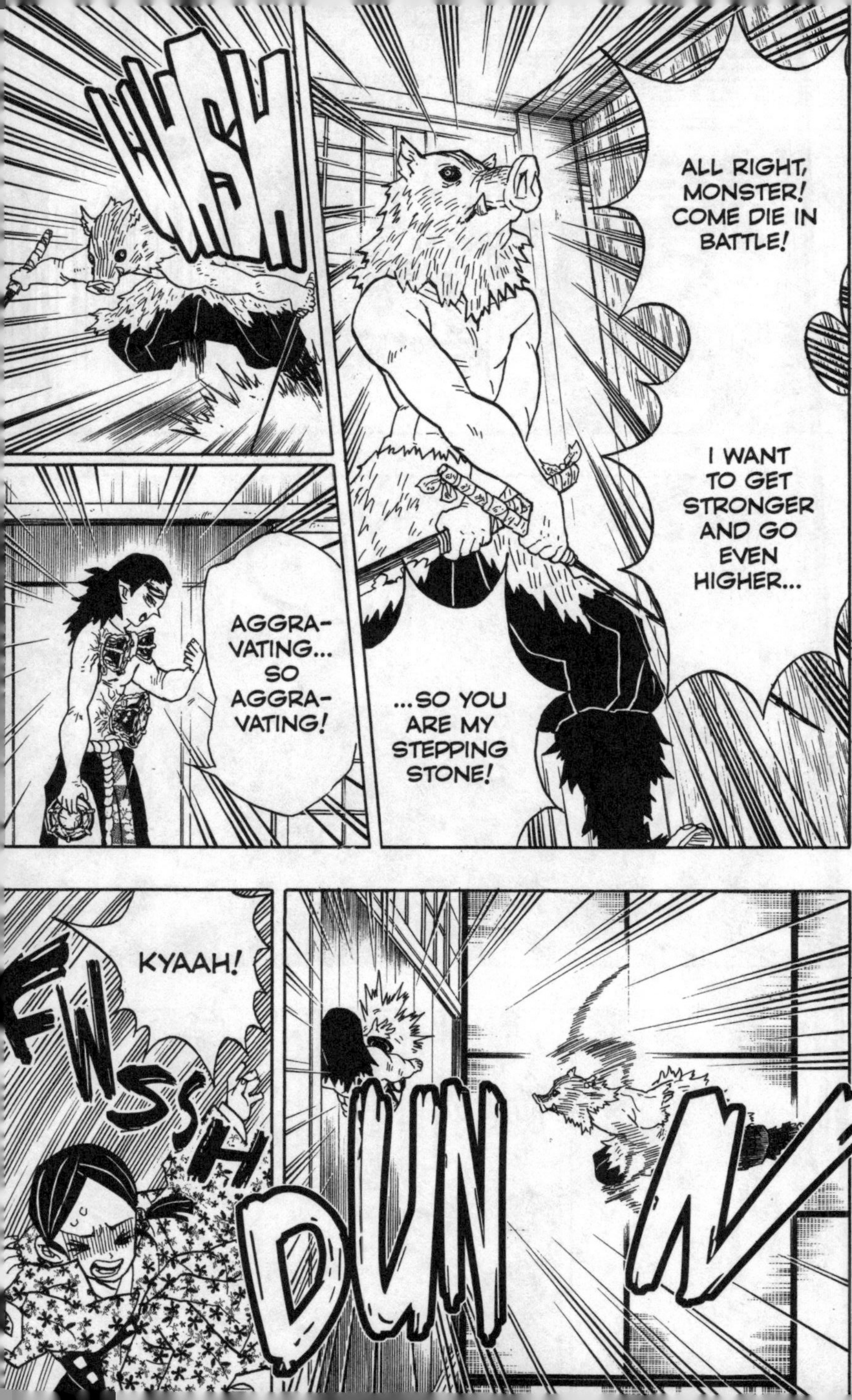
ALL RIGHT, MONSTER! COME DIE IN BATTLE!
I WANT TO GET STRONGER AND GO EVEN HIGHER...
...SO YOU ARE MY STEPPING STONE!
AGGRA-VATING... SO AGGRA-VATING!
DUNN
KYAAH!
FWSSH

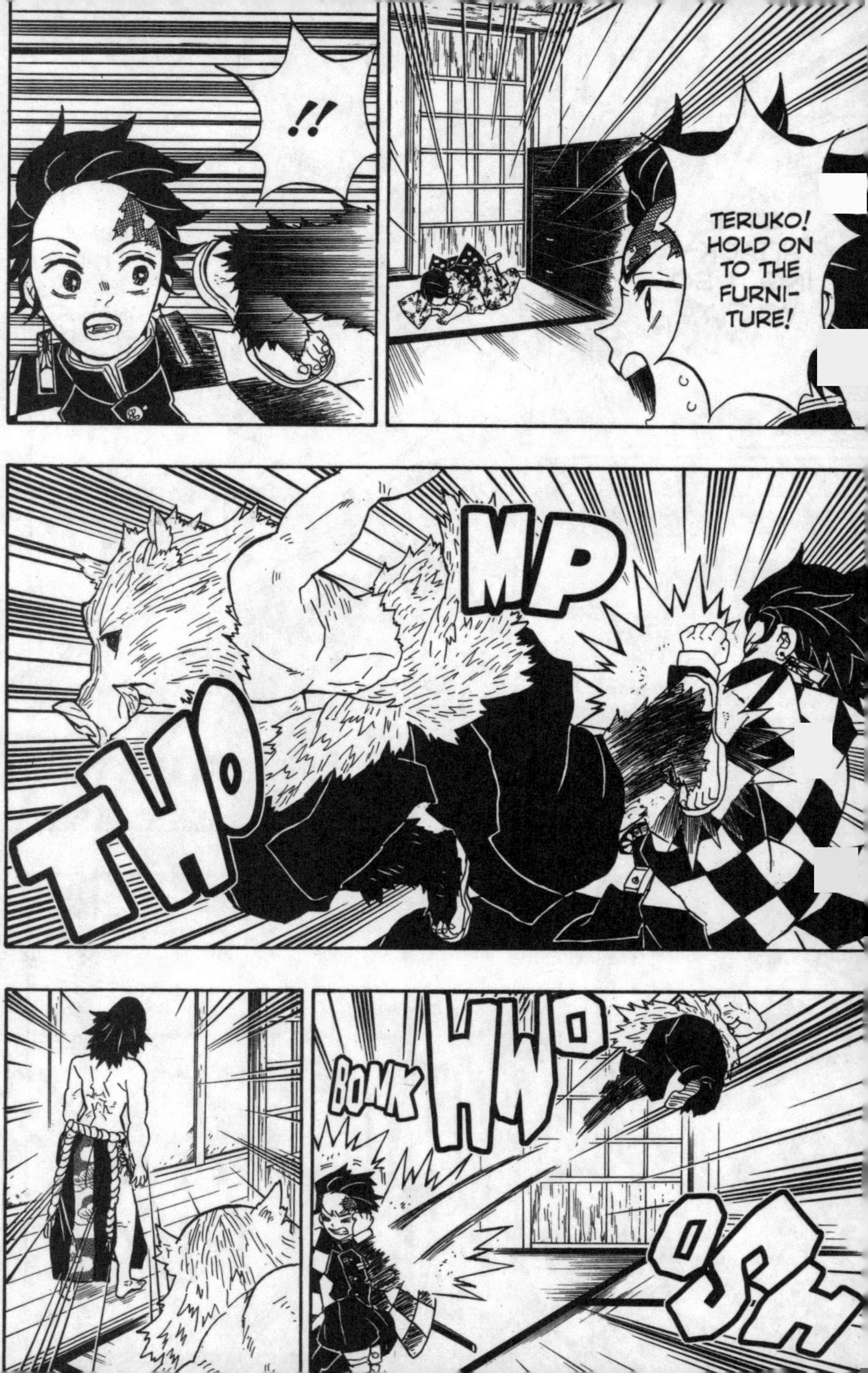
TERUKO! HOLD ON TO THE FURNITURE!
!!
THOMP
BONK
WHOOSH

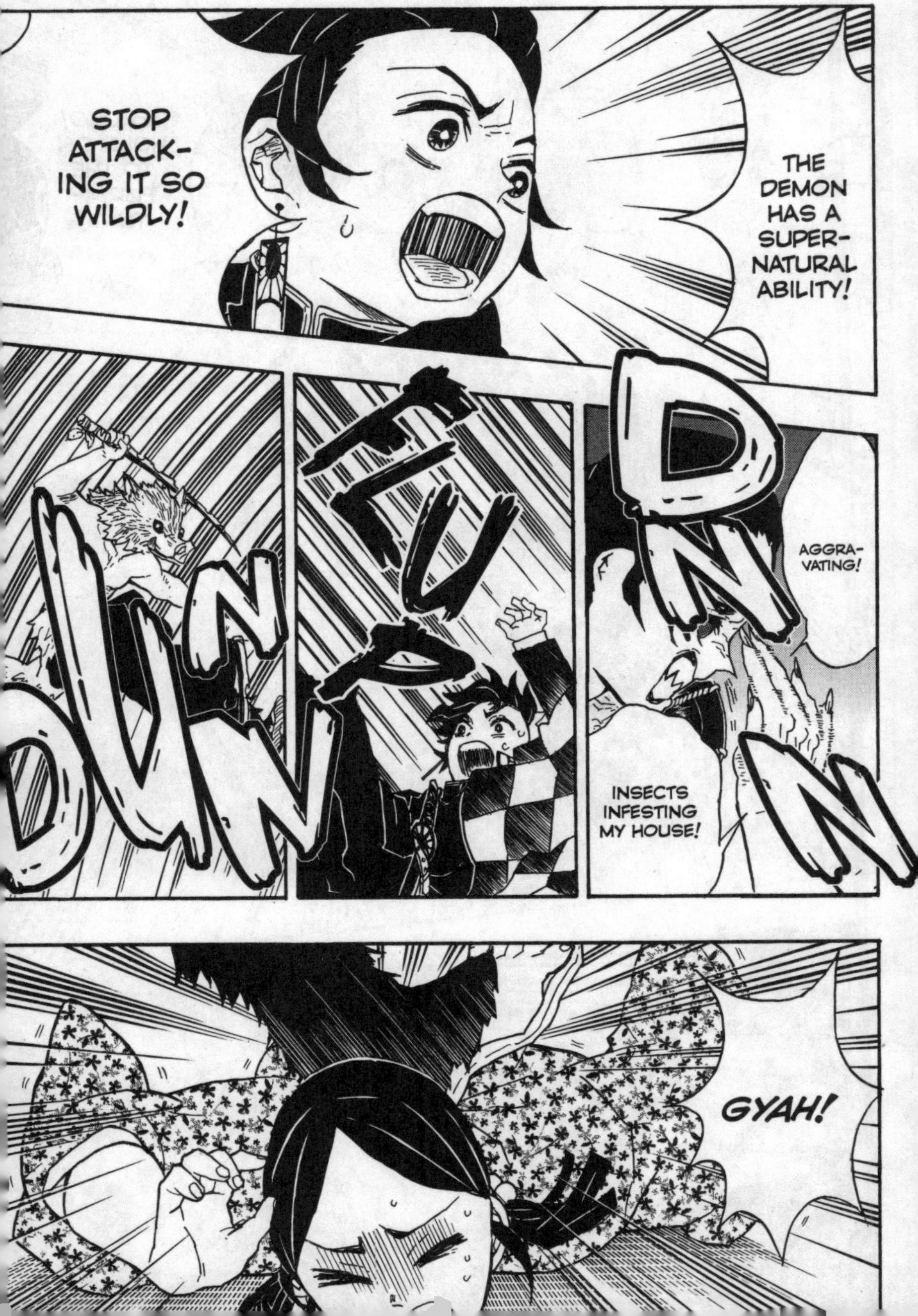
THE DEMON HAS A SUPER-NATURAL ABILITY!
STOP ATTACK-ING IT SO WILDLY!
AGGRA-VATING!
INSECTS INFESTING MY HOUSE!
GYAH!

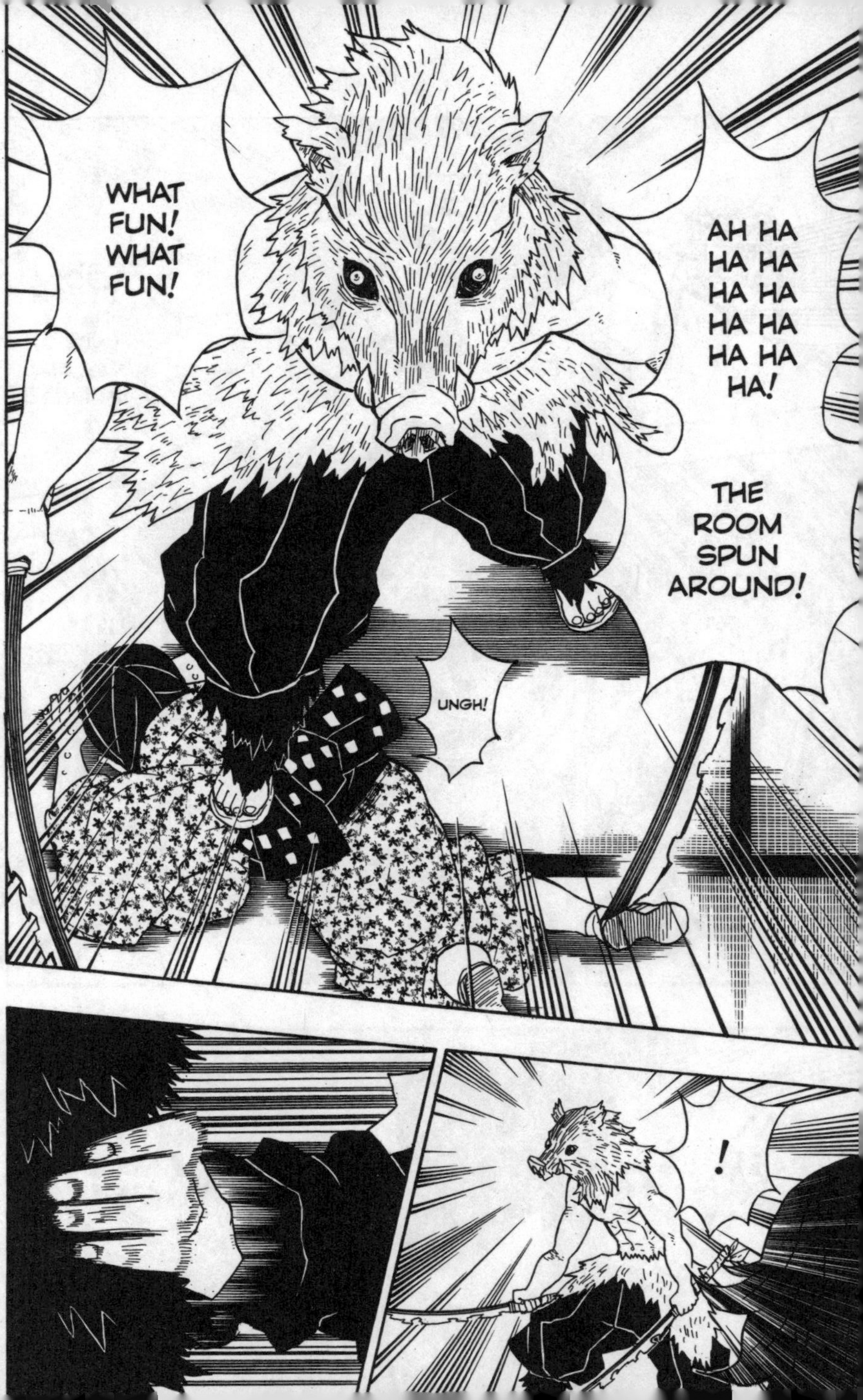
AH HA HA HA HA HA HA HA HA HA HA!
WHAT FUN! WHAT FUN!
THE ROOM SPUN AROUND!
UNGH!
!

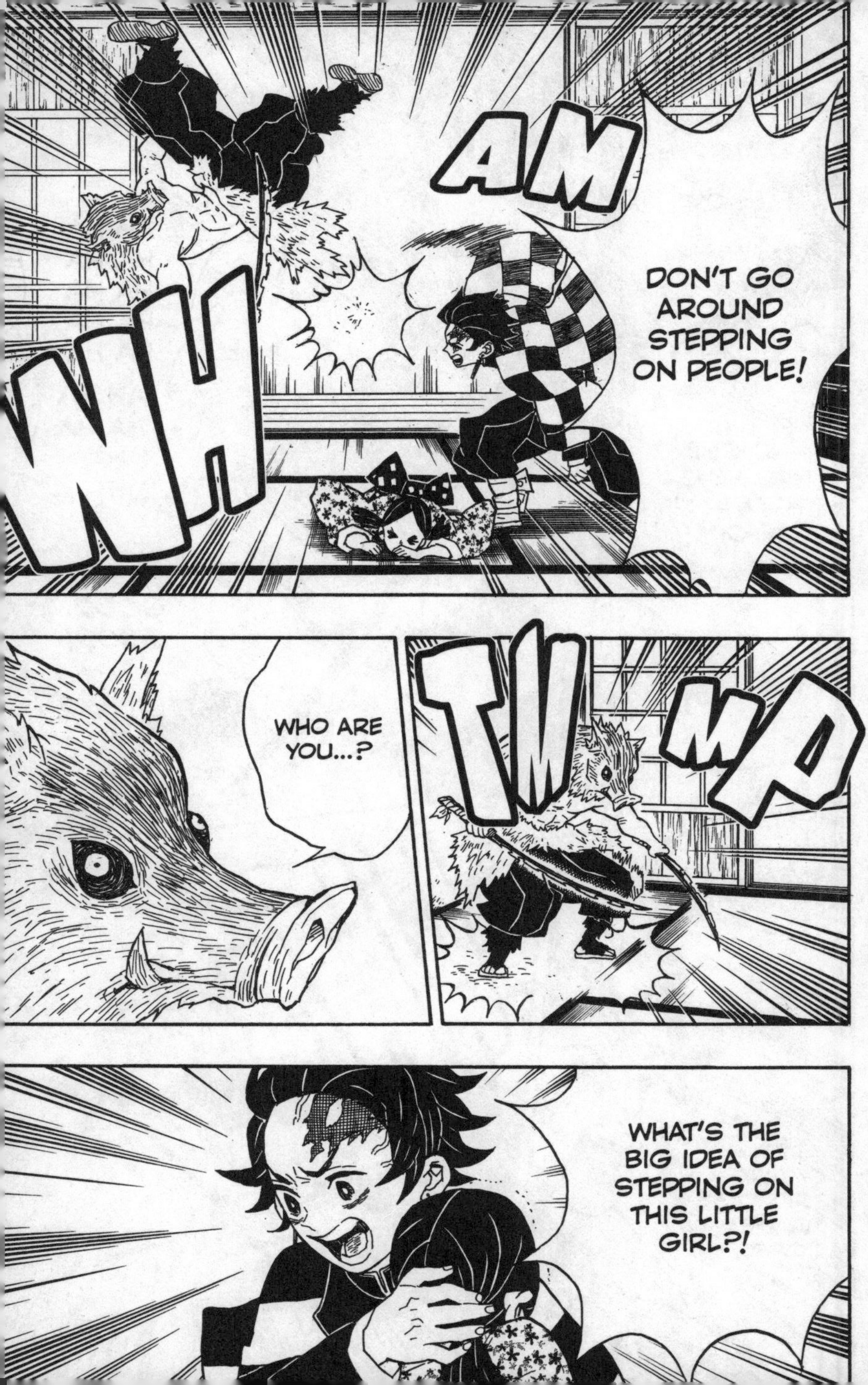
DON'T GO AROUND STEPPING ON PEOPLE!
WHAM
WHO ARE YOU...?
WHAT'S THE BIG IDEA OF STEPPING ON THIS LITTLE GIRL?!

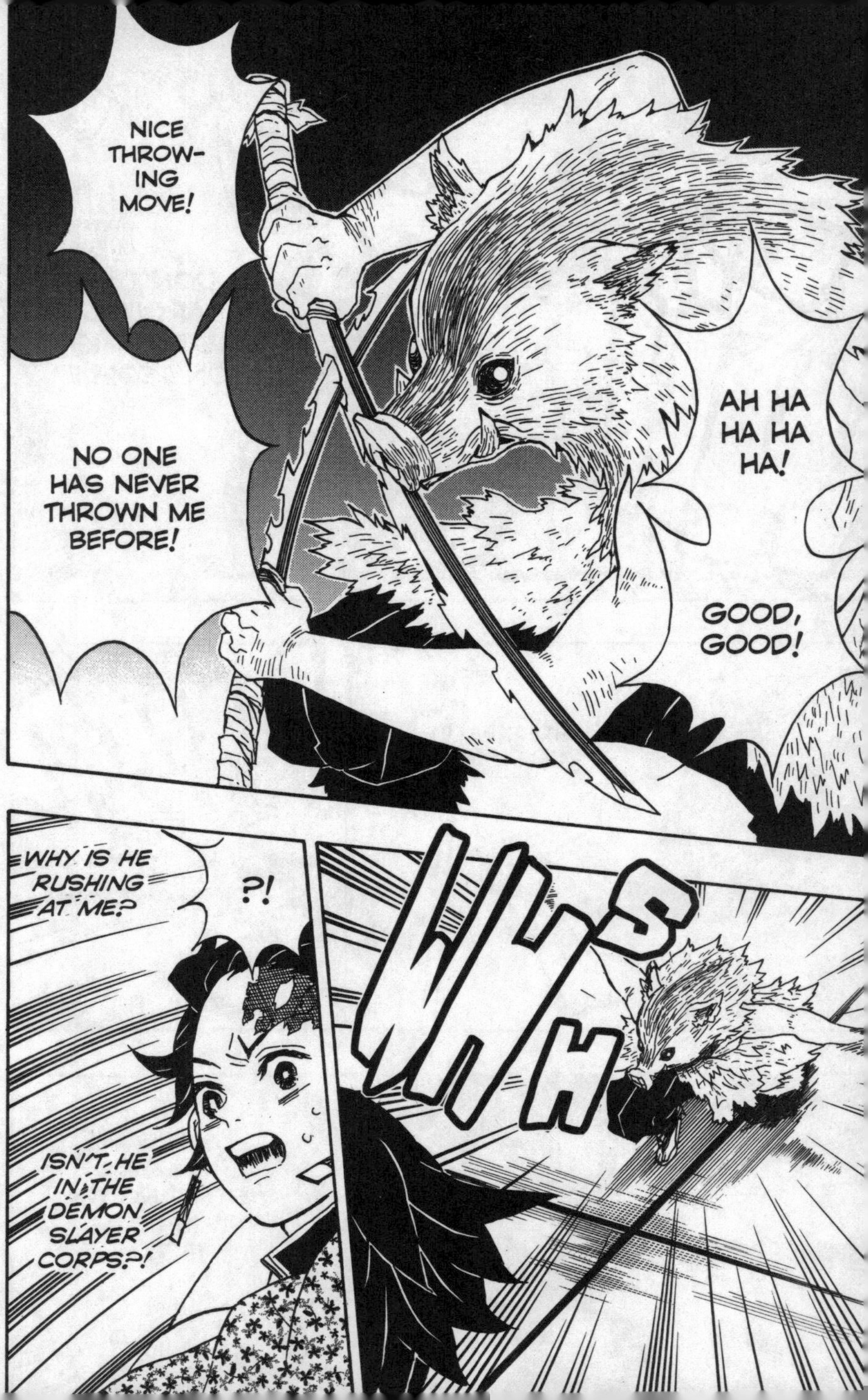
AH HA HA HA HA!
GOOD, GOOD!
NICE THROWING MOVE!
NO ONE HAS NEVER THROWN ME BEFORE!
WHSH
?!
WHY IS HE RUSHING AT ME?
ISN'T HE IN THE DEMON SLAYER CORPS?!

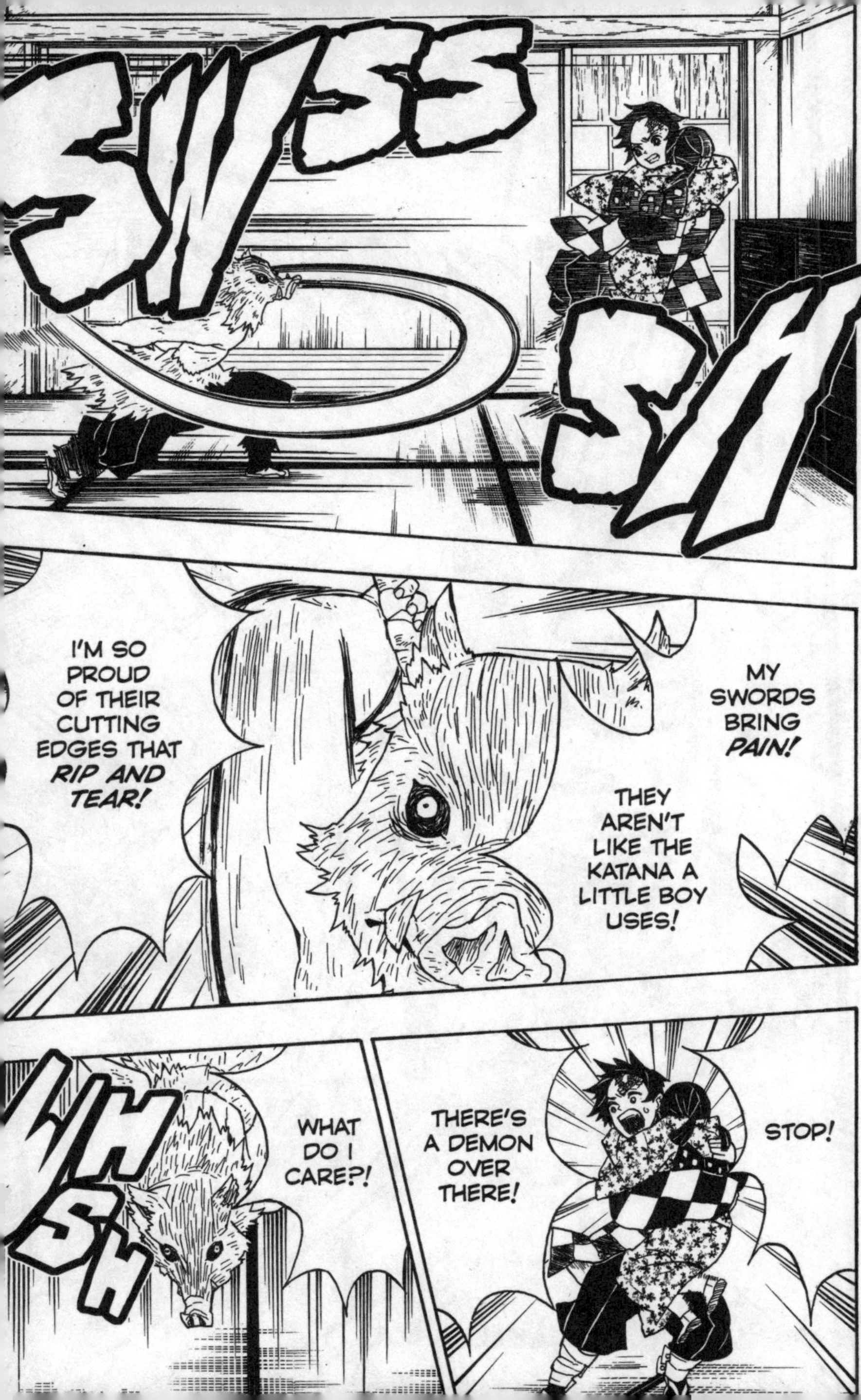
SHING
SHA
MY SWORDS BRING *PAIN!*
THEY AREN'T LIKE THE KATANA A LITTLE BOY USES!
I'M SO PROUD OF THEIR CUTTING EDGES THAT *RIP AND TEAR!*
STOP!
THERE'S A DEMON OVER THERE!
WHAT DO I CARE?!
WHSH

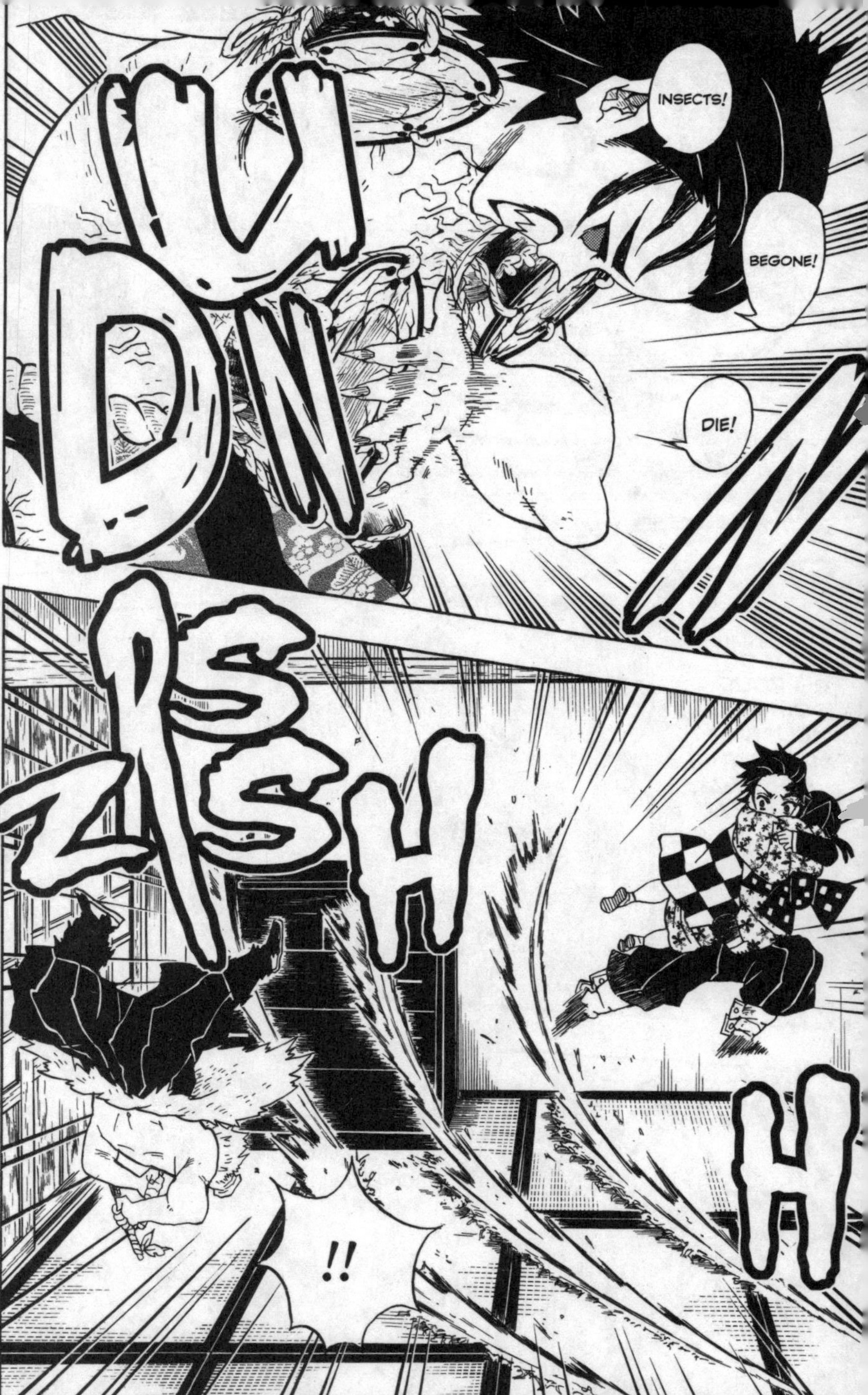
INSECTS!
BEGONE!
DIE!
ZISH
H
!!

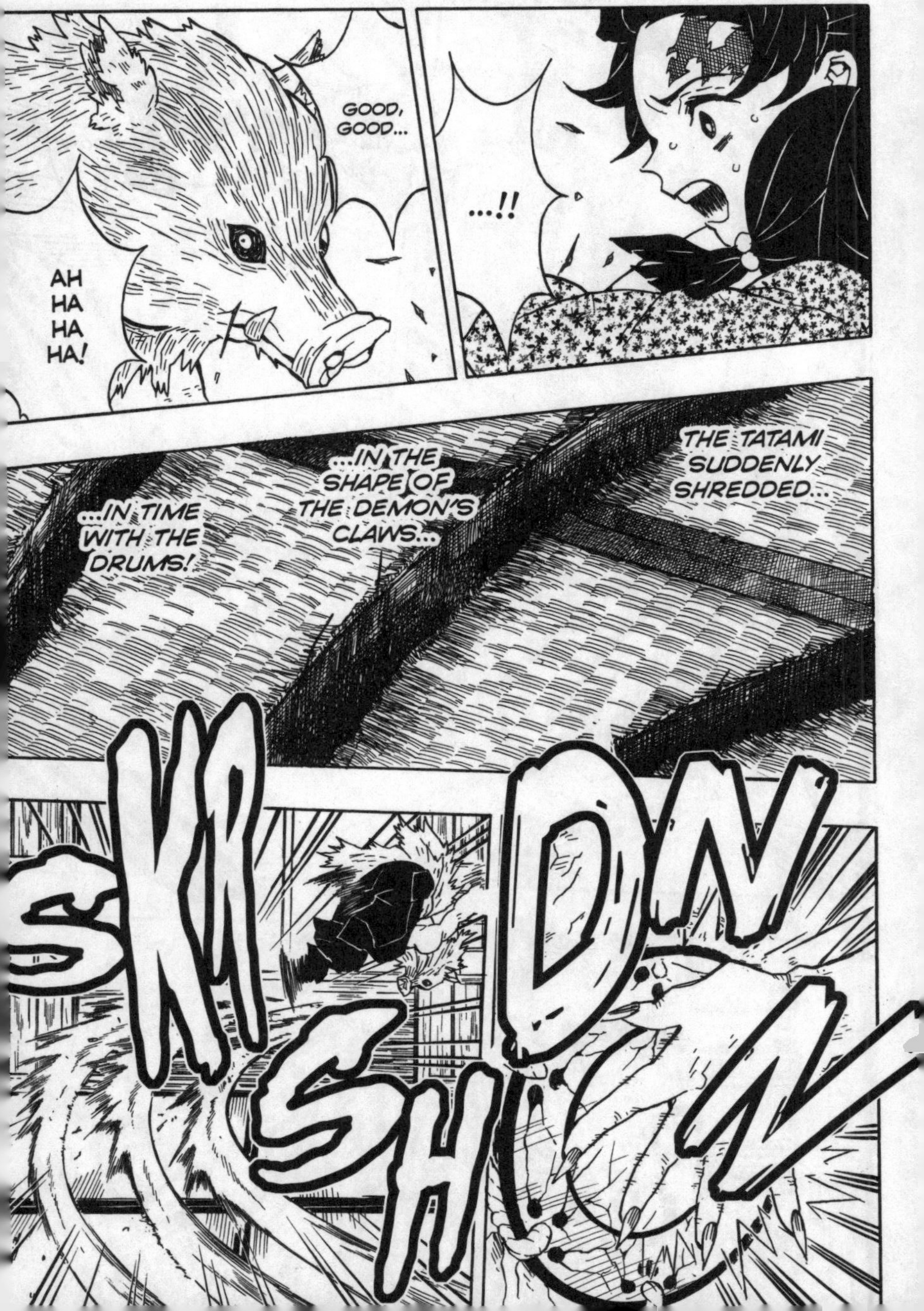
...!!
GOOD, GOOD...
AH HA HA HA!
THE TATAMI SUDDENLY SHREDDED...
...IN THE SHAPE OF THE DEMON'S CLAWS...
...IN TIME WITH THE DRUMS!

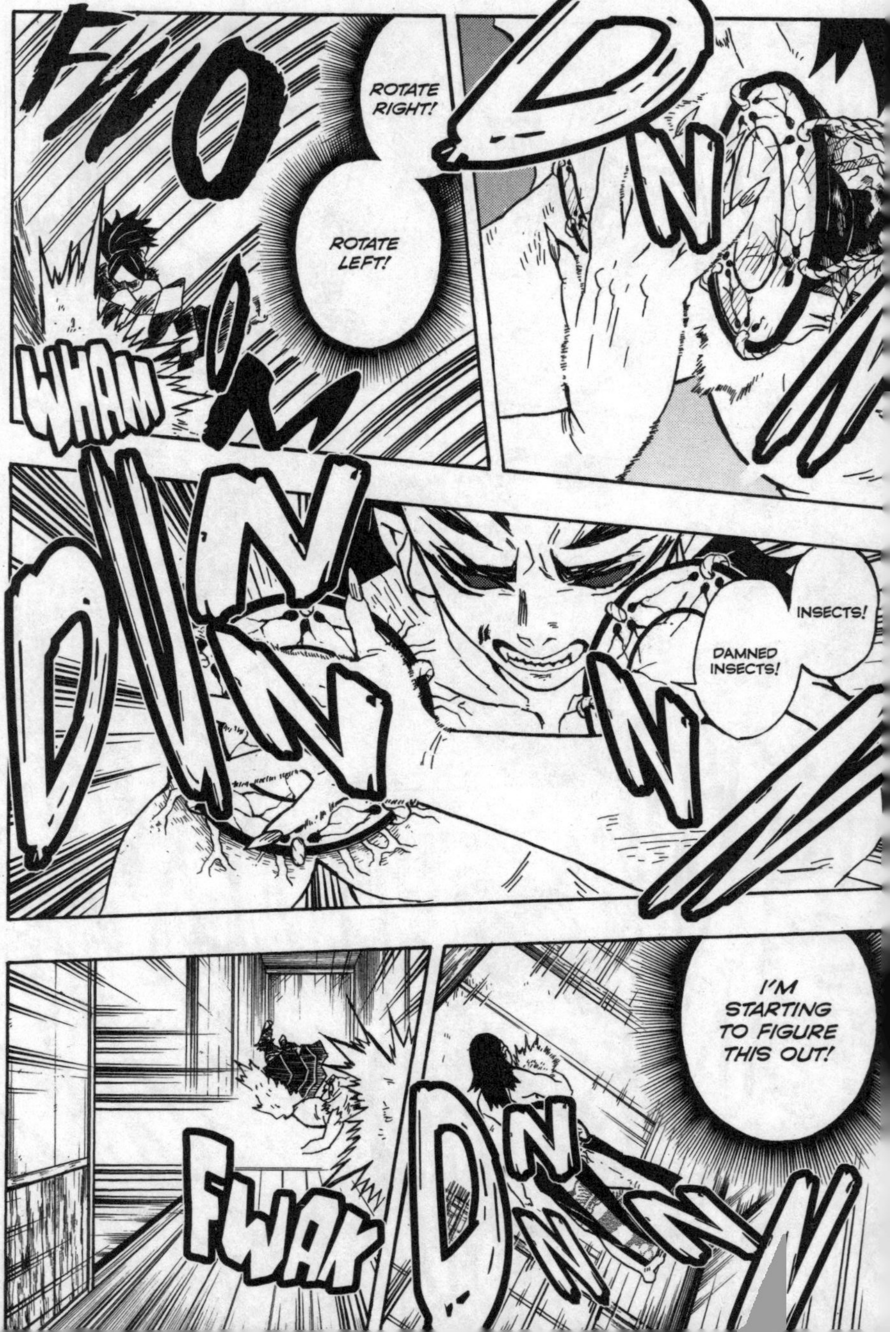
ROTATE RIGHT!
ROTATE LEFT!
FWO
WHAM
INSECTS!
DAMNED INSECTS!
I'M STARTING TO FIGURE THIS OUT!
FWAK

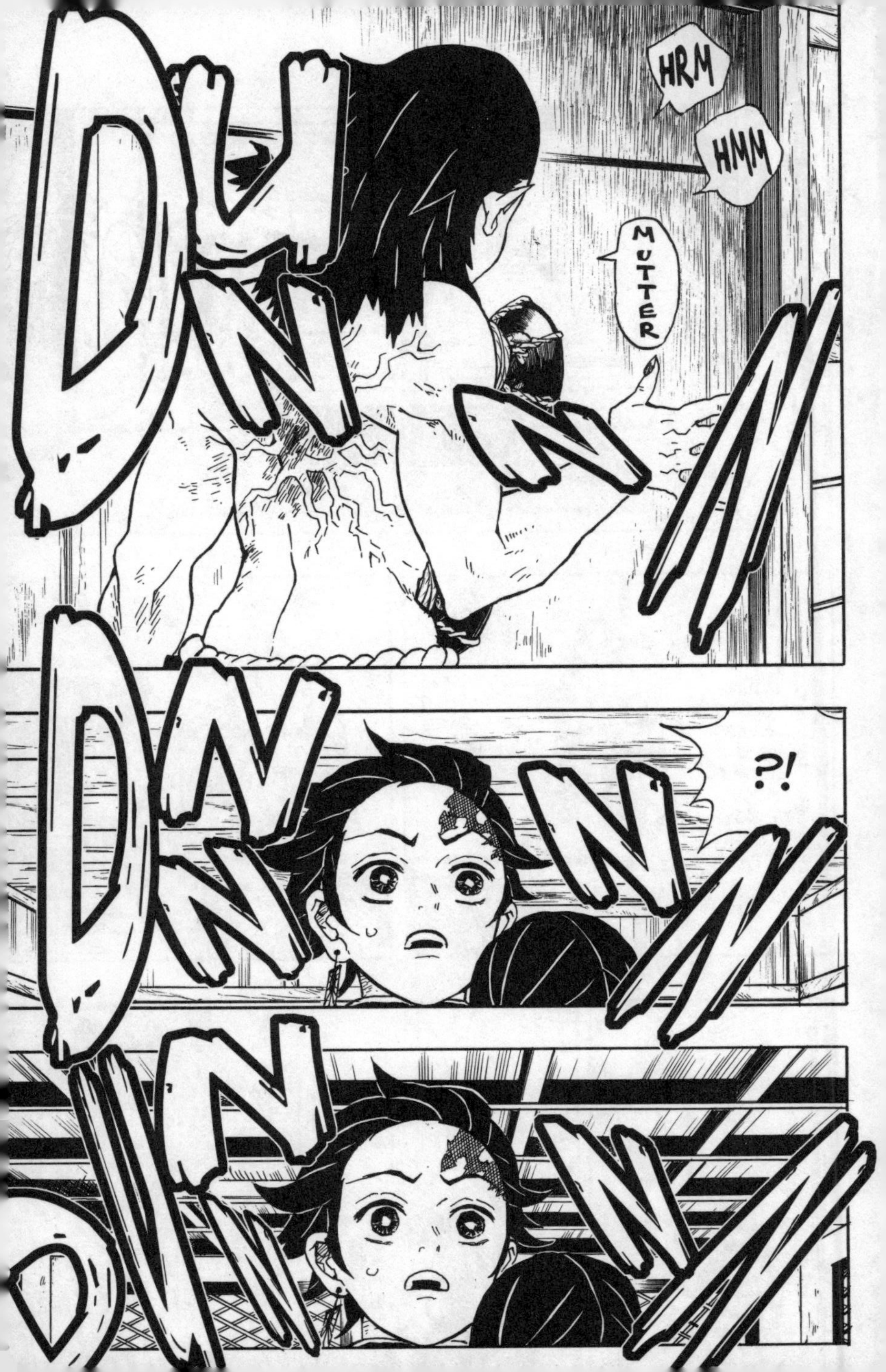
HRM
HMM
MUTTER
DWNNN
?!
DWNNNN
DWNNNN

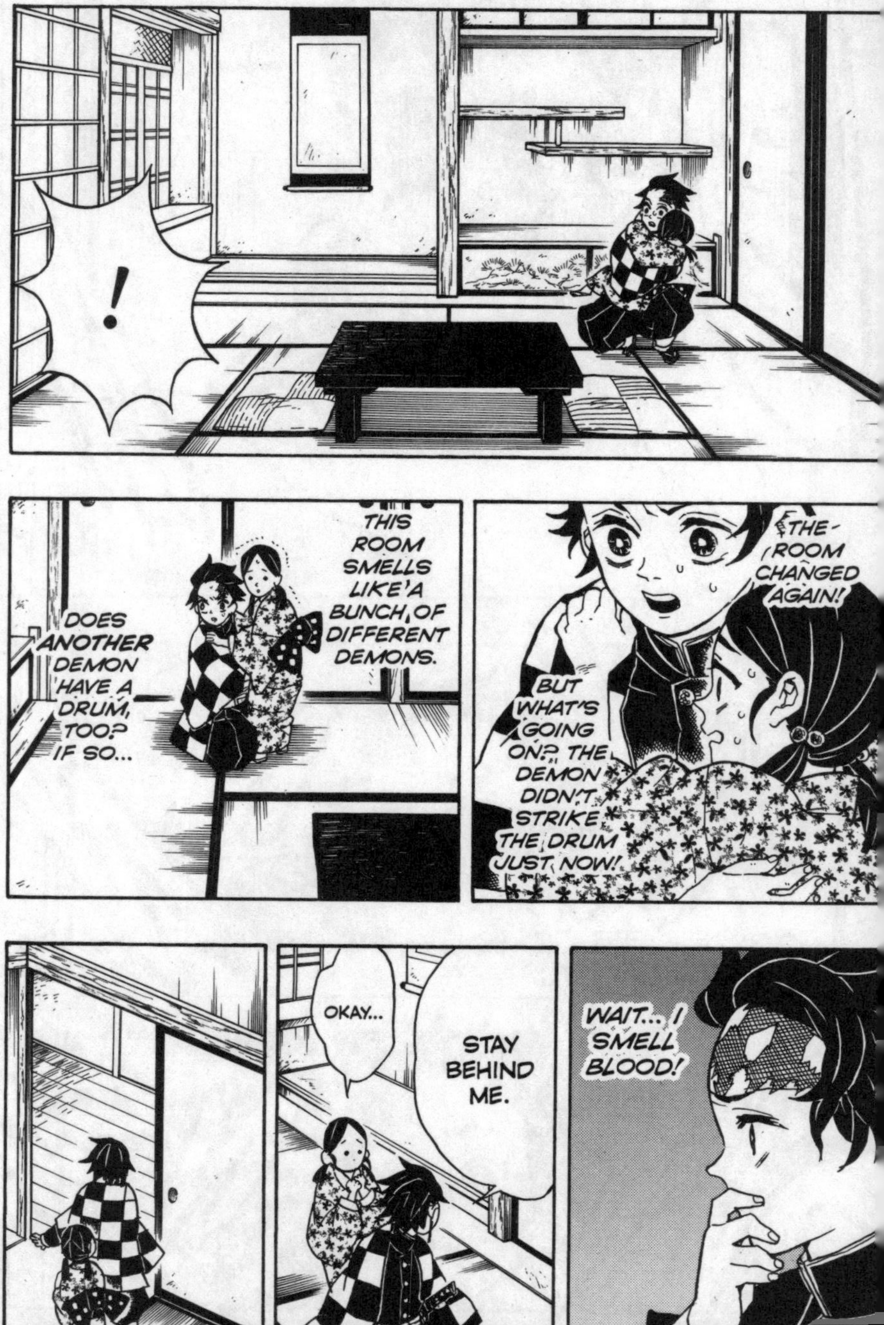
!
THE ROOM CHANGED AGAIN!
BUT WHAT'S GOING ON?! THE DEMON DIDN'T STRIKE THE DRUM JUST NOW!
THIS ROOM SMELLS LIKE A BUNCH OF DIFFERENT DEMONS.
DOES ANOTHER DEMON HAVE A DRUM, TOO? IF SO...
WAIT... I SMELL BLOOD!
STAY BEHIND ME.
OKAY...

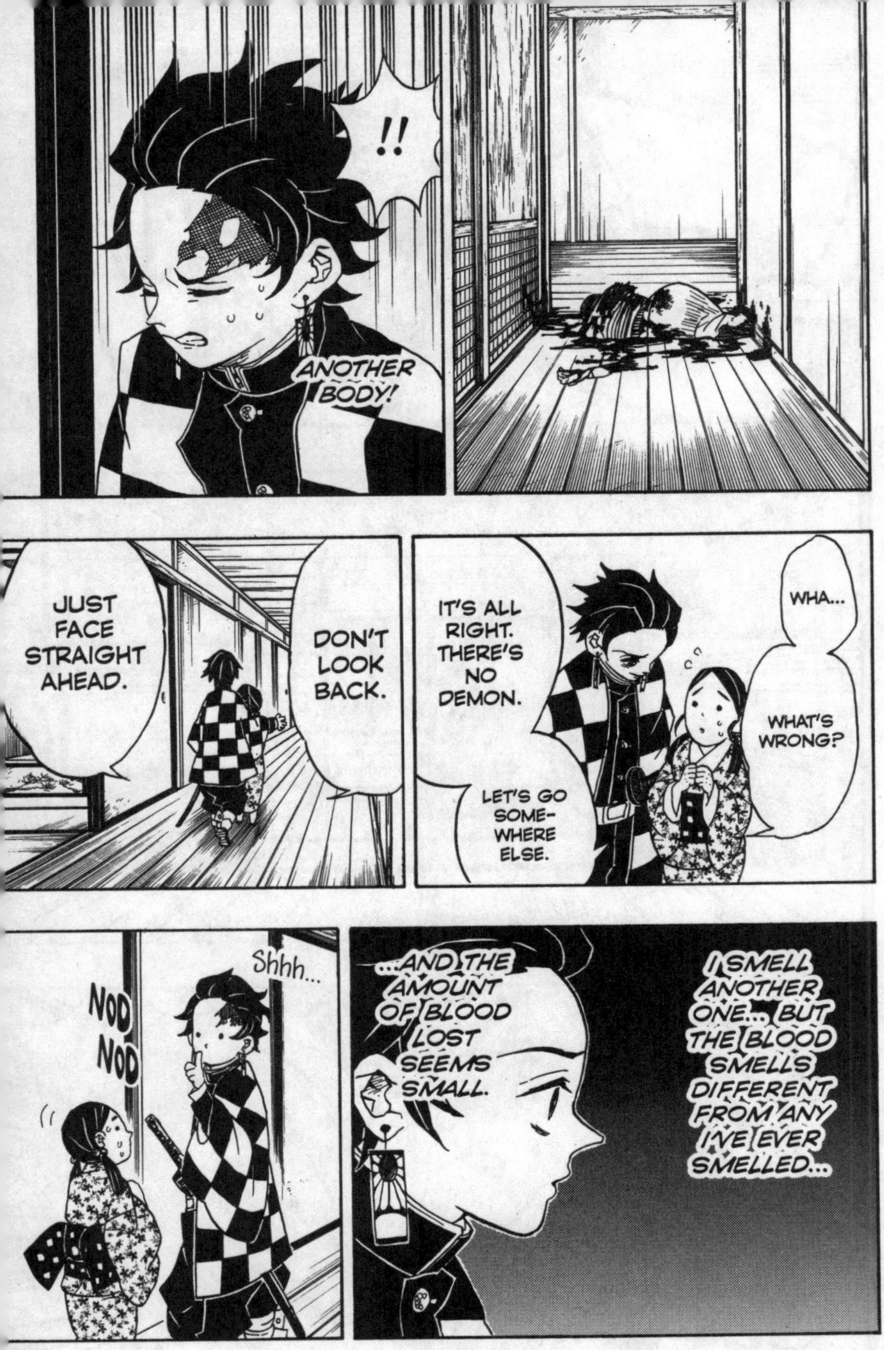
!!
ANOTHER BODY!
WHA...
WHAT'S WRONG?
IT'S ALL RIGHT. THERE'S NO DEMON.
LET'S GO SOME-WHERE ELSE.
DON'T LOOK BACK.
JUST FACE STRAIGHT AHEAD.
I SMELL ANOTHER ONE... BUT THE BLOOD SMELLS DIFFERENT FROM ANY I'VE EVER SMELLED...
...AND THE AMOUNT OF BLOOD LOST SEEMS SMALL.
Shhh...
NOD NOD

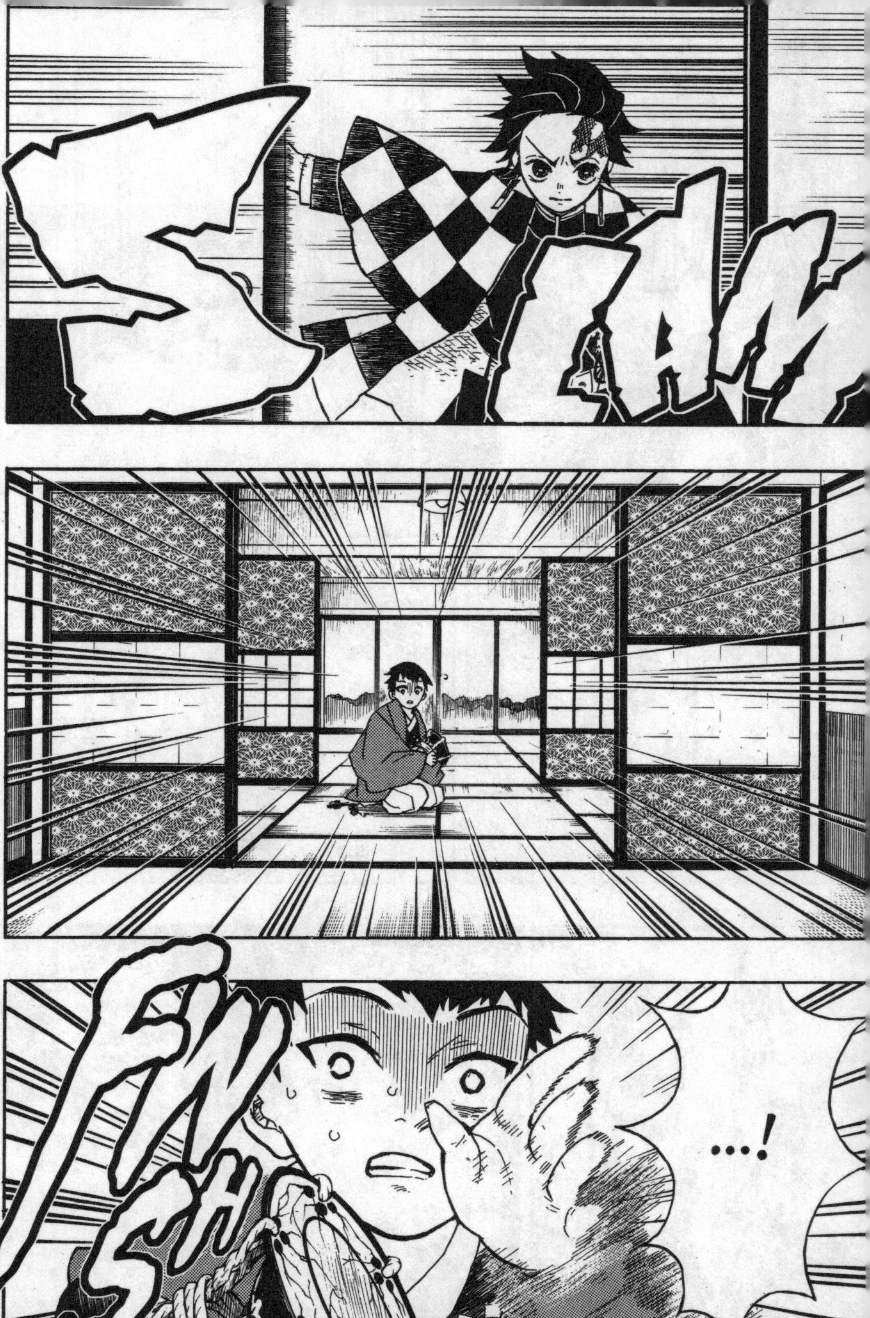
SLAM
FWSH
...!

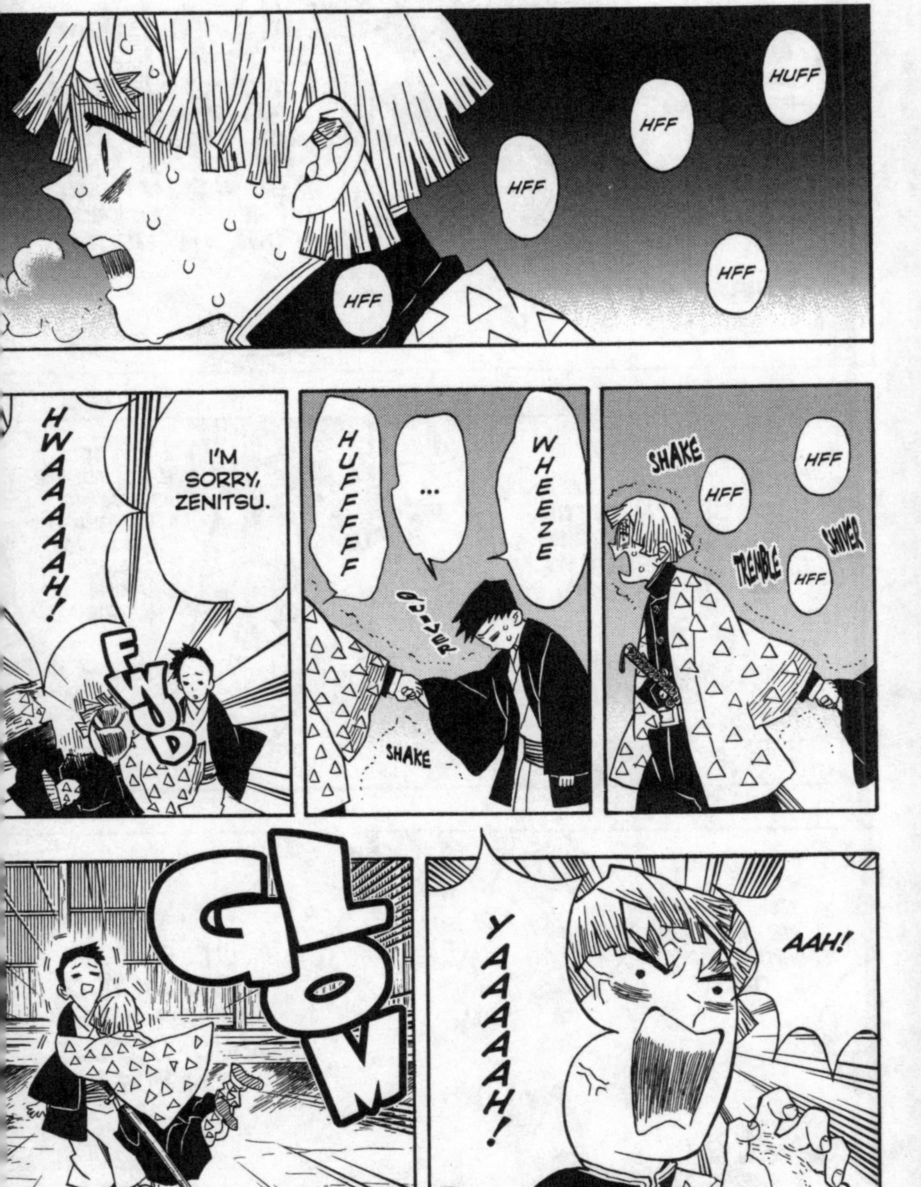
HUFF
HFF
HFF
HFF
HFF
HFF
HFF
SHAKE
TREMBLE
SHIVER
HFF
WHEEZE
...
HUFFFFF
QUIVER
SHAKE
HWAAAAAAH!
I'M SORRY, ZENITSU.
FWUD
AAH!
YAAAAAAH!
GLOOM

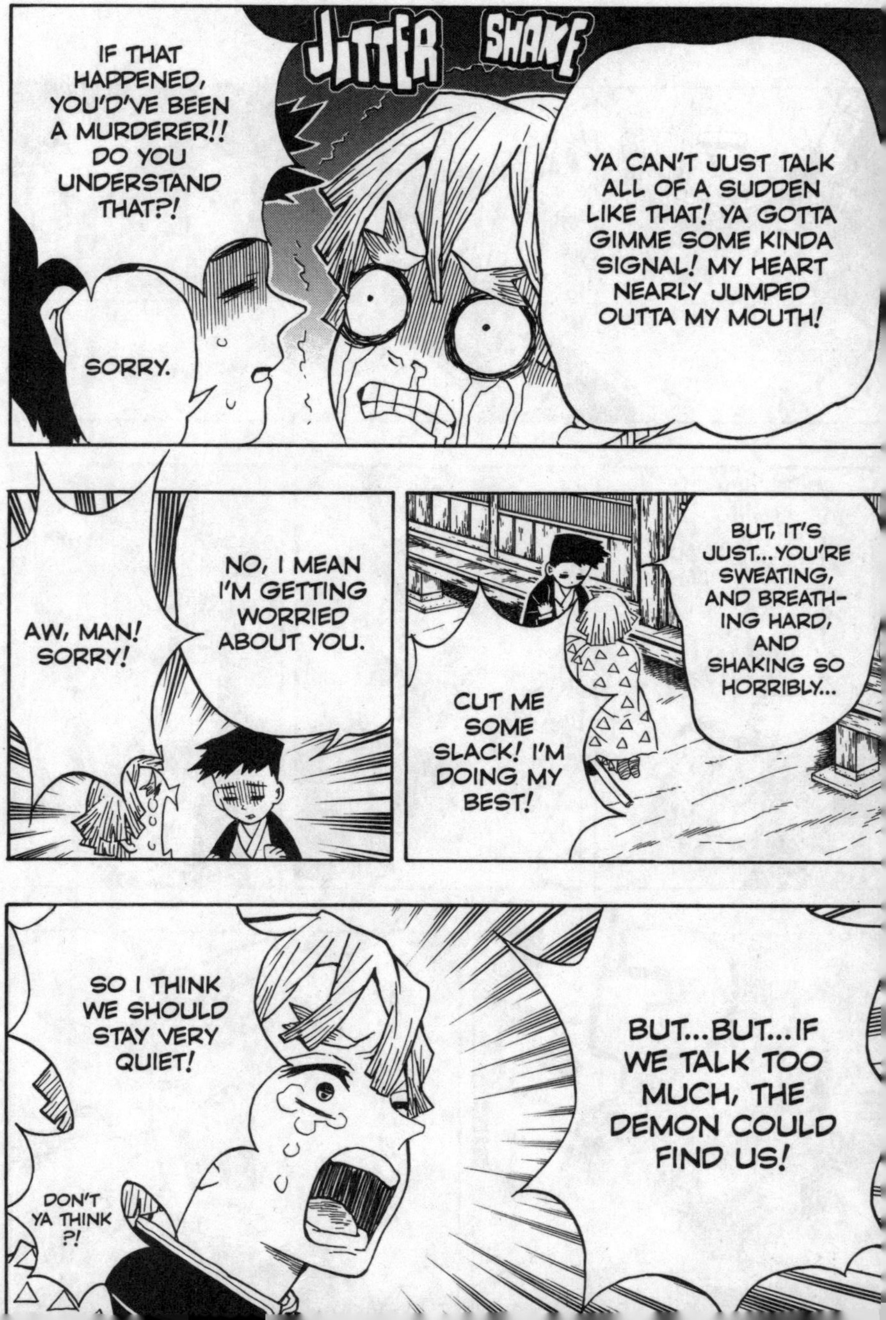
JITTER
SHAKE
YA CAN'T JUST TALK ALL OF A SUDDEN LIKE THAT! YA GOTTA GIMME SOME KINDA SIGNAL! MY HEART NEARLY JUMPED OUTTA MY MOUTH!
IF THAT HAPPENED, YOU'D'VE BEEN A MURDERER!! DO YOU UNDERSTAND THAT?!
SORRY.
BUT, IT'S JUST...YOU'RE SWEATING, AND BREATHING HARD, AND SHAKING SO HORRIBLY...
CUT ME SOME SLACK! I'M DOING MY BEST!
NO, I MEAN I'M GETTING WORRIED ABOUT YOU.
AW, MAN! SORRY!
BUT...BUT...IF WE TALK TOO MUCH, THE DEMON COULD FIND US!
SO I THINK WE SHOULD STAY VERY QUIET!
DON'T YA THINK?!

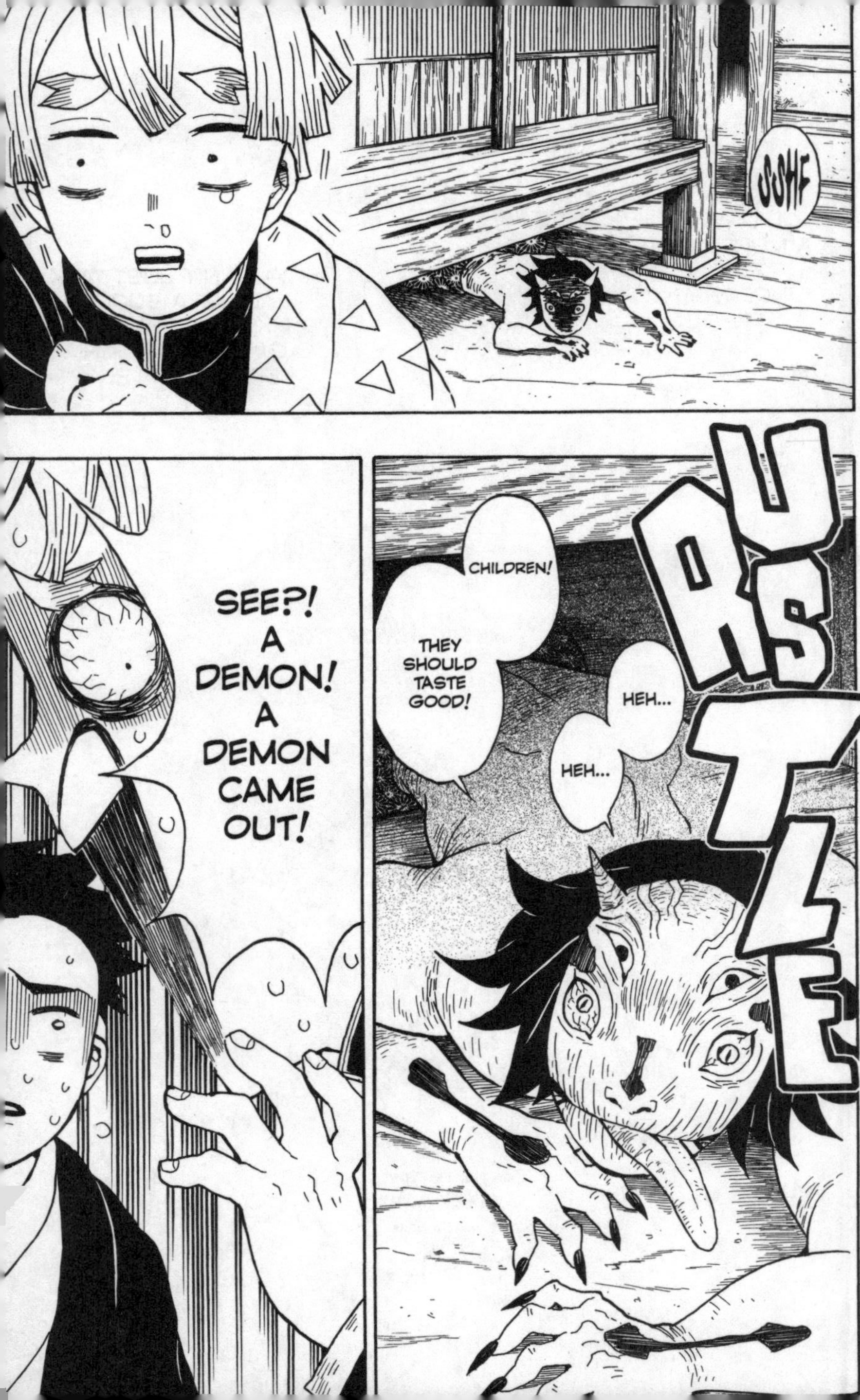
SSHF
RUSTLE
CHILDREN! THEY SHOULD TASTE GOOD!
HEH...
HEH...
SEE?! A DEMON! A DEMON CAME OUT!

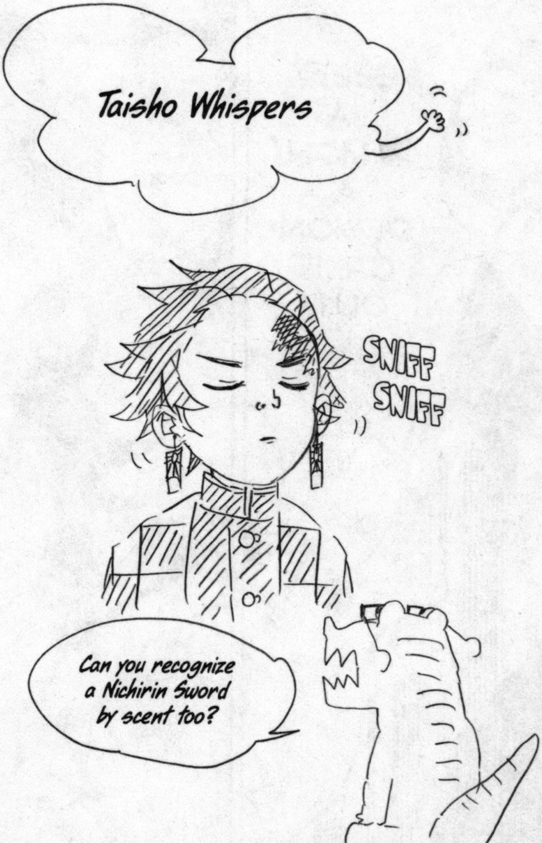
Taisho Whispers
SNIFF
SNIFF
Can you recognize a Nichirin Sword by scent too?

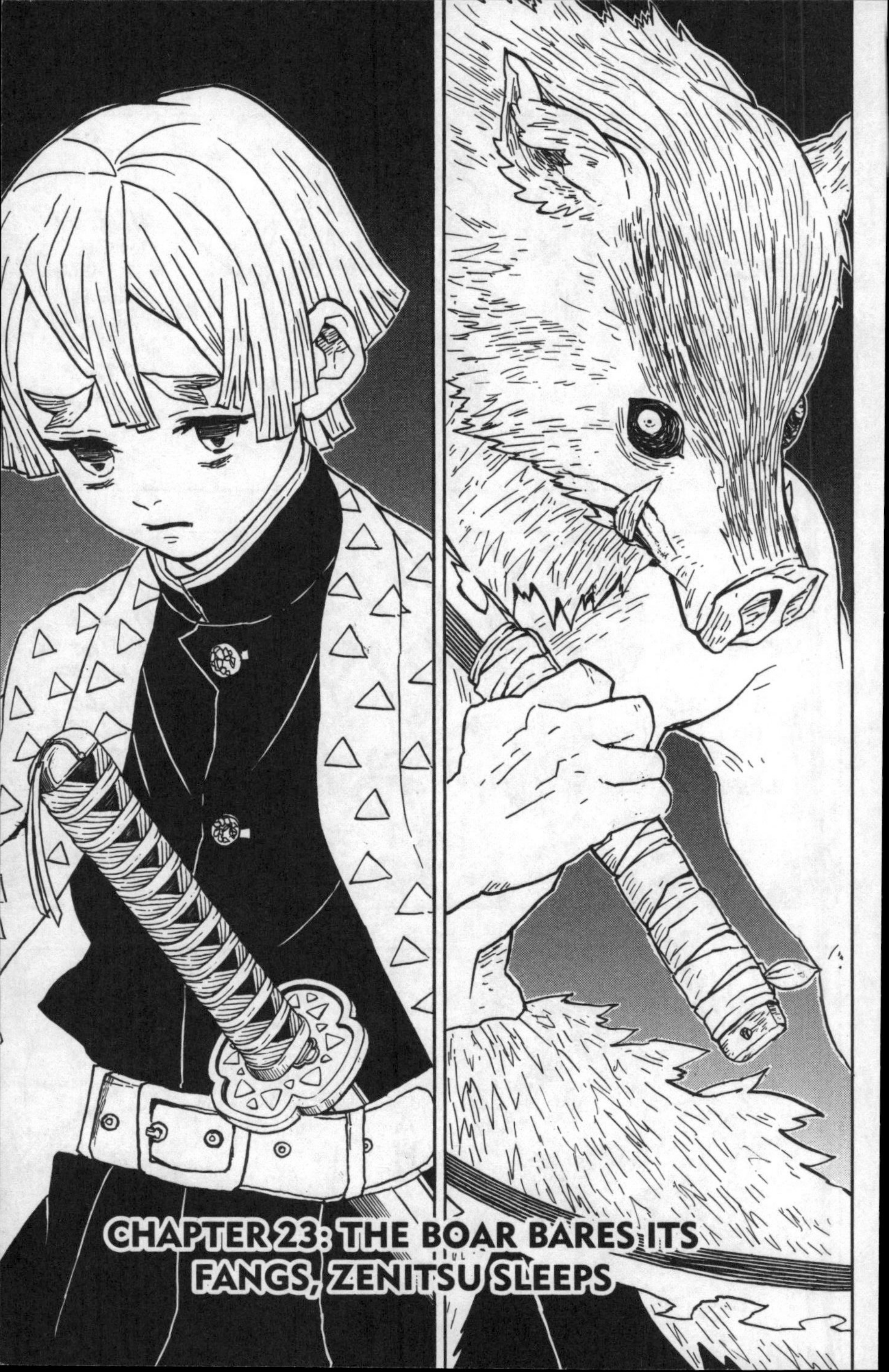
CHAPTER 23: THE BOAR BARES ITS
FANGS, ZENITSU SLEEPS

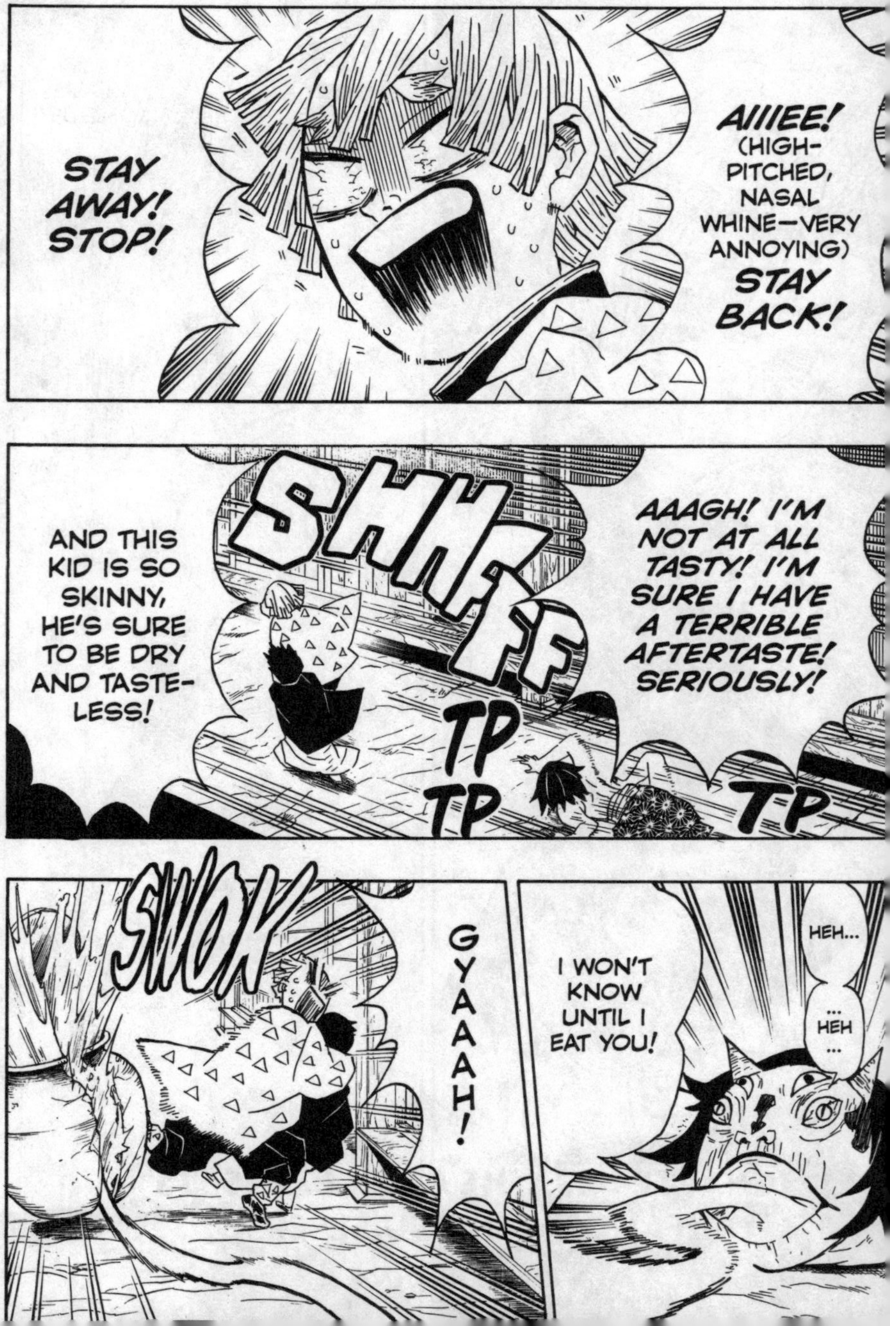
AIIIEE! (HIGH-PITCHED, NASAL WHINE—VERY ANNOYING) STAY BACK!
STAY AWAY! STOP!
AAAGH! I'M NOT AT ALL TASTY! I'M SURE I HAVE A TERRIBLE AFTERTASTE! SERIOUSLY!
SHHFF
TP TP
TP
AND THIS KID IS SO SKINNY, HE'S SURE TO BE DRY AND TASTELESS!
HEH...
...HEH...
I WON'T KNOW UNTIL I EAT YOU!
GYAAAH!
SWOK

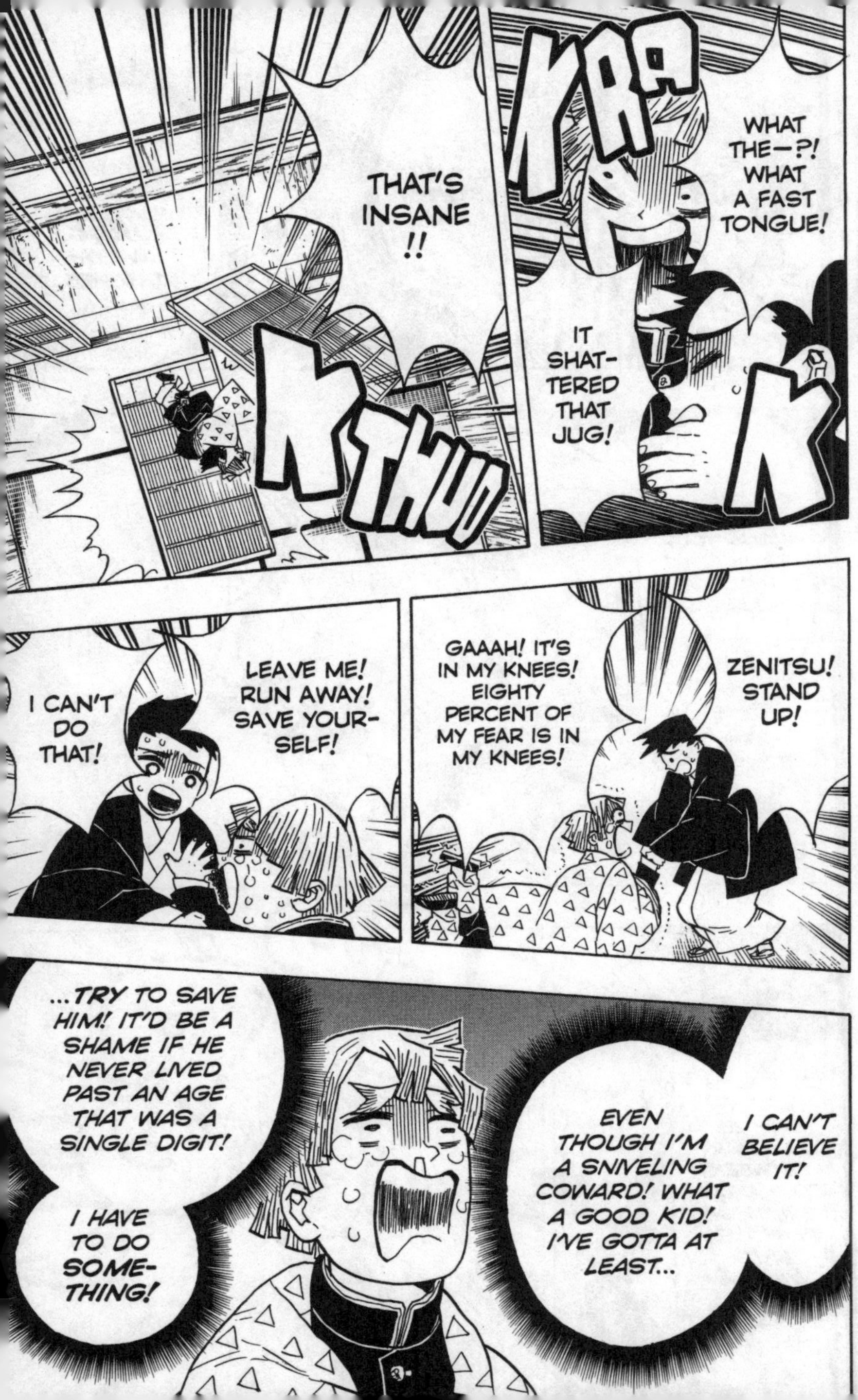
KRA
WHAT THE—?! WHAT A FAST TONGUE!
K
IT SHATTERED THAT JUG!
THAT'S INSANE!!
THUD
ZENITSU! STAND UP!
GAAAH! IT'S IN MY KNEES! EIGHTY PERCENT OF MY FEAR IS IN MY KNEES!
LEAVE ME! RUN AWAY! SAVE YOURSELF!
I CAN'T DO THAT!
I CAN'T BELIEVE IT!
EVEN THOUGH I'M A SNIVELING COWARD! WHAT A GOOD KID! I'VE GOTTA AT LEAST...
...TRY TO SAVE HIM! IT'D BE A SHAME IF HE NEVER LIVED PAST AN AGE THAT WAS A SINGLE DIGIT!
I HAVE TO DO SOMETHING!

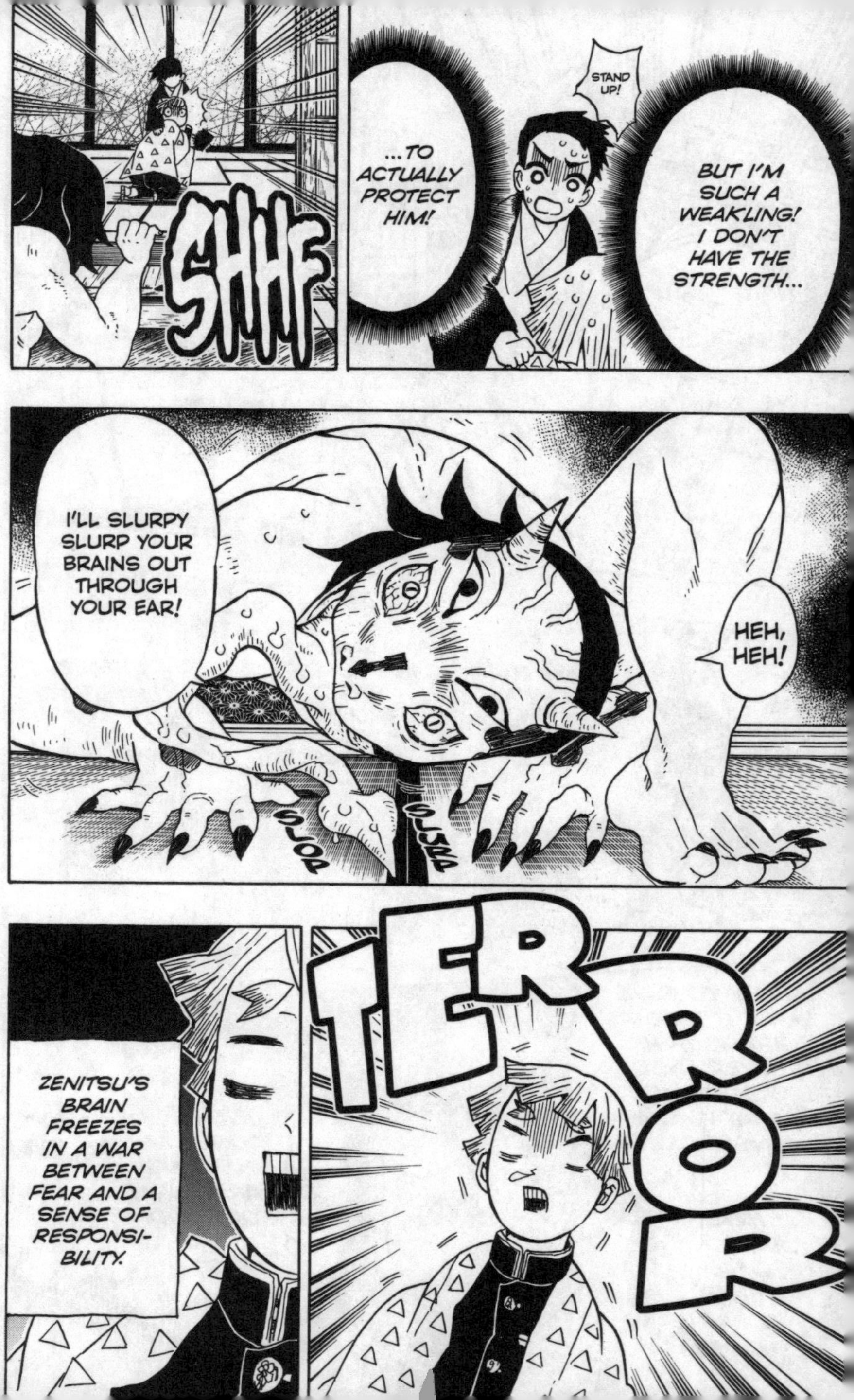

STAND UP!
BUT I'M SUCH A WEAKLING! I DON'T HAVE THE STRENGTH...
...TO ACTUALLY PROTECT HIM!
SHHF
HEH, HEH!
I'LL SLURPY SLURP YOUR BRAINS OUT THROUGH YOUR EAR!
SLURP
SLOP
TERROR
ZENITSU'S BRAIN FREEZES IN A WAR BETWEEN FEAR AND A SENSE OF RESPONSI-BILITY.

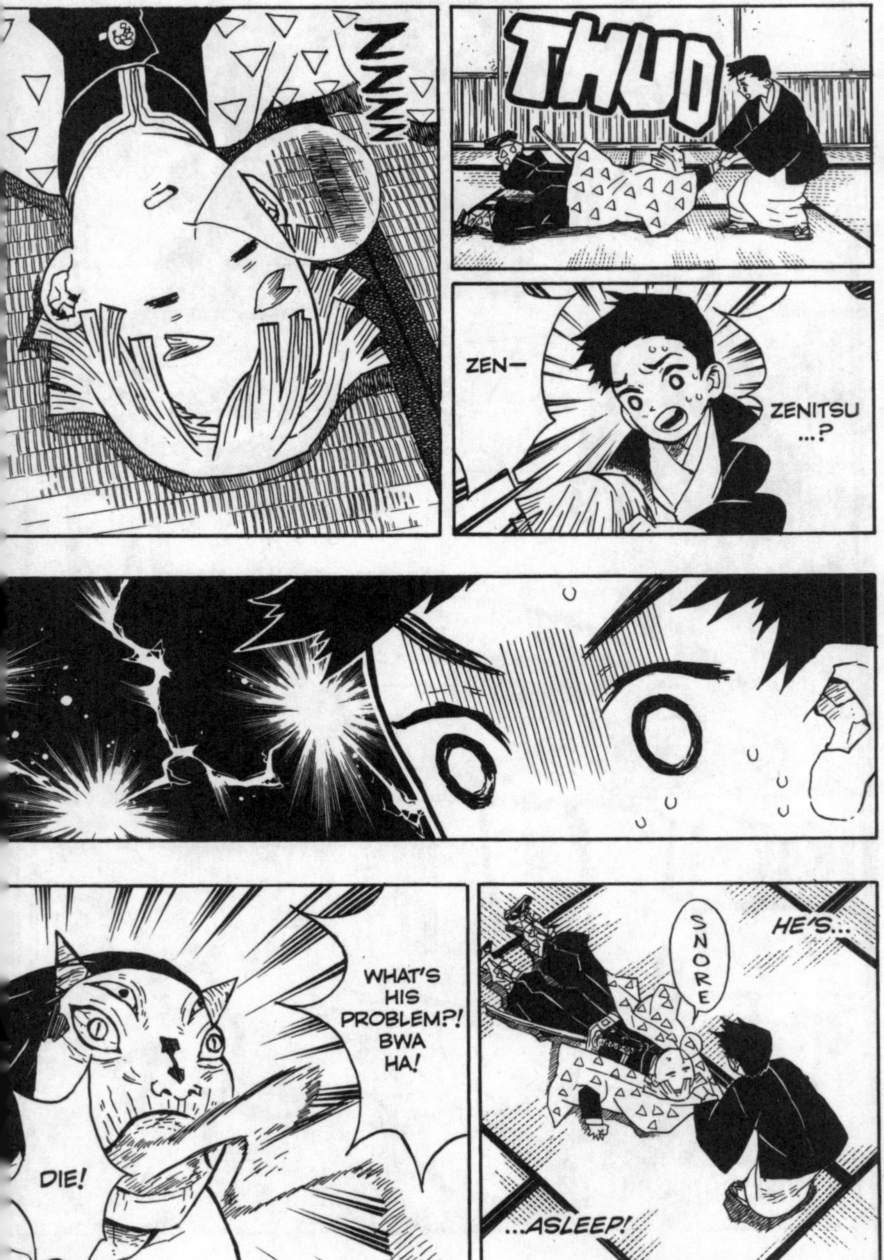
THUD
ZEN—
ZENITSU ...?
ZZZZ
HE'S...
SNORE
...ASLEEP!
WHAT'S HIS PROBLEM?! BWA HA!
DIE!

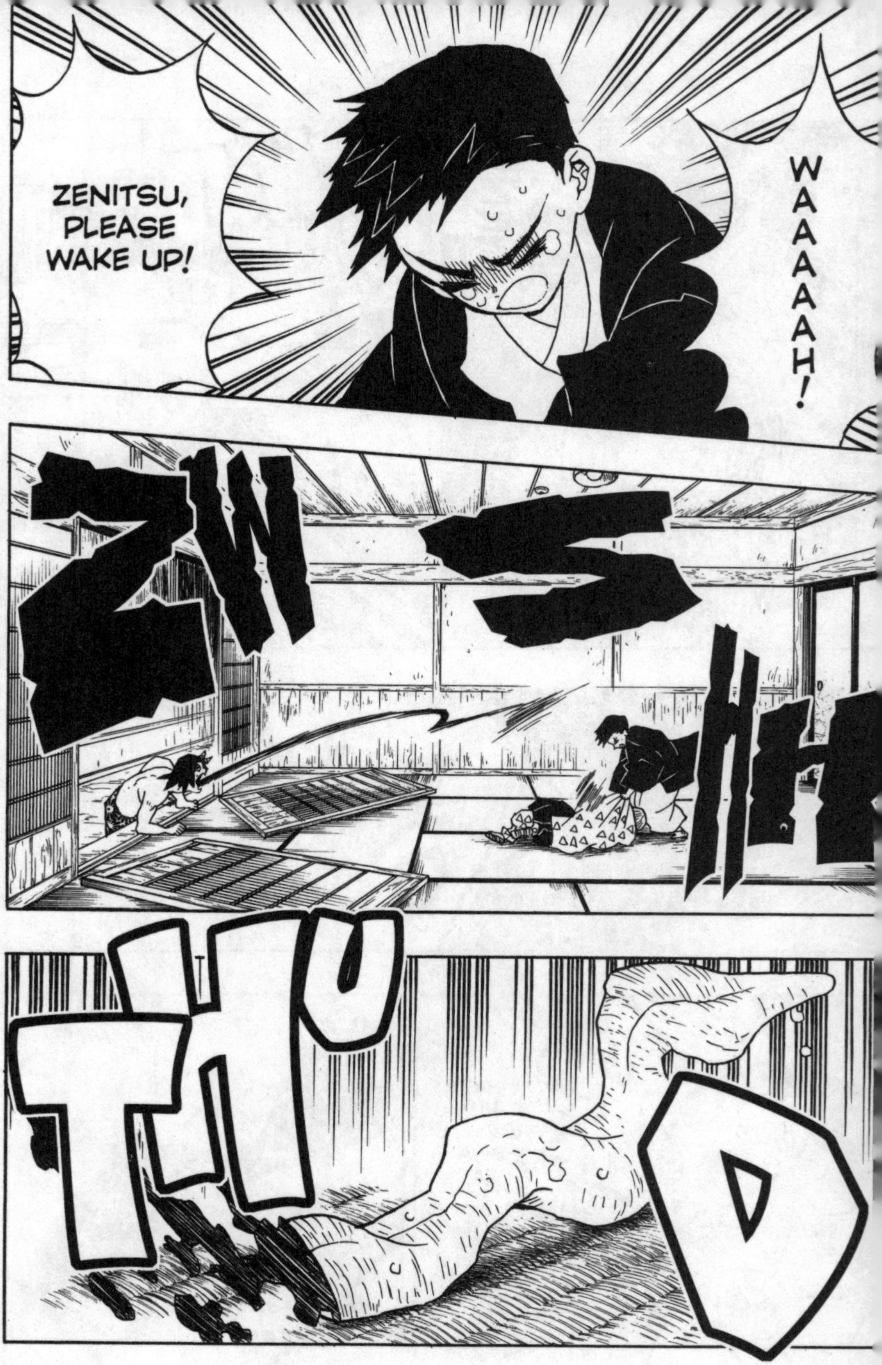

WAAAAAH!
ZENITSU, PLEASE WAKE UP!
ZWSHH
THUD

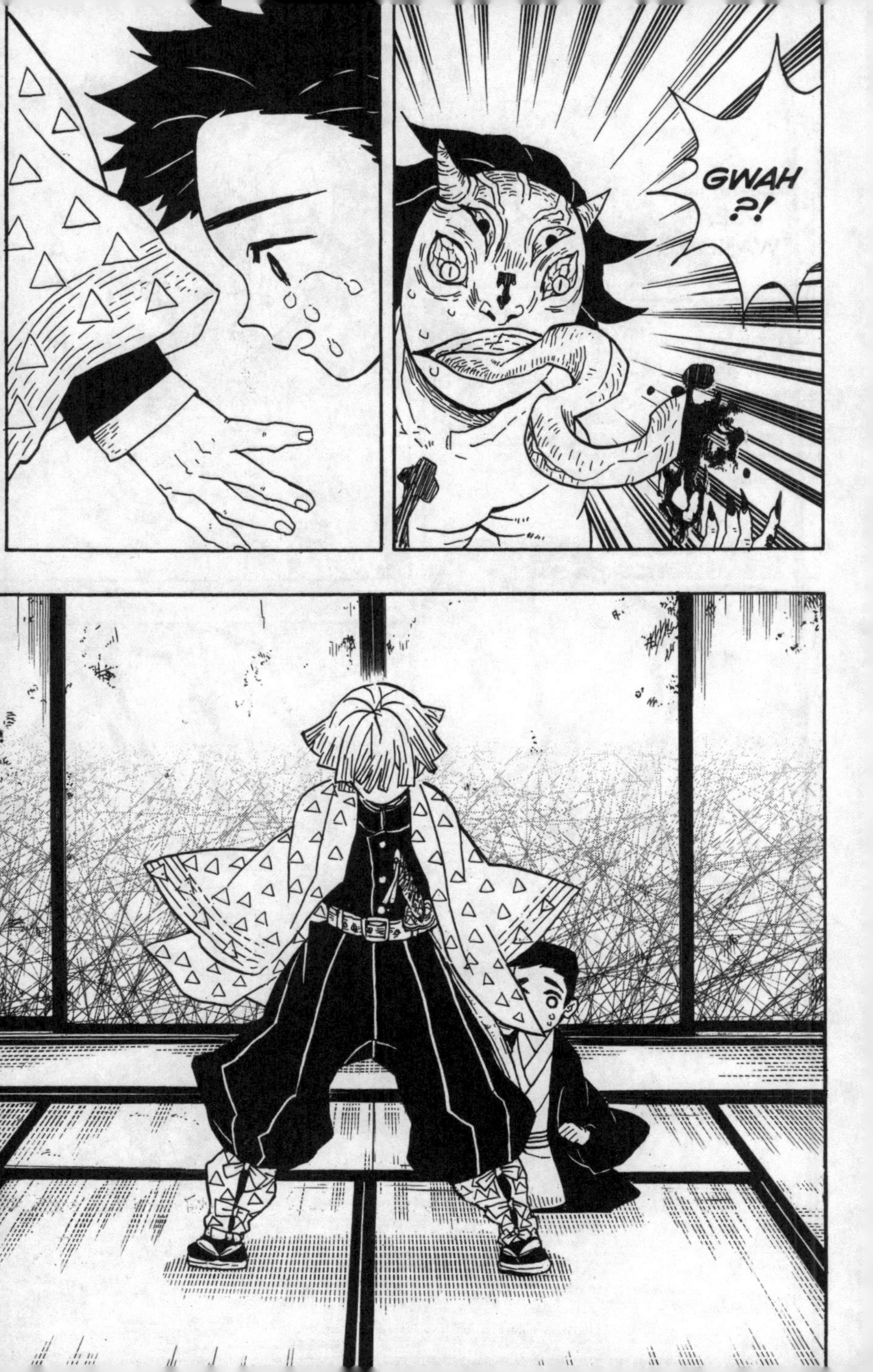
GWAH ?!

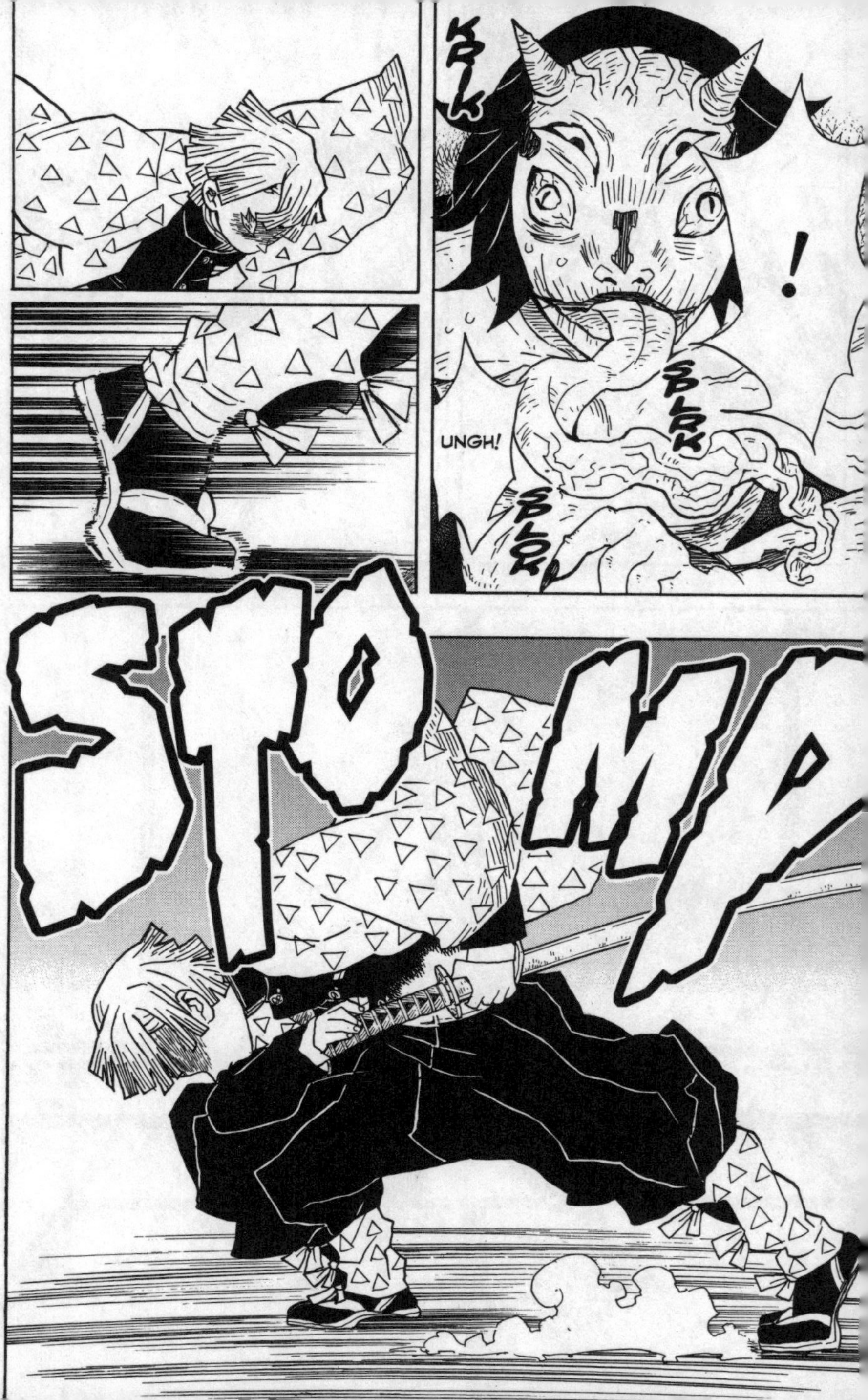
!
SPLRK
UNGH!
STOMP

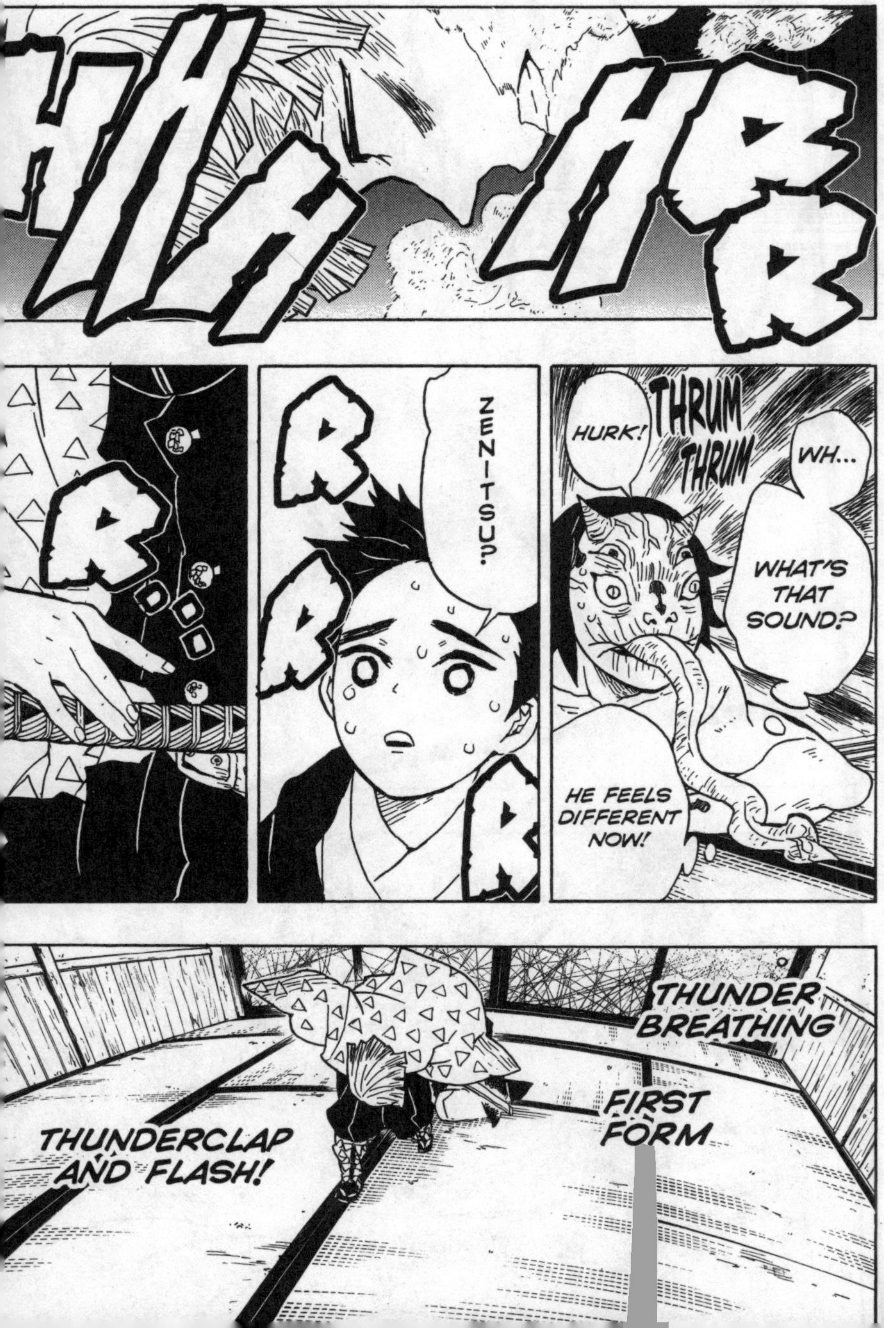
WH...
WHAT'S THAT SOUND?
THRUM THRUM
HURK!
HE FEELS DIFFERENT NOW!
ZENITSU?
THUNDER BREATHING
FIRST FORM
THUNDERCLAP AND FLASH!

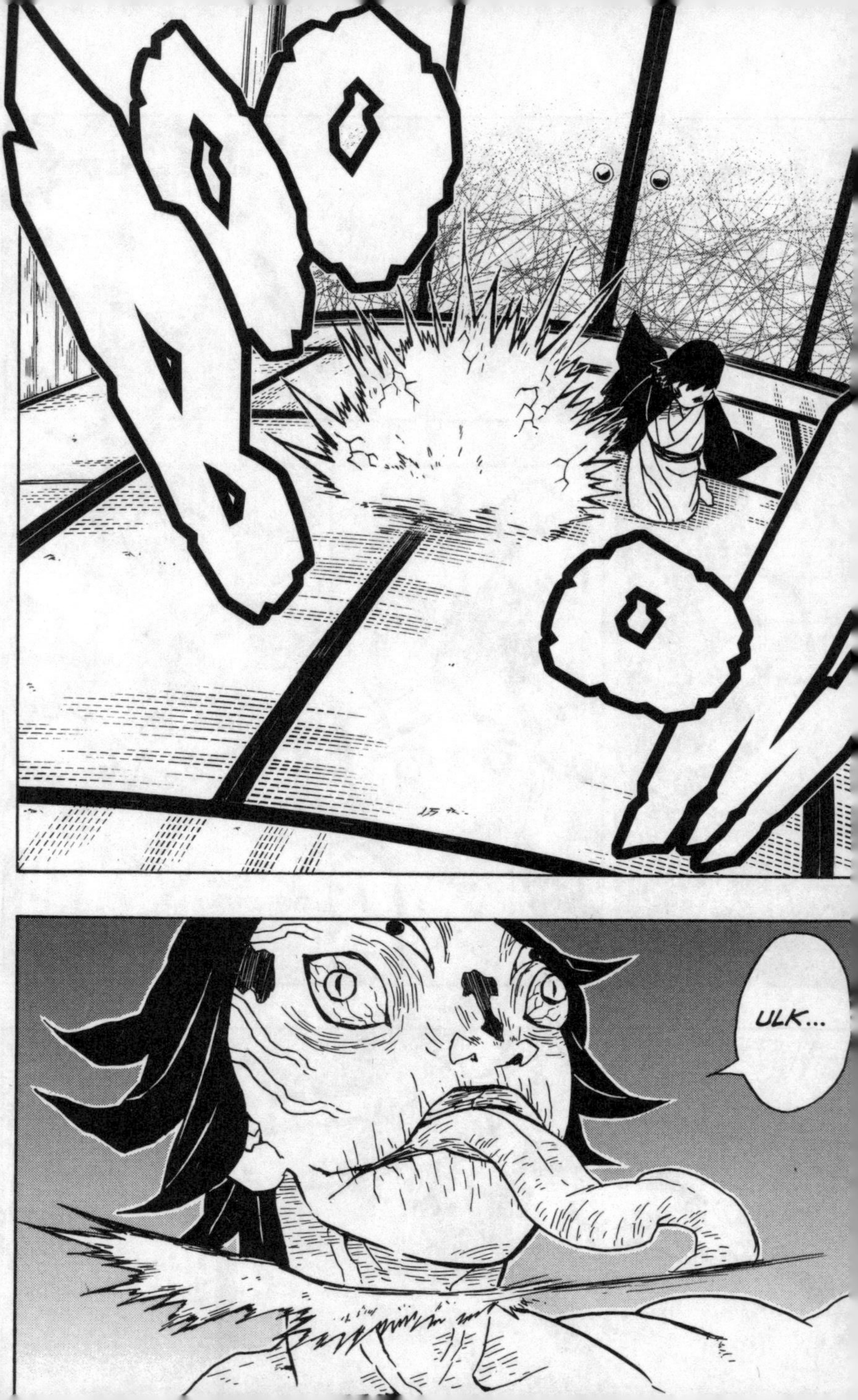
ULK...

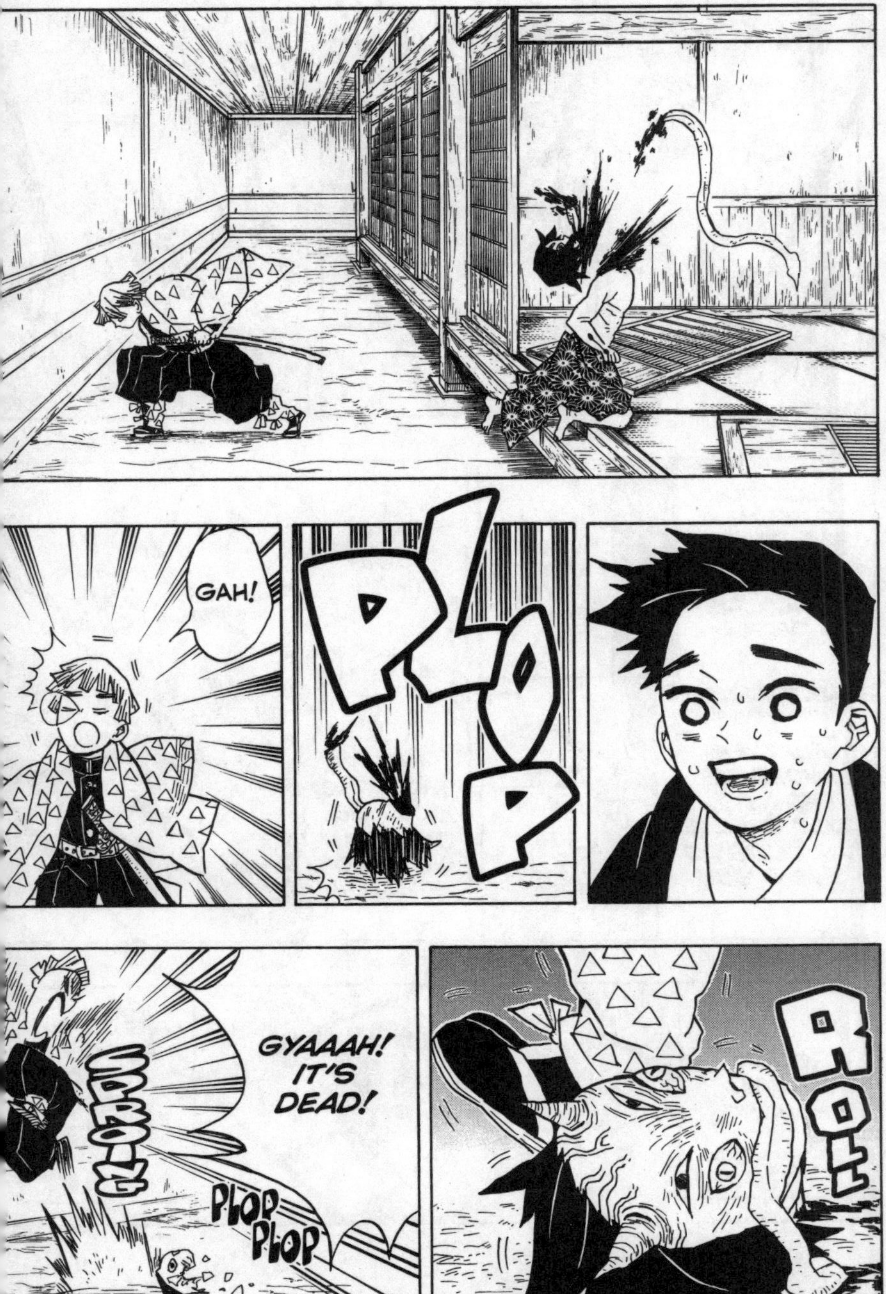
PLOP
GAH!
ROLL
GYAAAH! IT'S DEAD!
PLOP PLOP

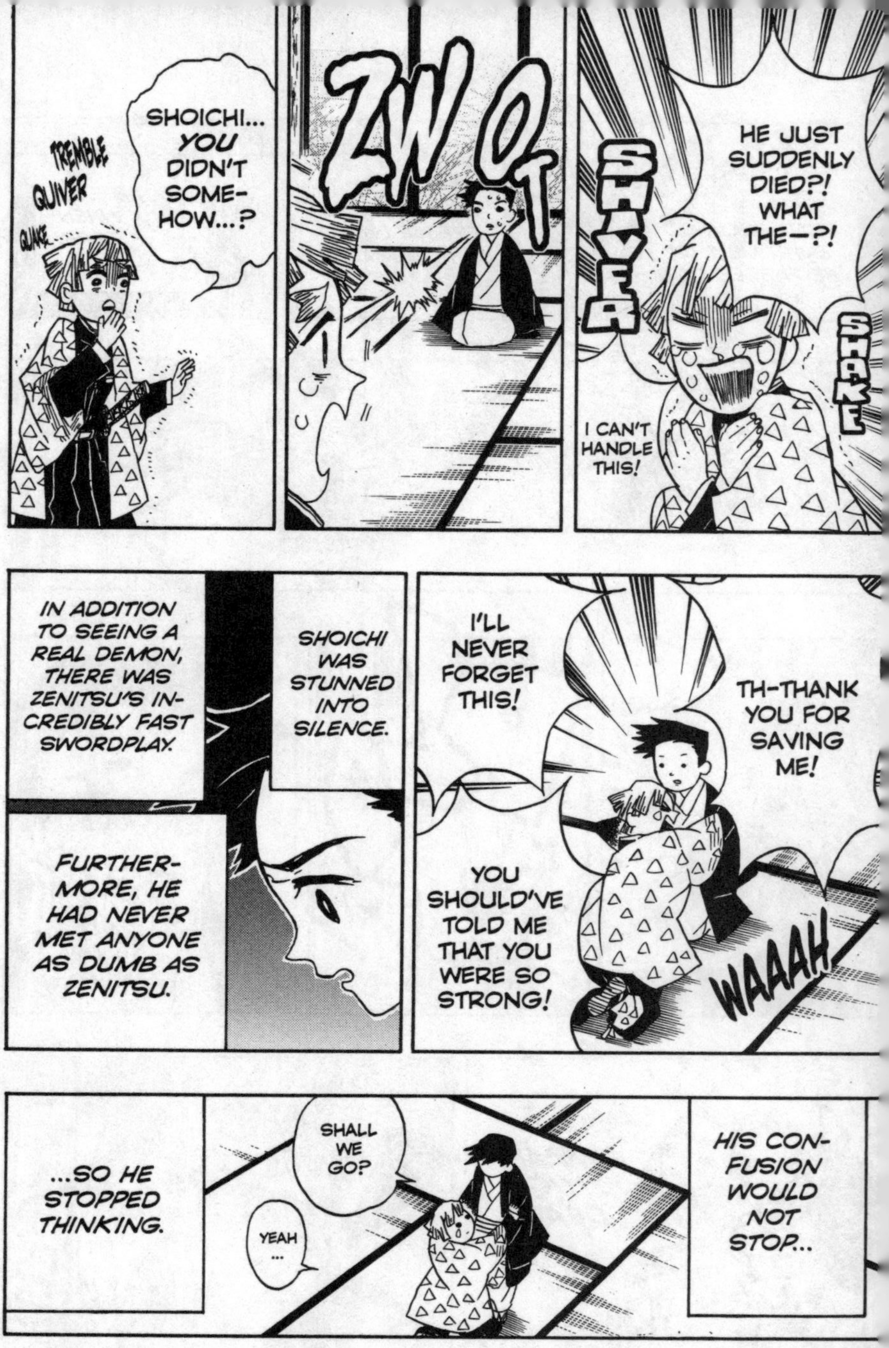
HE JUST SUDDENLY DIED?! WHAT THE—?!
SHIVER
SHAKE
I CAN'T HANDLE THIS!
ZWOT
SHOICHI... YOU DIDN'T SOMEHOW...?
TREMBLE
QUIVER
QUAKE
TH-THANK YOU FOR SAVING ME!
I'LL NEVER FORGET THIS!
YOU SHOULD'VE TOLD ME THAT YOU WERE SO STRONG!
WAAAH
SHOICHI WAS STUNNED INTO SILENCE.
IN ADDITION TO SEEING A REAL DEMON, THERE WAS ZENITSU'S INCREDIBLY FAST SWORDPLAY.
FURTHERMORE, HE HAD NEVER MET ANYONE AS DUMB AS ZENITSU.
HIS CONFUSION WOULD NOT STOP...
SHALL WE GO?
YEAH...
...SO HE STOPPED THINKING.

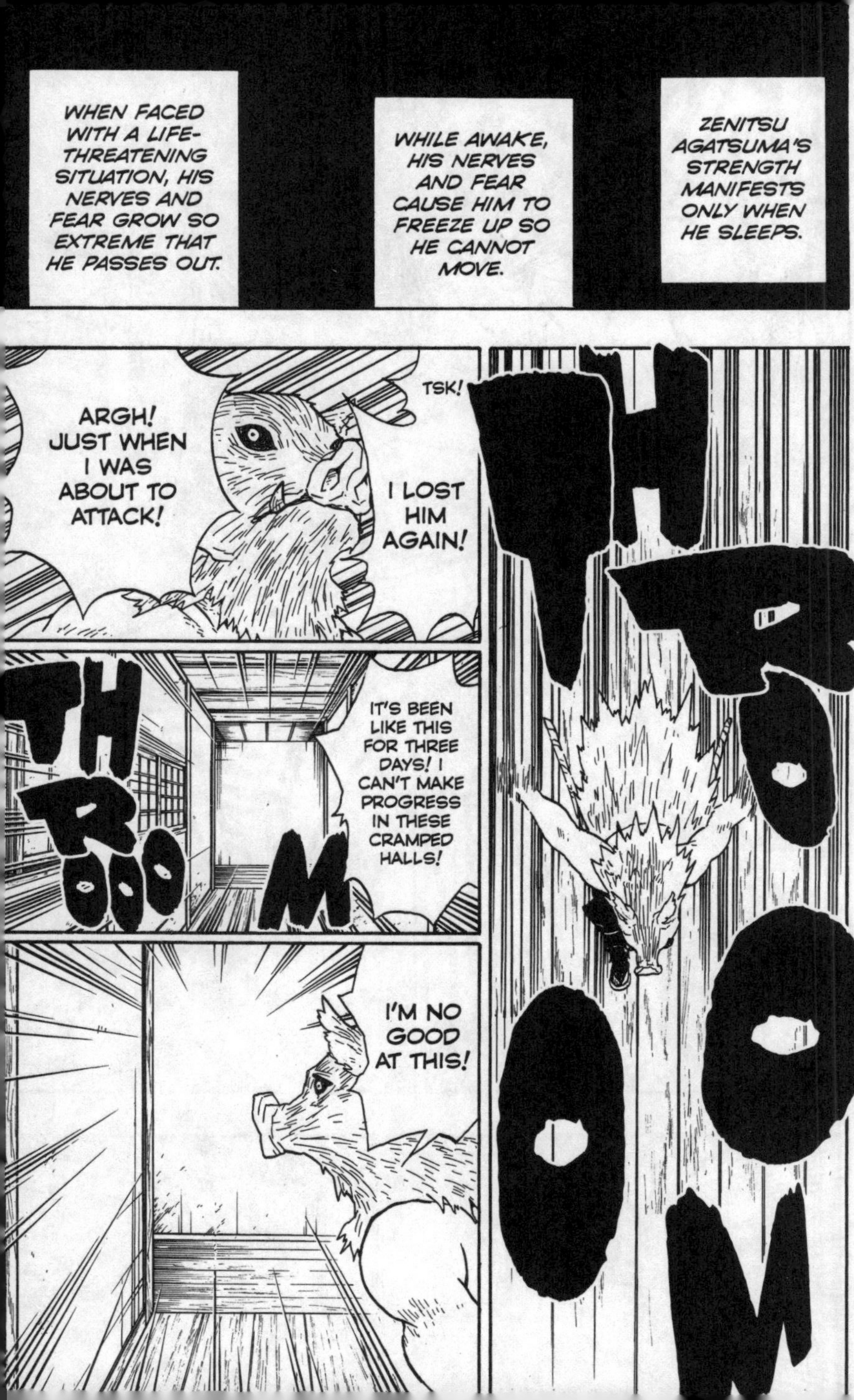
ZENITSU AGATSUMA'S STRENGTH MANIFESTS ONLY WHEN HE SLEEPS.
WHILE AWAKE, HIS NERVES AND FEAR CAUSE HIM TO FREEZE UP SO HE CANNOT MOVE.
WHEN FACED WITH A LIFE-THREATENING SITUATION, HIS NERVES AND FEAR GROW SO EXTREME THAT HE PASSES OUT.
THROOOM
TSK!
I LOST HIM AGAIN!
ARGH! JUST WHEN I WAS ABOUT TO ATTACK!
IT'S BEEN LIKE THIS FOR THREE DAYS! I CAN'T MAKE PROGRESS IN THESE CRAMPED HALLS!
THROOOM
I'M NO GOOD AT THIS!

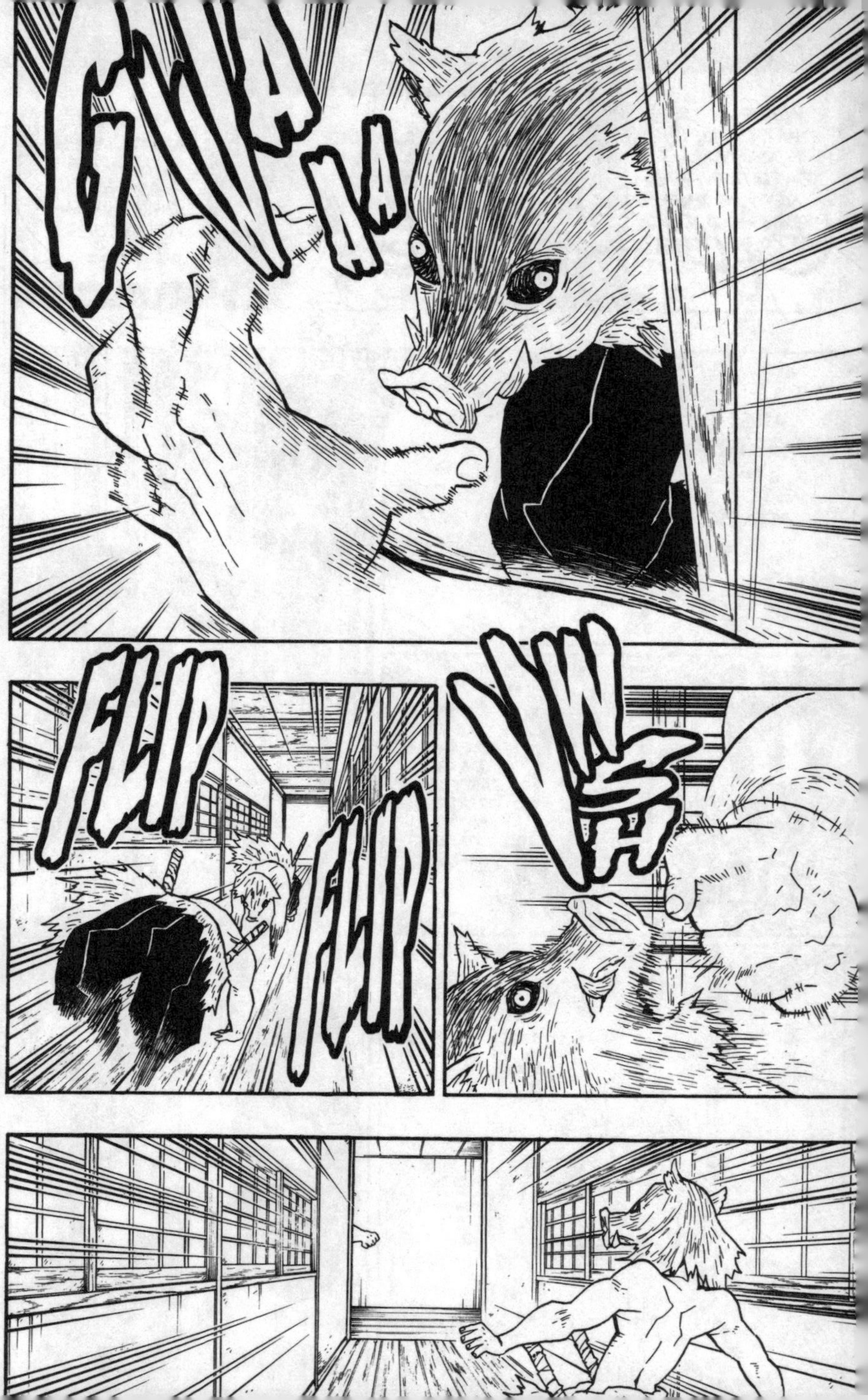
GWAAA
WSH
FLIP
FLIP

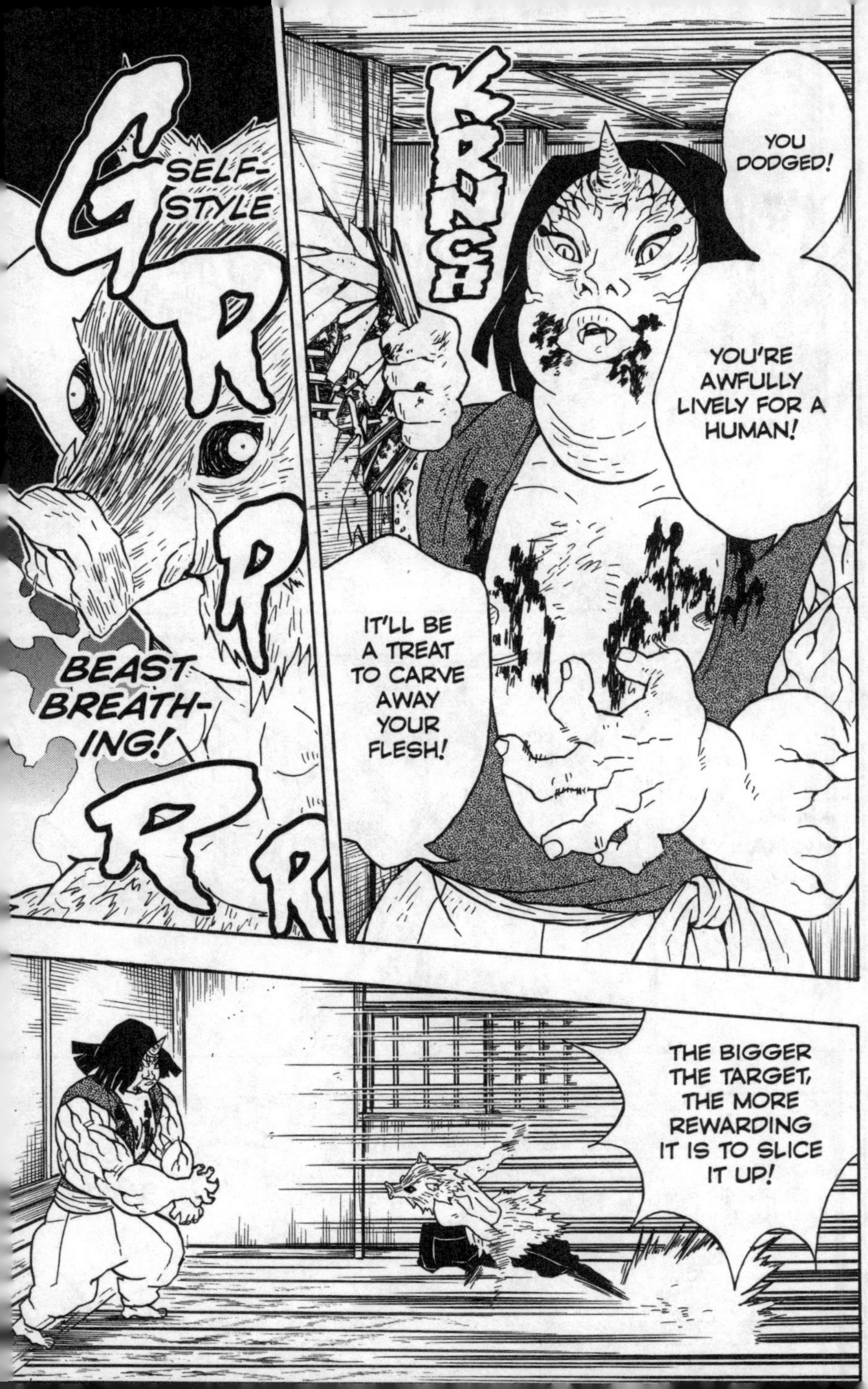
YOU DODGED!
KRNCH
YOU'RE AWFULLY LIVELY FOR A HUMAN!
IT'LL BE A TREAT TO CARVE AWAY YOUR FLESH!
SELF-STYLE
BEAST BREATHING!
GRRR
THE BIGGER THE TARGET, THE MORE REWARDING IT IS TO SLICE IT UP!

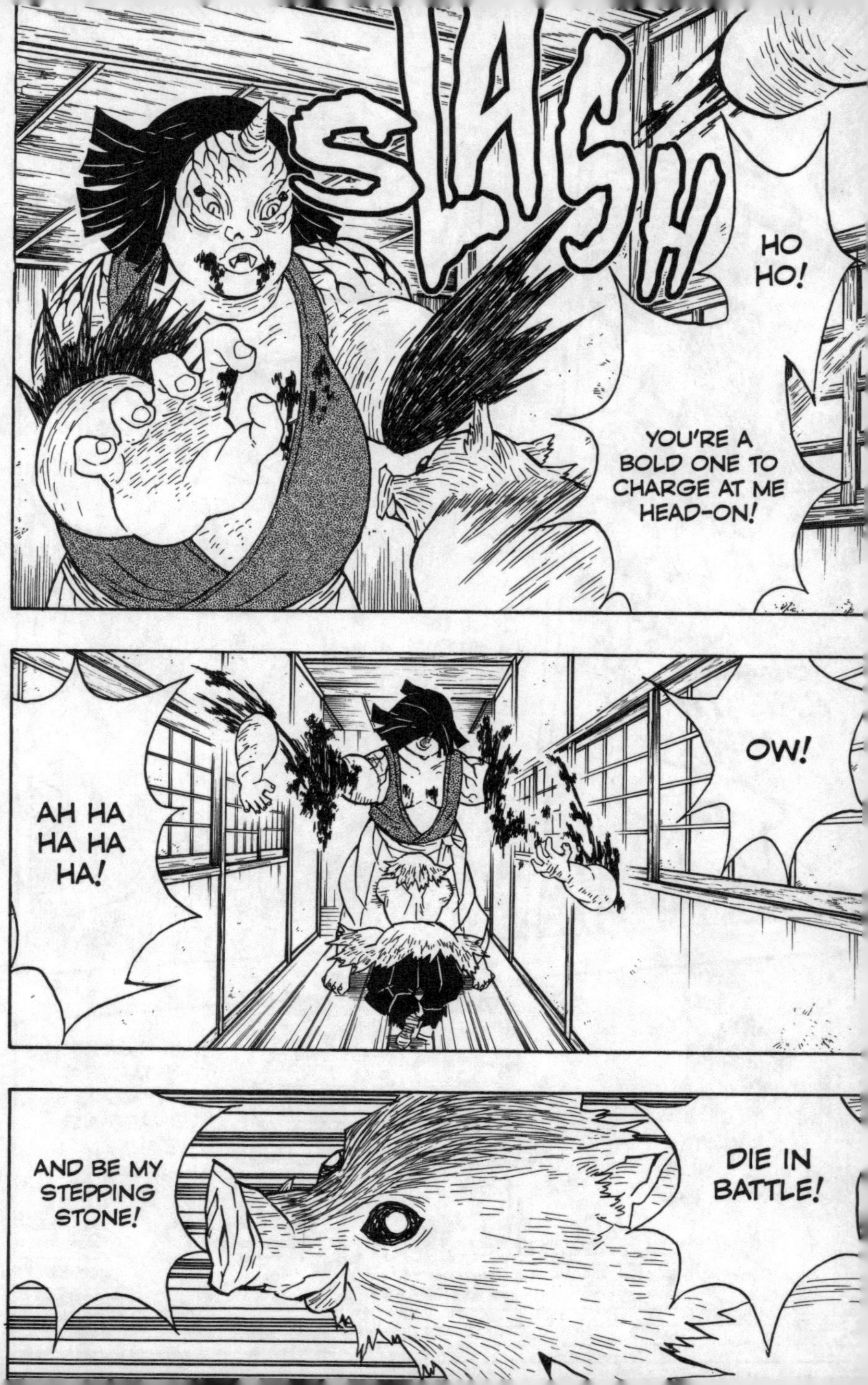
SLASH
HO HO!
YOU'RE A BOLD ONE TO CHARGE AT ME HEAD-ON!
OW!
AH HA HA HA HA!
DIE IN BATTLE!
AND BE MY STEPPING STONE!

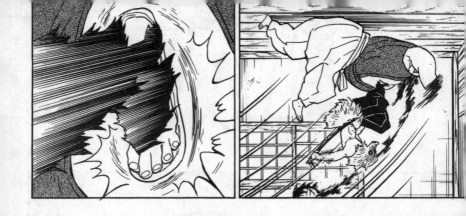

DEVOUR!

FANG THREE

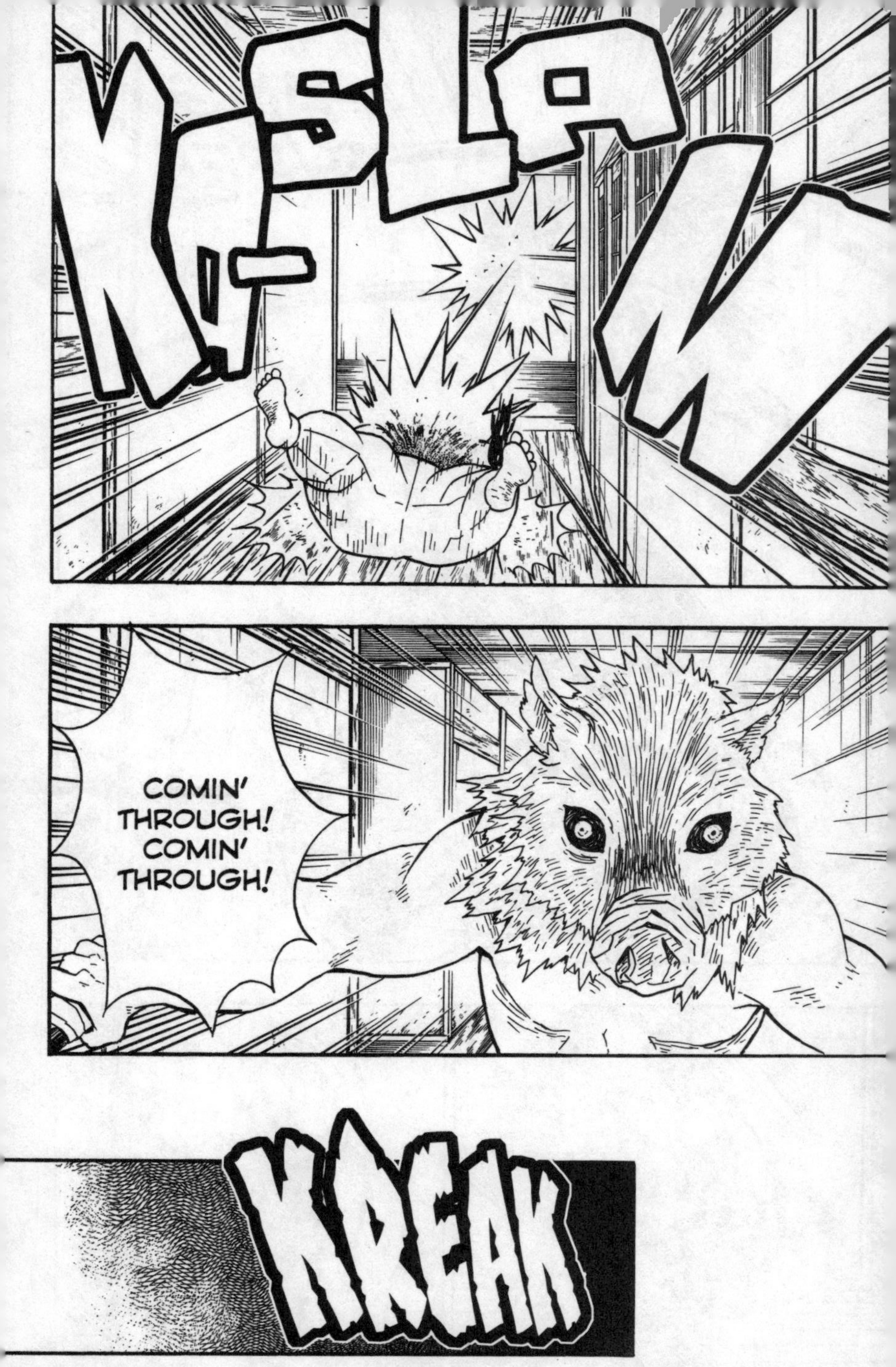
K-SLAM
COMIN' THROUGH! COMIN' THROUGH!
KREAK

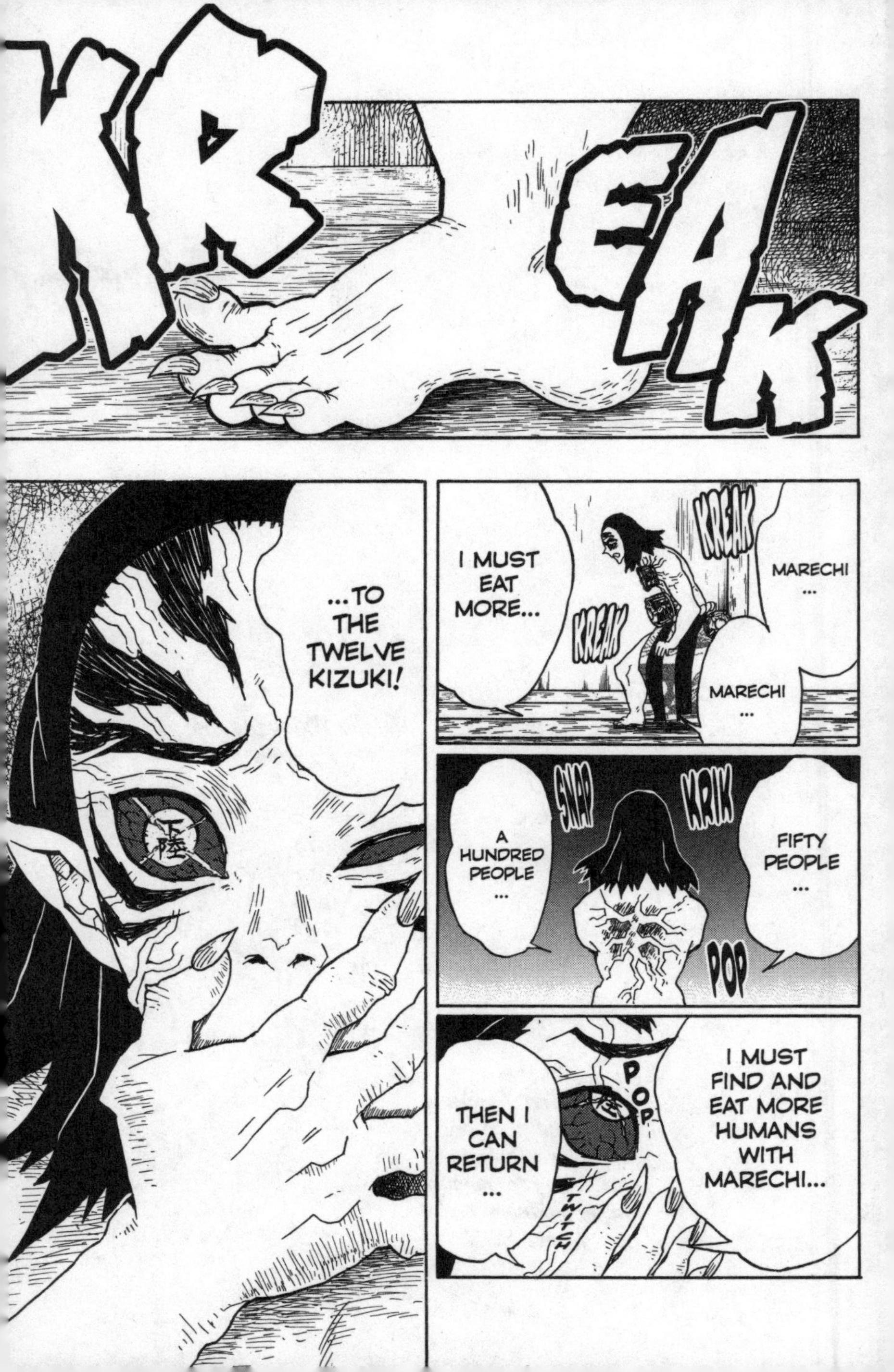
KREAK
MARECHI ...
KREAK
KREAK
MARECHI ...
I MUST EAT MORE...
FIFTY PEOPLE ...
KRIK
SNAP
A HUNDRED PEOPLE ...
POP
I MUST FIND AND EAT MORE HUMANS WITH MARECHI...
POP
TWITCH
THEN I CAN RETURN ...
...TO THE TWELVE KIZUKI!
下陸

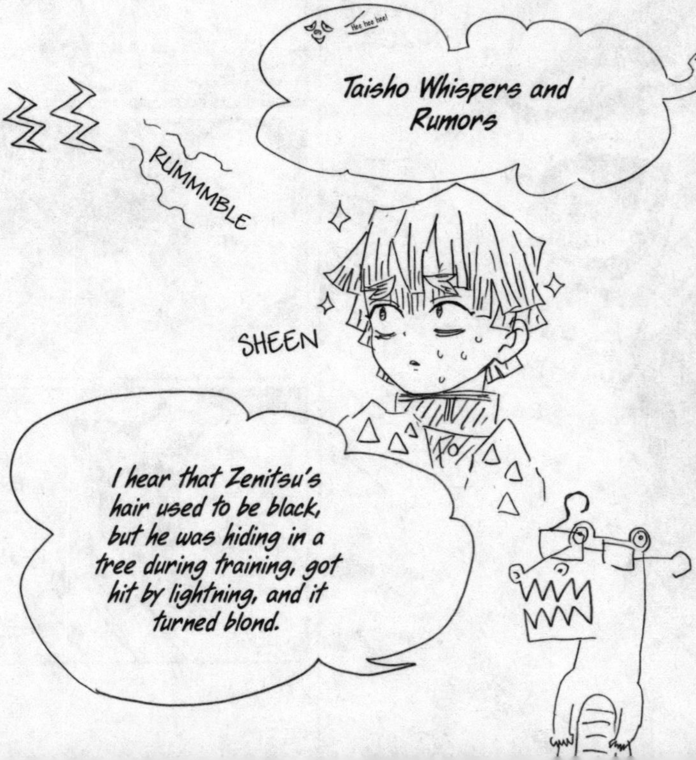

Hee hee hee!
Taisho Whispers and Rumors
RUMMMBLE
SHEEN
I hear that Zenitsu's hair used to be black, but he was hiding in a tree during training, got hit by lightning, and it turned blond.

CHAPTER 24: FORMER MEMBER OF THE TWELVE KIZUKI

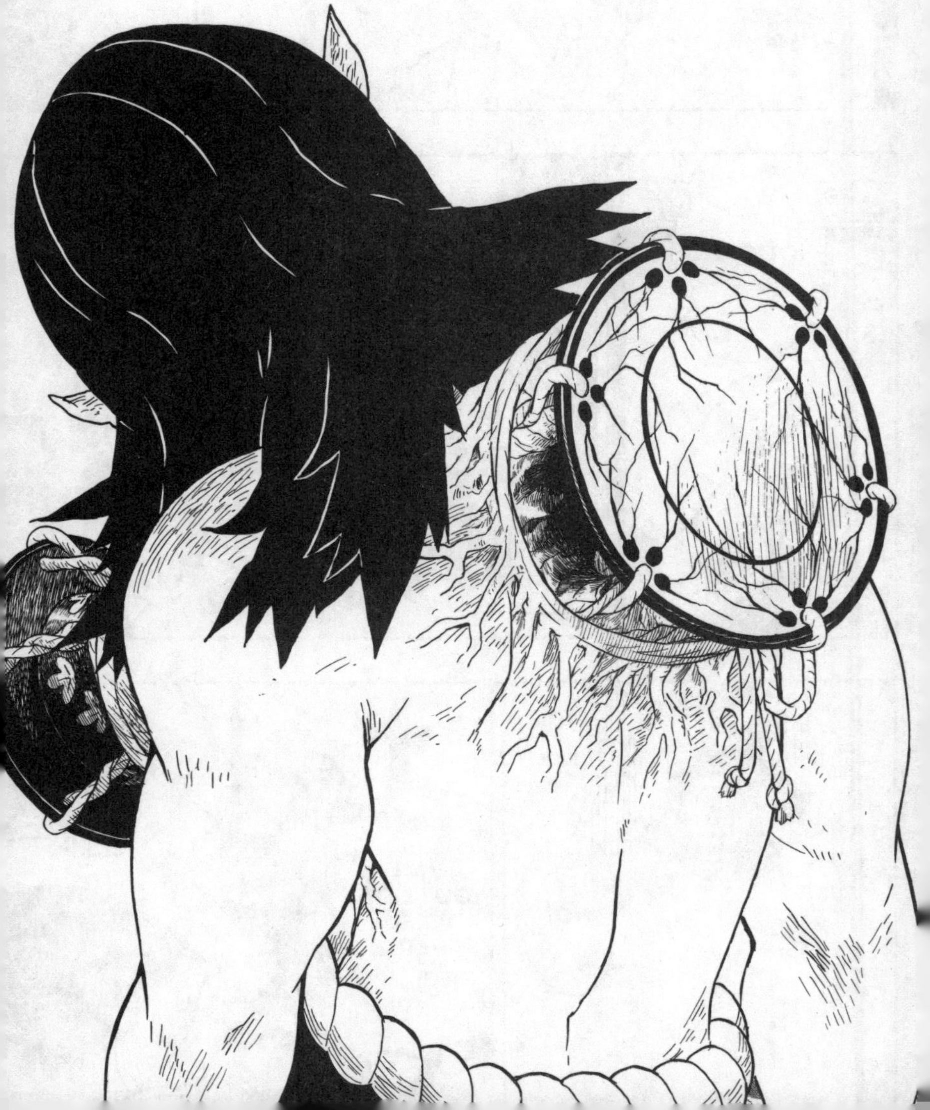

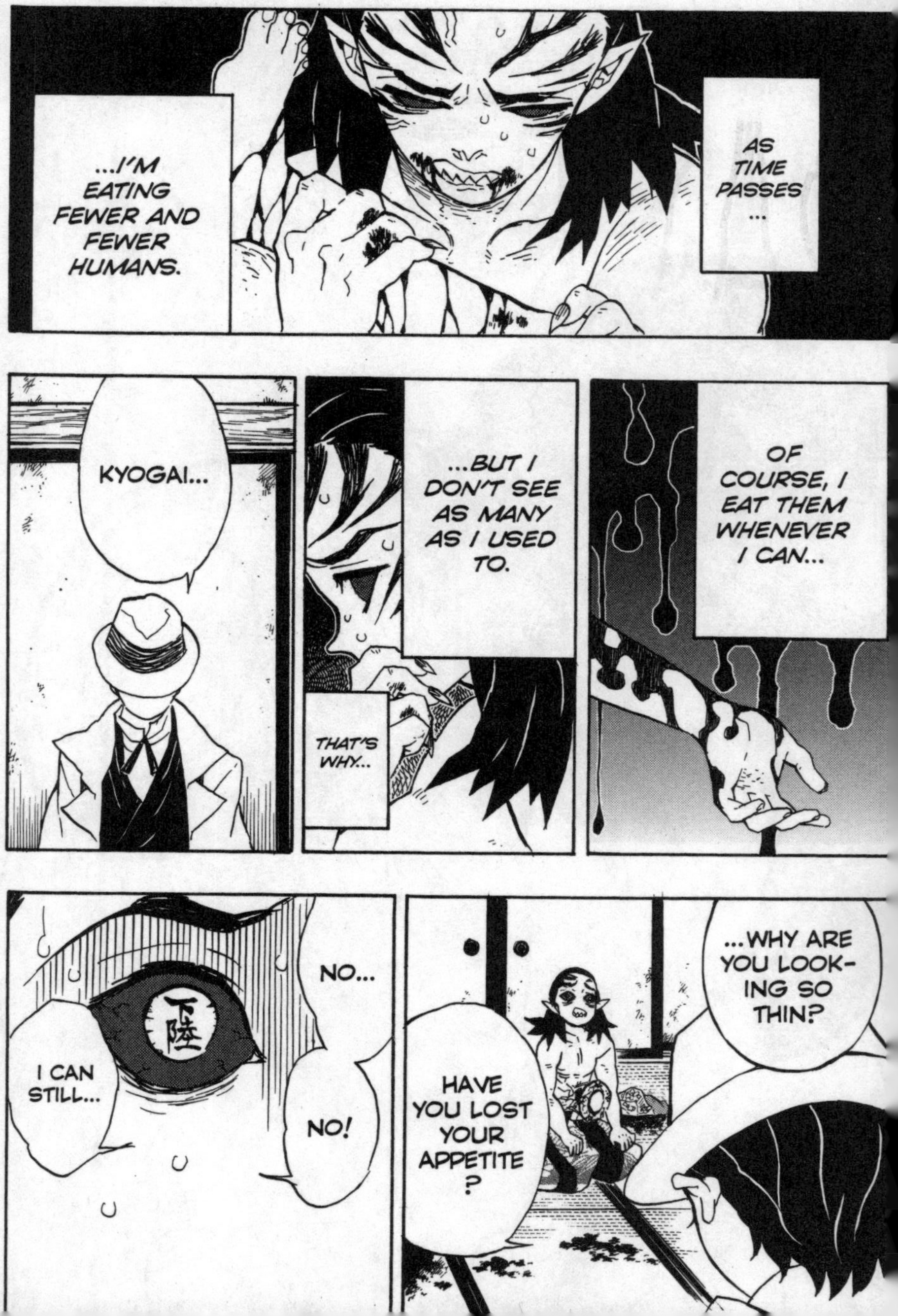
AS TIME PASSES ...
...I'M EATING FEWER AND FEWER HUMANS.
OF COURSE, I EAT THEM WHENEVER I CAN...
...BUT I DON'T SEE AS MANY AS I USED TO.
THAT'S WHY...
KYOGAI...
...WHY ARE YOU LOOKING-ING SO THIN?
HAVE YOU LOST YOUR APPETITE?
NO...
NO!
下陸
I CAN STILL...

SLASH
GYAH!
...!
P-PLEASE! JUST WAIT A LITTLE LONGER...
NO, THAT'S ENOUGH.
YOU'VE SHOWN ME YOUR LIMITS.
I'M STRIPPING YOU OF YOUR NUMBER!

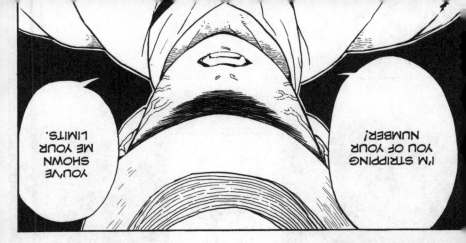

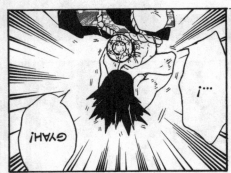

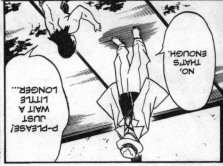

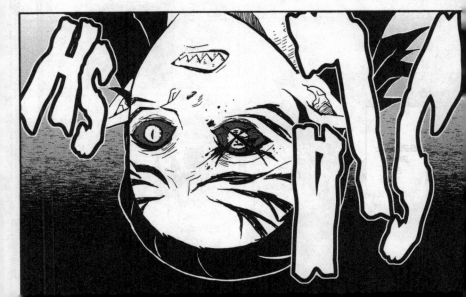

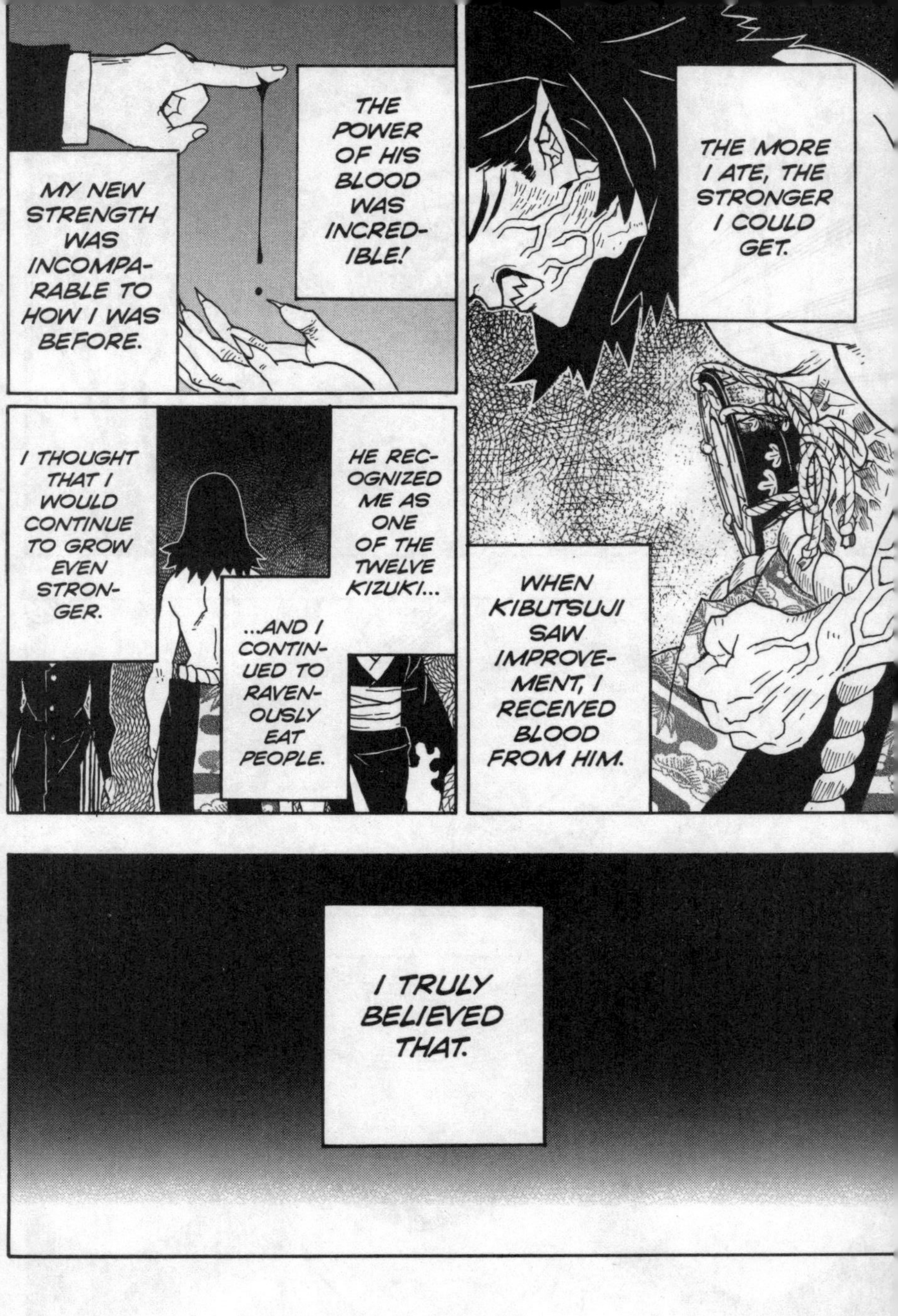
THE MORE I ATE, THE STRONGER I COULD GET.
WHEN KIBUTSUJI SAW IMPROVEMENT, I RECEIVED BLOOD FROM HIM.
THE POWER OF HIS BLOOD WAS INCREDIBLE!
MY NEW STRENGTH WAS INCOMPARABLE TO HOW I WAS BEFORE.
HE RECOGNIZED ME AS ONE OF THE TWELVE KIZUKI...
...AND I CONTINUED TO RAVENOUSLY EAT PEOPLE.
I THOUGHT THAT I WOULD CONTINUE TO GROW EVEN STRONGER.
I TRULY BELIEVED THAT.

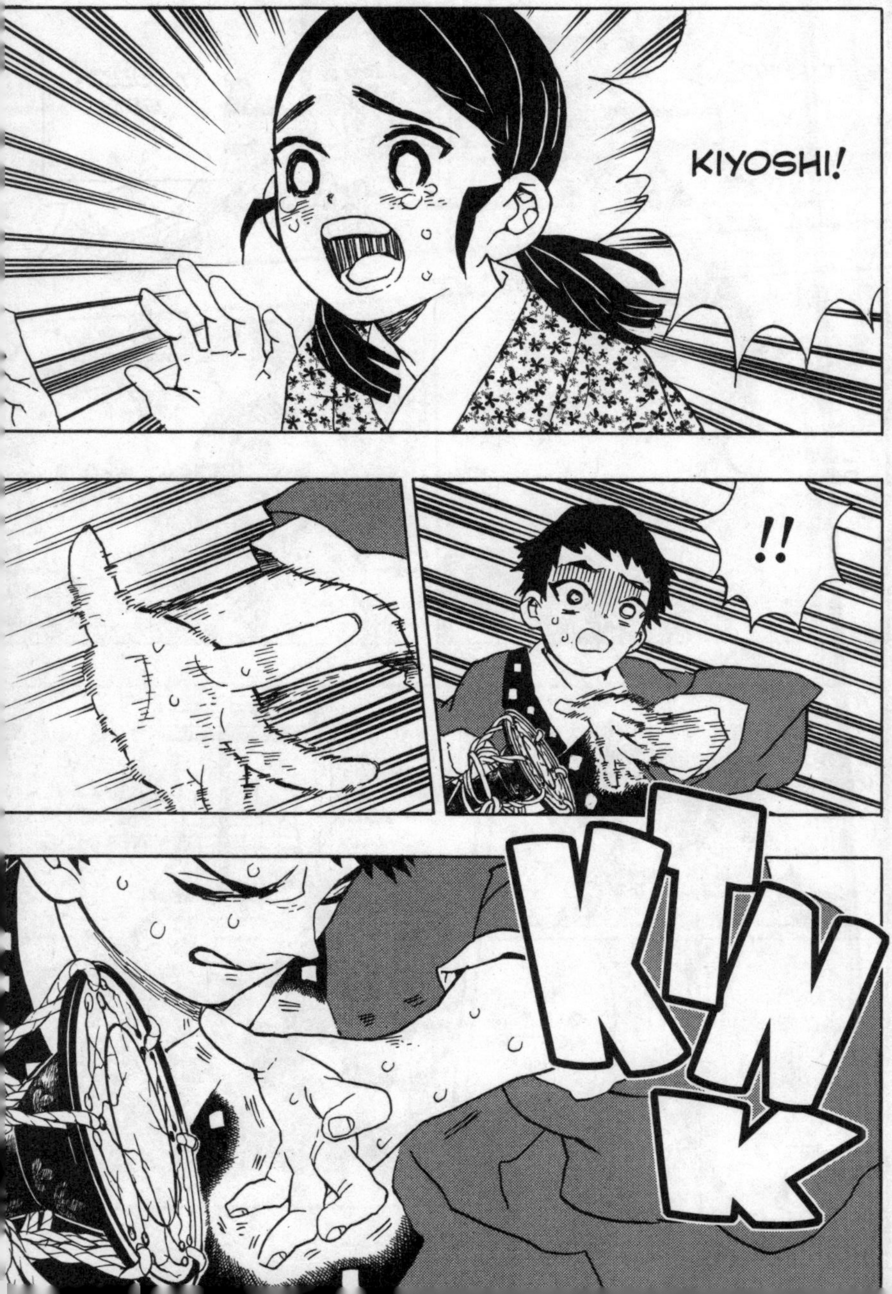
KIYOSHI!
!!
KLINK

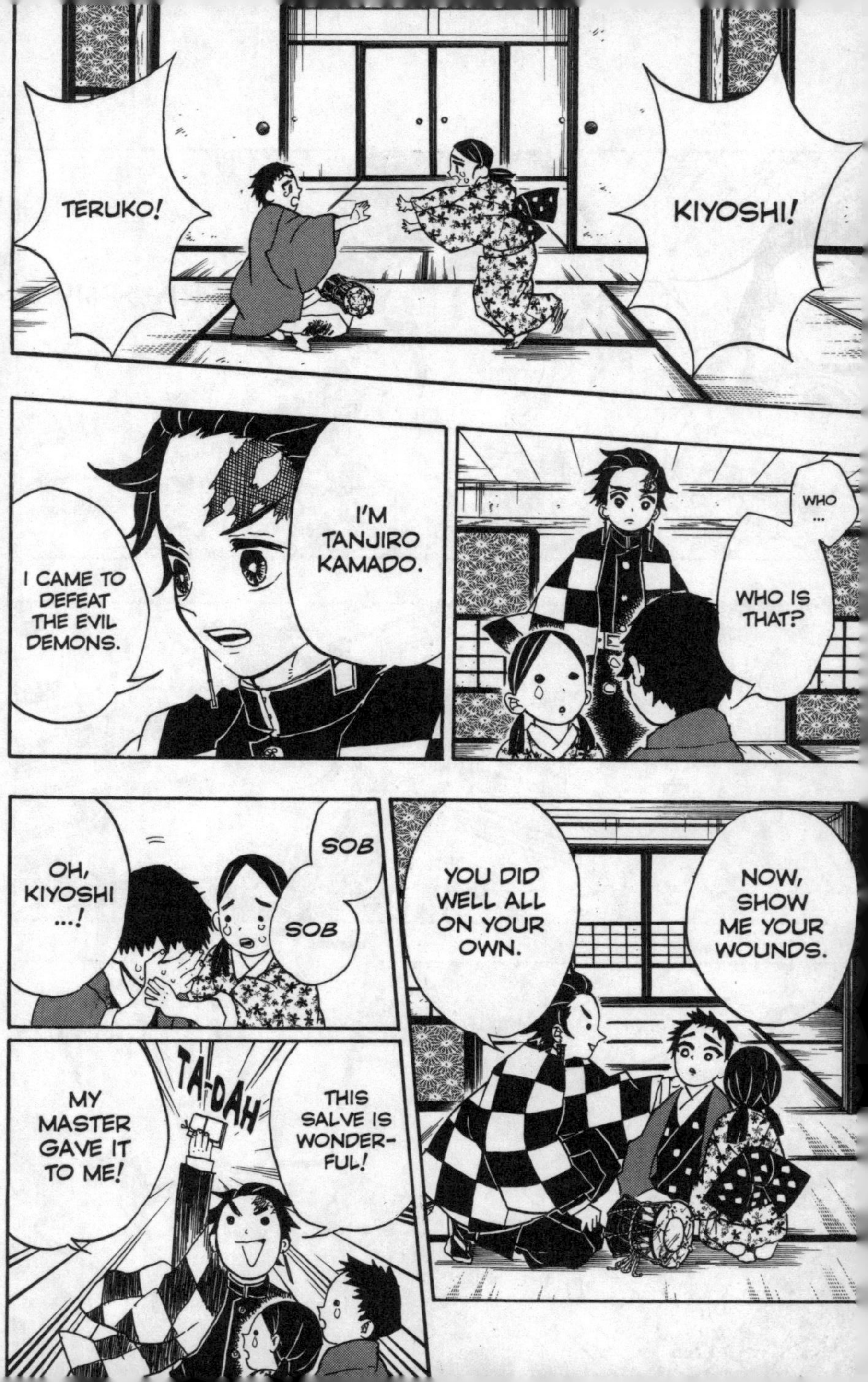
KIYOSHI!
TERUKO!
WHO ...
WHO IS THAT?
I'M TANJIRO KAMADO.
I CAME TO DEFEAT THE EVIL DEMONS.
NOW, SHOW ME YOUR WOUNDS.
YOU DID WELL ALL ON YOUR OWN.
SOB
SOB
OH, KIYOSHI ...!
TA-DAH
THIS SALVE IS WONDER-FUL!
MY MASTER GAVE IT TO ME!

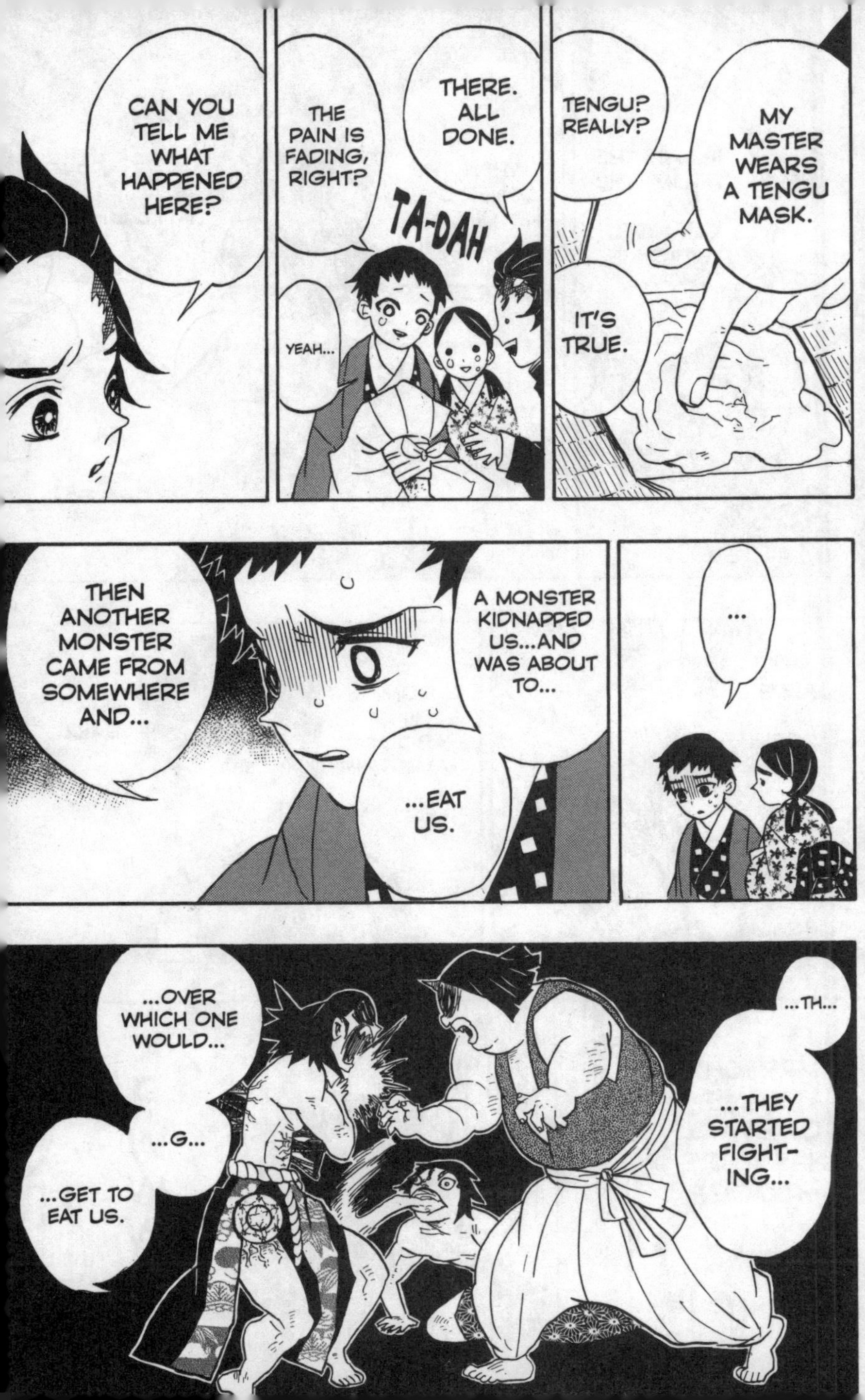
MY MASTER WEARS A TENGU MASK.
IT'S TRUE.
TENGU? REALLY?
THERE. ALL DONE.
TA-DAH
THE PAIN IS FADING, RIGHT?
YEAH...
CAN YOU TELL ME WHAT HAPPENED HERE?
...
A MONSTER KIDNAPPED US...AND WAS ABOUT TO...
...EAT US.
THEN ANOTHER MONSTER CAME FROM SOMEWHERE AND...
...TH...
...THEY STARTED FIGHT-ING...
...OVER WHICH ONE WOULD...
...G...
...GET TO EAT US.

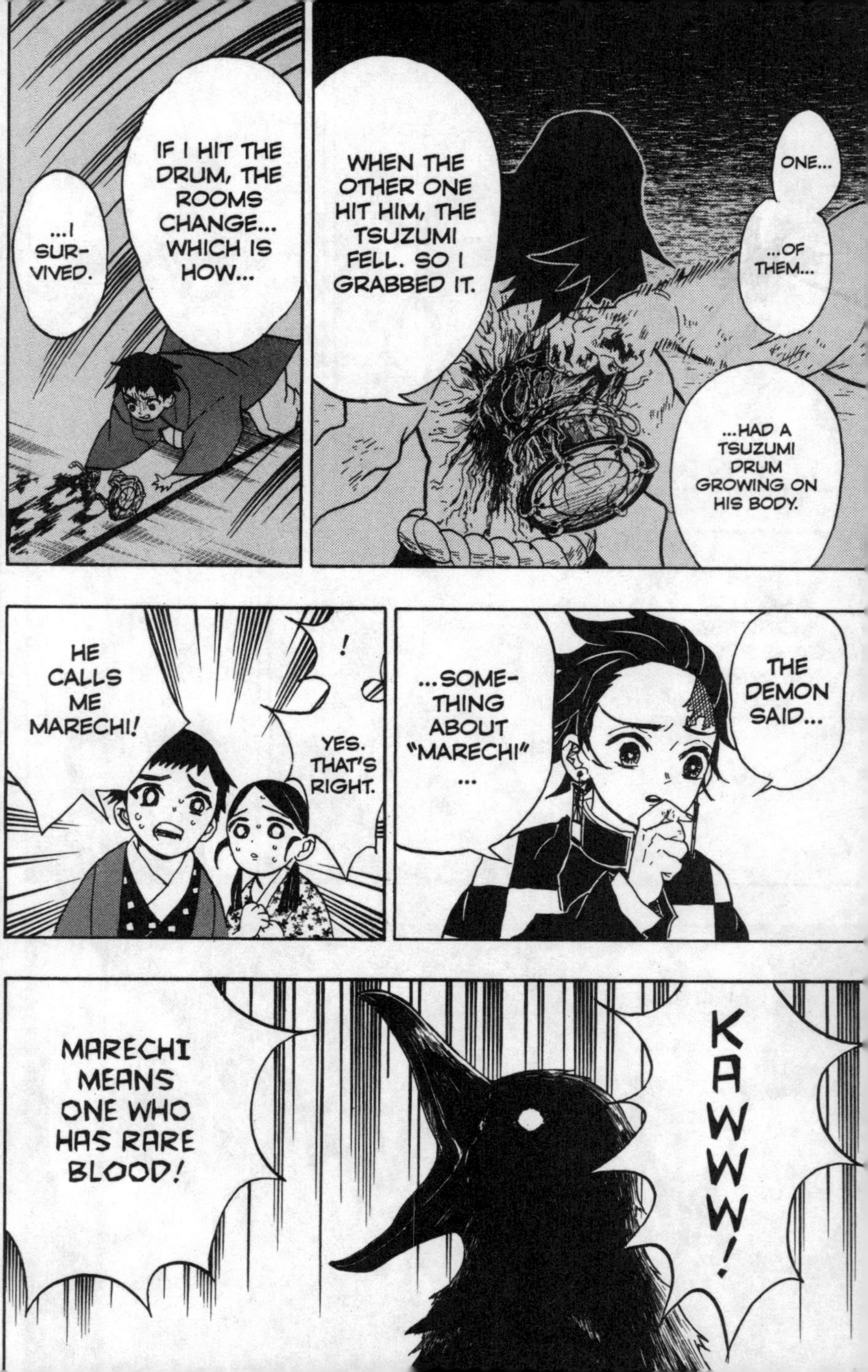
ONE...
...OF THEM...
...HAD A TSUZUMI DRUM GROWING ON HIS BODY.
WHEN THE OTHER ONE HIT HIM, THE TSUZUMI FELL. SO I GRABBED IT.
IF I HIT THE DRUM, THE ROOMS CHANGE... WHICH IS HOW...
...I SURVIVED.
THE DEMON SAID...
...SOMETHING ABOUT "MARECHI"...
!
YES. THAT'S RIGHT.
HE CALLS ME MARECHI!
KAWWW!
MARECHI MEANS ONE WHO HAS RARE BLOOD!

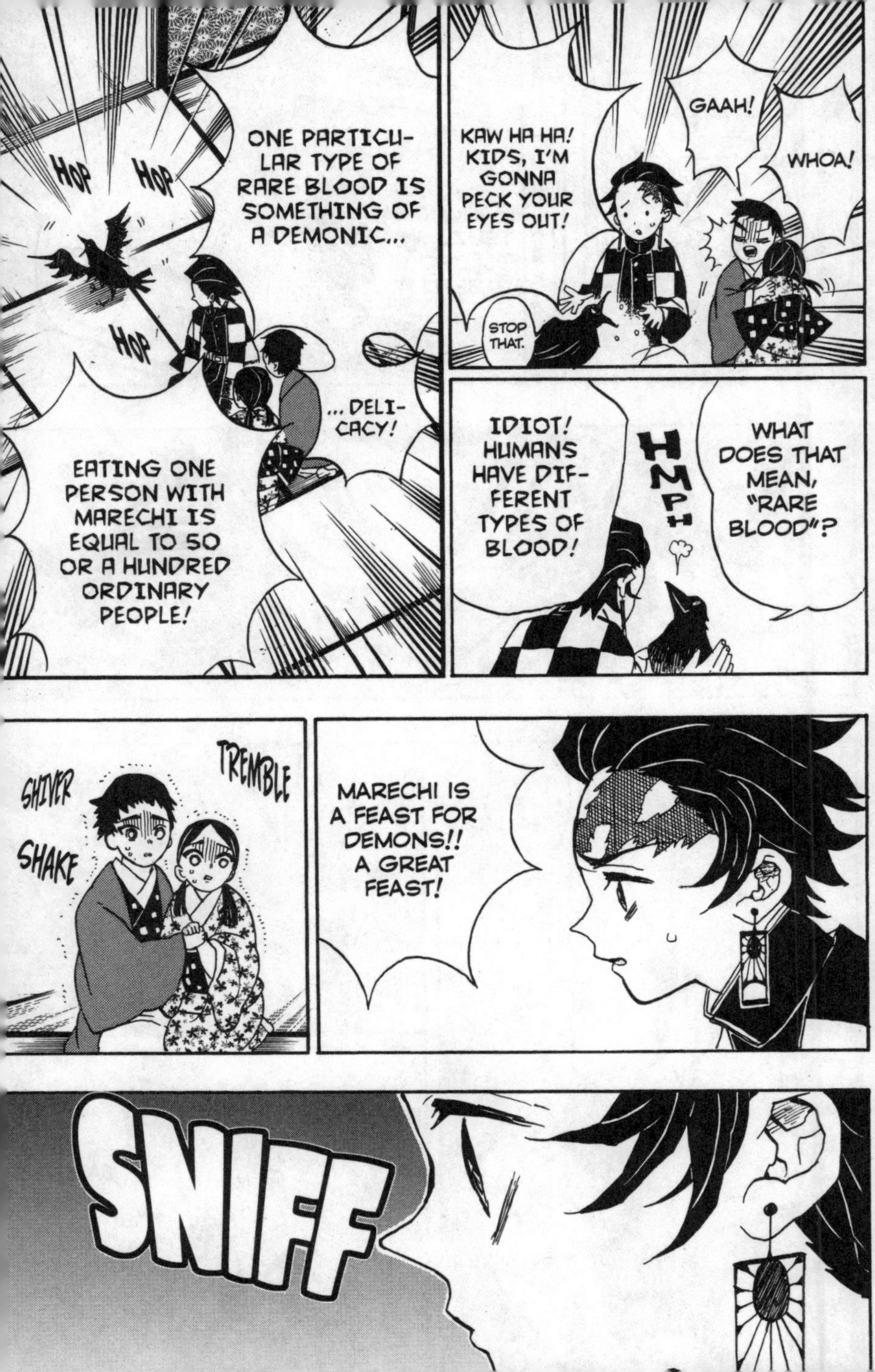
GAAH!
WHOA!
KAW HA HA! KIDS, I'M GONNA PECK YOUR EYES OUT!
STOP THAT.
WHAT DOES THAT MEAN, "RARE BLOOD"?
HMPH
IDIOT! HUMANS HAVE DIF-FERENT TYPES OF BLOOD!
HOP
HOP
ONE PARTICU-LAR TYPE OF RARE BLOOD IS SOMETHING OF A DEMONIC...
HOP
...DELI-CACY!
EATING ONE PERSON WITH MARECHI IS EQUAL TO 50 OR A HUNDRED ORDINARY PEOPLE!
MARECHI IS A FEAST FOR DEMONS!! A GREAT FEAST!
TREMBLE
SHIVER
SHAKE
SNIFF

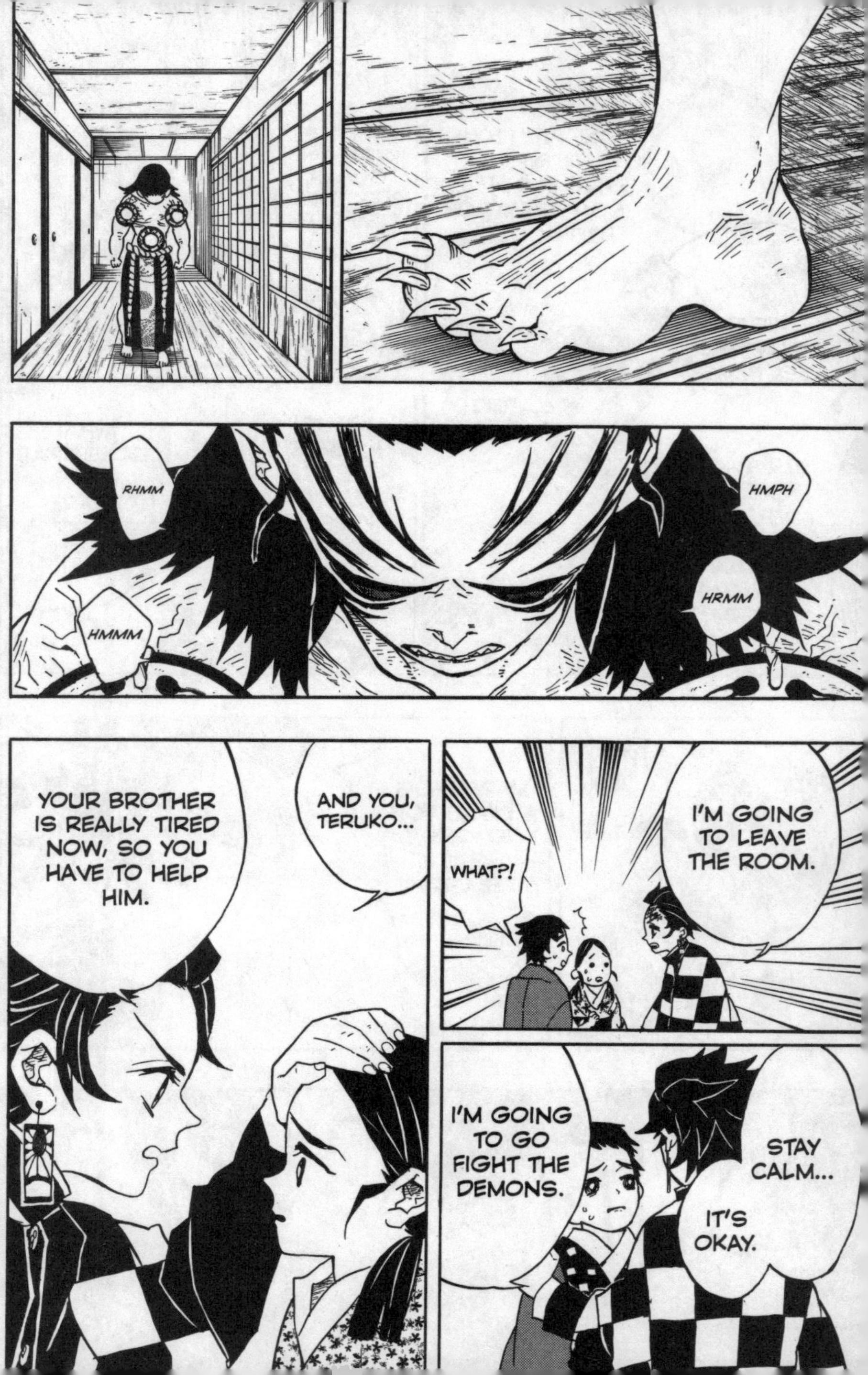
HMPH
HRMM
RHMM
HMMM
I'M GOING TO LEAVE THE ROOM.
WHAT?!
STAY CALM...
IT'S OKAY.
I'M GOING TO GO FIGHT THE DEMONS.
AND YOU, TERUKO...
YOUR BROTHER IS REALLY TIRED NOW, SO YOU HAVE TO HELP HIM.

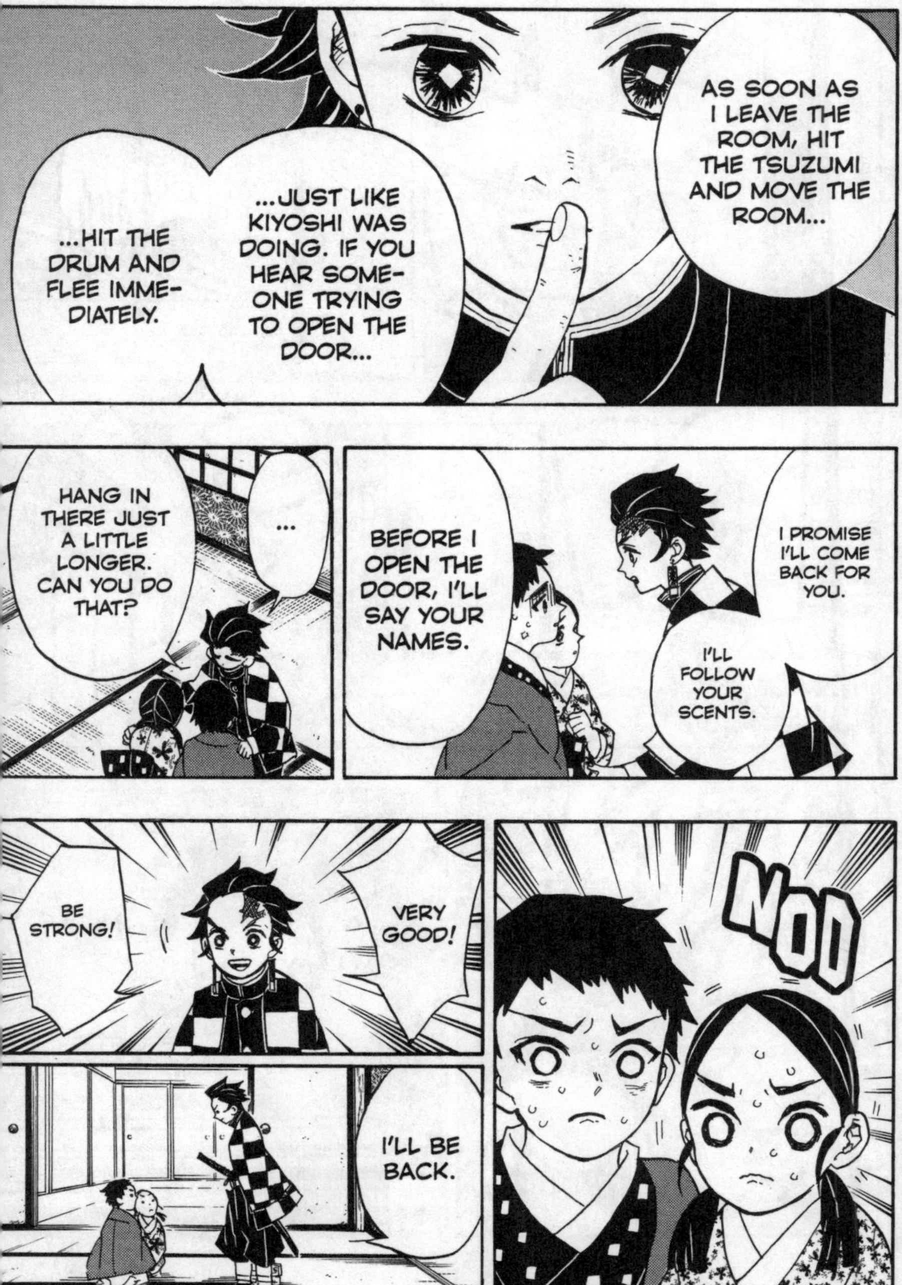
AS SOON AS I LEAVE THE ROOM, HIT THE TSUZUMI AND MOVE THE ROOM...
...JUST LIKE KIYOSHI WAS DOING. IF YOU HEAR SOME-ONE TRYING TO OPEN THE DOOR...
...HIT THE DRUM AND FLEE IMME-DIATELY.
I PROMISE I'LL COME BACK FOR YOU.
I'LL FOLLOW YOUR SCENTS.
BEFORE I OPEN THE DOOR, I'LL SAY YOUR NAMES.
...
HANG IN THERE JUST A LITTLE LONGER. CAN YOU DO THAT?
NOD
VERY GOOD!
BE STRONG!
I'LL BE BACK.

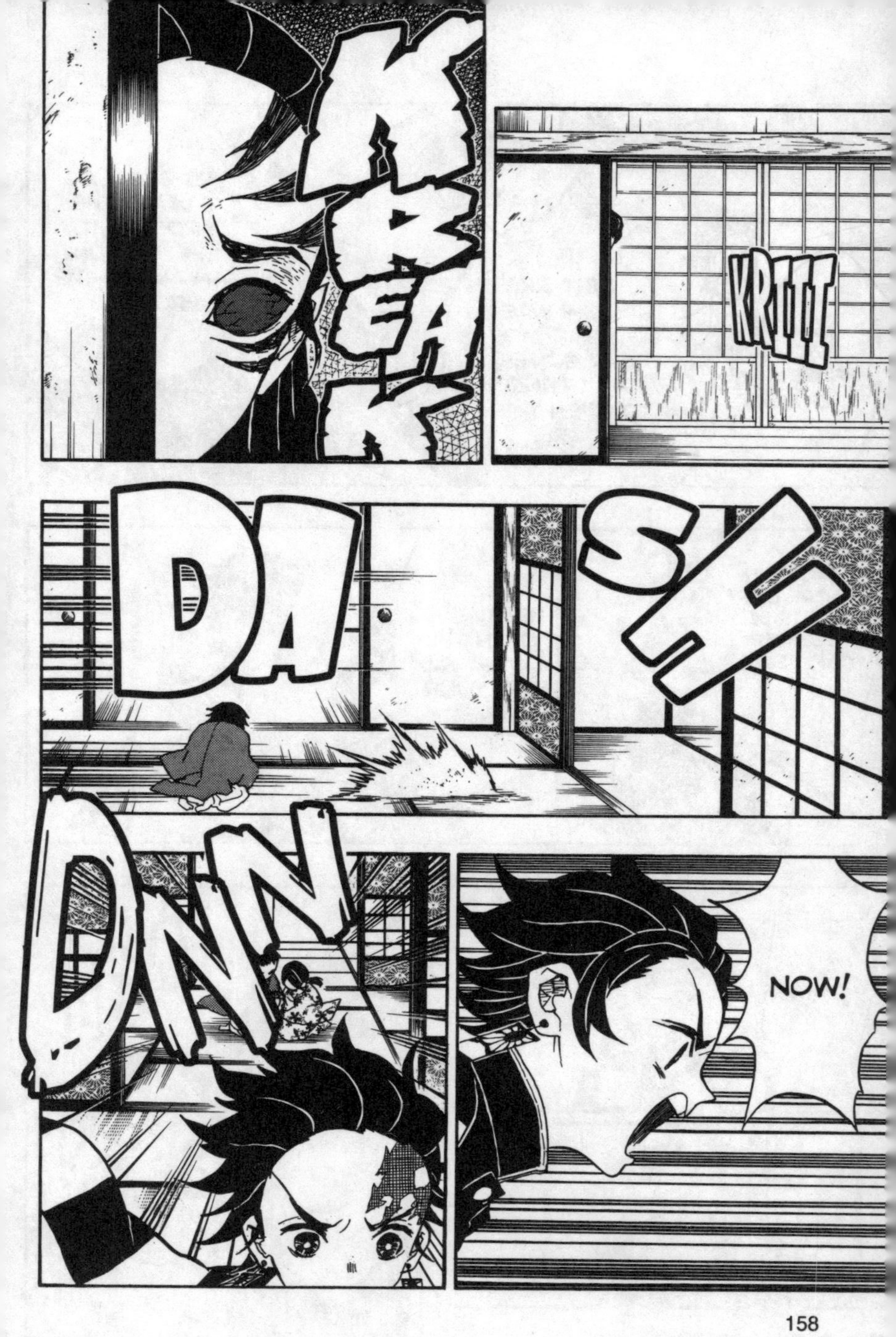
KRIII
KREAK
DASH
NOW!
DNN

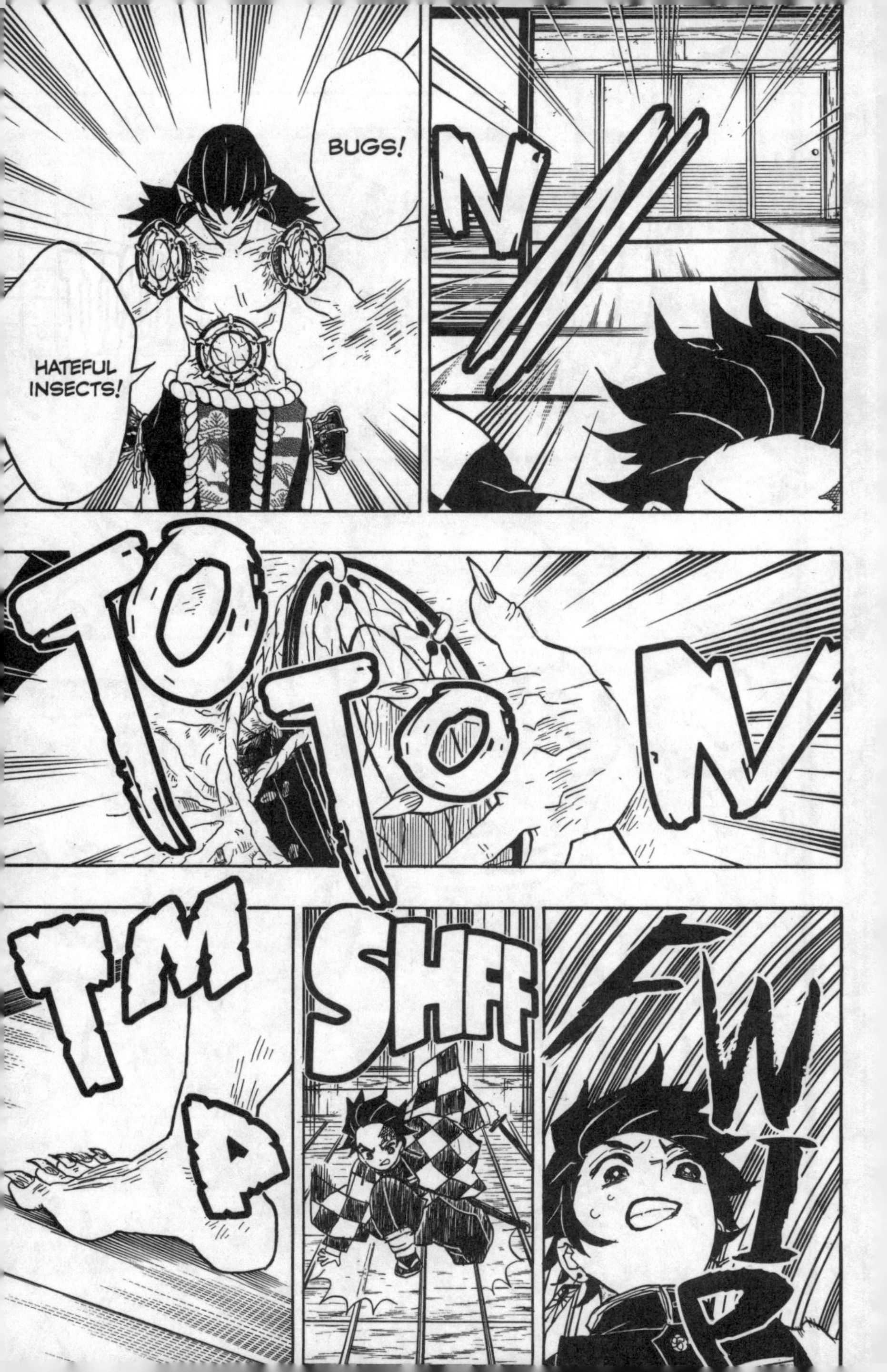
N
BUGS!
HATEFUL INSECTS!
TOTON
WIP
SHFF
TMP

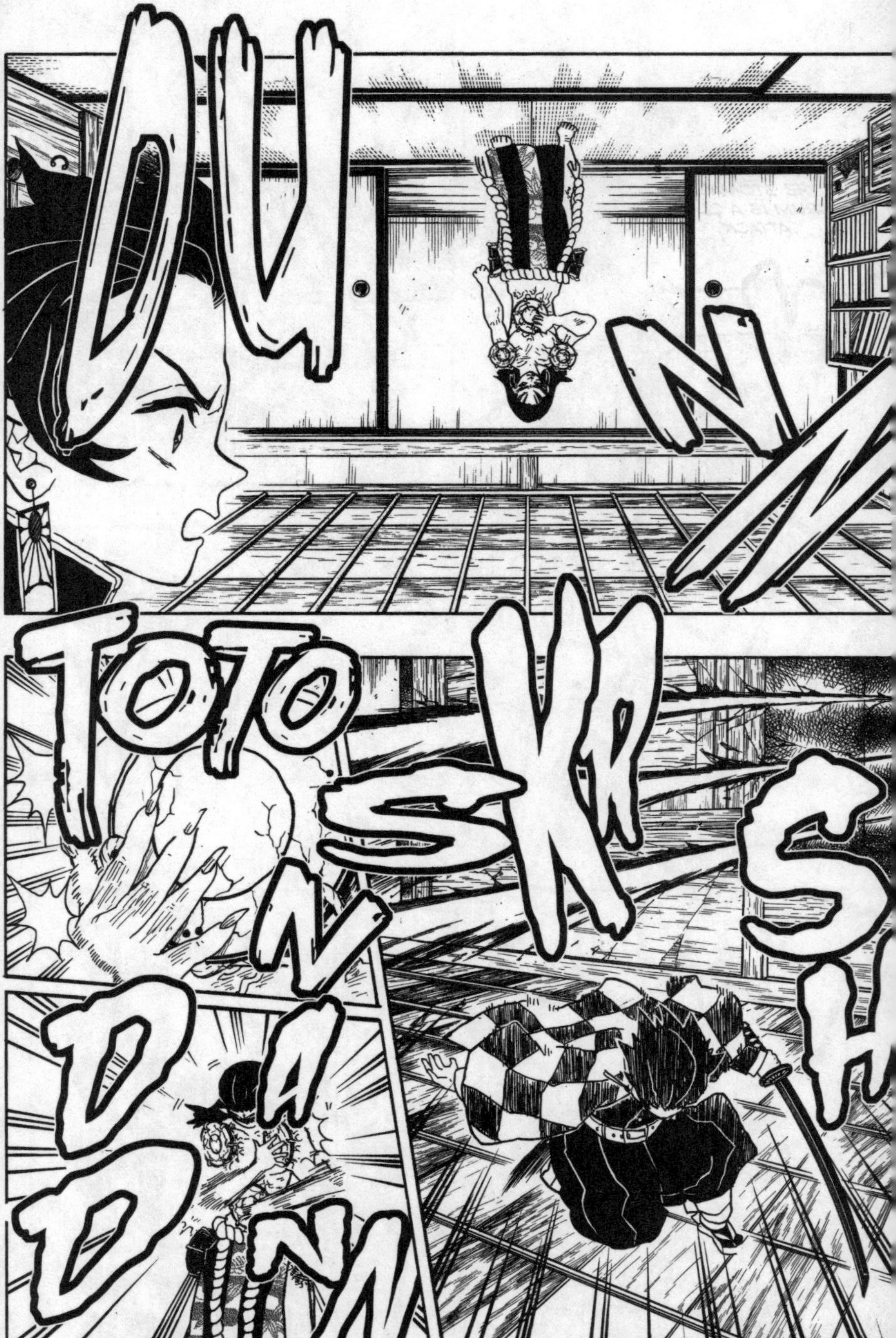
TOTON

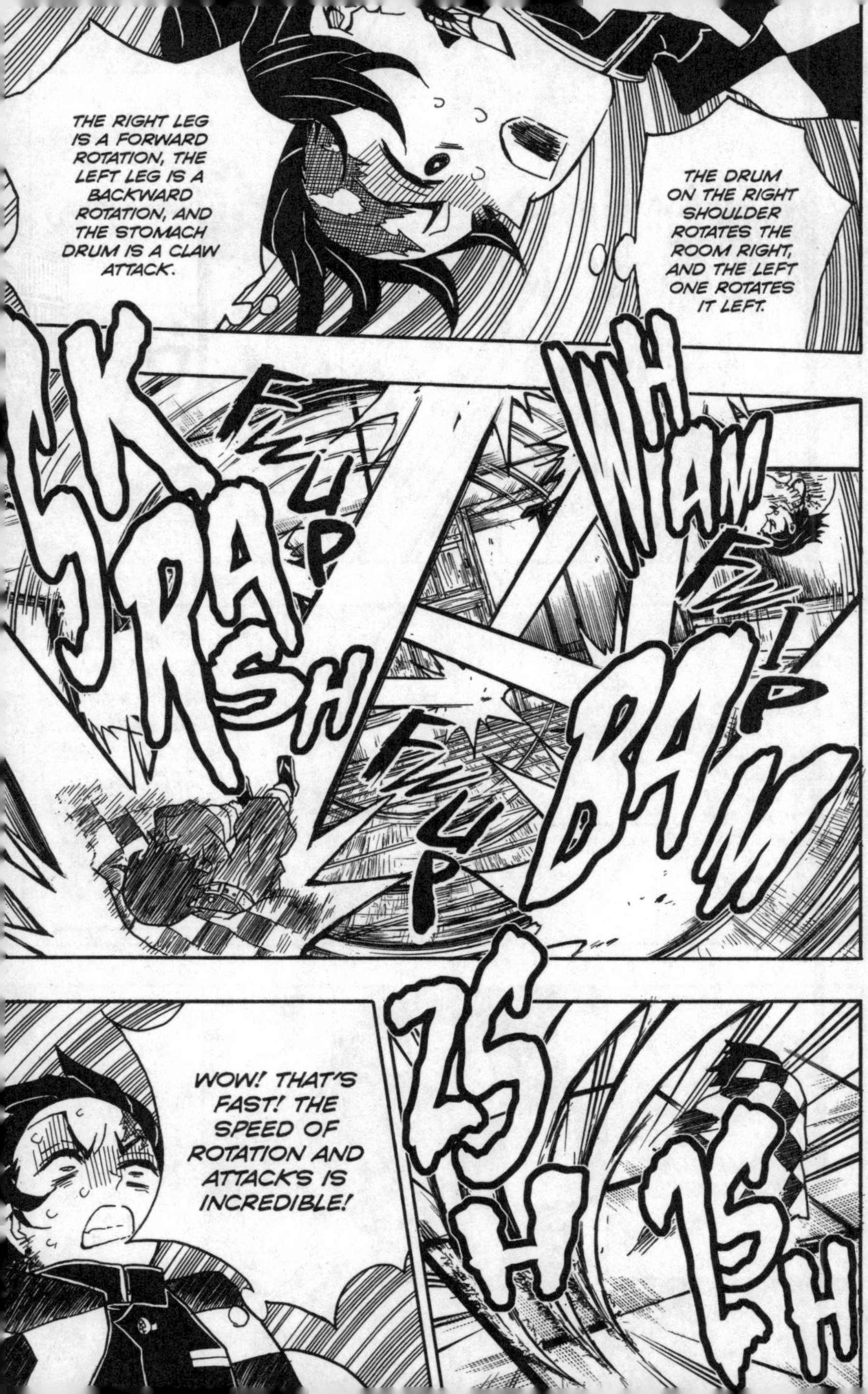
THE DRUM ON THE RIGHT SHOULDER ROTATES THE ROOM RIGHT, AND THE LEFT ONE ROTATES IT LEFT.
THE RIGHT LEG IS A FORWARD ROTATION, THE LEFT LEG IS A BACKWARD ROTATION, AND THE STOMACH DRUM IS A CLAW ATTACK.
WHAM
FWIP
BAM
FWUP
SKRASH
FWUP
ZSH
ZSH
WOW! THAT'S FAST! THE SPEED OF ROTATION AND ATTACKS IS INCREDIBLE!

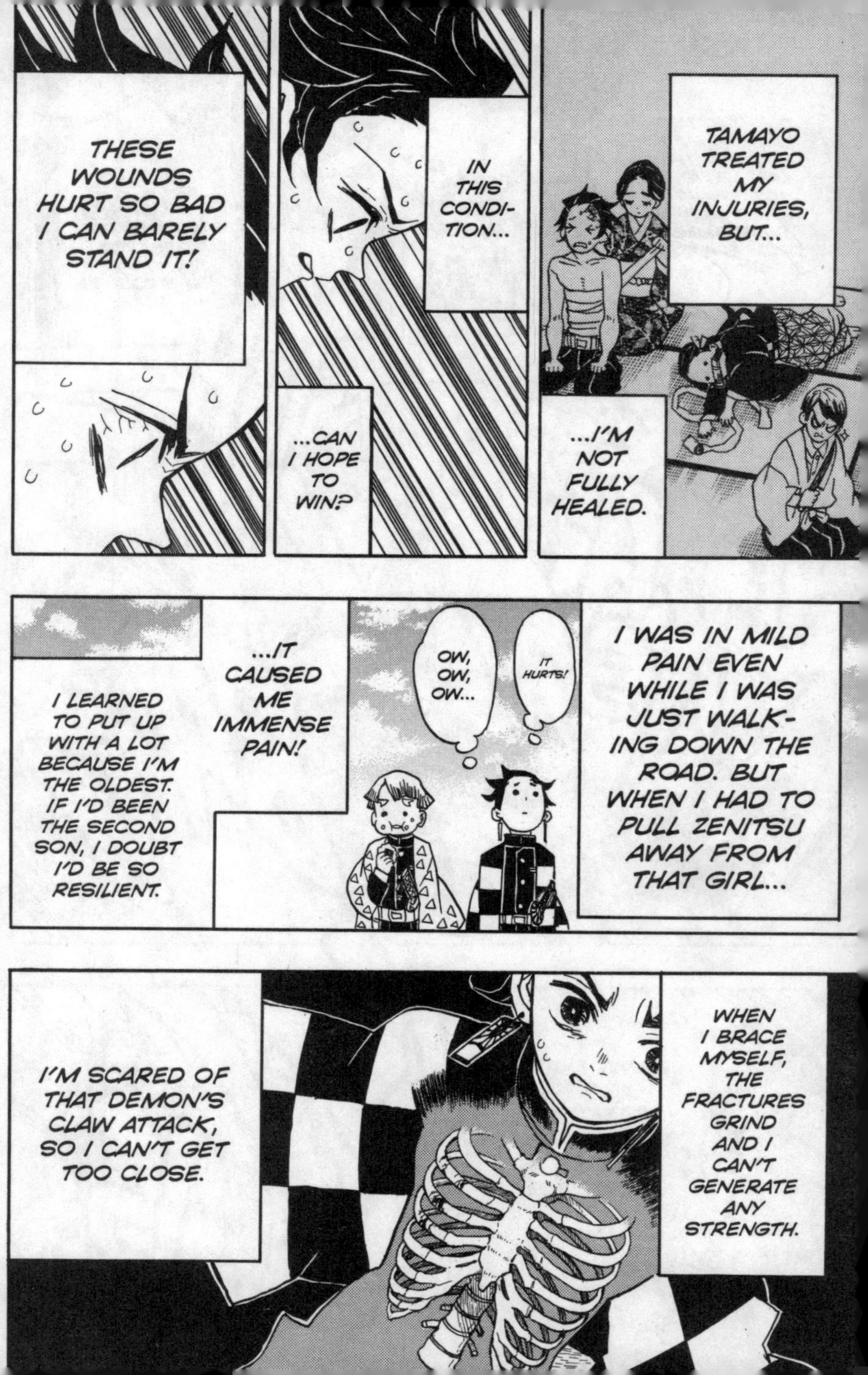
TAMAYO TREATED MY INJURIES, BUT...
...I'M NOT FULLY HEALED.
IN THIS CONDITION...
...CAN I HOPE TO WIN?
THESE WOUNDS HURT SO BAD I CAN BARELY STAND IT!
I WAS IN MILD PAIN EVEN WHILE I WAS JUST WALKING DOWN THE ROAD. BUT WHEN I HAD TO PULL ZENITSU AWAY FROM THAT GIRL...
IT HURTS!
OW, OW, OW...
...IT CAUSED ME IMMENSE PAIN!
I LEARNED TO PUT UP WITH A LOT BECAUSE I'M THE OLDEST. IF I'D BEEN THE SECOND SON, I DOUBT I'D BE SO RESILIENT.
WHEN I BRACE MYSELF, THE FRACTURES GRIND AND I CAN'T GENERATE ANY STRENGTH.
I'M SCARED OF THAT DEMON'S CLAW ATTACK, SO I CAN'T GET TOO CLOSE.

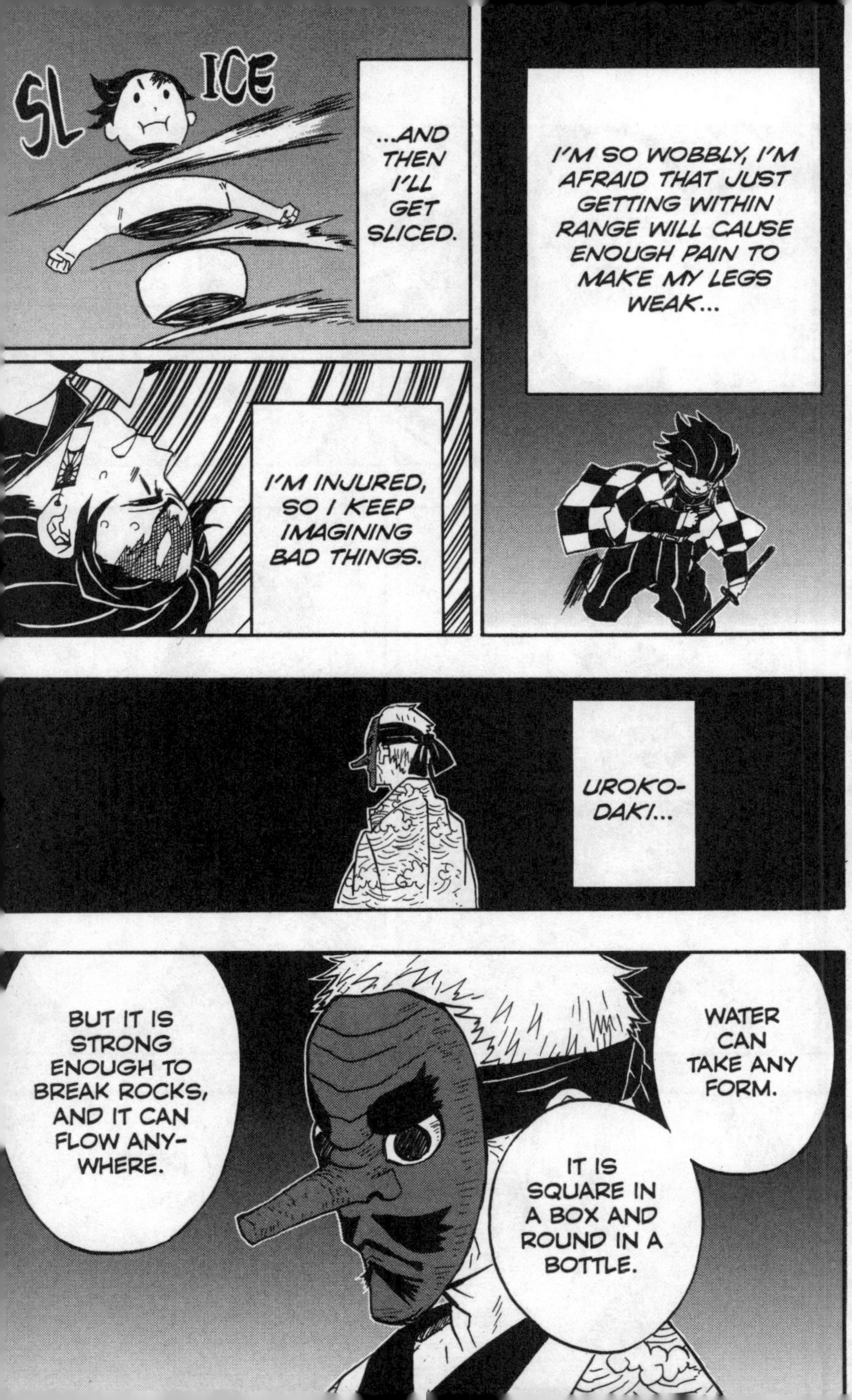
I'M SO WOBBLY, I'M AFRAID THAT JUST GETTING WITHIN RANGE WILL CAUSE ENOUGH PAIN TO MAKE MY LEGS WEAK...
...AND THEN I'LL GET SLICED.
SL ICE
I'M INJURED, SO I KEEP IMAGINING BAD THINGS.
UROKO-DAKI...
WATER CAN TAKE ANY FORM.
IT IS SQUARE IN A BOX AND ROUND IN A BOTTLE.
BUT IT IS STRONG ENOUGH TO BREAK ROCKS, AND IT CAN FLOW ANY-WHERE.

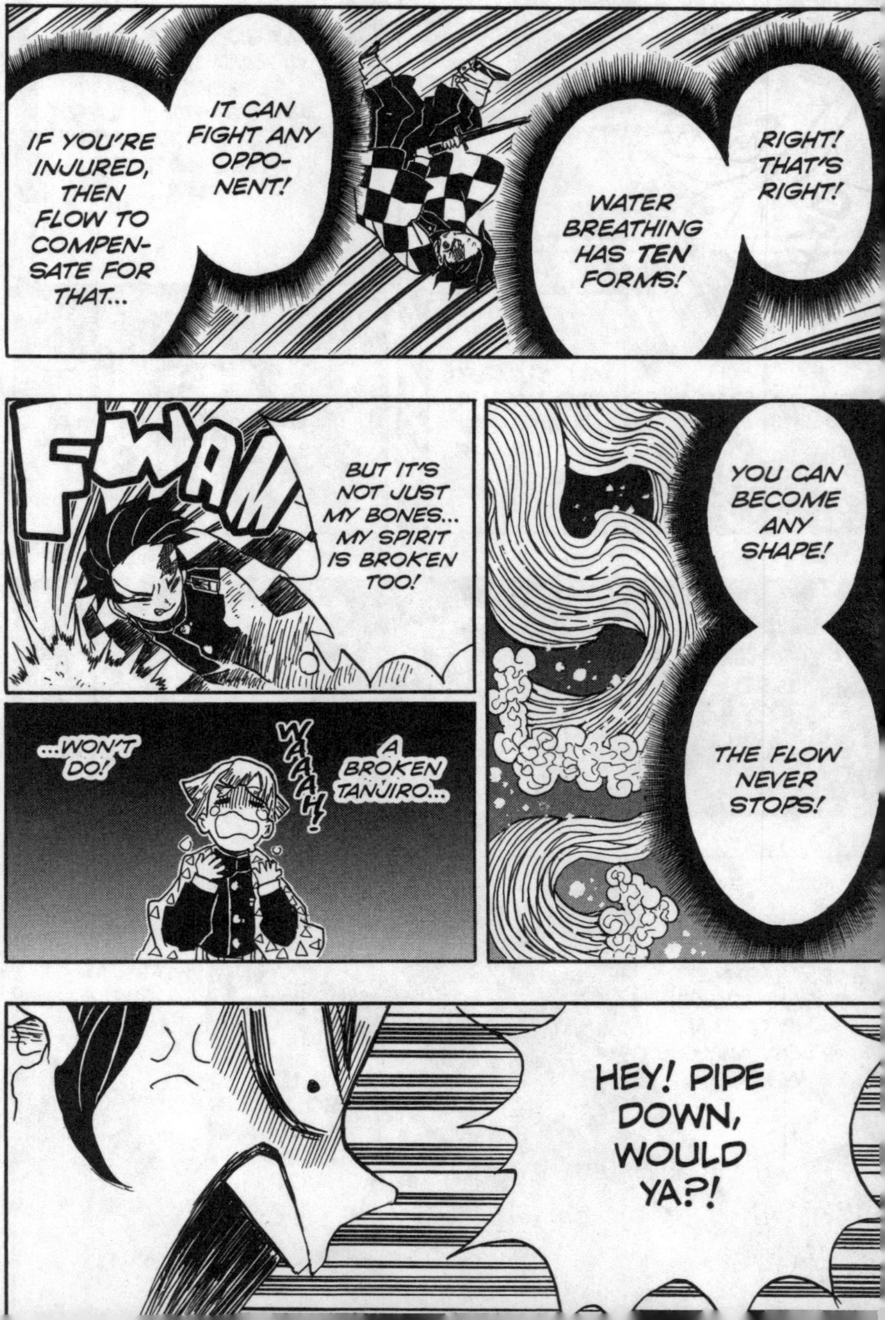
RIGHT! THAT'S RIGHT!
WATER BREATHING HAS TEN FORMS!
IT CAN FIGHT ANY OPPO-NENT!
IF YOU'RE INJURED, THEN FLOW TO COMPEN-SATE FOR THAT...
YOU CAN BECOME ANY SHAPE!
THE FLOW NEVER STOPS!
F-WAM
BUT IT'S NOT JUST MY BONES... MY SPIRIT IS BROKEN TOO!
A BROKEN TANJIRO...
WAAAAH!
...WON'T DO!
HEY! PIPE DOWN, WOULD YA?!

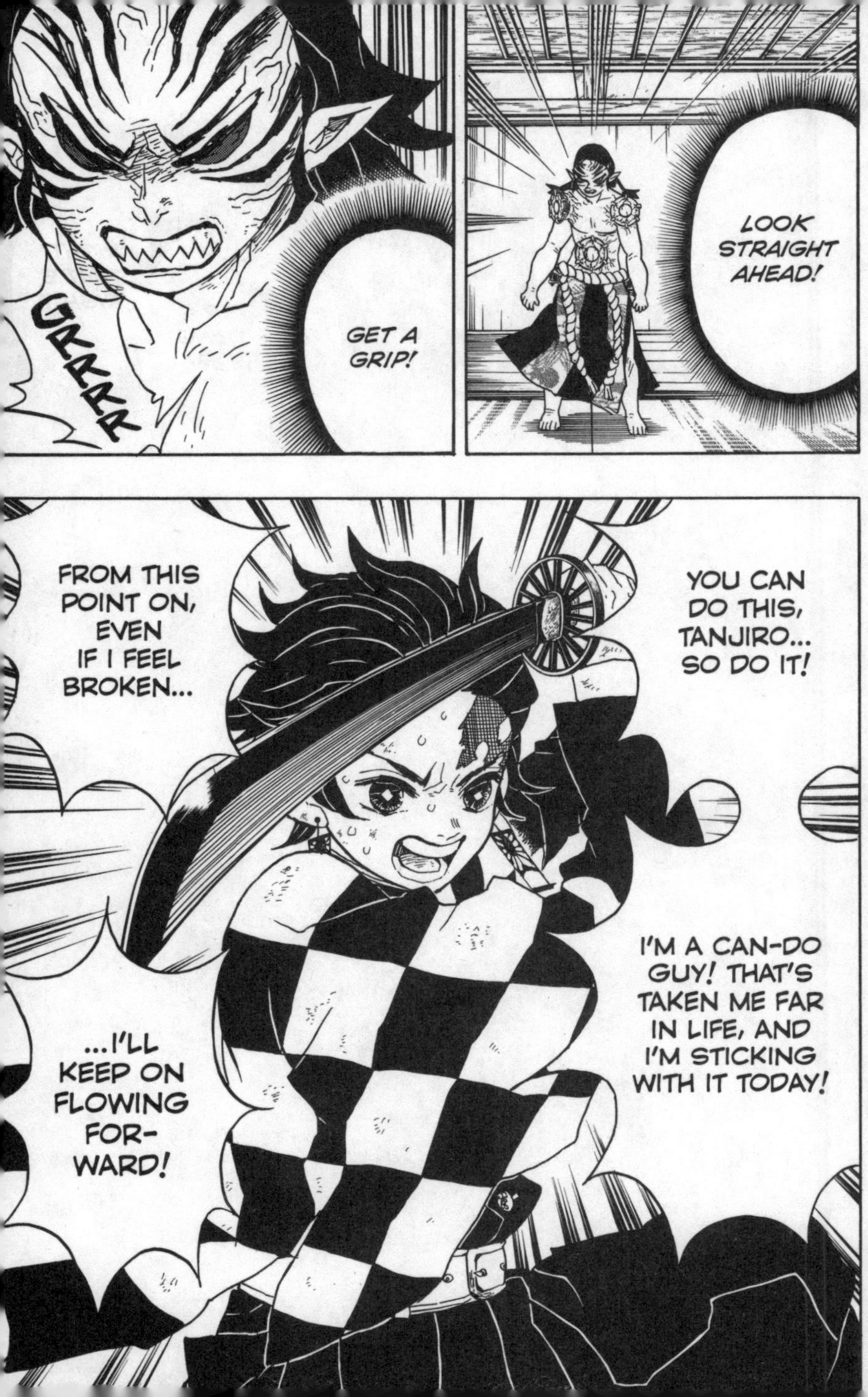
LOOK STRAIGHT AHEAD!
GET A GRIP!
GRRRR
YOU CAN DO THIS, TANJIRO... SO DO IT!
I'M A CAN-DO GUY! THAT'S TAKEN ME FAR IN LIFE, AND I'M STICKING WITH IT TODAY!
FROM THIS POINT ON, EVEN IF I FEEL BROKEN...
...I'LL KEEP ON FLOWING FOR-WARD!

Raaah!

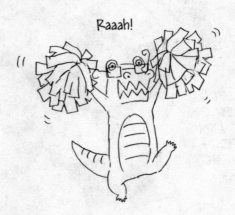

CHAPTER 25: BELIEVE IN YOURSELF

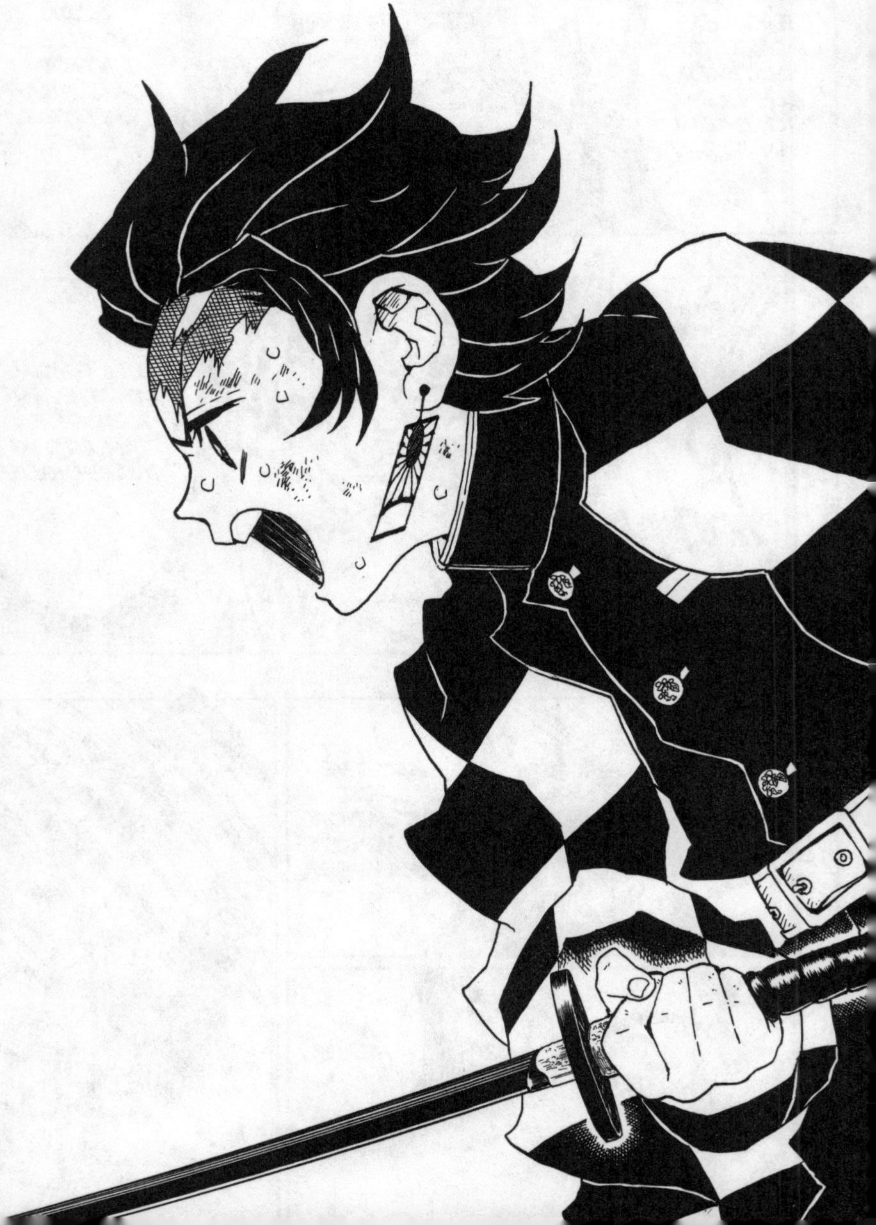

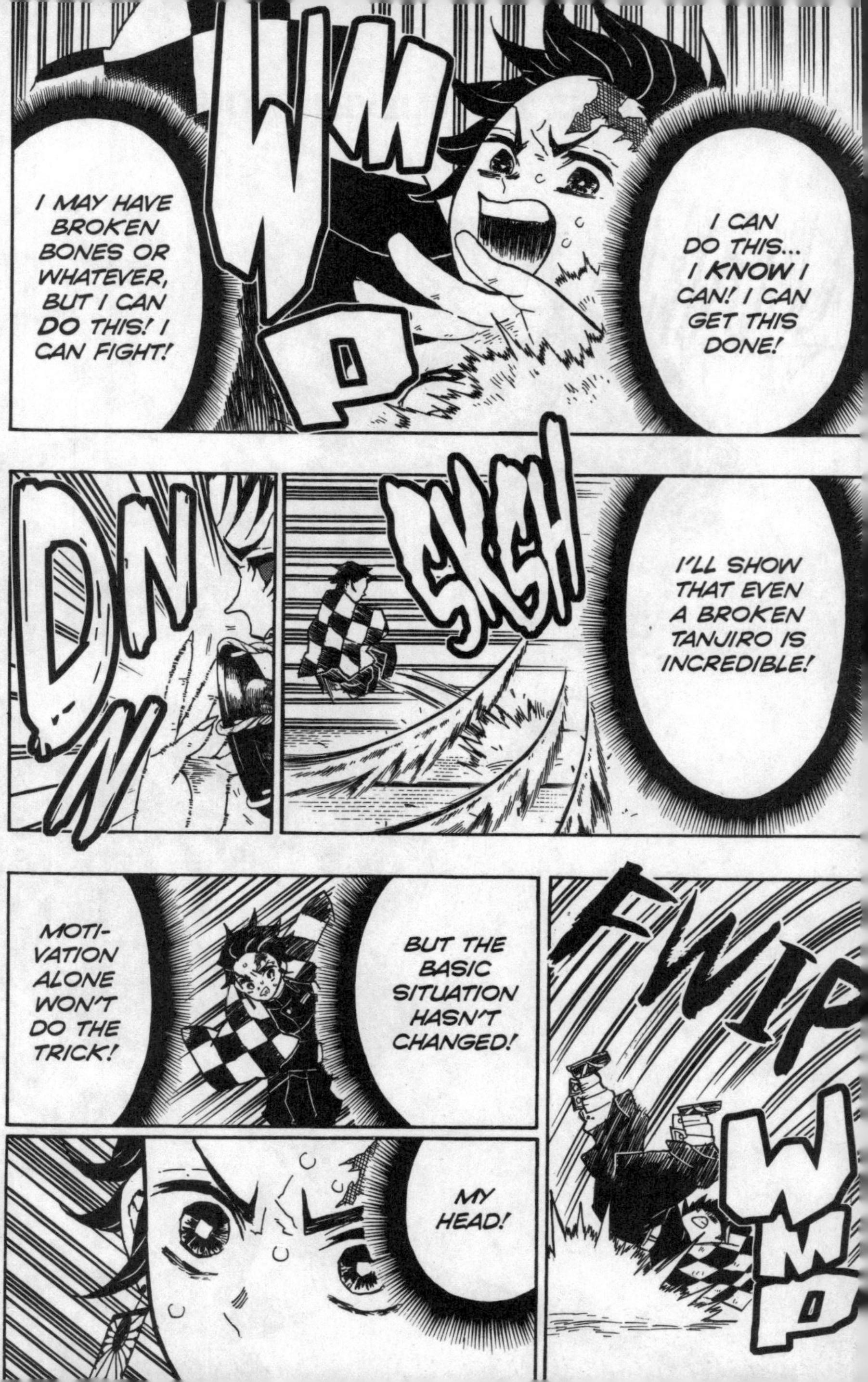
I CAN DO THIS... I KNOW I CAN! I CAN GET THIS DONE!
WMP
I MAY HAVE BROKEN BONES OR WHATEVER, BUT I CAN DO THIS! I CAN FIGHT!
I'LL SHOW THAT EVEN A BROKEN TANJIRO IS INCREDIBLE!
SKSH
DNN
FWIP
WMP
BUT THE BASIC SITUATION HASN'T CHANGED!
MOTI-VATION ALONE WON'T DO THE TRICK!
MY HEAD!

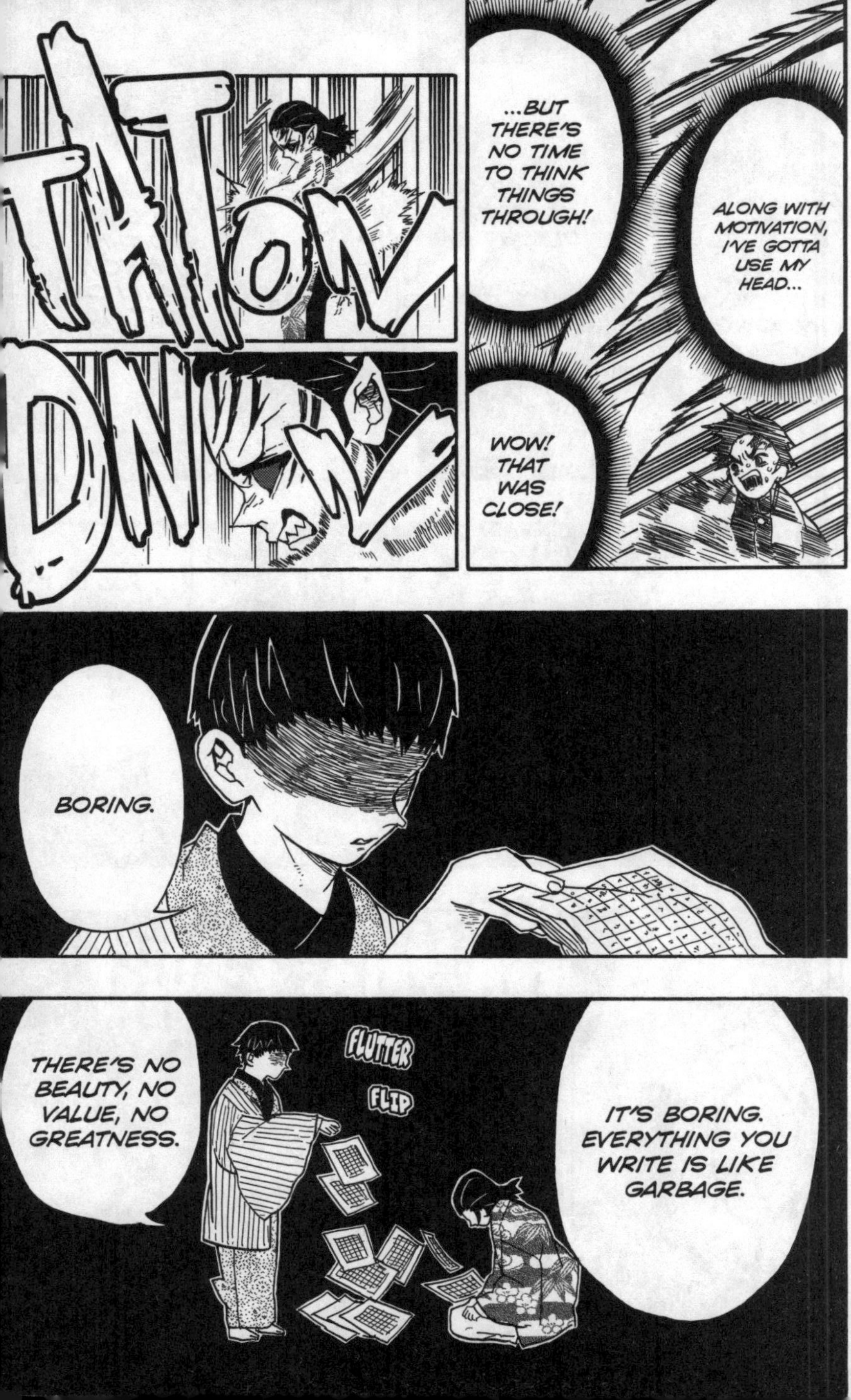
ALONG WITH MOTIVATION, I'VE GOTTA USE MY HEAD...
...BUT THERE'S NO TIME TO THINK THINGS THROUGH!
WOW! THAT WAS CLOSE!
BORING.
IT'S BORING. EVERYTHING YOU WRITE IS LIKE GARBAGE.
FLUTTER
FLIP
THERE'S NO BEAUTY, NO VALUE, NO GREATNESS.

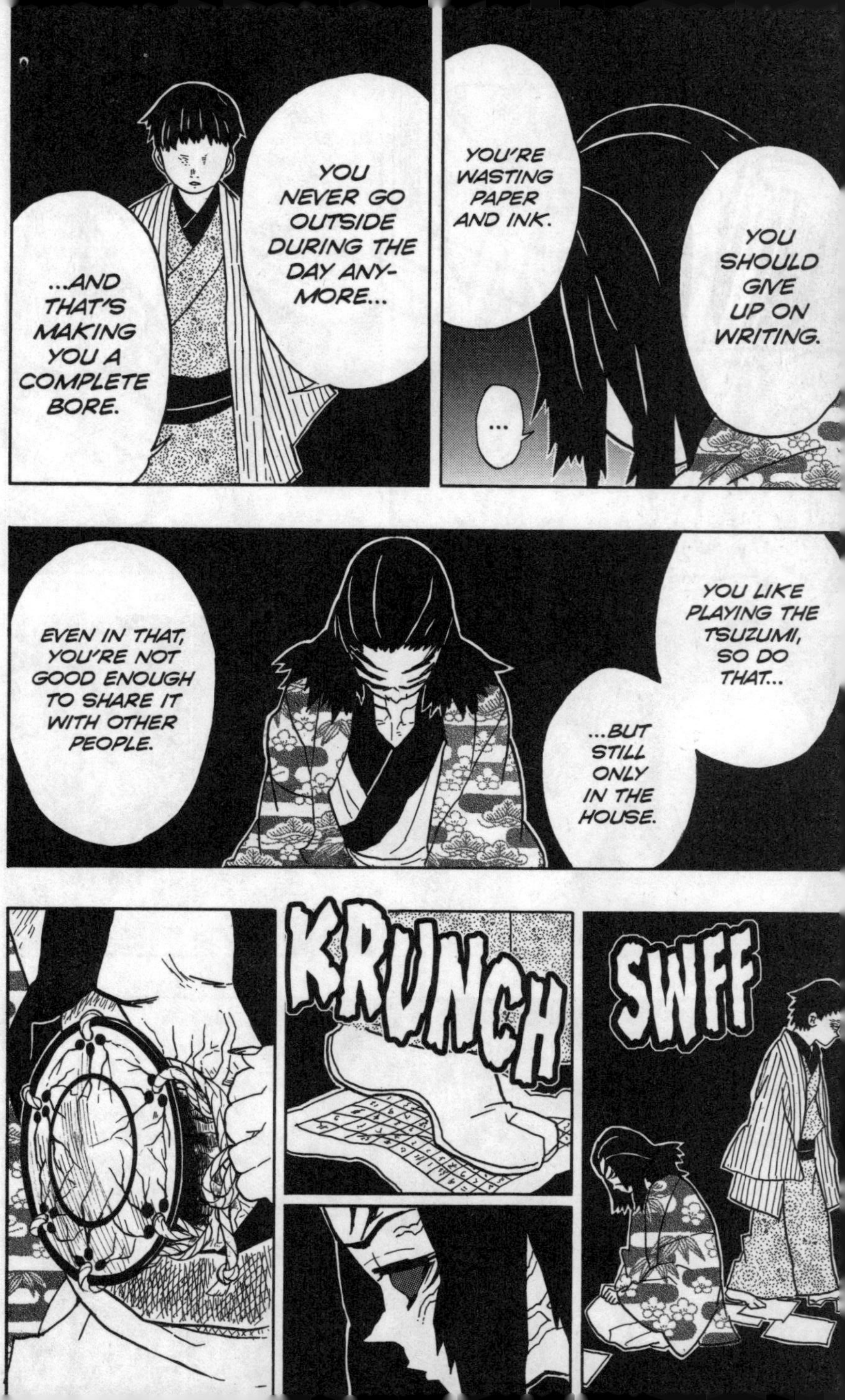
YOU SHOULD GIVE UP ON WRITING.
YOU'RE WASTING PAPER AND INK.
...
YOU NEVER GO OUTSIDE DURING THE DAY ANY-MORE...
...AND THAT'S MAKING YOU A COMPLETE BORE.
YOU LIKE PLAYING THE TSUZUMI, SO DO THAT...
...BUT STILL ONLY IN THE HOUSE.
EVEN IN THAT, YOU'RE NOT GOOD ENOUGH TO SHARE IT WITH OTHER PEOPLE.
SWFF
KRUNCH

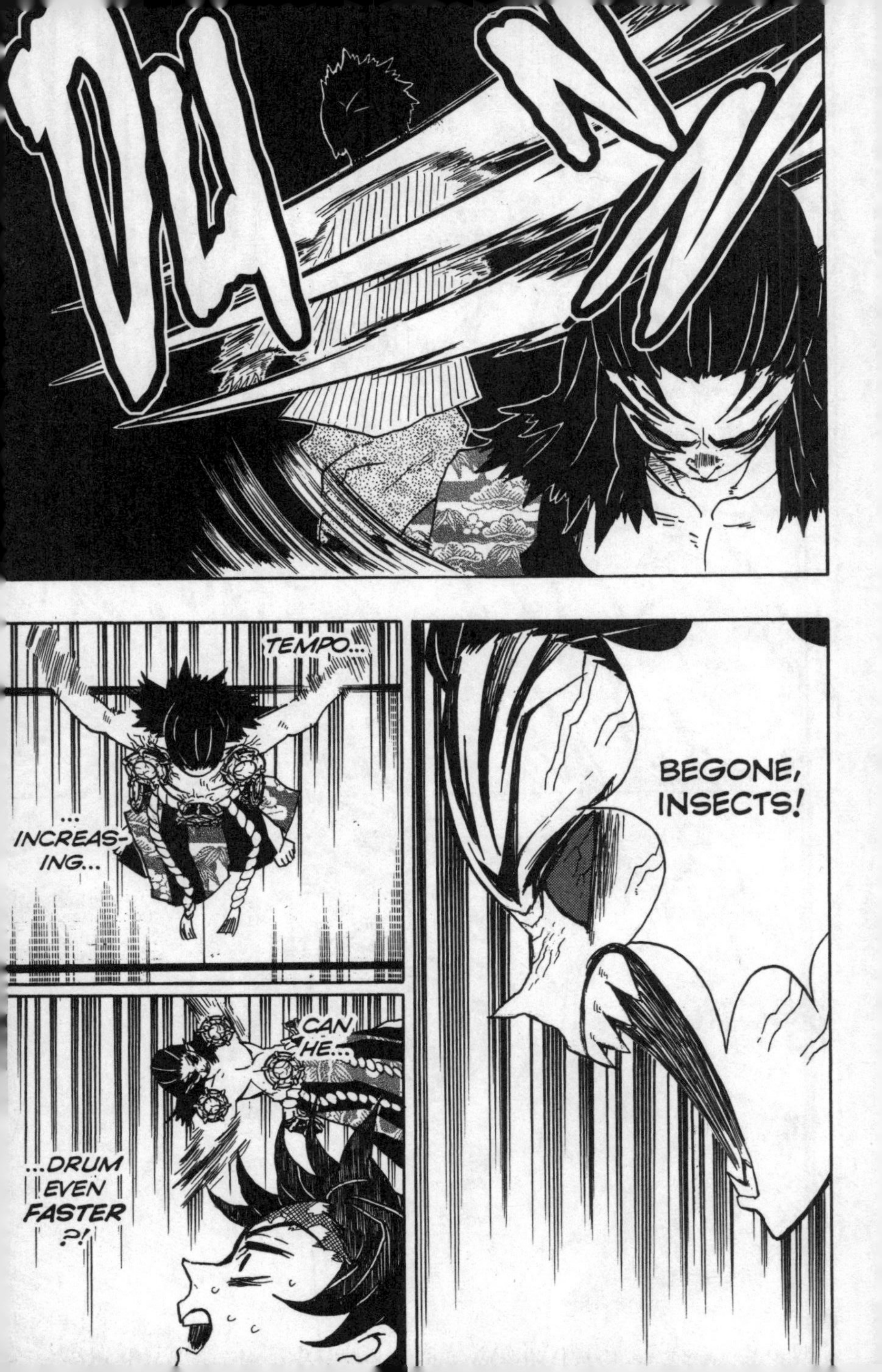
DAN
BEGONE, INSECTS!
TEMPO...
...INCREAS-ING...
CAN HE...
...DRUM EVEN FASTER?!

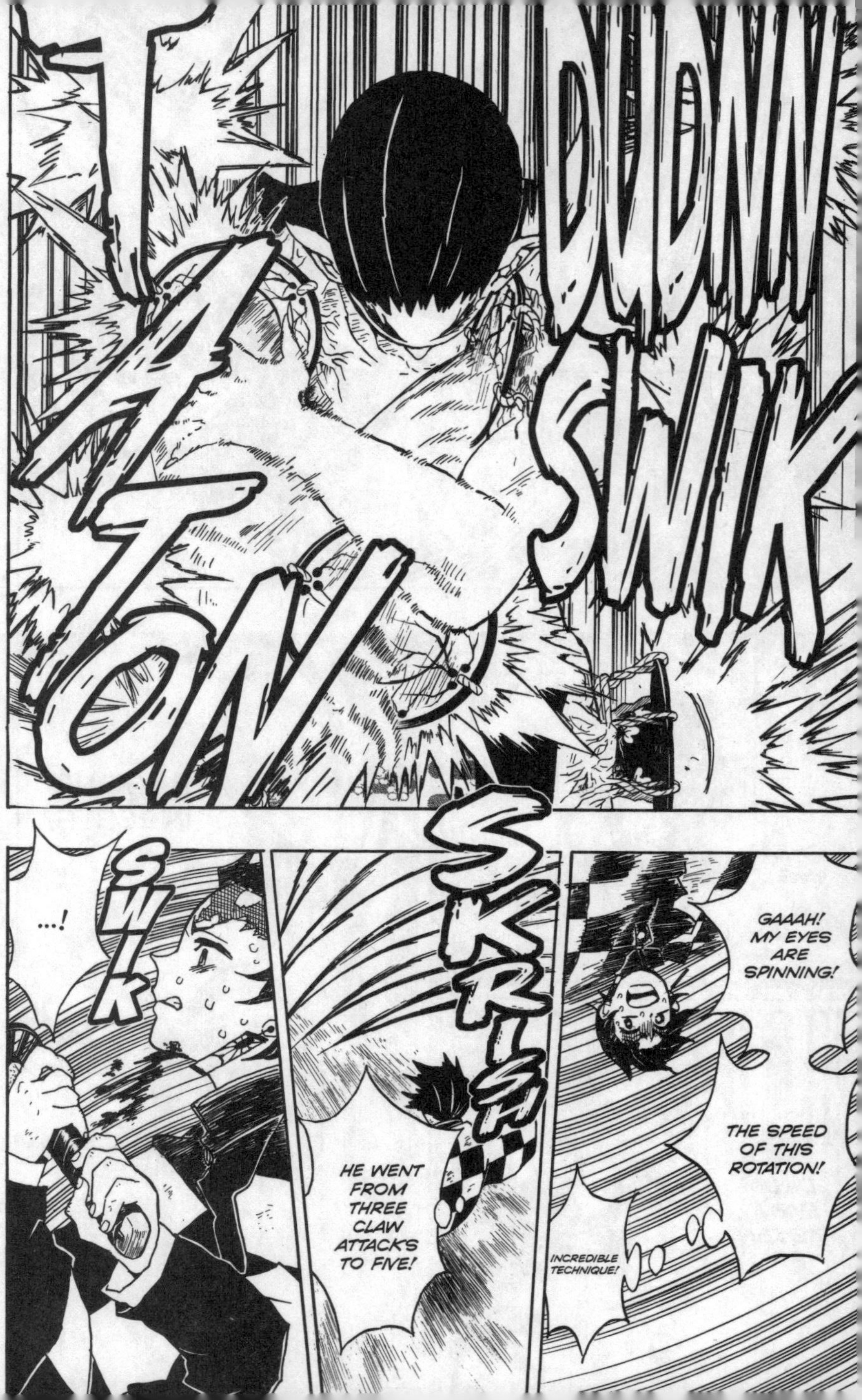
SWIK
GAAAH! MY EYES ARE SPINNING!
THE SPEED OF THIS ROTATION!
INCREDIBLE TECHNIQUE!
SKRISH
HE WENT FROM THREE CLAW ATTACKS TO FIVE!
SWIK
...!

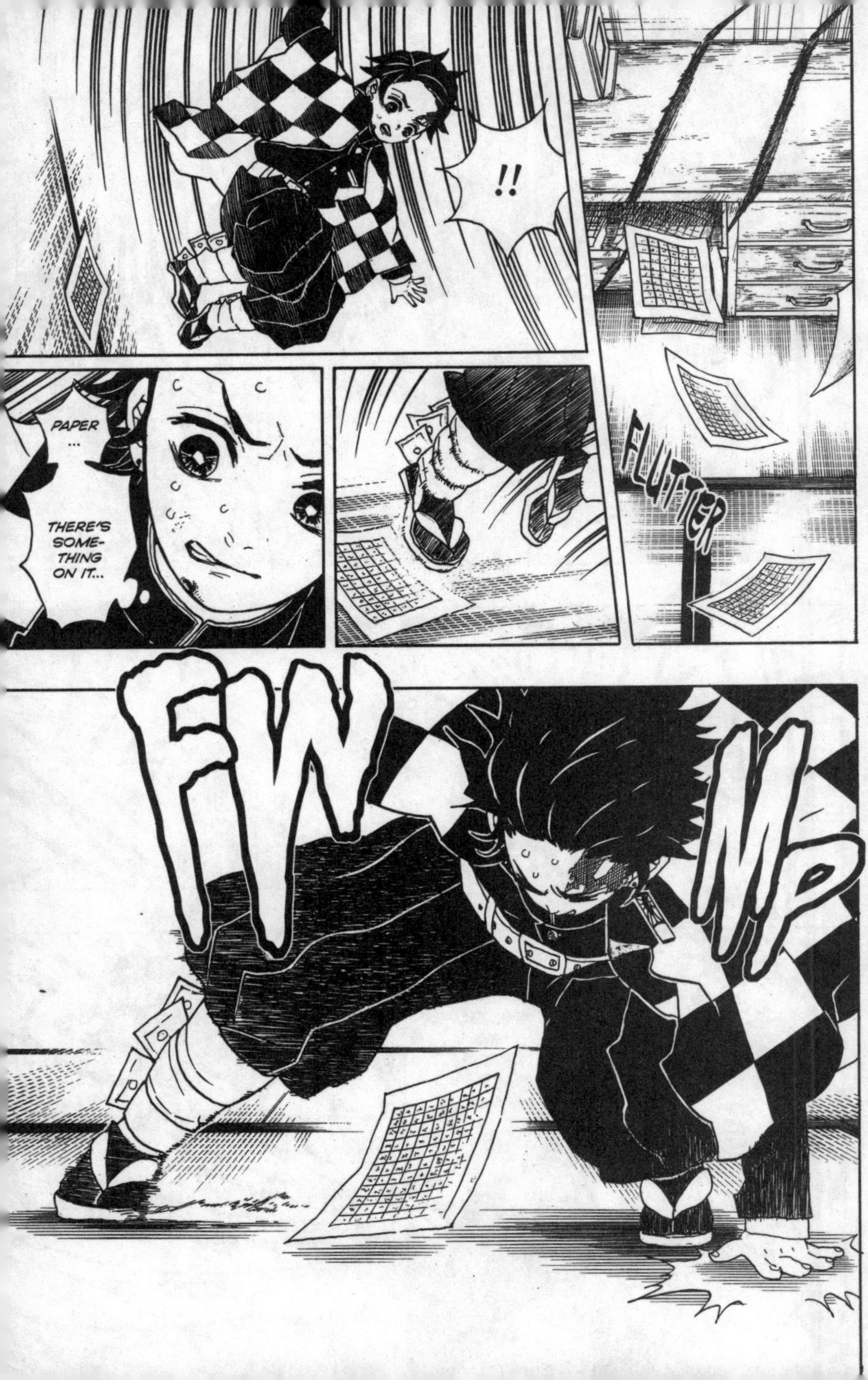
FLUTTER
!!
PAPER ...
THERE'S SOME-THING ON IT...
FWMP

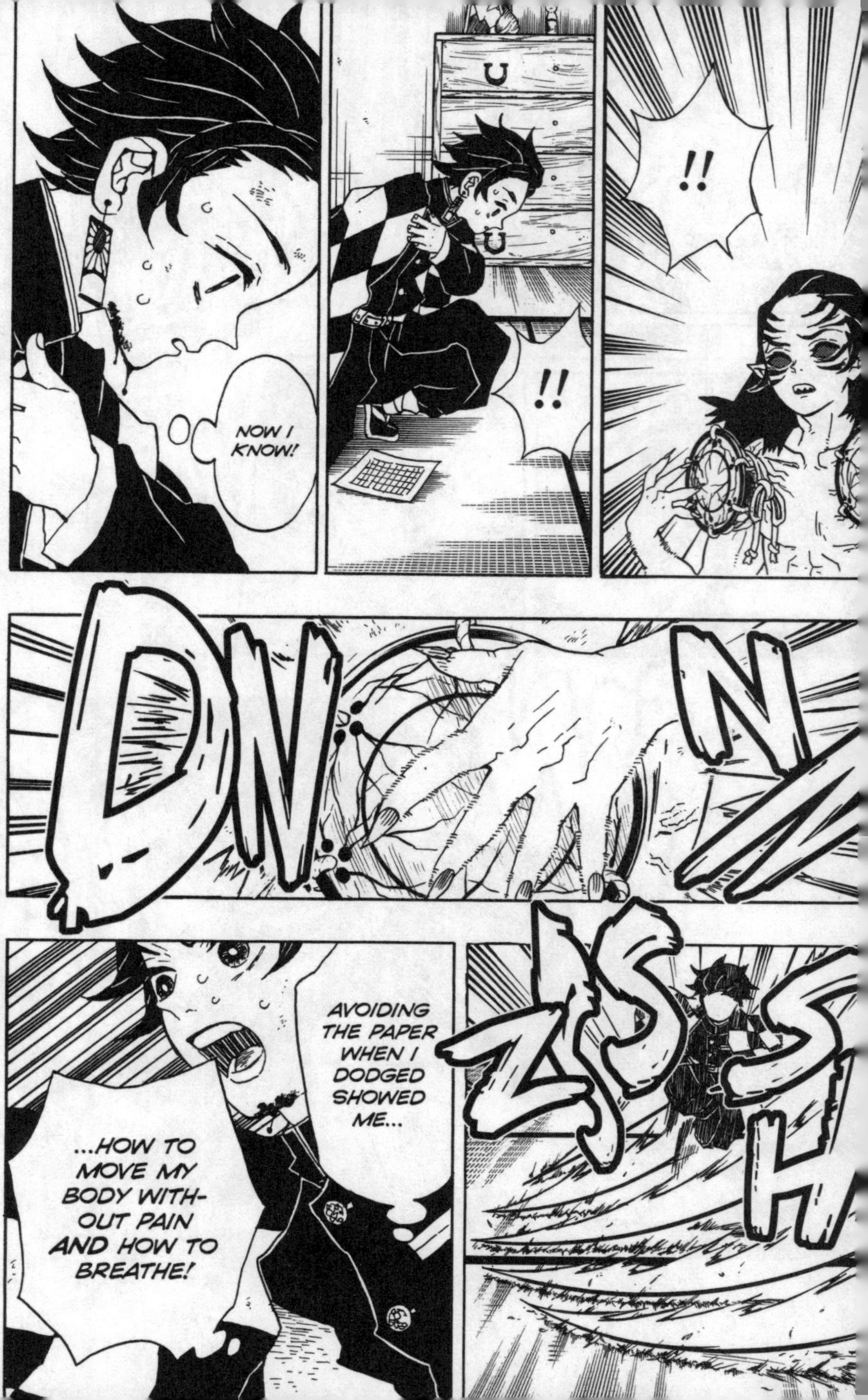
!!
!!
NOW I KNOW!
DNN
ZSSH
AVOIDING THE PAPER WHEN I DODGED SHOWED ME...
...HOW TO MOVE MY BODY WITH-OUT PAIN AND HOW TO BREATHE!

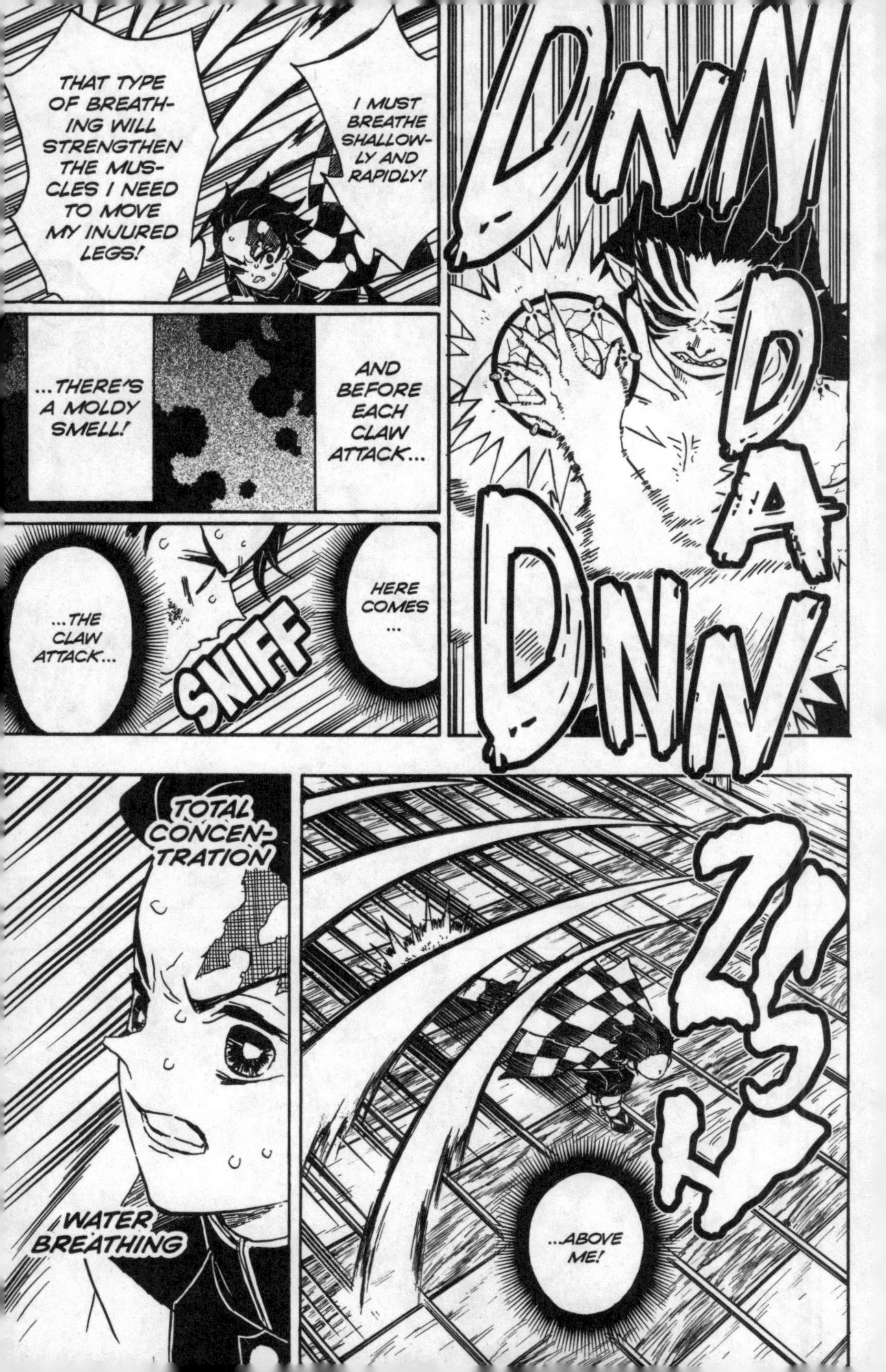
DNN
DA
DNN
I MUST BREATHE SHALLOW-LY AND RAPIDLY!
THAT TYPE OF BREATH-ING WILL STRENGTHEN THE MUS-CLES I NEED TO MOVE MY INJURED LEGS!
AND BEFORE EACH CLAW ATTACK...
...THERE'S A MOLDY SMELL!
HERE COMES ...
SNIFF
...THE CLAW ATTACK...
ZSH
...ABOVE ME!
TOTAL CONCEN-TRATION
WATER BREATHING

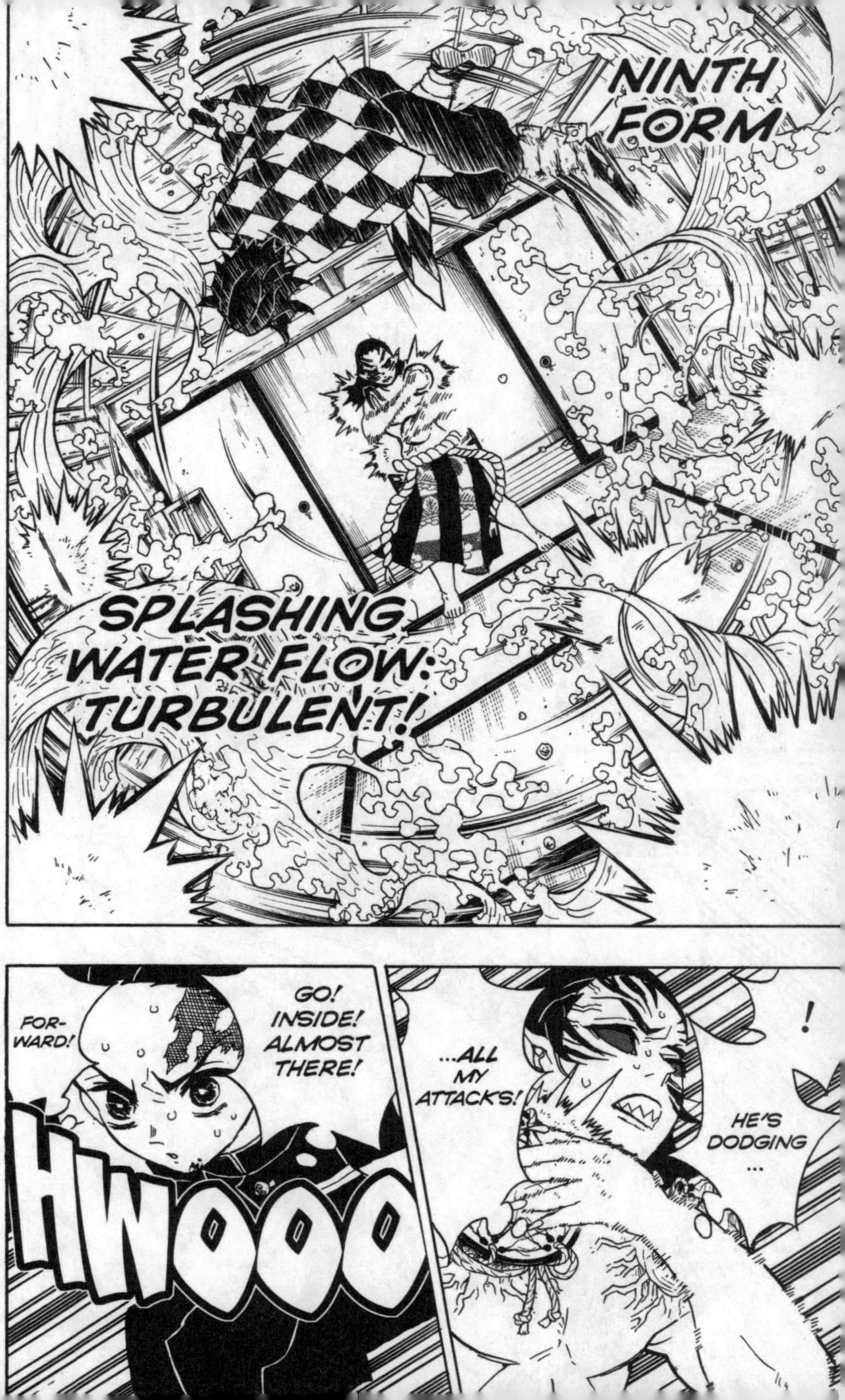
NINTH FORM
SPLASHING WATER FLOW: TURBULENT!
!
HE'S DODGING ...
...ALL MY ATTACKS!
GO! INSIDE! ALMOST THERE!
FOR-WARD!
HWOOO

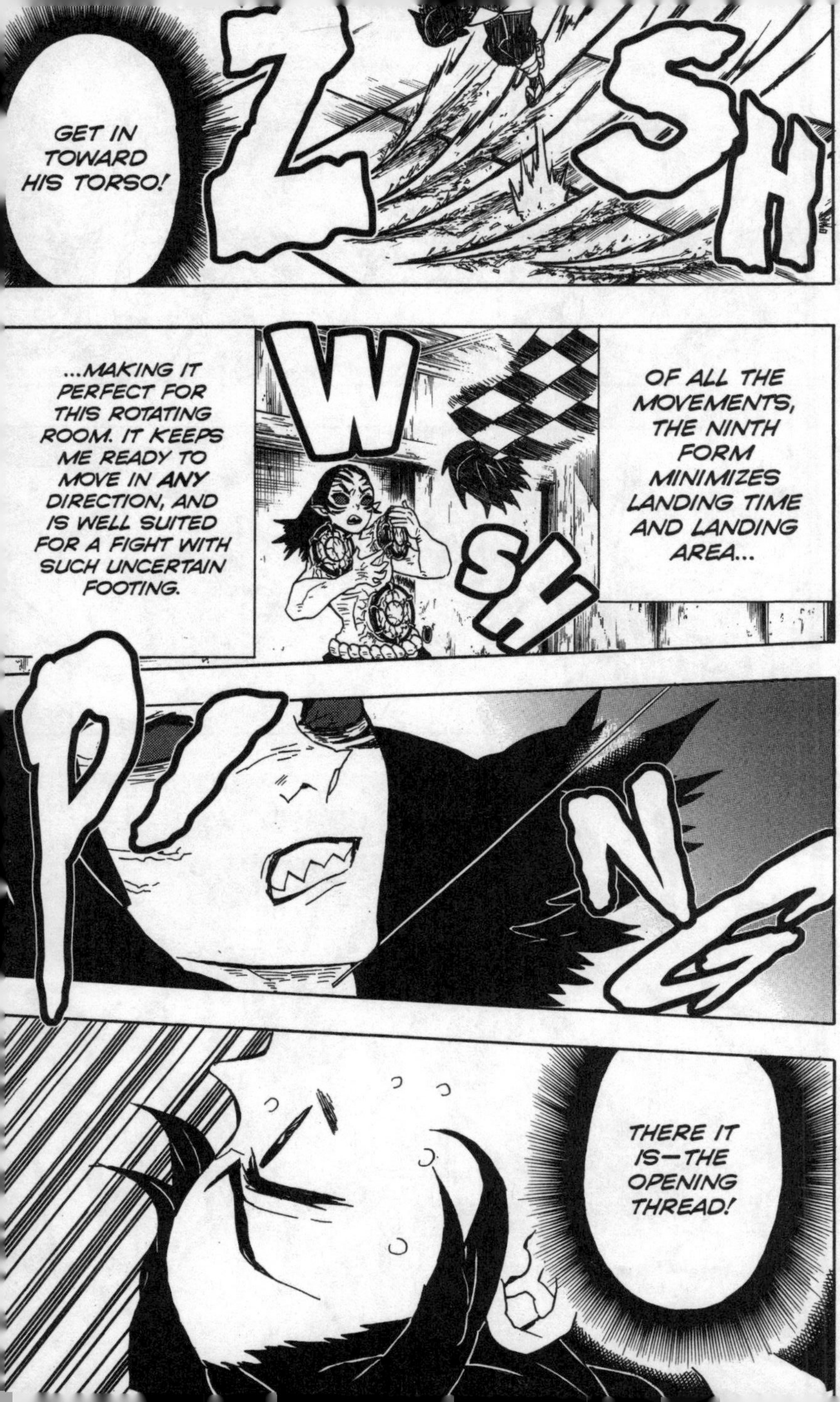
ZSH
GET IN TOWARD HIS TORSO!
OF ALL THE MOVEMENTS, THE NINTH FORM MINIMIZES LANDING TIME AND LANDING AREA...
WSH
...MAKING IT PERFECT FOR THIS ROTATING ROOM. IT KEEPS ME READY TO MOVE IN ANY DIRECTION, AND IS WELL SUITED FOR A FIGHT WITH SUCH UNCERTAIN FOOTING.
PING
THERE IT IS—THE OPENING THREAD!

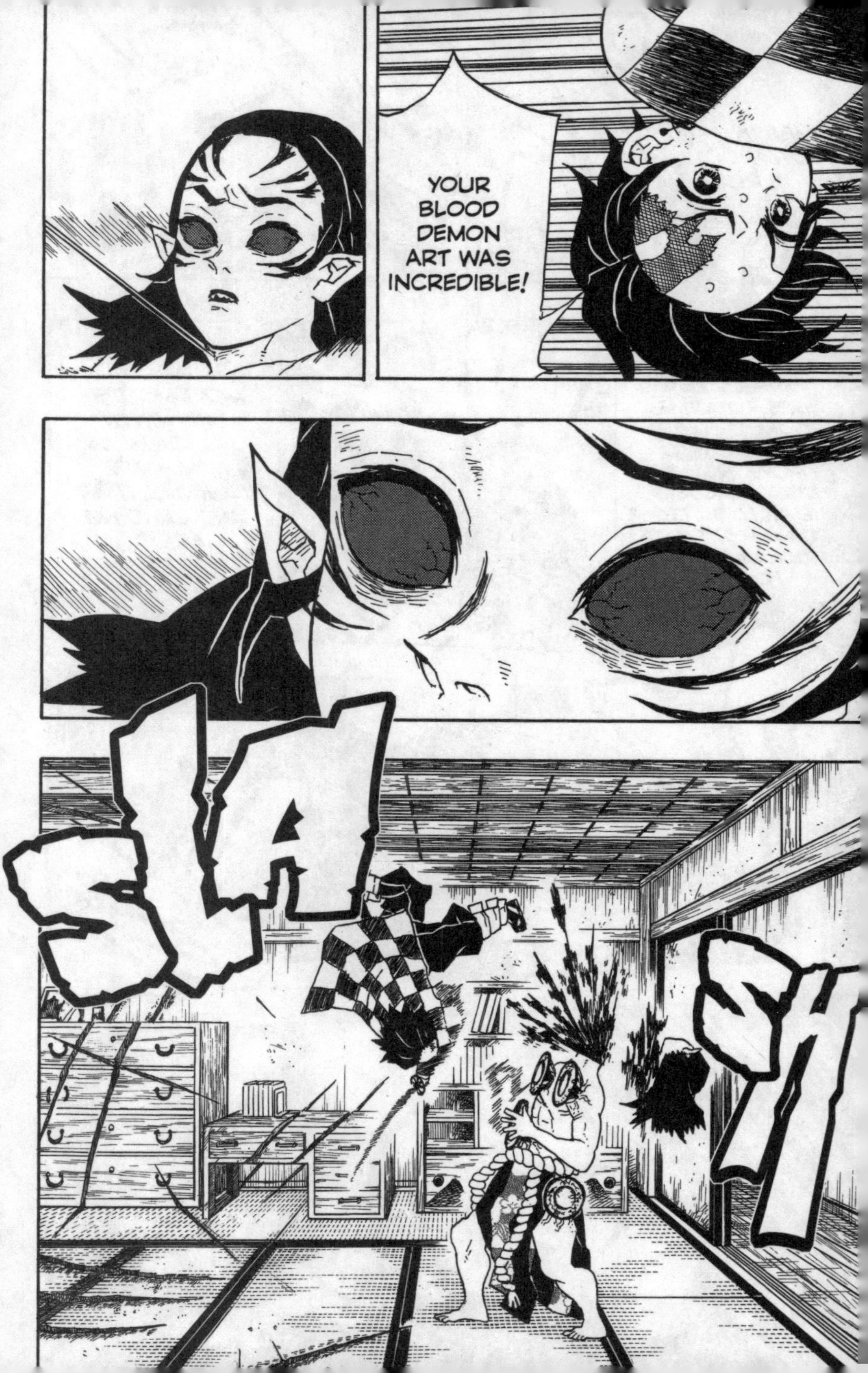
YOUR BLOOD DEMON ART WAS INCREDIBLE!
SLA
SH

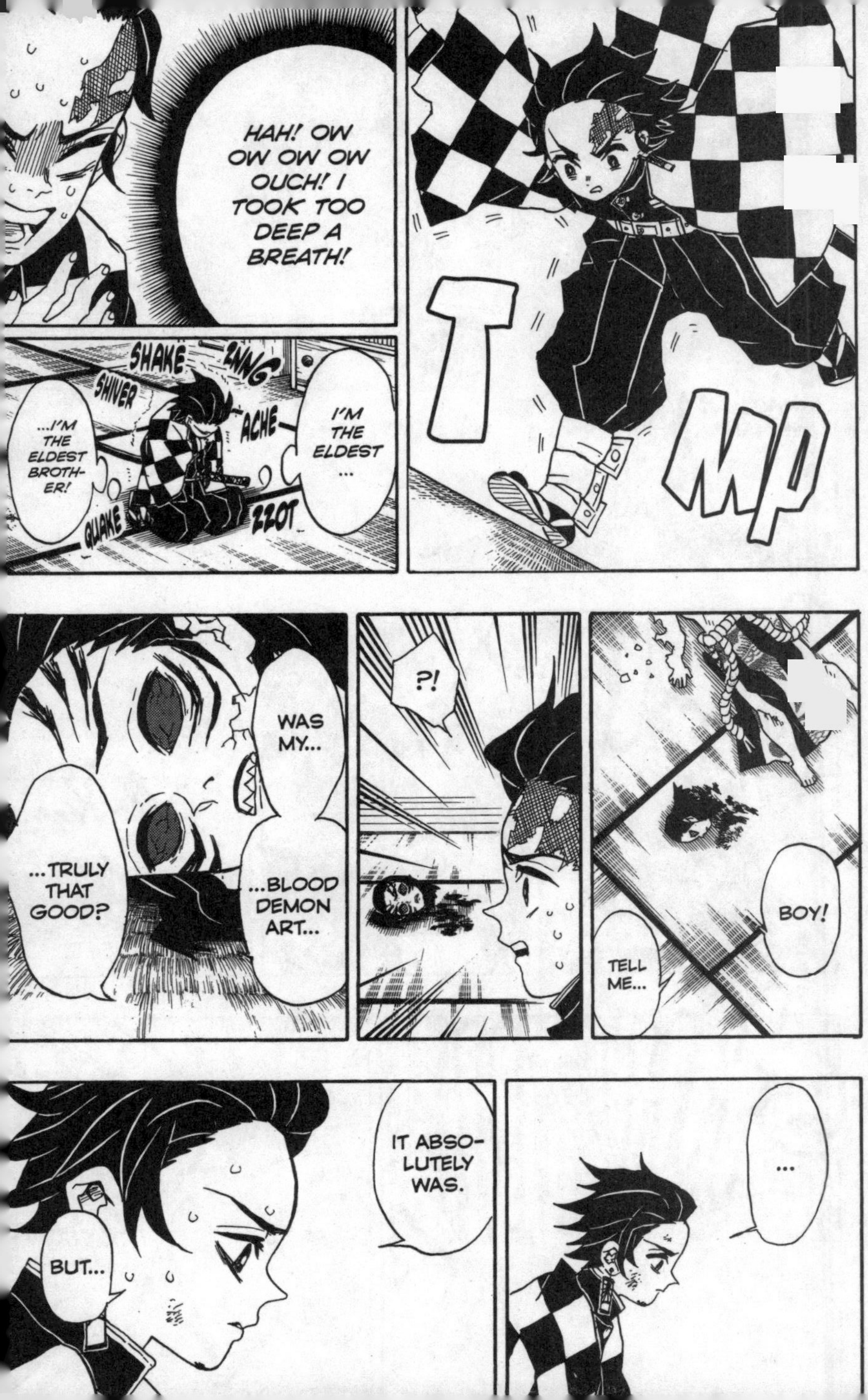
TMP
HAH! OW OW OW OW OUCH! I TOOK TOO DEEP A BREATH!
ZNNG
SHAKE
I'M THE ELDEST ...
ACHE
SHIVER
...I'M THE ELDEST BROTHER!
ZZOT
QUAKE
BOY!
TELL ME...
?!
WAS MY...
...BLOOD DEMON ART...
...TRULY THAT GOOD?
...
IT ABSOLUTELY WAS.
BUT...

...I CANNOT ALLOW THE DEATH...

...OF INNOCENT HUMANS.

FW UP

OH, RIGHT. THIS SHOULD DO.

I THOUGHT SO...

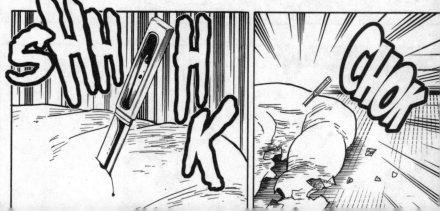

SHHHK

CHOK

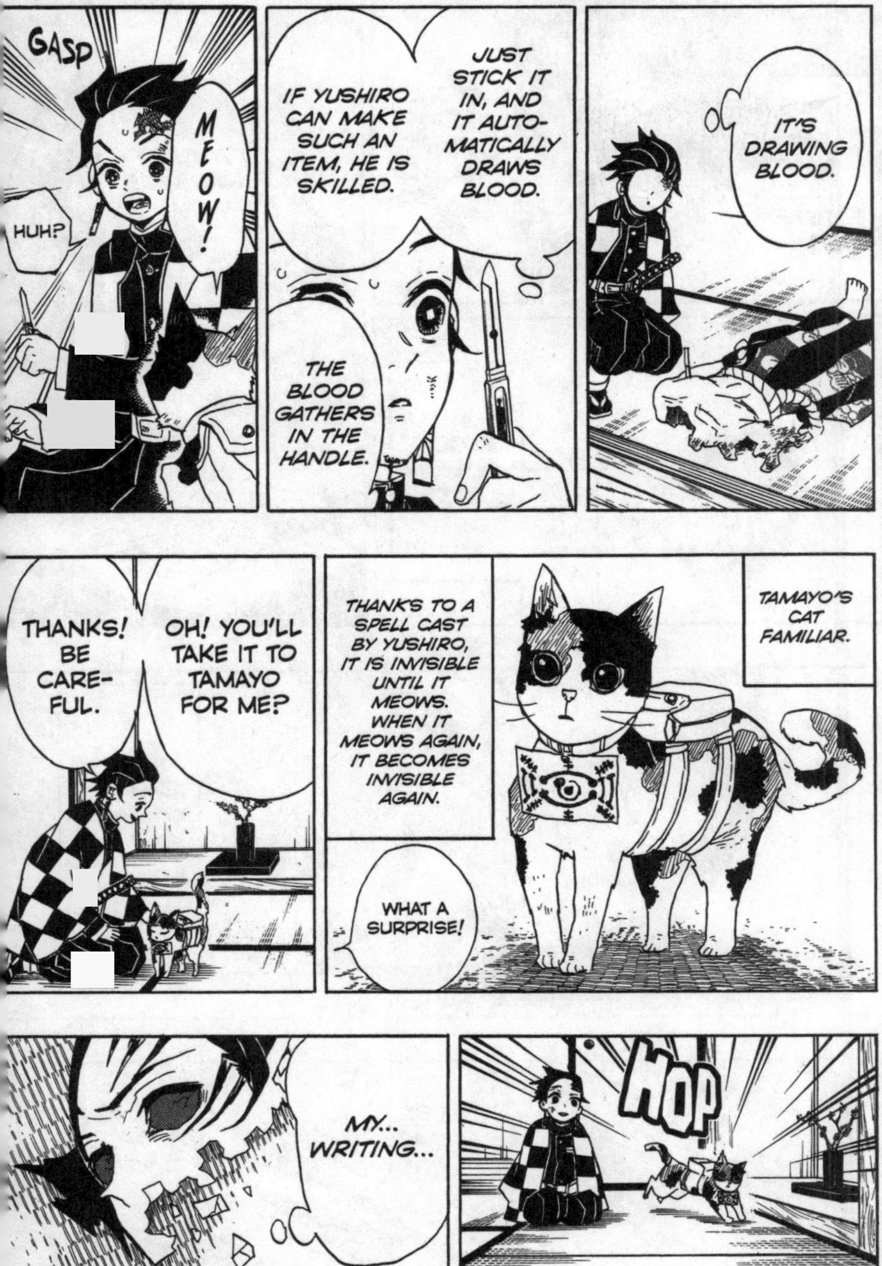
IT'S DRAWING BLOOD.
JUST STICK IT IN, AND IT AUTOMATICALLY DRAWS BLOOD.
IF YUSHIRO CAN MAKE SUCH AN ITEM, HE IS SKILLED.
THE BLOOD GATHERS IN THE HANDLE.
GASP
MEOW!
HUH?
TAMAYO'S CAT FAMILIAR.
THANKS TO A SPELL CAST BY YUSHIRO, IT IS INVISIBLE UNTIL IT MEOWS. WHEN IT MEOWS AGAIN, IT BECOMES INVISIBLE AGAIN.
WHAT A SURPRISE!
OH! YOU'LL TAKE IT TO TAMAYO FOR ME?
THANKS! BE CARE-FUL.
HOP
MY... WRITING...

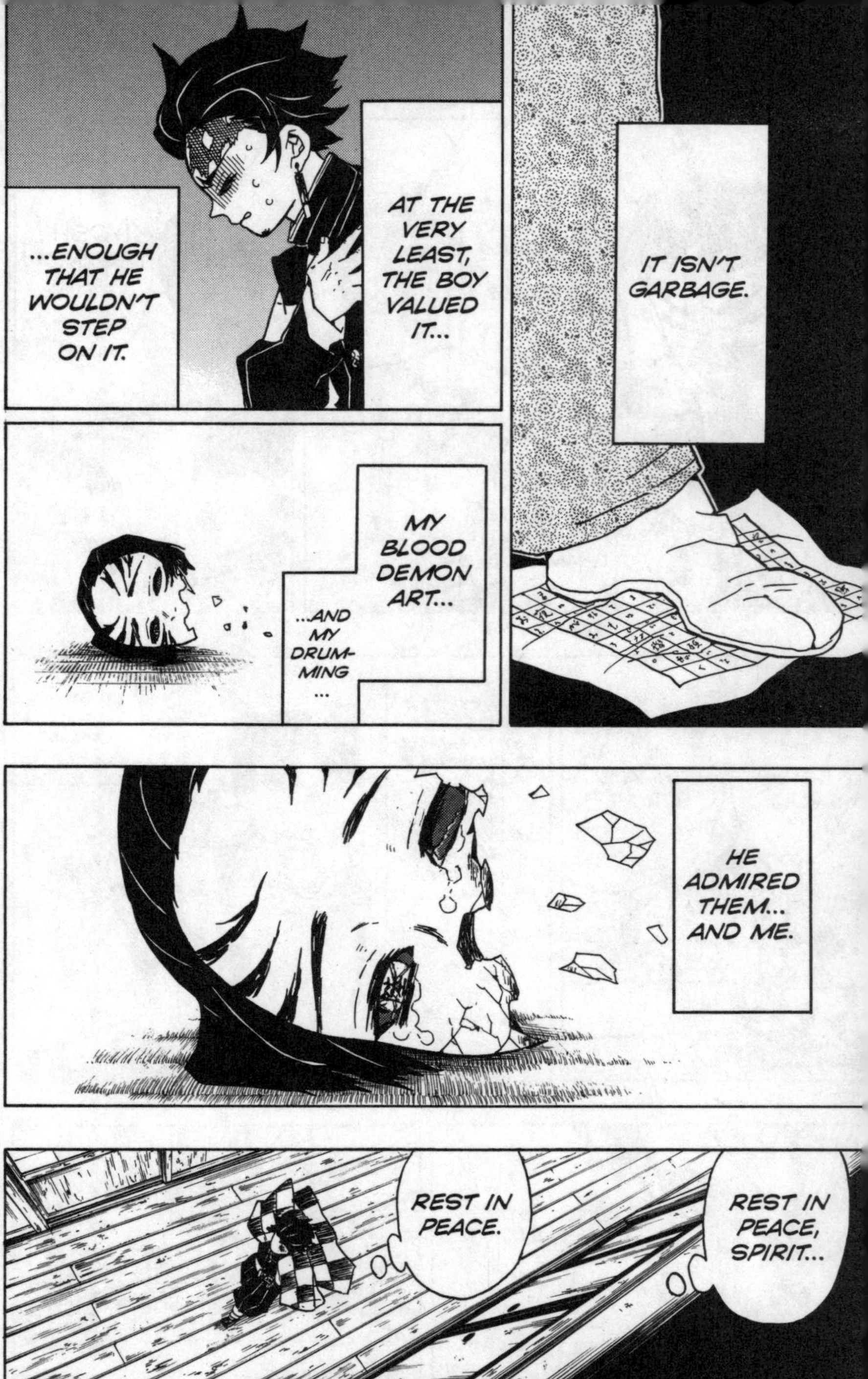
IT ISN'T GARBAGE.
AT THE VERY LEAST, THE BOY VALUED IT...
...ENOUGH THAT HE WOULDN'T STEP ON IT.
MY BLOOD DEMON ART...
...AND MY DRUMMING...
HE ADMIRED THEM... AND ME.
REST IN PEACE, SPIRIT...
REST IN PEACE.

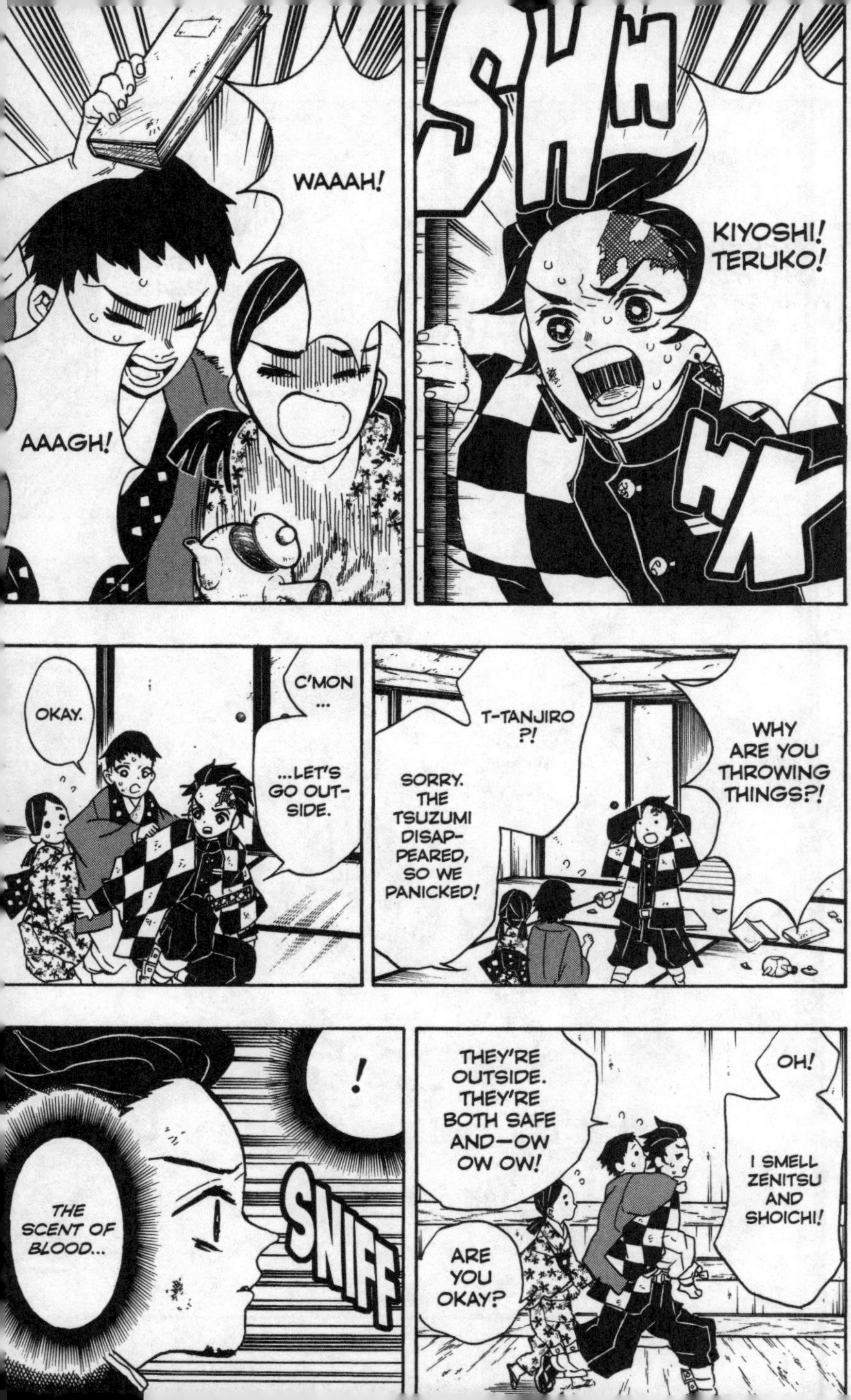
SHH
KIYOSHI! TERUKO!
HK
WAAAH!
AAAGH!
WHY ARE YOU THROWING THINGS?!
T-TANJIRO ?!
SORRY. THE TSUZUMI DISAPPEARED, SO WE PANICKED!
C'MON ...
...LET'S GO OUTSIDE.
OKAY.
OH!
I SMELL ZENITSU AND SHOICHI!
THEY'RE OUTSIDE. THEY'RE BOTH SAFE AND—OW OW OW!
ARE YOU OKAY?
!
SNIFF
THE SCENT OF BLOOD...

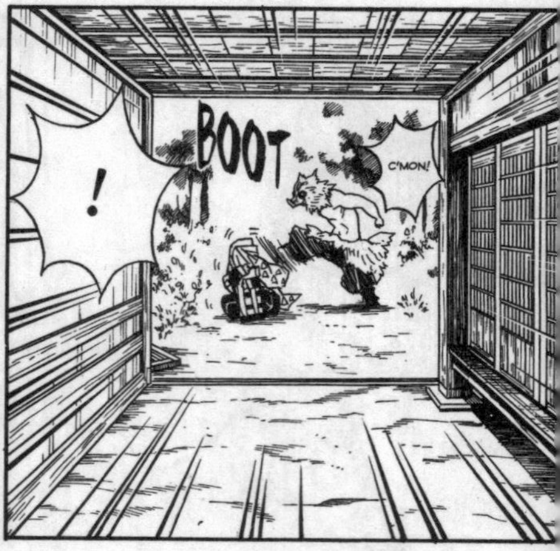
C'MON!
BOOT
!

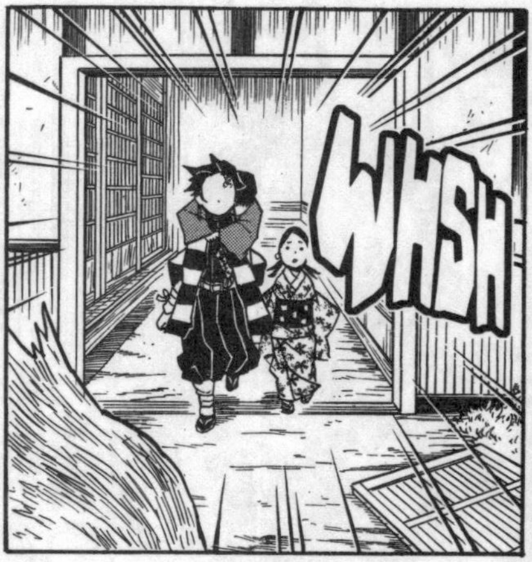
WHSH

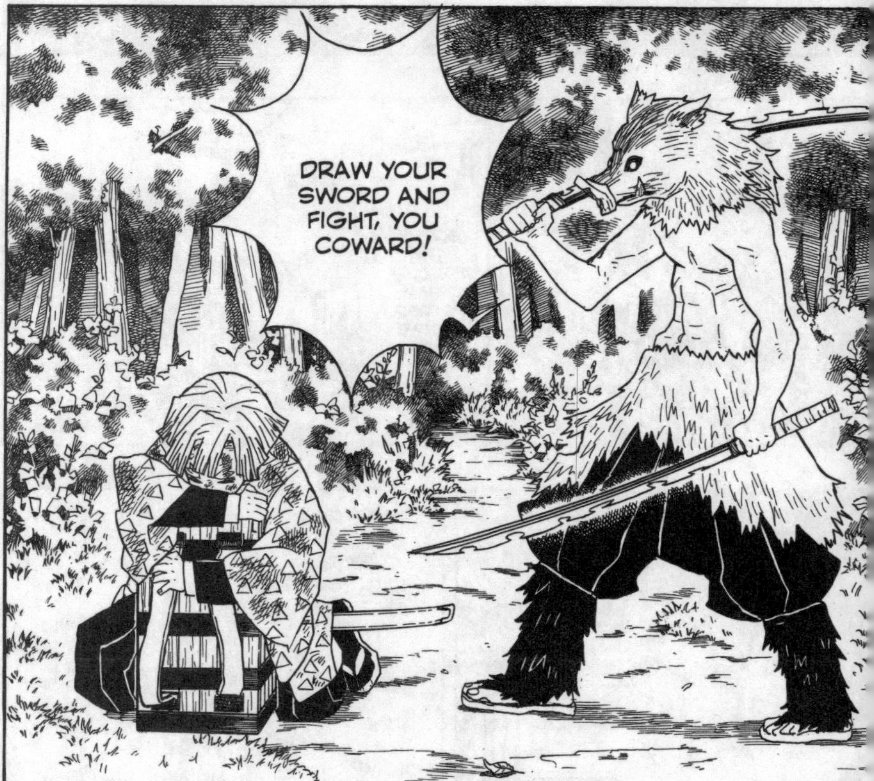
DRAW YOUR SWORD AND FIGHT, YOU COWARD!

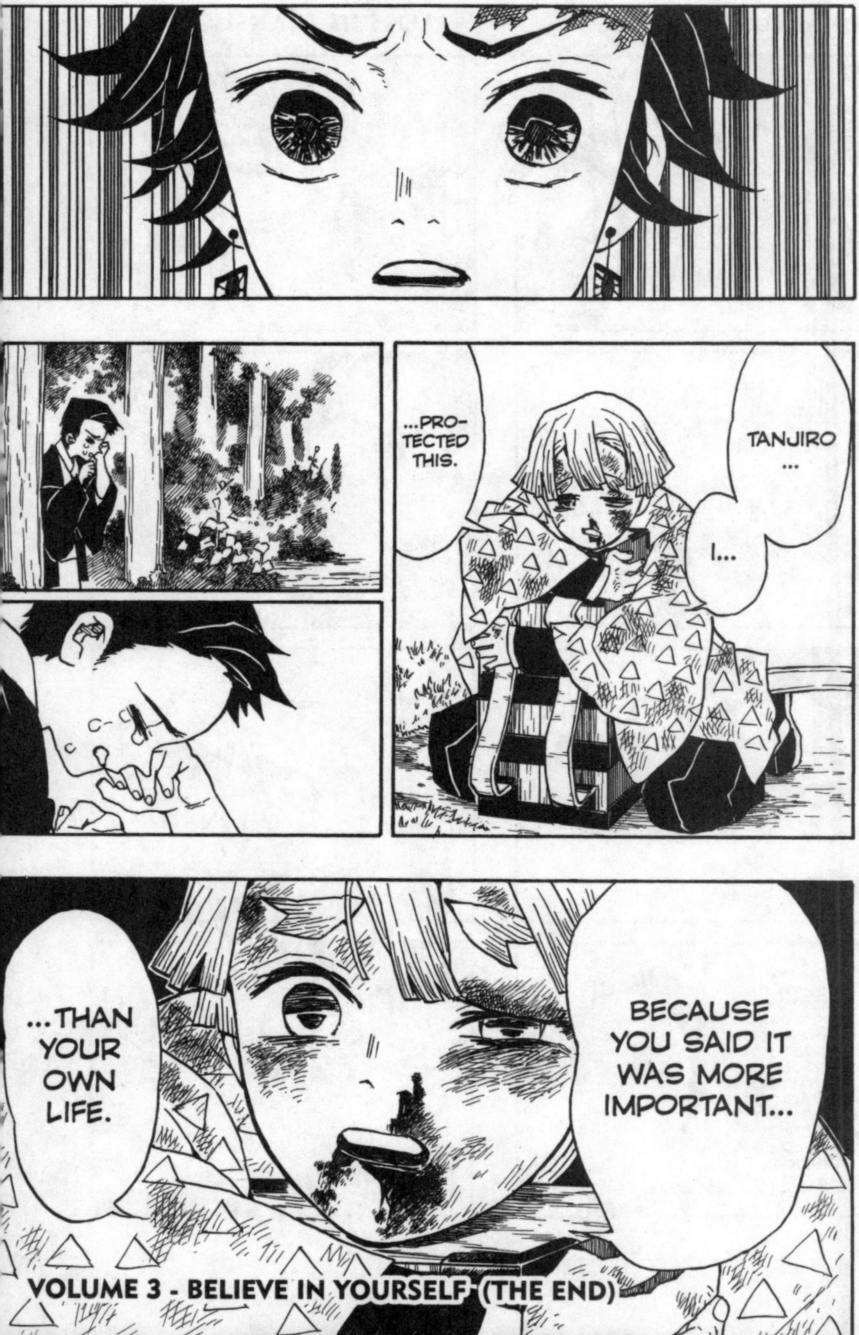
TANJIRO...
I...
...PROTECTED THIS.
BECAUSE YOU SAID IT WAS MORE IMPORTANT...
...THAN YOUR OWN LIFE.
VOLUME 3 - BELIEVE IN YOURSELF (THE END)

JUMP GIGA 2016 VOL. 1 BONUS COMIC STRIPS

LOST IN TRANSLATION

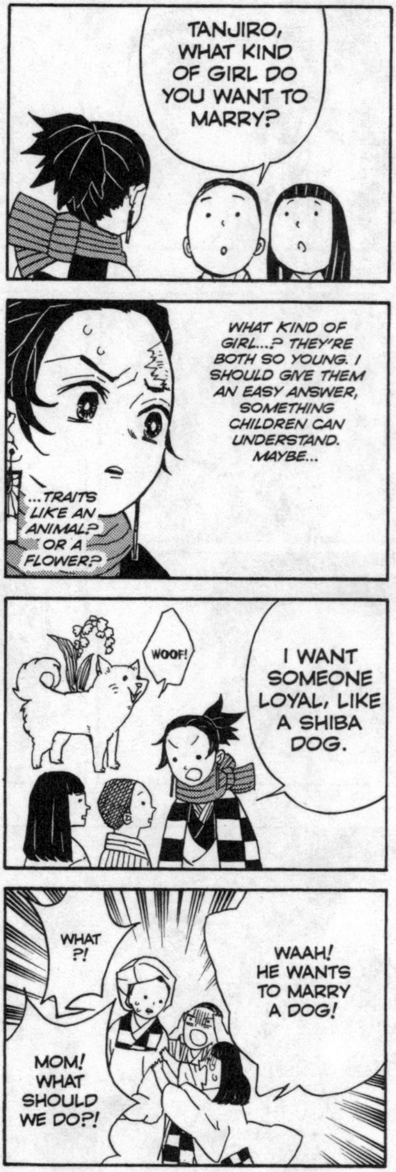
TANJIRO, WHAT KIND OF GIRL DO YOU WANT TO MARRY?
WHAT KIND OF GIRL...? THEY'RE BOTH SO YOUNG. I SHOULD GIVE THEM AN EASY ANSWER, SOMETHING CHILDREN CAN UNDERSTAND. MAYBE...
...TRAITS LIKE AN ANIMAL? OR A FLOWER?
I WANT SOMEONE LOYAL, LIKE A SHIBA DOG.
WOOF!
WAAH! HE WANTS TO MARRY A DOG!
WHAT ?!
MOM! WHAT SHOULD WE DO?!

NEZUKO'S IDEAL

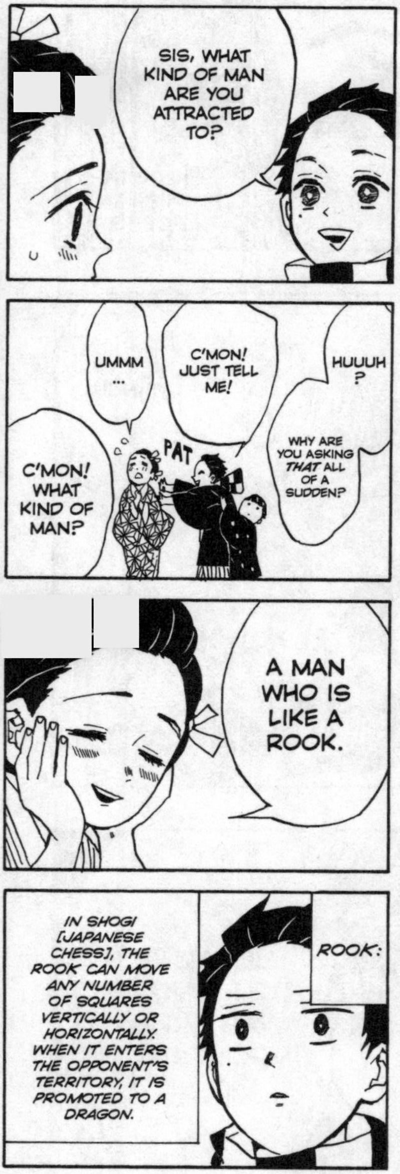
SIS, WHAT KIND OF MAN ARE YOU ATTRACTED TO?
HUUUH ?
WHY ARE YOU ASKING THAT ALL OF A SUDDEN?
C'MON! JUST TELL ME!
UMMM ...
PAT
C'MON! WHAT KIND OF MAN?
A MAN WHO IS LIKE A ROOK.
ROOK:
IN SHOGI [JAPANESE CHESS], THE ROOK CAN MOVE ANY NUMBER OF SQUARES VERTICALLY OR HORIZONTALLY. WHEN IT ENTERS THE OPPONENT'S TERRITORY, IT IS PROMOTED TO A DRAGON.

THE LOVE OF GOSSIP

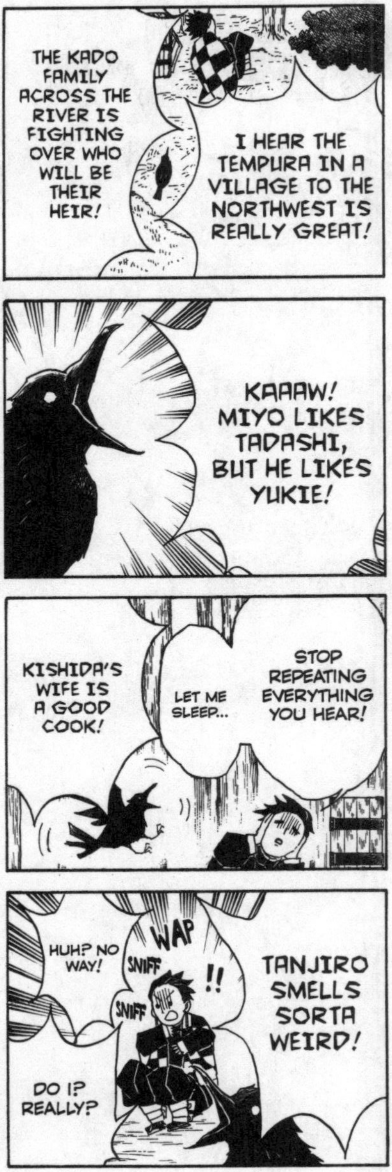
I HEAR THE TEMPURA IN A VILLAGE TO THE NORTHWEST IS REALLY GREAT!
THE KADO FAMILY ACROSS THE RIVER IS FIGHTING OVER WHO WILL BE THEIR HEIR!
KAAAW! MIYO LIKES TADASHI, BUT HE LIKES YUKIE!
STOP REPEATING EVERYTHING YOU HEAR!
LET ME SLEEP...
KISHIDA'S WIFE IS A GOOD COOK!
TANJIRO SMELLS SORTA WEIRD!
!!
WAP
HUH? NO WAY!
SNIFF
SNIFF
DO I? REALLY?

DOCTOR CONSULTATION

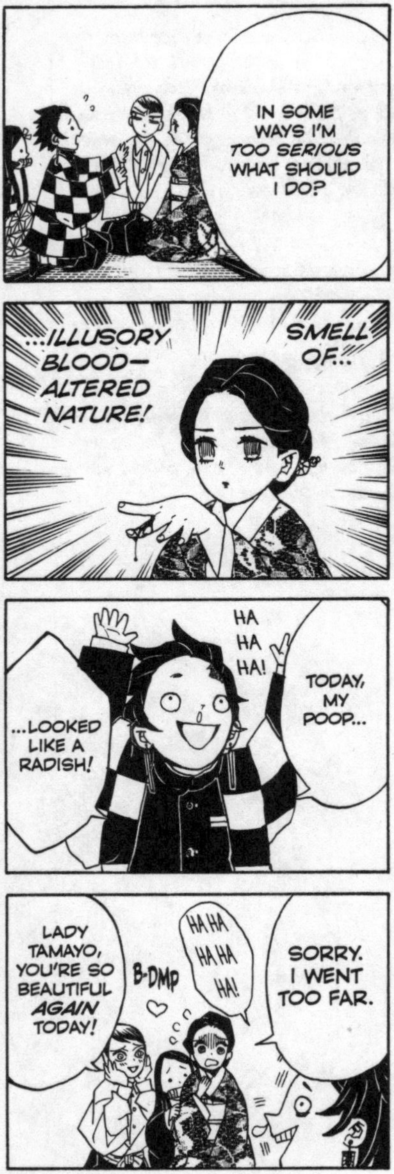
IN SOME WAYS I'M *TOO SERIOUS* WHAT SHOULD I DO?
SMELL OF...
...ILLUSORY BLOOD—ALTERED NATURE!
TODAY, MY POOP...
HA HA HA!
...LOOKED LIKE A RADISH!
SORRY. I WENT TOO FAR.
HA HA HA HA HA!
B-DMP
LADY TAMAYO, YOU'RE SO BEAUTIFUL *AGAIN* TODAY!

THE END

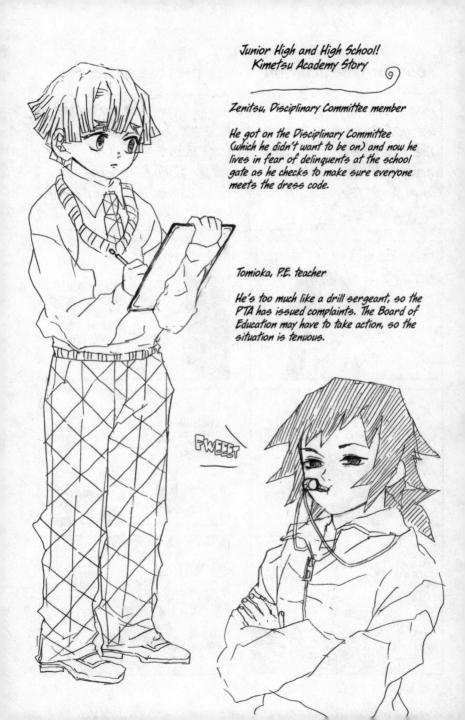

Junior High and High School! Kimetsu Academy Story

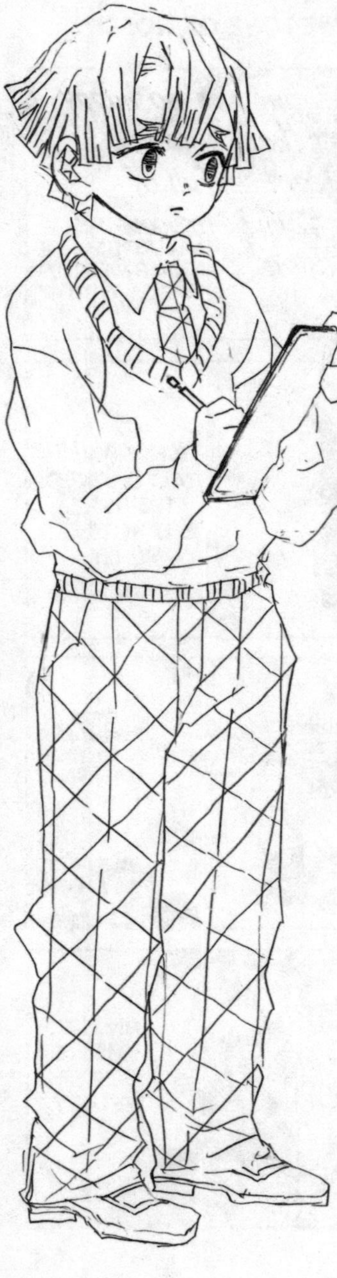

Zenitsu, Disciplinary Committee member

He got on the Disciplinary Committee (which he didn't want to be on) and now he lives in fear of delinquents at the school gate as he checks to make sure everyone meets the dress code.

Tomioka, P.E. teacher

He's too much like a drill sergeant, so the PTA has issued complaints. The Board of Education may have to take action, so the situation is tenuous.

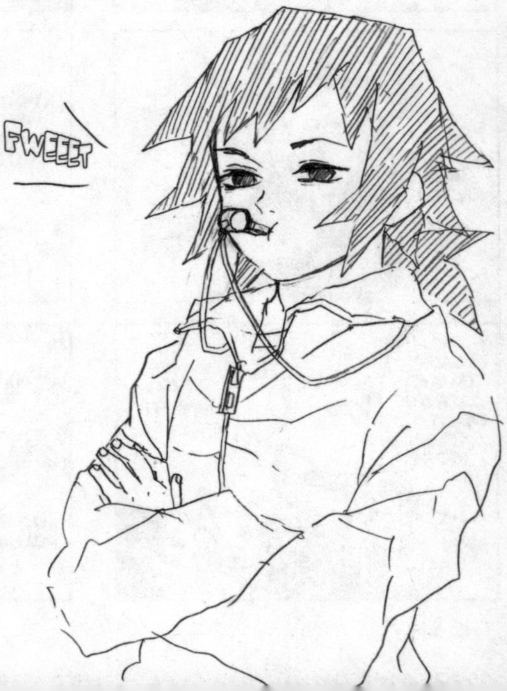
FWEEET

Words of Gratitude

How's everyone doing? I'm Gotouge, and I'm so happy we got to release volume 3! It's all thanks to you, the readers, so... Thank you! My heart is full of gratitude. Thank you for the letters, illustrations, and tasty treats! Tokyo is a land I don't know at all and at first I was lonely here. Now I'm really happy every day. Sorry I can't reply to you all individually. But I'll work my hardest to give you a story worth reading, so please stick with me!

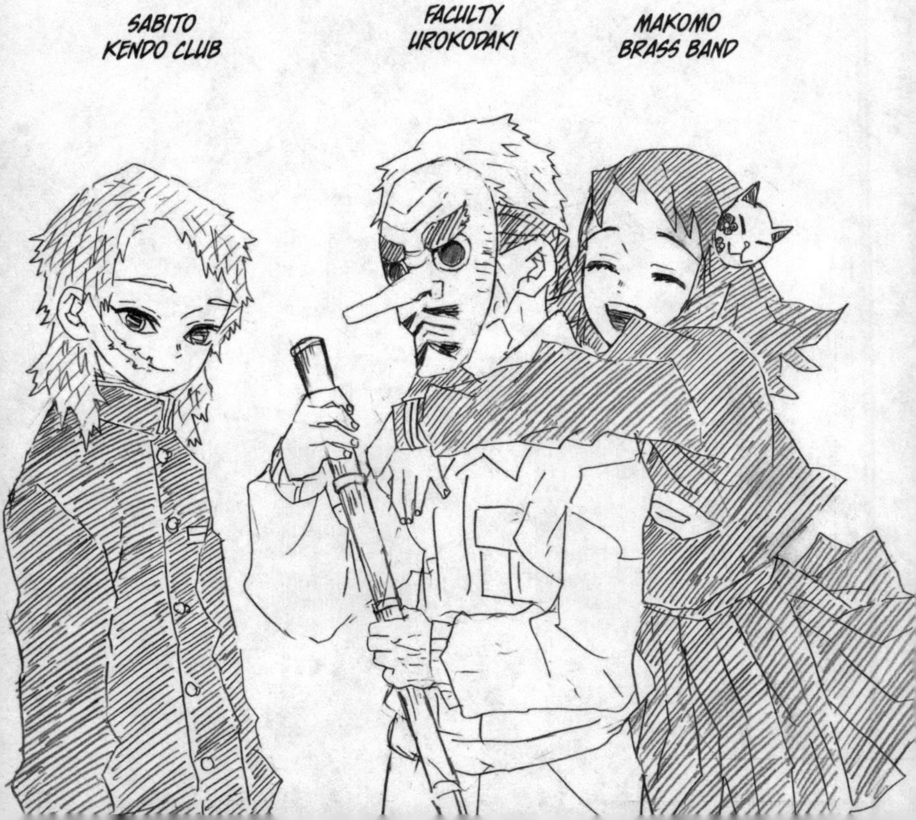
SABITO
KENDO CLUB
FACULTY
UROKODAKI
MAKOMO
BRASS BAND

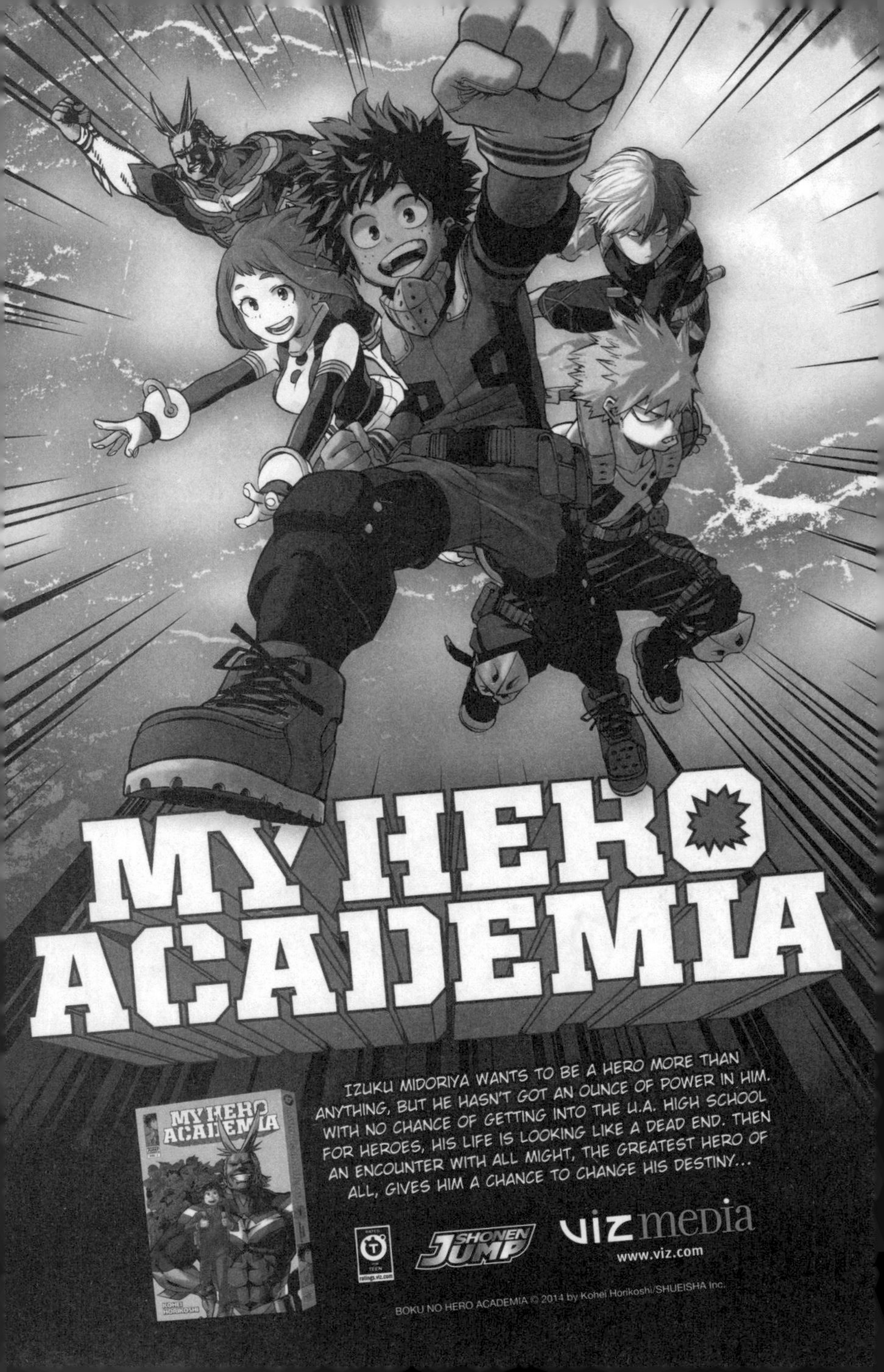
MY HERO ACADEMIA
IZUKU MIDORIYA WANTS TO BE A HERO MORE THAN ANYTHING, BUT HE HASN'T GOT AN OUNCE OF POWER IN HIM. WITH NO CHANCE OF GETTING INTO THE U.A. HIGH SCHOOL FOR HEROES, HIS LIFE IS LOOKING LIKE A DEAD END. THEN AN ENCOUNTER WITH ALL MIGHT, THE GREATEST HERO OF ALL, GIVES HIM A CHANCE TO CHANGE HIS DESTINY...
MY HERO ACADEMIA
KOHEI HORIKOSHI
RATED T TEEN
ratings.viz.com
SHONEN JUMP
viz media
www.viz.com
BOKU NO HERO ACADEMIA © 2014 by Kohei Horikoshi/SHUEISHA Inc.

YOU'RE READING THE
WRONG WAY!

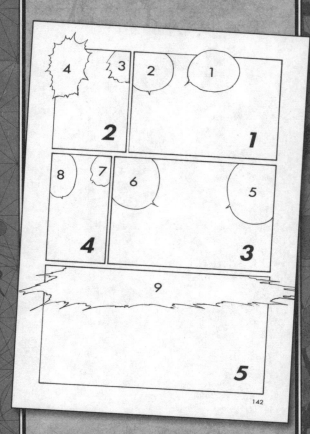

DEMON SLAYER: KIMETSU NO YAIBA
reads from right to left, starting in the
upper-right corner. Japanese is read from
right to left, meaning that action, sound
effects and word-balloon order are com-
pletely reversed from English order.